American
Social Welfare
Institutions

American Social Welfare Institutions

RUSSELL E. SMITH
Professor, Sacramento State College
School of Social Work

DOROTHY ZIETZ
Professor, Sacramento State College
School of Social Work

HV
95
S58
C. 2

John Wiley & Sons, Inc.
New York / London / Sydney / Toronto

Library of Congress Catalog Card Number: 74-118625
ISBN 0-471-80195-X

Printed in the United States of America

10 9 8 7 6 5 4 3 2 1

To

*Dorothy, Mary Ann, Kent,
Samuel, Nathan, and Rachel
who not only tolerated the
writing of this book but, on
occasion, gave assistance and
support to the authors.*

Foreword

Few fields of human endeavor have been so thoroughly and unanimously relegated to the depths of the national dog house during the decade of the '60's as has social welfare and, specifically, public welfare. As this is being written, the national scene presents an unprecedented paradox. A conservative President and a Southern Chairman of the House Ways and Means Committee have come together on a plan to reform the welfare system which, in its provision of a program of income supplements for the working poor, represents a startling departure from traditional American values regarding the necessary tie between work and income. The Nixon welfare proposals offer, philosophically at least, the most significant reforms in our tired and creaky welfare system since the passage of the original Social Security Act in 1935 and, no matter what their ultimate form, will exert pressures for change throughout the entire complex system in the years immediately ahead.

Has America really come of age in its recognition that money is required for the maintenance of life, and that the commitment of an unstinting portion of our national wealth to the poor is a fact of modern life? Have we at last come to realize that welfare is merely one of the prices that we must pay for capitalism? Has the advent of a gross national product flirting with the trillion dollar mark brought us finally to the point of generosity with our wealth? Have we finally sloughed off the myth of the "idle poor," and along with it the steadfast conviction that the "sturdy beggar" of history still lurks among us?

Alas, on closer examination of Nixon's contribution to welfare reform, we discover that all is not well—that these myths die harder than we thought. In the legislation, still much alive, is the ancient notion that the poor are different from everyone else, in that they will be encouraged to work only under the whiplash of economic desperation. In fact, the current proposals carry with them the threat of a triple whiplash—grant levels pegged at less than half the poverty line accepted by the federal government itself, a harsh work incentive feature, and a fifty percent tax on income earned above the basic grant level of $1,600.

Other proposals abound and will continue to proliferate in the next few years. But dollars for the care of people must take second place to the demand for national security, to vast sums committed for our war in Southeast Asia, and to efforts to shove back man's frontier in outer space. At the same time, competition for both the dollars and the dedicated energies of those who would change the world comes from a new and unexpected source—the ecology movement. The long overdue recognition that our national environment is being depleted and destroyed at an alarming rate has led many to the obvious conclusion that social reform must once more be delayed, since if there is no physical environment human life cannot be sustained at all.

The youthful reformer comes easily and logically to this conclusion. It is easy to commit oneself to the movement to save the natural environment because in that effort there is excitement as well as the support that comes from the knowledge that not only are Ralph Nader, and the Sierra Club committed to the battle, but also Governor Reagan, President Nixon, and General Motors. It is not so easy, for many reasons, to announce one's commitment to the equally important goals of completely turning our social institutions around so that they serve human beings instead of destroying them.

Despite stupendous advances in knowledge about people and what they need in order to grow and change, our social institutions whose task it is to care for those who have fallen by the way remain monuments to the past. Our prisons and youth correction systems are an international shame and disgrace; our child-care institutions lag far behind those of other Western nations; our mental hospitals have moved ahead but little since the mid-nineteenth century; and, although it may be on the verge of significant advances, our public income maintenance system continues to view the poor as if they were thieves bent on raiding the public treasury.

Perhaps there is room for a joining of the concern for the physical environment with the commitment of humanizing the environment of social institutions. There are other lessons to be learned from the discovery that D.D.T. released with the best intentions upon the farmland of the nation, can ultimately infest the cells of simple marine organisms dwelling deep in the oceans or from the recognition that industrial smoke released into the atmosphere in our cities has both immediate and long-range effects on the health of people in the surrounding countryside. Rather than being a retardant to the development of public concern and political action directed toward the needs of people, it is possible that the awakened interest in the natural environment may be transferred to a desire to change our social institutions. It is true that we cannot live without air and water. It is also true that we will destroy ourselves if we save our air and water and neglect our relationships with one another and, specifically, if we let languish our institutions designed to care for the poor, the aged, the disabled, and children.

It is possible, therefore, that the newly awakened commitment of young people to the fight for preservation of our natural world may be translated into an equivalent concern for preserving the quality of human life through the development of social institutions that truly minister to human needs. There are encouraging signs that this is beginning to happen. Young social workers have joined with clients in pressing for changes in public assistance through the national welfare rights movement, public welfare workers' unions in some communities have demonstrated as much concern for clients' welfare as for the job security and working conditions of their membership, and there is evidence of a growing political sophistication on the part of young people in social work and related fields.

These are important signs of change, but represent only a beginning. Far more in the way of energy and commitment will be required if our basic people-serving institutions are to undergo the changes required to modernize, upgrade, and humanize them. At this point in history, a commitment on the part of young people to engagement in macro-social change seems far more gripping and "relevant," and offers ready-made outlets for the expression of youthful radicalism and revolutionary spirit. Commitment to changing the world through the ecology movement, or the peace movement, is probably more attractive to young people than the steady, often hum-drum, day-to-day slogging demanded of us when we try to change our prisons, our mental hospitals, and our public welfare system.

But changes in the larger society and changes in its institutional parts move along together. A broadened ideological view of the world on the part of youth, marked by a new and expanded concept of the possibilities inherent in human life, can and must be translated into a commitment to the development of new programs for social welfare. The incessant demand for reform of social welfare institutions now being experienced will increase and will take on a new shape as we become aware as a nation that people in mass society require a variety of human services as essential public utilities, not as mere gratuities or charities the purpose of which are to keep the poor tranquil. We will come to recognize that we cannot depend on an ever-expanding production of consumer goods to provide jobs for people, and that we must increasingly depend on the growth of human services for the creation of new jobs.

The variety of proposals currently before Congress for revision of our public income maintenance system suggests systematic and continued change, if not radical and rapid change, in our public programs for the relief of poverty in the years immediately ahead. Reforms in income maintenance will not eliminate economic poverty, but will result in a process of income redistribution that will begin to bring about significant new opportunities and changes in life style for those currently in poverty. Along with such changes will come an increasing demand for effective, widespread, and easily available social, psychological, and health services.

These services will need people with tremendous creative energy, deep commitment, and, most important, new knowledge. A radically changed community will demand an approach to the social services only faintly envisioned by those of us in positions of leadership on the current scene. Russell Smith and Dorothy Zietz have put together a document that will prove valuable to the serious student and practitioner of social welfare in gaining an introduction to the breadth and complexity of the field, and in helping with the design and management of future programs that avoid the mistakes and advance the sucesses of the past.

ALAN D. WADE
Dean, School of Social Work
Sacramento State College
Sacramento, California

Preface

In writing this book we have tried to provide a view of the past, knowledge of the present, and some ideas about possibilities for the future of both the institution of social welfare and social work as a profession. Institutional patterns are viewed as the result of political developments, legal system alterations, economic forces, and religious-ethical ideas which, we feel, have been of primary import in producing a certain constellation of services and have molded a profession to provide for social needs.

In offering a developmental perspective we are mindful of the present changes and demands to which the contemporary social worker must respond. We have therefore attempted to create a neotraditional stance that moves the social worker from the role of reformer or clinician to that of social advocate and socially aware practitioner.

Throughout we have had to select those programs, events, and individuals considered by us to be the most significant. In so doing it is inevitable that some readers will be dissatisfied with the selections made and that some favorites will have been overlooked or slighted. Some conclusions that might be drawn from the material have not been drawn, whereas others may appear to be tenuously made. We take comfort, however, in the knowledge that further explication and exploration will be done by both the teacher and the learner using the volume.

This book has been separated into two parts; the first gives primary emphasis to the institution of social welfare, and the second deals with the profession charged with responsibility for program execution within the institution. It is hoped that such an organization will provide the creative teacher with many options and be more understandable to the student.

Bibliographical material reflects the principal sources used in individual chapters but does not include the wealth of additional material available in both popular and professional magazines and journals. For further work, reference to periodicals is indispensable in the study of the history, the current status, and the future of the institution and the profession.

In any writing the authors are conscious of omissions and the probability of errors and misinterpretation of facts. Some conscious exclusions—for example, the absence of charts and graphs, and detailed descriptions of programs and agencies—may cause dissatisfaction with the way the book is written. Because such material is generally available in other sources more current than a textbook, we believe such exclusions to be justified. If we have provided a resource for understanding the past and present as a springboard for the future, we are content with our undertaking.

We should like to acknowledge our debt to Mrs. Helen I. Clarke, Mr. David Humphers, Dr. Ivor Kraft, Mr. David L. Blicker, Dr. Howard Hartman, Dr. Sidney Eisenberg, Dr. Marc Tool, Miss Barbara Merritt, and Mr. Louis Lee, who read parts of the manuscript and made valuable suggestions about both content and style. We are also appreciative of the work done by Mrs. Donna Campbell and Mrs. Carole Larsen in typing and correcting an ever-changing manuscript.

Because a book of this nature rests on the scholarship and writing of others, we are indebted to all our sources and to the librarians who contributed so much time and made many helpful suggestions about resource material. The staff at the Harry S. Truman Library in Independence, Missouri, at the Boonslick Regional Library in Warsaw, Missouri, at Sutro Library in San Francisco, and at the University of Missouri in Kansas City were most accommodating. At our own school Miss Leah Freeman took many patient hours to search out obscure writings, legal materials, and documents, and Mrs. Dorothy Wooldridge was consistently cheerful in tracking down recent and, in some instances, uncataloged materials.

We should also like to offer our thanks to the Dean of the School of Social Work at Sacramento State College, Dr. Alan D. Wade, for encouragement given during the writing and to the faculty and administration of the college for granting us sabbatical and research leaves to complete the book. We acknowledge the debt owed to Dr. Charles Guzzetta, who read the entire manuscript and made many valuable suggestions for changes in both writing style and content emphases. Although errors in fact and interpretations are the exclusive responsibility of the authors, many of the improvements over the original manuscript are attributable to Dr. Guzzetta. His critical comments and his humor in pointing out mistakes and misjudgments made the undertaking less grim. Finally, we should like to thank Mr. Ronald St. John and Mr. William Gum for their considerable help and encouragement.

RUSSELL E. SMITH
DOROTHY ZIETZ

Sacramento, California
April 1970

Contents

I

The Development of Social Welfare Institutions

Chapter One

The Dual Tradition of American
Social Welfare Development

Social work as an identifiable profession had its point of origin in the final decade of the nineteenth century. The feeling of charity toward one's fellow man and actions based on that feeling, however, had their origins in antiquity. The philanthropic impulse, the love of mankind that is manifested in beneficent deeds has, it appears, always been a part of human nature—an essential ingredient of the mixture of emotions and beliefs that makes man human. As the motivation has persisted in human nature, so has the movement toward institutionalization of the process through which society acts collectively to help those who suffer a breakdown in social functioning. This process of institutionalization, that is, the organizing of formal structures or agencies and laws designed to regulate social behavior, has taken place as social relationships have increased in complexity. The performance of charitable acts has been carried out under the aegis of voluntary and governmental organizations throughout history; the need for giving help and the acceptance of responsibility to do so has been a constant in human society.

But to be human is to err, and in the history of man's intrinsic desire to benevolently assist his fellow man, he has frequently been something less than divine. In the perspective of time, man has generally acted with compassion toward the less fortunate, but the rationale for doing so has varied from time to time and from place to place. One constant characteristic throughout the ages, along with the recognition that some are worthy of concern, is the ambivalence about who is to be adjudged "worthy."

Today in every industrial nation and in many preindustrial societies there exist, perhaps alongside voluntary associations and agencies, publicly financed social welfare systems. Established to meet the particular needs of each society, the social services institutionalize, as public policy, the philanthropic impulse. In Western society, however, the organization and management of social services vary considerably and reflect the different nations' legal systems, religious heritage, political systems, and economic conditions. These factors place limitations both on what a society is able to do and what the people are willing to do for others. It is in the will to do that we find in Western society a dual tradition involving a sense of obligation coupled with internal strains that make the left hand anxious to take away what the right has given freely.

This dual tradition derives from the moral and humanitarian imperative that is also identified with the religious and moral requirement that you should be your brother's keeper. A second, and less perfectly articulated tradition in the United States, is the democratic ideal that holds that members of a society, by virtue of membership in the extended group, have a right to participate in the social system. Although both rationales contain the basis for a humane system of social welfare programs, both also accommodate contradictions of democratic humanitarianism.

3

IN THE BEGINNING

As early as 2000 B.C. the rulers and important men of Egypt included, in their last wills, declarations of virtuous acts that were recitations of the good deeds performed by them on behalf of the poor.[1] These declarations were made as a kind of "insurance" for the hereafter in that it was hoped that the doing of good works in this life would be assurance of the peaceful repose of the soul. There was, it appears, a religious and perhaps a social obligation for the wealthy to share with the less fortunate. Early biblical references admonished the Hebrews to provide alms for those in need and spelled out their duties toward the blind, the lame, the widow, and the traveler. If alms were not given, homes were to be open to the traveler, and the needy were to be allowed to glean the fields. The nineteenth chapter of Leviticus put it succinctly and included the implication of punishment for the miscreant:

When you reap the harvest of your land, you shall not reap your field to its very border, neither shall you gather the gleanings after your harvest. And you shall not strip your vineyard bare, neither shall you gather the fallen grapes of your vineyard; you shall leave them for the poor and for the sojourner: I am the Lord your God.

In Judaism there was allowance for the accumulation of wealth by the individual and a corresponding necessity that help be given to those in need. There was not, as there was in Christianity, the foundation for the prohibition of charging interest in financial transactions or the concept of poverty as penance, which led to monasticism and asceticism. But there were in Judaism, hence in Christianity, two views of the cause of poverty and misfortune. As Edgar May has pointed out, throughout the centuries of Western civilization man has struggled to decide whether the cause and cure of social distress are as described in the sixth chapter of Proverbs, which advises:

Go to the ant, O sluggard; consider her ways, and be wise. Without having any chief, officer or ruler, she prepares her food in summer, and gathers her sustenance in harvest. How long will you lie there, O sluggard? When will you arise from your sleep? A little sleep, a little slumber, a little folding of the hands to rest, and poverty will come upon you like a vagabond, and want like an armed man.

Or, alternately, is one bound by the admonishment in the twenty-fifth chapter of Leviticus, which says, "And if thy brother be waxen poor and

[1] Karl de Schweinitz, *Social Security for Egypt* (Washington, D.C.: Government Printing Office, August 1952), p. 5.

fallen in decay with thee, then thou shalt relieve him." Depending on the camp to which one belonged, biblical references could be used at different times and in different countries to justify a harsh and punitive attitude toward the socially disadvantaged or a humanitarian approach to social problems. The moral and religious ambiguity remains evident today.[2]

The democratic imperative of the right of an individual to society's help derives from the Greco-Roman tradition of our culture. In early Athens, the welfare of a citizen was considered the proper concern of the state. Help was given to individuals and families, not for religious reasons, but because it was felt that all citizens had a right to share in the benefits of a democratic society. However this excluded the many who were not citizens—notably the slaves. Thus within the democratic heritage, as in the religious inheritance, the opportunity existed for treating some members of society in one fashion while those who were equally (or more) needy could be logically excluded. The noncitizen in Greece and later in Rome did enjoy a kind of social security in that masters were considered to have an obligation to their inferiors. The concept of obligation between a patron and his freeholder in Roman society was later incorporated into feudal society. One modern remnant of the notion of *noblesse oblige* is the twentieth century idea that the corporation has a duty to society that can be discharged through philanthropic giving.

In the Roman Empire, which was eventually to be the vehicle for the amalgamation of religious and secular ideas of charity, there were examples of both public and private concern for the disadvantaged and the introduction of the concept of the matching of public funds to private beneficence. As an example, in the town of Como in the first century A.D., the Younger Pliny put up a third of the money for the expense of hiring an instructor for a school, but stipulated that his fellow townsmen must raise the balance of the funds.

In addition to the schools, libraries, and baths provided by public-spirited Romans, the State also engaged in philanthropic acts, although the motivation generally was the political exigencies of the moment. Grain was distributed to the poor, and no charge was made for admission to the circuses or theaters. One enduring project was instituted during the reign of Trajan at the turn of the first century: the equivalent of the imperial budget for one year was used to establish a system of low-cost farm loans, and the interest from the loans was used to support orphans and the children of the poor.[3] Grants were higher for boys, and children who were illegiti-

[2] Edgar May, "The Disjointed Trio: Poverty, Politics and Power," *The Social Welfare Forum, 1963,* Official Proceedings of the 90th National Conference on Social Welfare (New York: Columbia University Press, 1963), pp. 47–61.
[3] Moses Hadas, *Imperial Rome* (New York: Time Inc., 1965), pp. 65–67.

mate received less than girls. This program of public support for children, known as the Alimanta, was expanded by Trajan's successors and was in effect for almost 200 years.

Christians in Rome, being ineligible for participation as citizens, took active responsibility for the welfare of their less fortunate brethren. Mutual aid funds were created to help aged household slaves, orphans, widows, and others in need. This voluntary system of assistance, a creature of necessity, became superfluous in the early part of the fourth century when Constantine was converted to Christianity. As the first Christian emperor he decreed that all charity, public and private, should be channeled through the church. Thus the power of the state and the organization of the Christian church were, by government decree, blended into a religious-secular system of organized charity. Following the pattern dictated by Constantine, social welfare was made the function of the Church during the Medieval period. But it was a function that was, through the centuries, increasingly supplemented by legal and political dicta that spelled out mutual obligations between classes and between individuals. Laws regulating social relationships and responsibilities, it should be noted, are in themselves evidence that a society is in the process of change, and legal statements are needed when the accepted system is in a state of flux—or disintegration. Convents were assigned specific tasks by the state for the care of widows and the aged, and *each* monastery was required to maintain a guesthouse for travelers, a nascent form of present-day traveler's aid societies. By the eleventh and twelfth centuries, it was necessary for the Church to found *hôtels de Dieu* to care for orphans, abandoned children, the old, the infirm, the disabled, the sick, and homeless pregnant women.[4] Increasingly, financial supplements were made by the State to support these institutions, and the fact that they were needed was a recognition of the failure of earlier laws and the changed social system.

Another element that acted as an agent of social change was the recurrence of the bubonic plague, which decimated the population of Europe toward the end of the Middle Ages. The first severe outbreak occurred in 1348, and periodic visitations occurred through the seventeenth century. A marked decrease in the number of available workers acted to place a premium on agricultural service, with a concomitant increase in wages and heightened mobility as workers moved from town to town seeking higher payment. England's Edward III, reacting to the change taking place in society, enacted the Statute of Labourers in 1349. This provided that every man and woman under the age of 60 who had no craft or land could be bound to a landowner and required to serve, taking "only the wages . . .

4 Walter A. Friedlander, *Individualism and Social Welfare* (Free Press of Glencoe, 1962), pp. 1–2.

which were accustomed to be given in the places where he oweth to serve. . . ." [5] Failure to work as required or attempts to get increased wages were punishable by imprisonment. In a society that operated on the basis of custom and tradition, the idea of mobility, bargaining for labor, or a status independent of land ownership was, if not criminal, incomprehensible.

THE RELIGIOUS SOCIETY

Up to the time of the Reformation, as monasteries and convents spread throughout Western Europe, religious orders such as the Franciscans cooperated with secular and religious institutions to provide for the needy. Along with this institutional pattern of providing for the poor, voluntary giving, characterized by the growth of charitable foundations, grew apace. Although the accepted pattern was to channel voluntary giving through the Church, this concept was increasingly ignored in England. Capital was increasingly concentrated in the hands of fewer individuals, and money was available for private causes, especially after the discoveries of America and the trade routes to the Orient. A dramatic increase in private philanthropy was possible because of the resources available and the rejection, especially in England, of the notion that philanthropy was the sole province of the church. It was possibly also encouraged by the resentment and "hatred of rich people, especially of the new rich, who were then very numerous." [6] Guilt came to be attached to conspicuous wealth, and the religious society had always maintained as a cardinal tenet that those with means held property as a stewardship bestowed by God. Therefore wealth depended on God's grace, and to withhold alms from the poor was deemed a mortal sin. The idea of stewardship and the fear of retribution now and later extended to the growing merchant class as well. In the fourteenth century poem, "Piers Plowman," the well-to-do were advised:

Therefore I warn you rich, have ruth on poor folk; Though you are mighty in the moot-hall be meek in your judgements; For the measures that you mete shall be meted to you; Your weights shall weigh you when the hour is ready.[7]

The changing attitude between the classes from acceptance to resentment, the increased commerce and flow of trade, new communication

[5] Karl de Schweinitz, *England's Road to Social Security* (New York: A. S. Barnes & Co., a Perpetua Book, 1943), p. 6.

[6] Johan Huizinga, *The Waning of the Middle Ages* (New York: Doubleday & Co., 1956), p. 28.

[7] William Langland, *The Vision of Piers Plowman* (New York: Greenwood Press, 1968), p. 16.

technology, and the hold of the churches on property, brought increased friction in European society during the fourteenth and fifteenth centuries.[8] The changing economics ran contrary to the religious aura of mystical glamour that had traditionally surrounded both poverty and the compassion through which poverty was relieved. In the Church's traditional teaching poor men were seen as being God's special friends, and the existence of the poor was sometimes conceived of as being a possible test of the rich man's religious convictions. In other words, God might have placed the poor on earth in order to test the devotion of the more affluent. It was also conceded in the traditional theology that forces beyond man's control, or perhaps the elements of nature and an imperfect society, could be responsible for individual poverty; therefore lack of this world's goods was not necessarily a reflection of personal failure or evidence of a sinful nature. It was generally felt that the prayers of the poor were especially efficacious in absolving the sin of the cheerful giver. Good works were highly esteemed and felt to be, in the sight of God, essential for salvation. Increasing sale of indulgences, concentration on the doing of good works, and the venality of the Church led to the possibility for reformation—a possibility seized upon by Martin Luther in the sixteenth century.

THE REFORMATION

Martin Luther's quarrel with the Church in the first quarter of the sixteenth century came at a time when national states and their kings and princes were becoming increasingly restive under the sometimes harsh control from Rome. Political considerations gave added fuel to the discontent with the Church and its doctrines. Furthermore the economic system had changed to such a degree that the realities of society required some kind of accommodation that would allow for usury and the accumulation of capital. In England the development through the centuries of the common law and the rights of man made the situation there especially grave, but the English king's traditional right to name bishops and his control over the religious made the reforming of the church, in the eyes of the political leaders there, less imperative than in Germany.

Luther, born in 1483, the son of a Saxon miner, abandoned his intention of entering the law and came to the Church after a conversion reminiscent of that of St. Paul. Driven by a sense of sinfulness and God's majesty, Luther approached his study of Scripture with a driving passion and developed the doctrine of justification by faith as his central idea. The emphasis on faith rather than works led him to reject the practice of the sell-

[8] Marshall McLuhan, *The Gutenberg Galaxy* (Toronto: University of Toronto Press, 1962).

ing of indulgences and, ultimately, to a position that assigned to the State the responsibility for dispensing charity. This was done to keep the religious sphere uncorrupted although Luther, who felt that the highest form of charity was private, believed that "good works do not make a man good, but a good man does good works." Believing that charity had been used by the Church to corrupt men, and emphasizing the "priesthood of all believers," Luther insisted that each man was responsible for his own salvation. He was more concerned about man's relationship with God than man's relationship with his fellow man. Luther saw himself as a reformer within Roman Catholicism who was attempting to return the Church to an earlier and purer religious core of belief. In like manner, as a descendent of peasant stock, he yearned for the earlier system of social relationships, undisturbed by the post-Renaissance breakdown of the feudal system. Although his denial of centrality to the clergy contributed to the Protestant ethic of work as a means of salvation, and in spite of his teaching that man's soul belonged to the Church, whereas his body was consigned to the world, it was Luther's follower, Calvin, who provided the basis for the hard core of the Protestant ethic.

John Calvin was born in France in 1509, the son of a middle-class notary; he was educated as a lawyer, although he originally intended to enter the priesthood. His father, who was excommunicated in 1528 for refusing to open his books of accounts of properties that had been left to his employer, the Noyon cathedral, played a decisive role in changing his career intentions. John Calvin studied law in Orleans and traveled in Germany, where he came under the influence of the Lutheran Wolmar. By 1534 Calvin had joined the ranks of Protestantism, and in 1536 he published *Institutes of the Christian Religion*, one of the few books to profoundly affect the course of history. Through syndics and councils, Calvin established in Geneva the Christian community he had envisaged; in it, the religious and the civil community were synonymous. There was no toleration for dissent, and persons of good repute were to be appointed in all parts of the city to oversee the conduct of all citizens. If admonishment of the wayward did not produce the desired change of conduct, banishment by the consistory was possible and the burning of heretics, such as the unitarian Servetus, was acceptable.

In Geneva the first free and compulsory public school system was established, the manufacture of cloth was introduced to provide a livelihood for the unemployed poor, and provision was made for a charity hospital, a house for travelers, and a pesthouse. A physician and surgeon were appointed to care for patients in the hospital and for the poor in their homes.

Although charity was not scorned in Geneva, Calvin maintained that there were no outward signs of inner grace; therefore the giving of alms did not mean that the giver absolved himself of his sins. Calvin taught that at the moment of birth a person is predestined either to salvation as an act of grace by a merciful God or foredoomed to destruction as a reprobate. One could not be certain of the category to which he belonged, outward signs of wealth and godliness being no insurance. As Calvin saw it, "If God does not make us prosper in a worldly way we must not grieve . . ." Although the faithful might be vexed with poverty while the ungodly prospered, the former could take comfort in dire poverty because they were assured that God was with them.[9] With the passing of time, and especially in England, where Calvinism was introduced by John Knox, the teachings were gradually altered to the point that it came to be accepted that there were indeed outward signs of inner grace—that, in fact, a person's status in society reflected his personal qualities and inadequacies.[10] The emphasis on work, which was later of such import in Puritan America, derived from Calvin's refutation of the Medieval idea of being born to a permanent class or station in life. Calvin believed that "whatever of worldly goods we handle or possess, our function with them is one of stewardship. We and our possessions together belong to God." This involved the hallowing of each man's vocation, and although it was the "post assigned" and to be faithfully exercised, it could be changed for God's glory. The determination of God's glory was left up to the individual conscience.[11]

From the ideas of Luther and Calvin came the concepts of the importance of the individual, the primacy of work, and the freedom from religious control of much of secular life. The mercantile class in particular found the new theology suited to the ends they wished to pursue. The developing middle class took comfort in the ideas that made their efforts in this life noble in God's sight and profitable on earth.

The Reformation in England followed a different pattern from that on the Continent. The superfluity of monasteries and the venality of the religious community acted to encourage the change in temper and mental activity of the lower classes in England, to the point that the peasant community more openly challenged not only the Church authorities but the landlords and royal authorities as well. Although Lollardry (a 14th century religious protest movement which decried the church's wealth amidst the poverty of the people) had subsided by the time of Henry VIII, the middle class had upward strivings that added impetus to Henry's decision to break with the Church. The development of the common law and equity, added to the command that the King was able to exercise over

---

[9] John T. McNeill, *The History and Character of Calvinism* (New York: Oxford University Press, 1954), p. 223.

[10] George L. Mosse, *The Reformation* (New York: Henry Holt & Co., 1953), p. 44.

[11] McNeill, *op. cit.*, p. 221.

his subjects, made it possible for him to retain more control over the break with Rome than had been true on the Continent. This allowed the monarch to expand his authority while contributing to the economic reorganization of society.

When Henry VIII was excommunicated in 1533, land held by monasteries and religious societies was given over to private individuals or reserved to the Crown which made it into a financial resource. The dispensing of lands indebted the recipients to the central authority, and tenure depended on the good will of the King. In order to consolidate the kingdom, land and charitable institutions passed into hands outside the Church, and financial resources were denied traditional sources of relief for the needy. Henry, like Luther, would have preferred that relief giving be a voluntary act of conscience but, again like Luther, found it was necessary for either the Church or State to intervene in behalf of the poor. Initially, Parliament passed laws decreeing that alms be collected by the Church of England for the poor and discouraging all unlicensed begging.

The Justices of the Peace, civil officers appointed by the Crown to circumvent ecclesiastical courts centuries before, were in Elizabeth's reign responsible for appointing Overseers of the Poor. By the time of Elizabeth I the overseers were dispensing tax funds levied on local communities for the care of the needy poor, and an office of correction was set up to provide work for the indigent in the almshouses. The latter were antecedents of the poorhouses and were, as in medieval France, places of lodging for the old, the orphaned, the infirm, and the sick—the "worthy poor." The "ablebodied poor" were required to return to their own parishes for relief and, according to the "Act for the Punishment of Vagabonds," were, if above the age of 14, to be whipped and burned through the gristle of the right ear. After age 18, the "sturdy beggar," should "he fall again into a roguish life, he shall suffer death as a felon, unless some credible person will take him into service for two years."

During the time of the Reformation and the rise of the capitalist economic system, it is important to note the shift in attitude toward the poor. A changing economic system, necessitated by the first stirrings of the Industrial Revolution, was changing the nature of society. Private property, rather than largess from God consigned to man's stewardship for the benefit of all society, was to become John Locke's foundation for all social order. The amassing of wealth was increasingly seen as an outward sign of inner grace, and moral and political philosophy changed to accommodate a changing social structure.

Henry VIII's mentor and teacher, Cardinal Latimer, had advised that "the poor man hath title to the rich man's goods; so that the rich man ought to let the poor man have part of his riches to help and to comfort him withal." [12] Less than 100 years later, religious writers were more concerned with the souls of the poor and felt that giving alms or aid only corrupted an already vicious nature. Thus in the course of the Reformation, the greatest of evils became idleness; severity in dealing with the poor became a duty rather than a sin. The poor became the victims, not of circumstances or God's greater design for man, as they were seen earlier, but of their own "idle, irregular and wicked courses." The truest charity became not to enervate them by relief but to reform their characters so that giving financial aid would be unnecessary. As R. H. Tawney, the English economist, has stated: "A society which reverences the attainment of riches as the supreme felicity will naturally be disposed to regard the poor as damned in the next world, if only to justify itself for making their life a hell in this." [13]

During the sixteenth century in England a number of laws were passed to try to bring some order to the chaos. The obligation of landowner to tenant that had existed in earlier days was being upset by the importation of the Belgian method of weaving, and the enclosure of land was accelerated, with the concomitant severing of any bonds that existed between servant and master. Large numbers of people were thrown off the land and forced to go into the cities to seek work. Bickering and fighting among the adherents of various religious groups, notably between Catholics and Anglicans and Anglicans and Puritans, added to the general confusion of the times.

THE ELIZABETHAN POOR LAW

Although numerous laws were passed to try to deal with the social, religious, and economic problems, the single piece of legislation that has had the most impact on welfare both in England and the United States was 43 Elizabeth, or the 1601 Poor Law, as it is commonly known. This law, which brought together much old practice and some new ideas, was not designed to be the sole measure for coping with economic distress; however, it became such in England and the American colonies. Although its purpose was to provide relief, it was but the last link in a chain of measures intended to mitigate the forces that made relief necessary. Among these were the prevention of evictions and the control of food supplies and prices in an attempt to stabilize employment and check unnecessary dismissals of workmen. We must also remember that apart from the Poor Law, the first 40 years of the seventeenth century were prolific in the de-

[12] R. H. Tawney, *Religion and the Rise of Capitalism* (New York: New American Library, a Mentor Book, 1954), p. 217.
[13] *Ibid.*, p. 222.

velopment of private charity, which founded almshouses and hospitals and established private funds to provide employment or to otherwise aid struggling tradesmen.

According to 43 Elizabeth, each county was to have an Overseer of the Poor appointed by the Justice of the Peace; overseers were to be responsible for setting to work all children whose parents were unable to keep and maintain them. Thus the State rather than the Church became the ultimate guardian of the children. Furthermore, the Overseer of the Poor was to set to work all such persons, married or unmarried, who had no means of maintaining themselves. Each parish could purchase a stock of flax, wool, iron, or other supplies to set the poor to work as a test of need and worthiness. In line with this, there was the pervasive idea (which remains today) that factories could be created to provide work and thus obviate the need for supporting the poor by taxation. The factories were unsuccessful, however, because those lines of activity that were profit producing were generally already in existence under the sponsorship of private enterprise. The characteristics of the poverty-stricken, then as now, made their employment difficult if not impossible.

An important feature of the Poor Law was the fact that it was a national program, intended to extend to every parish in the nation. Although this was never accomplished in fact, it is important to note that the English in dealing with problems of the poor received and accepted national direction even though the activities themselves were carried out in the community by appointees of the central government.

Money to pay for the cost of welfare was to be raised by taxation on the landowners. This kind of tax was easy to collect and was justified intellectually on the basis that the landlords were the ones creating the problems through enclosure and should therefore pay for the needs of the poor. Also important, though infrequently mentioned, was the practical reason that Elizabeth I was having difficulties with landowners and vindictiveness was not a quality foreign to her. Today in the United States some welfare programs and portions of others, such as the categorical aids that provide for the blind, the disabled, the aged, and dependent children, are financed in the amount required from local sources through property taxes.

The giving of "indoor relief" was espoused, and according to the law "it shall be lawful for the overseer to build and set out places of habitation for housing the impotent poor." [14] These shelters were essentially the almshouses in which the old, young, lame, mentally ill, blind, and other needy were housed to remove them from society. Although this was justi-

[14] The term "indoor relief" was used to denote assistance given in institutions such as the almshouse or the workhouse. "Outdoor relief" was assistance given to individuals and families in their own homes.

fied as a test of need and an economical system of relief giving, it is apparent that the focus was not so much on helping individuals as it was to remove them from the body politic and protect the latter from their corruption or, at least having to view them. Even today in the United States the case can still be made that our homes for the aged, camps for migrant farm workers, and institutions for the mentally ill are placed outside the urban centers and off the main highways so that we do not have to think about their problems.

Relatives were responsible for their kin and this extended to grandparents as well as parents and children. Children were liable to be bound out or indentured, and the system of categories of the needy can be traced to the 1601 Poor Law; for example, dependent young people could be apprenticed to learn a trade and were obliged to serve until the age of 24 in the case of boys and until 21 for girls or until they married. Up to the present time the granting of aid has continued to be governed by whether a person fits neatly into a category rather than by eligibility based on need alone.

In the Settlement Act of 1662 each parish was assigned the responsibility for those having legal residence within its bounds. The concept of settlement was based on the premise that a community ought not have to provide for those who did not "belong" to it. The intent of the legislation, in some respects a refinement of the provisions of 1349 in the Statute of Labourers, was to prevent "squatters" from taking over untilled land, discourage vagabondage by the unemployed, and prevent movement to the cities. The needy could be forcibly returned by Justices of the Peace to the places in which they had legal settlement.

Residence within a state was, until 1969, when it was outlawed by a U.S. Supreme Court decision, required in all public welfare programs, and in some states, in general assistance programs, the notion of settlement remained; for instance, a family that had not resided in a state with a residence law for 365 days (the maximum under federal regulations), but who became needy, would be returned to the state in which it had lived a full year for help through the Aid to Families with Dependent Children program. This was the idea of residence and incorporated the concept as spelled out in the 1662 English law. The idea of settlement was exemplified by the 1962 *Laws of Wisconsin Relating to the Institutions and Agencies Charitable, Curative, Reformatory and Penal*, which described in terms reminiscent of the 1662 legislation how legal settlement was determined within the state. They further provide:

> When a dependent person, other than a recipient of old age assistance, aid to blind, aid to dependent children, or aid to totally and permanently disabled persons is receiving relief elsewhere than at his place of settlement

and refuses to return thereto, the officer or agency of the place administering relief or of the place of settlement may petition the judge of the county court or the judge of any other court of record of the county in which the relief is furnished for an order directing such person to return to his place of settlement.

Residence laws, settlement restrictions, and other provisions derived from the 1601 Poor Law or before remain in effect in many social welfare programs in the United States. Most are irrelevant for today's conditions and are increasingly being successfully challenged in our courts. But society, no less than the individual, is the hostage of the past. Queen Elizabeth I may have died 400 years ago, but the system spawned in her name remains with us.

AMERICAN PROGRESS AND POVERTY

The Puritans in the Massachusetts Bay Colony brought with them the theology of Calvin, the social attitudes of the English middle classes, and the welfare machinery of Queen Elizabeth. It was not until several years had passed before the colonies began enacting their own poor relief legislation. Persons who became mentally ill or physically handicapped were returned to England if their legal settlement was there. Orphans and children whose parents were unable to provide for them were ordered by the magistrate to live with families and learn a vocation. The fear of the town fathers, motivated both economically and religiously, was that a young person might reach his majority without a trade or "calling." Consequently if parents neglected to provide what society considered to be an appropriate trade education, the community could intervene to provide this. The town records of Boston in 1656 contained the following about an unemployed child whose mother was remiss in her duties:

> It is agreed upon the complaint against the son of Goodwife Samon living withoutt a calling, that if shee dispose nott of him in some way of employ before the next meeting, that then the townemen will dispose of him to some service according to law.[15]

The number of persons in need did not yet justify the construction of almshouses, and the cost of such institutions would have been prohibitive for the colonists. Thus "outdoor relief" was the principal vehicle of institutionalized aid giving. Supplying the needed articles or "in kind" charity was commonplace. Persons wishing to move into a community frequently

[15] Ralph E. Pumphrey and Muriel W. Pumphrey, *The Heritage of American Social Work* (New York: Columbia University Press, 1961), p. 21.

had to post bond or otherwise prove that within a specified length of time neither they nor their dependents or servants woud become charges on the town. Freedom of movement was severely restricted, and persons who were considered potentially dependent were "warned out" from communities.

The aged were provided for in various ways, but one of the most common practices was to place them in the homes of townsmen who would provide for them on contract. In the Fairfield, Connecticut, town records of 1685 the following description is found of the way in which care was contracted for one Joseph Patchin:

> The Towne are willing to give Thomas Bennet Thirteen pounds provided he mayntayn ol patchin with meat drink clothing washing and Lodging for the Term of Twelve Month: and render him clothing at the years end as he is at this present.[16]

One way in which relief giving differed from England, was that in the early days there was little private philanthropy in America. Individuals in the early Colonial days did not have the wherewithal to sponsor private charities on any significant scale. Thus it was not until much later that the English system of foundations and voluntary services became important in the New World. It is interesting to note that many examples of early charitable works took the form of cooperative ventures between philanthropists and various units of government, rather than individual acts of charity.

The dual and cooperative nature of the growth of services, made necessary by the increase in population and the gaining of a settlement in America, is well illustrated in the creation of the first public hospital in the colonies. The Pennsylvania Hospital in Philadelphia was created in the fifth decade of the eighteenth century, the impetus for its erection coming from Dr. Thomas Bond and his friend Benjamin Franklin. When private donations for the building lagged, Franklin persuaded the colony's assembly to match the money from private citizens with a like donation from the public treasury. The hospital was set up to serve the physically and mentally ill, and the use of public funds was justified on the basis that "the saving and restoring useful and laborious members to a community, is a work of public service, and the relief of the sick poor is not only an act of humanity, but a religious duty. . . ." [17] Furthermore the care of the sick was extended to those coming to the colony, and the isolation of the persons with communicable diseases was noted as an additional benefit for the protection of the community. The rationale for the care of the sick was

---

[16] *Ibid.*, p. 22.
[17] *Ibid.*, p. 42.

based on the idea of protecting society, rehabilitating the dependent person so that he might be productive again, the humanitarian impulse for relieving misery, and the religious imperative to help those in need. Throughout the history of the nation these same motives have intertwined to create the basis for social welfare institutions.

Pennsylvania approached the problem of the dependent person somewhat more realistically and humanely than the other colonies. Nevertheless, it is generally correct to characterize the attitude of society toward the indigent as one in which poverty and misfortune were considered to be individual matters and usually indicative of some personal and moral flaw. Given this premise, it naturally followed that the giving of help should be as unpalatable as possible for the recipient, and that wide publicity of the names of those who needed help would discourage idleness and would be a lesson to youth on the consequences of profligacy and sin. The attitude toward youth in keeping with Calvinist precepts, was one of tender concern for their education so that they might be able to read the Bible, attention through laws in all colonies for their apprenticeship and indenture, and control of delinquent behavior when they strayed from the paths of righteousness. An example of delinquency control was a law enacted in the 1640's in the Massachusetts Bay Colony wherein a stubborn and rebellious son could be brought to the magistrates and either be severely punished or put to death.

The periods before and after the Revolution were characterized by vast increases in immigration, partly through deception by agents who induced Europeans, especially the Germans, to come to America. The conditions on shipboard defy description. Those who survived undoubtedly found, however, a better condition than that which they had endured in Europe. Writing before the Revolution, J. Hector St. John de Crevecoeur described the scene that greeted the immigrant as follows:

> Here he beholds fair citizens, substantial villages, extensive fields, an immense country filled with decent houses, good roads, orchards, meadows, and bridges, where an hundred years ago all was wild, woody, and uncultivated. . . . He is arrived on a continent; a modern society offers itself to his contemplation, different from what he had hitherto seen. It is not composed, as in Europe, of great lords who possess everything, and of a herd of people who have nothing. Here are no aristocratical families, no courts, no kings, no bishops, no ecclesiastical dominion, no invisible power giving to a few a very visible one; no great manufacturers employing thousands, no great refinements of luxury. The rich and the poor are not so far removed from each other as they are in Europe.[18]

[18] J. Hector St. John de Crevecoeur, *Letters from an American Farmer* (New York: E. P. Dutton & Co., 1957), pp. 35–36.

The idea of education, first given religious sanction in New England, was enlarged by Thomas Jefferson and given a social philosophy that made education a necessary requisite for maintaining the democracy. The matching of funds concept used in building the Pennsylvania Hospital was extended by Jefferson in the Northwest Ordinance, drawn up before the adoption of the Constitution, which provided that the government would set aside one section of each township—640 acres—for the creation and maintenance of public schools. Jefferson's concern for democracy and education also extended to the care of the poor, and his description of poor relief in Virginia is one of the best examples of how organized charity, local in character, operated in the first days of the Republic:

> The poor unable to support themselves, are maintained by an assessment on the tithable persons in their parish. This assessment is levied and administered by twelve persons in each parish, called vestrymen, originally chosen by the housekeepers of the parish, but afterwards filling vacancies in their own body by their own choice. These are usually the most discreet farmers, so distributed through their parish, that every part of it may be under the immediate eye of some one of them. They are well acquainted with the details and economy of private life, and they find sufficient inducements to execute their charge well, in their philanthropy, in the approbation of their neighbors, and the distinction which that gives them. The poor who have neither property, friends, nor strength to labor, are boarded in the houses of good farmers, to whom a stipulated sum is annually paid. To those who are able to help themselves a little, or have friends from whom they derive some succors, inadequate however to their full maintenance, supplementary aids are given which enable them to live comfortably in their own houses, or in the houses of their friends. Vagabonds without visible property or vocation, are placed in work houses, where they are well clothed, fed, lodged, and made to labor. Nearly the same method of providing for the poor prevails through all our states; and from Savannah to Portsmouth you will seldom meet a beggar. In the large towns, indeed they sometimes present themselves. These are usually foreigners, who have never obtained a settlement in any parish. I never yet saw a native American begging in the streets or highways. A subsistence is easily gained here; and if, by misfortunes, they are thrown on the charities of the world, those provided by their own country are so comfortable and so certain, that they never think of relinquishing them to become strolling beggars.[19]

This description, although perhaps overly optimistic, reflects a general feeling that the needy were taken care of and helps explain why the Constitution makes no mention of the creation of social welfare institutions

---

[19] Thomas Jefferson, *Notes on the State of Virginia*, William Peden, ed. (Chapel Hill, N.C.: University of North Carolina Press, 1955), p. 133.

other than the broadly construed and very useful statement in the Preamble that government can "promote the general welfare."

No less a democrat than Jefferson, but less acceptable to his contemporaries in his adopted homeland, was Thomas Paine. While antagonizing the clergy and the religious, Paine spent his life in search of the "perfect society" and found it briefly in America and for a time in revolutionary France. Although his impact extended to many areas other than social welfare, it is interesting to note his concern for the welfare of his fellow man and what he considered to be the rights of man. Paine foreshadowed contemporary proposals for what is called the negative income tax and the children's allowance scheme as well. He recommended the abolition of "poor-rates entirely, and in lieu thereof, to make a remission of taxes to the poor of double the amount of the present poor-taxes. . . . [20] He also favored the graduated and progressive tax and proposed payment of "four pounds a-year for every child under fourteen years of age enjoining the parents of such children to send them to school, to learn reading, writing, and common arithmetic." [21] This plan was advanced for the young as a means of reducing poverty; Paine also planned for the second group of numerous needy—the aged. He divided them into two groups, those who at age 50 were less vigorous as workers and those at 60 for whom "labor ought to be over, at least from direct necessity." He considered the most humane method of help for both groups to be a form of guaranteed income for the former and a pension for the latter "not as a matter of grace and favour, but of right." [22] For those in between youth and old age, Paine advocated a form of a guaranteed right to work that did not receive serious consideration until the middle of the twentieth century.

The general feeling of contentment with the existing system, the agricultural basis of society, the consolidation of the political system after adoption of the Constitution, the erection of the legal system based on defining the purpose of the U.S. Supreme Court, and general prosperity, caused little challenge to the *status quo* in the early days of the Republic. The general pattern followed the system of the mother country, and lack of clarity about the nature of the new democracy caused the federal government to move cautiously in the first years of the nineteenth century. However, after the Constitution went into effect in March 1780, Congress increasingly became involved in legislating for social problems. An early act passed in behalf of one special category of the population authorized the secretary of war, in 1832, to provide for the vaccination of Indians against smallpox. Another group singled out for special consideration were

[20] Thomas Paine, *The Rights of Man* (New York: E. P. Dutton & Co., 1951), p. 247.
[21] *Ibid.*, p. 249.
[22] *Ibid.*, p. 251.

veterans; in 1833 Congress established a national pension system for the relief of veterans who became mentally or physically disabled while in the service of their country. From this modest beginning, focused on compensation for loss of personal functioning rather than for loss of productive power, as in the case of the post-World War II GI Bills, grew the Veterans Administration of the twentieth century.

The movement toward government intervention was matched in the early years of the nineteenth century by the reform movement, which called into question all sectors of American social life. This movement, later constricted and channeled into the all-consuming problem of Negro slavery, had several characteristics that made it different from later reform periods but similar in some of its goals. This period of reforming zeal was remarkable in American life in that it was an expression of the Transcendental philosophy, which was a denial of Puritan and Calvinist precepts and was led in large measure by New England clergymen. The belief in man's inherent goodness rather than dwelling on his depravity, springing from original sin, is all the more remarkable because of the localization of the roots of the reform philosophy in New England. Although Calvin's ideas and corruptions and refinements of his theology had proved to be ideally suited to frontier conditions, the blending of a doctrine of historical inevitability along with a determination to shape the future proved to be too much of an intellectual straitjacket for democratic descendents of the Puritans. The reform movement took place outside the political framework, although many of the ends sought, such as women's suffrage, legal equality for women in matters of property and custody of children, homestead rights, free public education, and prohibition, were achieved through political means sooner or later.[23]

Most of the early reformers, feeling that democracy had been thwarted by the political organizations, regarded the political system as an object of distrust and therefore believed that the route for providing the great society lay outside that system. The most extreme statement of the attitude and the cause that provided the most important rationale for it was expressed by Henry David Thoreau. Although Thoreau declared in *Walden*, "If I knew for a certainty that a man was coming to my house with the conscious design of doing me good, I should run for my life," [24] he was nonetheless exquisitely aware of society's contradictions and concerned for his fellow man. But he believed that the political system was only an expedient that could not be trusted so long as it tolerated slavery and

[23] Henry Steele Commager, *The Era of Reform 1830-1860* (New York: D. Van Nostrand Co., 1960).

[24] Henry David Thoreau, *Walden and Civil Disobedience*, Sherman Paul, Ed. (Boston: Houghton Mifflin Co., 1957), p. 51.

could, as did Massachusetts, pass a Fugitive Slave Law. Thoreau also articulated a concern that has continued throughout American history to be a question of vital concern—majority rule and minority rights. At a time when there is in America a minority poor, it is well to examine Thoreau's ideas about the question of minority rights versus majority-rule:

> After all, the practical reason why, when the power is once in the hands of the people, a majority are permitted, and for a long period continue, to rule is not because they are most likely to be in the right, nor because this seems fairest to the minority, but because they are physically the strongest. But a government in which the majority rule in all cases cannot be based on justice, even as far as men understand it. Can there not be a government in which majorities do not virtually decide right and wrong, but conscience?—in which majorities decide only those questions to which the rule of expediency is applicable? Must the citizen ever for a moment, or in the least degree, resign his conscience to the legislator? Why has every man a conscience, then? I think that we should be men first, and subjects afterwards. It is not desirable to cultivate a respect for the law, so much as for the right.[25]

This passage from *Civil Disobedience*, written in 1849, was Thoreau's reaction to having been imprisoned for failing to pay his tax to support the local church and "the state which buys and sells men, women, and children, like cattle at the door of its senate-house."

Some of the more enduring reforms of the period were possible because of political support or sponsorship. One of the more noteworthy was the program of prison reform effected by Edward Livingston. For a time, early in the century, America became the envy of other civilized nations in the rehabilitation provided to the incarcerated. Solitary confinement, many times without work, was originally practiced in Auburn, New York, and Pittsburgh, Pennsylvania prisons. However, under the influence of men such as Livingston, Louis Dwight, and Robert Vaux, the prisons in many parts of the United States adopted the later Auburn system, which called for common labor during the day and isolation at night. In addition, John Augustus, a shoemaker in Boston, in 1841 began acting as an informal probation agent to prevent imprisonment, and juveniles began to attract attention as requiring treatment separate from adult offenders. Juveniles were, in many states, confined in Houses of Refuge—boys up to the age of 16 and girls, to age 14. In a system highly reminiscent of the present, juveniles were given an indeterminate sentence to the Houses of Refuge, considered to be halfway between a school and a prison. Gustave de Beaumont, a Frenchman who toured the United States and observed

---

[25] *Ibid.*, p. 236.

penology practices before recommending their adoption by his country-men, described these institutions as follows:

> The young deliquents are received much less for punishment than to re-ceive that education which their parents or their ill fate refused them; the magistrates, therefore, cannot fix the duration of their residence in the house of refuge, because they cannot forsee how much time will be nec-essary to correct the children, and to reform their vicious dispositions.
>
> The office of judging whether a child is fit to leave the refuge, is left to the managers of the establishment. . . . But then even when a child leaves the house of refuge in consequence of good conduct, he does not cease to be under the supervision of the managers during minority; and if he does not realize the hopes which had been entertained, the latter have the right to call him back to the house of refuge, and may employ the most rigorous means in order to effect it.[26]

Interestingly enough, the matter of constitutionality which now sur-rounds the judicial proceedings for juvenile crime was equally in question 150 years ago. As de Beaumont pointed out:

> Some objections have been made in Pennsylvania against the right granted to the houses of refuge to receive individuals who had neither committed a crime nor incurred a conviction. Such a power, it was said, is contrary to the Constitution of the United States. . . .[27]

American leadership in the areas of prison reform and juvenile treat-ment died with the Civil War, but another reform movement, initiated shortly before that conflagration, had an enduring impact on the treatment of children. The Children's Aid Society of New York, under the leader-ship of Charles Loring Brace, pioneered, in a very rough sense, the system of foster care. Emphasis was placed, at least in theory, on finding suitable homes for New York's abandoned children. This is said, however, within the context of realizing that the whole point of the program was to move the children to some other place rather than attempt to help them in their native locale. In placing an estimated 50,000 children in the Midwest, the Society was unable, because of lack of staff and knowledge, to rise much above the earlier system of indenture. The essence of the movement and its importance for the present lies in the emphasis on home care at a time when the usual treatment for dependent children was the almshouse and the orphanage.

A movement that was characteristic of the first period of reform, vestiges of which remain today, were the utopian colonies. Some, such

---

[26] Gustave de Beaumont and Alexis de Tocqueville, *On the Penitentiary System in the United States and its Application in France* (Carbondale: Southern Illinois University Press, 1964), p. 139.

[27] *Ibid.*

as the Oneida Community in upstate New York, practiced social arrangements such as a complex marriage system wherein everyone in the colony was married to everyone else—which made the colonies unacceptable to surrounding citizens. Others, such as Brook Farm in Massachusetts, were inhabited primarily by intellectuals and were short-lived, sometimes because of ineptitude for communal living on the part of residents, sometimes because of inadequate financing. Others, such as Nashoba, the emancipation colony in Tennessee (founded by Frances Wright and supported by Robert Owen, founder of New Harmony in Indiana), antagonized the community by mixing races and floundered for want of adequate financial support. Romantic ideas about creating a perfect society, as in the case of Brook Farm, the failures of which were ably documented by Nathaniel Hawthorne in the novel *Blithedale Romance*, were not quite as serviceable under primitive conditions as the Puritan ethos. Despite the short life of many of the utopian communities, the idea of moving out of the established communities and demonstrating a superior organization for society has had a lasting impact on American life. In some respects the later settlement house movement can be compared to the utopian colonies in that settlements involved the physical movement of the reformer and an urge to live a simpler life for the benefit of mankind.

The distrust of the early reformers for government intervention was perhaps justified by the experience of Dorothea Dix in her efforts on behalf of the deaf and mentally ill. Although the central government had acted for groups of citizens early in the century, the willingness to do so dissipated in the argument over states' rights that preceded the Civil War. The abdication by the federal government of responsibility for social improvement is well illustrated by the 1854 veto by President Franklin Pierce of legislation which would have appropriated 12.5 million acres of public lands for the establishment of institutions for the care of the deaf and insane. Pierce's veto was based on the constitutional stand that charitable activities were reserved to the states since they were not specifically delegated to the federal government. In fact, federal intervention had been sought, and lobbied successfully through both houses of Congress by Miss Dix because of the refusal or inability of the several states to act. Traveling through most of the states, Miss Dix investigated the conditions in communities and presented memorials to the state legislatures outlining her findings. Her research showed that local resources were usually limited to jails and almshouses and that in the latter it was not unusual for paupers to be given responsibility by the Overseer of the Poor for the custody and restraint of the insane. Cost determined the quality of care given, and the conditions she described did not differ significantly from those in the seventeenth century or earlier. The use of paupers to care for the physically and mentally ill had its antecedents in England, where victims of the plague were consigned to the care of the poor because no one else wished to be exposed to the contagion.

THE EVE OF THE CIVIL WAR

By the end of the first half of the nineteenth century reform was centered on the question of slavery, and men such as William Lloyd Garrison, editor of *The Liberator*, helped to focus the attention of religious leaders and secular reformers on abolition. Some reforms turned out differently than envisioned by their proponents, as many reforms have had a way of doing. As a case in point, the agitation for state action for the mentally ill, necessitated by the Pierce veto, resulted in the creation of large state institutions, which were to become the "dumping ground" for counties and remain so in most states today. The care of the indigent remained a local concern, and taxation for their support either in their own homes or in almshouses was based on land ownership, as in Elizabethan days. The promise of democracy was stunted by the development of conservative counterforces that made action by the central government impossible so long as questions regarding the commitment of the several states to its perpetuation remained in doubt. The distrust of reformers and humanitarians for the ability of the government to act positively in behalf of citizens acted as a stumbling block in the development of affirmative government. Voluntary associations and private beneficence grew as the country grew, but it was not until after the Civil War, when the question of states' rights was (at least partially) answered, that further national legislation for social welfare could be secured. But the Civil War also raised even more important questions in that the economy began to move at a greatly accelerated speed toward industrialization, immigration increased and changed in composition, and the legal system became increasingly the creature and servant of the well-to-do. Furthermore, despite the Transcendentalist revolt against Puritanism, the Protestant ethic remained ingrained in the American mind. It was in the last half of the century that it was applied to the social sector with a vengeance—a development that would have lasting consequences for America.

Selected Bibliography

Ariela, Yehoshua. *Individualism and Nationalism in American Ideology*. Cambridge: Harvard University Press, 1964.
Bainton, Roland H. *The Reformation of the Sixteenth Century*. Boston: Beacon Press, 1952.

Barker, Sir Ernest. *Political Thought of Plato and Aristotle*. New York: Russell & Russell, 1959.
Bell, Walter George. *The Great Plague in London in 1665*. London: Bodley Head Ltd., 1951.
Beard, Charles A. *An Economic Interpretation of the Constitution*. New York: Macmillan Co., 1935.
Bornet, Vaughn Davis. *Welfare in America*. Norman: University of Oklahoma Press, 1960.
Bridenbaugh, Carl. *Cities in the Wilderness*. New York: Alfred A. Knopf, 1955.
Chambliss Rollin. *Social Thought From Hammurabi to Comte*. New York: Henry Holt and Co., 1954.
Clarke, Helen I. *Social Legislation*. New York: Appleton-Century-Crofts, 1957.
Commager, Henry Steele. *The Era of Reform 1830–1860*. New York: D. Van Nostrand Co., Inc., 1960.
Commons, John R. *A Documentary History of American Industrial Society*. New York: Russell & Russell, 1958.
Creech, Margaret D. *Three Centuries of Poor Law Administration In Rhode Island*. Chicago: University of Chicago Press, 1936.
Curti, Merle. *The Growth of American Thought*. New York: Harper & Row, 1951.
Deane, Herbert Andrew. *The Political and Social Ideas of St. Augustine*. New York: Columbia University Press, 1963.
de Beaumont, Gustave, and de Tocqueville, Alexis. *On the Penitentiary System in the United States and its Application in France*. Carbondale: Southern Illinois University Press, 1964.
de Crevecoeur, J. Hector St. John. *Letters From an American Farmer*. New York: E. P. Dutton & Co., 1957.
de Schweinitz, Karl. *England's Road to Social Security*. New York: A. S. Barnes & Company, a Perpetua Book, 1943.
de Schweinitz, Karl. *Social Security for Egypt*. Washington, D.C.: Government Printing Office, 1952.
Fishel, Leslie H., Jr., and Quarles, Benjamin. *The Negro American: A Documentary History*. New York: William Morrow & Co., 1967.
Friedlander, Walter A. *Individualism and Social Welfare*. New York: Free Press of Glencoe, 1962.
Gabriel, Ralph Henry. *The Course of American Democratic Thought*. New York: Ronald Press, 1956.
Griffin, Clifford S. *Their Brothers' Keepers*. New Brunswick, N.J.: Rutgers University Press, 1960.
Hadas, Moses. *Imperial Rome*. New York: Time Inc., 1965.
Hofstadter, Richard. *American Political Tradition*. New York: Vintage Books, 1960.
Huizinga, Johan. *The Waning of the Middle Ages*. New York: Doubleday & Co., Inc., 1956.

Jefferson, Thomas. *Notes on the State of Virginia.* Edited by William Peden. Chapel Hill: University of North Carolina Press, 1955.

Jordan, W. K. *Philanthropy in England, 1480–1660.* New York: Russell Sage Foundation, 1959.

Langland, William. *The Vision of Piers Plowman.* New York: Greenwood Press, 1968.

Latourette, Kenneth Scott. *A History of Christianity.* New York: Harper & Row, 1953.

Lewis, David W. *From Newgate to Dannemora.* Ithaca, N.Y.: Cornell University Press, 1965.

McGiffert, Arthur Cushman. *Martin Luther: The Man and His Work.* New York: D. Appleton-Century Company, 1941.

McLuhan, Marshall. *The Gutenberg Galaxy.* Toronto: University of Toronto Press, 1962.

McNeill, John T. *The History and Character of Calvinism.* New York: Oxford University Press, 1954.

May, Edgar. "The Disjointed Trio: Poverty, Politics and Power," *The Social Welfare Forum, 1963,* Official Proceedings of the 90th National Conference on Social Welfare. New York: Columbia University Press, 1963, pp. 47–61.

Mencher, Samuel. *Poor Law to Poverty Program.* Pittsburgh: University of Pittsburgh Press, 1967.

Mosse, George L. *Calvinism: Authoritarian or Democratic?* New York: Holt, Rinehart & Winston, 1961.

Mosse, George L. *The Reformation.* New York: Henry Holt & Co., 1953.

Niebuhr, Reinhold. *The Contribution of Religion to Social Work.* New York: Columbia University Press, 1932.

Ostrander, Gilman Marston. *The Rights of Man in America, 1606–1861.* Columbia: University of Missouri Press, 1960.

Paine, Thomas. *The Rights of Man.* New York: E. P. Dutton & Co., 1951.

Pumphrey, Ralph E., and Pumphrey, Muriel W. *The Heritage of American Social Work.* New York: Columbia University Press, 1961.

Rayback, Joseph G. *A History of American Labor.* New York: Macmillan Co., 1959.

Schlesinger, Arthur M., Jr. *The American as Reformer.* Cambridge: Harvard University Press, 1950.

Spitz, Lewis W., ed. *The Reformation: Material or Spiritual?* Boston: D. C. Heath & Co., 1962.

Tawney R. H. *Religion and the Rise of Capitalism.* New York: New American Library, a Mentor Book, 1954.

Thoreau, Henry David. *Walden and Civil Disobedience.* Edited by Paul Sherman. Boston: Houghton Mifflin Co., 1957.

Webb, Sidney, and Webb, Beatrice. *English Poor Law History.* New York: Longmans, Green, & Co., 1929.

Wright, Frances. *Views of Society and Manners in America.* Cambridge: Belknap Press, 1963.
Zweig, Stefan. *The Right to Heresy.* Boston: Beacon Press, 1951.

Chapter Two

Social Welfare in
Industrializing America

I N THE PERIOD from the Civil War to the time the nation became involved in World War I, social service programs developed and were integrated into America's social institutions. Social security programs were increasingly advocated by social critics, and many voluntary citizen's organizations developed in the states and on the national level to press for reform and improvement of the quality of life.[1]

During this time of expanding social welfare organization the nation was transformed from a predominantly agrarian and rural society into one with more people living in urban than in rural areas. By the end of the century more people were employed in manufacturing, construction, trade, and transportation than in agriculture. Furthermore the composition of the population was altered by a massive influx of immigrants, with a shift in the sources of immigration from northern to eastern and southern Europe.

This was a period of intellectual and social ferment in America. New ideas about man and society developed, including some that dealt with man's responsibility to his fellow man, to his community, and to his government. Different notions also evolved about the proper role of government in relation to the citizens and the reasons for having a government at all.

During this period of rather rapid change, many people and many organizations played a part in calling attention to the need for adjusting social institutions to the demands of industrialization and urbanization. In this era the profession of social work had its genesis, and social workers played an important part in calling society's attention to areas of need. Many believed that poverty, delinquency, mental illness, and other social problems could be prevented. Social workers and others interested in reform introduced a humanitarian approach to social problems that would be of continuing significance for the nation.

---

[1] Social institutions develop to perform certain functions for a society and come into being to help people work together to achieve common goals. The National Association of Social Workers, in its *Goals of Public Social Policy*, describes social institutions functionally to include "organized family, voluntary, economic, or governmental structures; attitudes, customs, or beliefs; and established patterns of relationship and interaction among any of these elements in a functioning society." National Association of Social Workers, *Goals of Public Social Policy* (New York: National Association of Social Workers, 1966), p. 7. Social services include all of the programs and activities that are aimed at furthering the welfare of the individual in society, and social security is used to denote programs provided by government at any level to provide income maintenance or economic security for the people. Helen I. Clarke, *Social Legislation* (New York: Appleton-Century-Crofts, 1957), p. 444. Social insurances are conditional programs under sponsorship of the state or federal government in the United States.

THE CIVIL WAR AND SOCIAL SERVICES

In 1854, the same year President Pierce vetoed the bill that would have involved the federal government in the care of the mentally ill and the deaf, Congress passed the Kansas-Nebraska Bill, which repealed the Missouri Compromise. From that time until the outbreak of hostilities between North and South, innovation or leadership by the central government became virtually impossible because the nature of the Union became the predominant concern. This political hiatus was paralleled in the field of social welfare by the slavery question. Social reform movements concerned with such things as legal equality for women or international peace were relegated to positions of secondary importance. While the question of whether the nation should continue to exist was debated, there was little possibility that Congress or the President would endanger a precarious balance by asserting federal primacy in social questions.

Once the conflict between the sections became a reality, however, the government in Washington, D.C., passed a succession of bills dealing with social problems. Some of these were concerned with problems attendant to prosecuting the war while others dealt with broad social issues in which the South had opposed federal action. Examples of the latter include the chartering of the Union and the Central Pacific Railroads by Congress in 1862 and passage of the Morrill Act in the same year. In promoting the construction of a transcontinental railroad system through loans and grants of land, congressional action had a number of social consequences. The growth of the transportation system led to an increase in immigration and laid the foundation for the development of heavy industry. The need for iron increased, partly in response to the needs of the railroad, and new agricultural lands were opened up as the railroads moved into areas remote from the rivers and canals. The demography of the nation was changed as cities such as Chicago and Kansas City developed in a few decades into metropolitan centers that owed their size and importance to the railroad lines. The Morrill Act was a continuation of the pattern established by Jefferson in the Northwest Ordinance wherein land was offered to the states to achieve a social objective. The Act made available to states 30,000 acres times the number of senators and representatives to Congress with the stipulation that colleges be established with the funds received from the sale of land to teach "agriculture and the mechanic arts". The intent of the Act was to make college education available to anyone wanting it, at the expense of the government, and to further promote agriculture and industry. The Act was important for the future in that it extended the concept of the federal-state "matching grant" and broadened the interpretation of the constitutional provision that Congress could "promote the general welfare" of citizens. It is apparent that the intent and method of the Morrill Act was not significantly different from the legislation that had been proposed by Dorothea Dix and vetoed as unconstitutional.

In addition to social legislation, two agencies—one privately sponsored and the other created by Congress—were developed during the Civil War, that were to provide examples of organization and action for succeeding generations. The first of these, the U.S. Sanitary Commission, was created on June 12, 1861. The Commission, patterned after the British Sanitary Commission, was a voluntary agency that fostered interest in later years in the American Red Cross and stimulated public concern about physical and mental health. The second agency, the Freedmen's Bureau, was authorized by legislation signed by President Abraham Lincoln on March 3, 1865. Through this bureau "the federal government would administer charity to the needy on a large scale." For the first time, citizens in a state were taxed from Washington through the temporary wartime enactment of an income tax to support the indigent population of other states.[2] Creation of the Freedmen's Bureau also opened the door for the expansion of the "police power" of the federal government in the administration of justice and provided a model for other future programs designed to benefit black and white alike.[3]

THE UNITED STATES SANITARY COMMISSION

The U.S. Sanitary Commission was developed under the initiative of Henry W. Bellows, a Unitarian minister from New York; the concept was supported by Dorothea Dix, who had been appointed Superintendent of Nurses by the government. The Commission was created to supplement the activities and correct the defects of the Medical Bureau of the War Department. Lincoln approved and sanctioned this civilian effort with mixed emotions, and this ambivalence toward the Commission permeated the executive branch. The organization aroused the suspicion and hostility of military men, and their cooperation was difficult to obtain.

Frederick Law Olmsted became secretary general of the Commission in 1861. He had achieved success as a writer on conditions in the antebellum South. He was also a city planner and conservationist whose

[2] George R. Bentley, *A History of the Freedmen's Bureau* (Philadelphia: University of Pennsylvania, 1955), p. 37.
[3] Through the years the police power has been a "flexible, constantly changing and enlarging concept." It is considered to be inherent in the sovereignty of the state and includes those things essential to public safety, health, and morals. In the United States it has developed to mean the right of the state to protect the public interest and includes the "power of the legislature to act for the protection of the general welfare." Clarke, *op. cit.*, p. 7.

achievements included the creation of Golden Gate Park in San Francisco and Central Park in New York City. Olmsted fashioned the Sanitary Commission into an effective agency that inspected the operations of the Medical Bureau, acted as the distributing agent of largess collected for the relief of service men, and made reports on morale and battle conditions. Although documents such as the *Report on the Demoralization of the Volunteers* provided insight into the weaknesses of the North's war efforts, they exacerbated the ill feelings existing between the Commission and military leaders.[4]

Acting in concert with other groups concerned with the medical needs of the soldiers, agents of the Commission such as Samuel Gridley Howe, Louisa Lee Schuyler, and Elisha Harris focused public attention on health needs and problems. Agents also gained experience in social welfare organization and methods of operation. Howe had achieved fame before the war as head of the Perkins School for the Blind and contributed his administrative ability to the work of the Commission. He also was experienced in working with opposition, having been involved with Horace Mann in Massachusetts during the campaign for better public schools. The experience was perhaps more significant for Miss Schuyler, who in the 1870s established the State Charities Aid Association in New York and opened the first nurses' training school in America at Bellevue Hospital in New York City. Harris was also profoundly affected by his work with the commission. A physician, he later became an important figure in tenement inspection and regulation in New York City. In that city he organized the first free public immunization service and helped found the American Public Health Association in 1872.

By disbursing money and supplies collected from state governments and benevolent societies, publishing medical monographs on hygiene and epidemiology, and introducing the practice of inspecting field facilities and hospitals, the Commission assisted in the war effort. The services it provided and the patterns of coordination it developed had a lasting impact. In addition to interesting the general public in health and sanitation matters, the Commission was one unifying force in the parts of the nation not directly affected by the war. Leaders in local programs of services related to health and welfare became aware of the activities of individuals in other parts of the nation.

By the end of the war the Commission had succeeded in forming more than 7000 aid societies, along with its affiliates, and had contributed more than $15 million in supplies. It had also supported 40 homes and lodges for soldiers, distributed reading matter, and given assistance to illiterate

[4] William Quentin Maxwell, *Lincoln's Fifth Wheel* (New York: Longmans, Green & Co., 1956), p. 23.

or incapacitated men wishing to write letters home.[5] Its work, and perhaps its conflict, with the Medical Bureau led to that service's reorganization and modernization. Agents also gained the cooperation, if not the whole-hearted support, of a nurse involved in ministering to soldiers—Clara Barton.

THE FREEDMEN'S BUREAU

The Bureau of Refugees, Freedmen, and Abandoned Lands was created within the War Department in 1865 and was to have continued in existence for one year after the end of the war. However, subsequent legislation extended the life of the bureau and it did not disappear until the end of June 1872.

Welfare activities were carried on by the military forces prior to 1865 as a matter of necessity. Refugees from the Confederacy and liberated Negroes were, in 1861 and 1862, a considerable problem, a problem which was magnified by the Emancipation Proclamation of January 1, 1863. During the war the Army constructed camps for the freedmen, and in a number of instances abandoned plantations were leased to Northerners and even freed Negroes by U.S. tax commissioners.[6] A futile attempt was made at colonization in Haiti, and attempts were made to disperse people who were technically "contraband property" throughout the country. These attempts were met with objections from laborers in the North who feared the competition of Negroes as much as they did the common practice of contracting convict labor to replace working men. Communities also expressed fear that relief might have to be given to indigents who did not have residence.

Alarmed over the actual and feared exploitation of Negroes, humanitarians such as Henry W. Bellows, Robert Dale Owen, Samuel Gridley Howe, and Henry Ward Beecher petitioned the President for governmental assumption of responsibility for the Negro. Pressure from state and local freedmen's aid societies in the North led to study commissions and new directives to military commanders and tax officials. It was not until the Bureau was actually created in 1865, however, that a comprehensive plan was devised for the new citizens. The National Freedmen's Relief Association, the Western Freedmen's Aid Commission, and numerous religious bodies pioneered in working with this needy group. Their efforts led to an increase in governmental concern and activity, a pattern that has not been unusual in the development of American social welfare services.

---

[5] *Ibid.*, p. 306.
[6] Laura Wood Roper, "Frederick Law Olmsted and the Port Royal Experiment," *Journal of Southern History*, Vol. 31, no. 3 (August 1965), pp. 272–84.

The office of administrator of the Freedmen's Bureau was filled by Major General Oliver Otis Howard, a military hero and openly pious man. Although not notably an abolitionist prior to 1865, he directed the 10 districts created by the legislation with dignity and conviction. Under his supervision the Bureau developed numerous programs to provide relief for the hungry, schools and orphan asylums for the young and illiterate, employment services for the freedmen, courts of justice, and legal aid for helping Negroes learn their rights as citizens.[7]

During its existence the Bureau distributed perhaps as much as $17 million in goods, services, and cash, operated 45 hospitals with a maximum of 4292 beds, transported 32,000 freedmen and white refugees, and helped provide 4000 teachers for schools in the South.[8] The scope and magnitude of the Bureau's work had no precedent in the United States and would not be approached again on a federal level until the New Deal of the 1930s.

Many of the social welfare programs of the Bureau ended before its dissolution in 1872. This was true of such things as federal aid for private housing, work projects, and government-sponsored medical care. Buildings to house the aged and infirm, however, continued to be used, and their financing was assumed by local communities. The same was true of the child care institutions that were constructed. Some land was redistributed by the Bureau, and vigorous, though futile, attempts were made to establish systems of tenant contracts and programs to regulate conditions of labor.[9] Colleges such as Howard, Fisk, and Atlanta were built with support from the Freedmen's Bureau, and, as long as the Bureau existed, attempts were made to help the Negro move into the mainstream of Southern life. Even with the demise of the Bureau and the end of Reconstruction, the spirit of cooperation endured until the appearance of "Jim Crow" separatism toward the end of the century.[10]

The significance of the Freedmen's Bureau for later social welfare developments lies in three areas. The first, previously mentioned, was the assumption of federal responsibility for a group of needy citizens. The second was the broadening of the police power of the state in elaborating the phrase in the Preamble of the Constitution that permits Congress to

[7] Victoria Olds, "The Freedmen's Bureau: A Nineteenth-Century Federal Welfare Agency," *Social Casework*, Vol. 44, no. 5 (May 1963), p. 251.

[8] *Ibid.*, p. 252.

[9] Gunnar Myrdal, Richard Sterner, and Arnold Rose, *An American Dilemma* (New York: Harper & Row, 1944), p. 227.

[10] C. Vann Woodward, *The Strange Career of Jim Crow* (New York: Oxford University Press, 1966), pp. 67-109.

pass laws and create programs "to promote the general welfare." [11] The third enduring contribution of the Freedmen's Bureau was the promotion of free public education in the South to the benefit of both Negroes and poor whites.

Before the war education for slaves was increasingly prohibited by law, and the lot of the Caucasian in the South was often only slightly better. Only North Carolina, which had a less rigid aristocracy than most other Southern states, showed much interest in the development of common schools. Even so, the school term in North Carolina was limited to four months, and the efforts of educators to improve the system encountered opposition from academies and other private schools as well as a lack of support from the upper class.[12] Most Southern states did not accept the common school idea until after the Civil War, when Congress required Southern states to establish and support public schools and to add to their constitutions "the requirement that taxes should be levied for public schools open to Negroes as well as whites." [13] Much of the interest in education was generated by the Freedmen's Bureau, which as late as 1870 operated 216 schools in the South.[14] Further support for education came from private groups such as the Quakers or from private philanthropic efforts such as the Peabody Education Fund. Although the South would continue to lag behind other sections in the development of public education, teachers sent there by the Bureau and other private and religious groups played an important part in changing the attitudes of the common man toward education. In some instances this change may have proceeded rather differently from what the teachers intended. Such was the case of the gentleman who, 50 years later, reminisced about his recognition of education as a positive value:

In 1876, I stood in Fayetteville, North Carolina, and saw white youth after white youth turned away from the polls because they could not read and write, while my horse-boy and other Negroes, taught by Northern teachers, were consistently admitted to the ballot. And I swore an oath that so long as my head was hot, I should never cease from fighting for

[11] Another constitutional development of significance during Reconstruction, although not connected to the Freedmen's Bureau, was the use of the amendment procedure to achieve social reform for the first time.

[12] Guion Griffis Johnson, *Ante-Bellum North Carolina* (Chapel Hill: University of North Carolina Press, 1937), pp. 271–78.

[13] Fletcher M. Green, "Cycles of American Democracy," *The Mississippi Valley Historical Review*, Vol. 48, no. 1 (June 1961), p. 16.

[14] *Report of the Commissioner of Education, 1870* (Washington, D.C.: Government Printing Office, 1870), p. 150.

schools until every white child born in the State had at least the surety of a common school education—and a chance to go as much further as he liked.[15]

Before the Civil War the slaveholding states, with less than half of the nation's population, had less than a third as many public schools and a fourth as many pupils.[16] By 1914 every Southern state had some form of uniform school system, providing education for nearly 8 million students—virtually the same proportion to population as in the rest of the nation.[17] By 1918 all states in the South had laws requiring compulsory school attendance—legislation pioneered by Massachusetts in 1852.[18]

CHANGING PATTERNS IN AMERICAN LIFE

Out of the Civil War and the era of Radical Reconstruction emerged a new nation—a nation with roots in an earlier day but concerned with the expansion of industry, the reformulation of democratic values and ideals, and the need to develop new institutions for the new society. As is generally the case, ideas and social institutions changed at a much slower pace than the expanding technology and economic reality.

One of the best indexes of the growth from a preindustrial, agrarian-oriented society to an urban industrial culture was the expansion of the railroad and the developments it spawned. In 1860 the nation had less than 40,000 miles of railroads, with a property investment of slightly over $1 million. By 1890 the mileage had increased to nearly 200,000, and the investment represented more than $10 million.[19] In addition to providing a system for moving goods to markets more efficiently than before, railroad construction added to the demand for iron and cheap labor through immigration and stimulated entrepreneurs to develop mass-production methods for mass markets.

The development of the railroads is only one example of the rapidly expanding economy. Developments and improvements in technology in many other areas served to raise the standard of living in America and promoted the growth of the industrial complex. Agriculture became more mechanized as interregional and overseas markets expanded.[20] Textile

---

[15] Quoted in W. J. Cash, The Mind of the South (Garden City, N.Y.: Doubleday Anchor Books, 1956), p. 180.

[16] Douglass C. North, Growth and Welfare in the American Past (Englewood Cliffs, N.J.: Prentice-Hall, 1966), p. 92.

[17] Cash, op. cit., p. 223.

[18] S. E. Frost, Jr., Historical and Philosophical Foundations of Western Education (Columbus, Ohio: Charles E. Merrill Books, 1966), p. 400.

[19] North, op. cit., pp. 112–13.

[20] Robert William Fogel, Railroads and American Economic Growth (Baltimore: Johns Hopkins Press, 1964), pp. 17–19.

manufacturing and the processing of agricultural products developed as regional specializations, as did the production and refining of petroleum.

As the growth of the industrial society accelerated, the city assumed an increasingly important role in the ecology of America. Although rural life continued to hold a place of esteem as the locus of political morality and the place where man's soul was refreshed through contact with the soil, the balance of political power shifted from the countryside to the urban center. The shift occurred as the cities became the centers of financial power, and business leaders on occasion exerted undue influence on political figures to gain favorable legislation or to block unwanted regulation. Into this maelstrom came many young people, who were offended by the sights and sounds of the burgeoning city. As Irvin G. Wyllie has pointed out, "It was sad but true, that if a country boy desired fortune he had to leave home to achieve it." [21] Many did achieve it and many more did not. A number did move into the urban middle-class reform movements that became increasingly important as the century drew to a close.

Part of the growth of the city may be attributed to internal migration and natural increase from a high birthrate that more than offset high infant and maternal mortality. Of overwhelming importance in boosting the population in urban centers was the increasing immigration from Europe. Some 600,000 men had died in the Civil War, and with no federal legislative restriction on immigration and with a growing need for unskilled laborers the non-English speaking southern and eastern Europeans came. The influx grew steadily to the peak year of 1907, when 1,285,000 newcomers arrived at Ellis Island. By 1910 nearly half of the nation's population of almost 92 million lived in cities. This represented a population increase of five and a half times and a fortyfold increase for urban communities.[22] The newer immigrants congregated in the ghettos of the cities and typically had different values and customs and spoke different languages. Furthermore, many of the immigrants were accustomed to political and religious patterns that differed from the American system of democracy, individual enterprise, and evangelical Protestantism.

The institutions of America were being changed by internal developments that were quite as important overall as the input from abroad. The occasion of the Civil War and the subsequent industrial explosion led first to the phenomenon of the self-made entrepreneur and then to the rise of the corporation. Both contributed to an increasing emphasis on materi-

[21] Irvin G. Wyllie, *The Self-Made Man in America* (New Brunswick, N.J.: Rutgers University Press, 1954), p. 29.
[22] Samuel Mencher, *Poor Law to Poverty Program* (Pittsburgh: University of Pittsburgh Press, 1967), p. 233.

alistic acquisition and, more important, the stressing of the acquisition of fortunes as an end in itself. As the century drew to a close, it was increasingly apparent that the open society was becoming blocked by huge fortunes and combinations in industry, and one could no longer take for granted "an open road to moderate success." [23] The American idea of an open class system has been termed perhaps the most important single contribution to the social thinking of Western civilization.[24] After the Civil War its reality appeared to many to be increasingly threatened.

Not only was access to wealth less open, but the new organization of industry produced a changed relationship between employers and employees. Dr. Leete, in Edward Bellamy's utopian romance, *Looking Backward* gave a vivid account of the way many perceived relationships to have changed:

> Before this concentration began, while as yet commerce and industry were conducted by innumerable petty concerns with small capital, instead of a small number of great concerns with vast capital, the individual workman was relatively important and independent in his relations to the employer. Moreover, when a little capital or a new idea was enough to start a man in business for himself, workingmen were constantly becoming employers and there was no hard and fast line between the two classes.[25]

What Bellamy did not see was that, imperceptibly, a status revolution was also taking place. Before the 1870s the broader diffusion of wealth, power, and status had made the man of only moderate means a leader in his community. The small manufacturer, the lawyer, and the minister were persons of local importance in "an age in which local eminence mattered a great deal." [26] Increasingly toward the end of the century, the local gentry came to be overshadowed by the national figure of the master of the great corporation. Although centralization did not necessarily mean that local leaders were growing poorer in absolute terms, they were dwarfed by comparison with new leaders with wealth and power. "They were less important, and they knew it." [27]

[23] Merle Curti, *The Growth of American Thought* (New York: Harper & Bros., 1951), p. 508.
[24] Ralph Henry Gabriel, *The Course of American Democratic Thought* (New York: Ronald Press Co., 1956), p. 16.
[25] Edward Bellamy, *Looking Backward* (New York: Houghton Mifflin Co., 1926), p. 52.
[26] Richard Hofstadter, *The Age of Reform* (New York: Alfred A. Knopf, 1956), p. 135.
[27] *Ibid.*, p. 137.

LABOR AND POLITICS IN THE POST-CIVIL WAR PERIOD

In this milieu of rapidly changing economic and social institutions, the first industrial depression occurred in 1873. Although depressions had occurred before the Civil War, the impact had been less dramatic when economic suffering struck the farms or villages than when it hit entire working-class neighborhoods in urban centers. The depression of 1873 was triggered by the failure of the New York City banking firm of Jay Cooke and Company. Economic hardship continued in succeeding years; by 1877 it was estimated that as many as one-fifth of the workingmen were unemployed and that only one-fifth worked regularly. For those who managed to find work, wages dropped significantly. Wages declined by 45 percent in textile mills, and railway workers had their salaries cut 30 to 40 percent.[28] Unemployed "tramps" roamed the country looking for a livelihood and constituted a threat to communities away from large urban centers. Some people living on the outskirts of New England towns abandoned their homes in terror and in Jacksonville, Illinois, a roaming band of marauders temporarily took over the town.

Embryonic national labor unions existed before the Civil War; the most successful in the immediate postwar period was the Knights of Labor. This organization, formed into a national group in 1878, grew out of the labor strife associated with depression conditions. The first nationwide strike occurred in 1877 and involved various railway unions and owners. Although violence and disorder prevailed in many cities, nowhere was it more severe than in Pittsburgh. In the course of a strike against the Pennsylvania Railroad, 26 members of a rioting mob were killed by federal troops, and three days of unrest and looting caused an estimated damage to property of $5 million dollars. "The divergence between the interests of employer and worker and the increasing loss of personal contact between the two sides of industry as the scale of manufacturing increased were helping to develop class feeling in the United States; but the great strikes of 1877 acted as a catalyst in making people consciously aware of social distinctions." [29]

In addition to creating a consciousness of social differences, the depression and hard times led to increased awareness of political structures among the working classes and the rise of socialist thought, much of

[28] Joseph G. Rayback, *A History of American Labor* (New York: Macmillan Co., 1959), p. 129.
[29] Henry Pelling, *American Labor* (Chicago: University of Chicago Press, 1960), p. 61.

which was brought to America by immigrants. New ideas and political configurations came into being in a period that was already in ferment. The period after the Civil War was characterized politically by the growth of city "bosses." The pursuit of wealth was considered by many to be a more noble undertaking than political endeavors although, on occasion, politicians were made wealthy by bestowing favors. The structure of the political system made the state the effective arena in which many economic benefits were conferred on corporations and private persons. State governments were frequently controlled by political machines in the cities, and both were apt to be "owned" by one or another vested interest. To the poor person especially, local ward politics were likely to have more meaning than the state or federal government.

The years between Reconstruction and the 1890s have been described as the "dreariest chapter" in American politics and a time when "major social problems inherent in an industrial society that had subjugated a vast continent were virtually ignored." [30] Perhaps it is true that without political machines and bosses, "the eleven million American families with an average income of $380 a year might well have voted themselves all kinds of remedies, well or ill advised, for their relative poverty." [31] Whatever the answer, it was true that the decades in question were characterized by the middle classes, and those aspiring to move into that economic world, dropping out of politics. Decision making in many large cities passed into the hands of political machines while workingmen, sensing that the new industrial system held the promise of a better life for all citizens, became increasingly desperate. Given this kind of situation, it was hardly surprising that socialist egalitarianism attracted many of the immigrants. Neither is it surprising that new ideas and changing social conditions produced a feeling of apprehension on the part of more established citizens.

Significant ideological challenges also came from native-born political theorists and thinkers who reacted to the "contrast between the realities of social tension and inherited ideals of a classless society." [32] In 1879 Henry George published *Progress and Poverty*, and in the 1880s came Bellamy's equally successful *Looking Backward*. To a society imbued with a reverence for private property and the ideal of the free individual, both authors seemed as radical as any hot-eyed, imported anarchist. In his diagnosis of society's ills, George observed:

[30] Arthur Schlesinger, Jr., and Fred L. Israel, eds., *The Chief Executive* (New York: Crown Publishers, 1965), p. 156.

[31] Thomas C. Cochran and William Miller, *The Age of Enterprise* (New York: Harper & Row, 1961), p. 267.

[32] Samuel P. Hays, *The Response to Industrialism, 1885–1914* (Chicago: University of Chicago Press, 1957), p. 38.

Poverty deepens as wealth increases, and wages are forced down while productive power grows, because land, which is the source of all wealth and the field of all labor, is monopolized. To extirpate poverty, to make wages what justice commands they should be, the full earnings of the laborer, we must therefore substitute for the individual ownership of land a common ownership.[33]

Throughout the 1880s and 1890s the writing of George and Bellamy had a considerable impact on all levels of American society. By 1906 *Progress and Poverty* had been through more than 100 editions and had been read by perhaps 6 million men and women. In 1900 Bellamy's book was still selling at the rate of 10,000 copies a week and had spawned some 150 Nationalist Clubs across the nation. By the turn of the century, associations for reform and combinations for collective action on questions of social and economic structure gained in membership and influence. Farmers grouped together in the Grange and the Farmers' Alliances. Workingmen were attracted to the Kights of Labor and to its successors, the American Railway Union, the United Mine Workers, and the American Federation of Labor. By the 1890s politics and political action increasingly attracted the attention of labor, agriculturists, and middle-class reformers.

The political reaction of the 1890s to the conditions of the previous decades is to be seen in the agrarian and small-town support given to the Populist party; a large segment of labor sought redress of grievances in various socialist parties. In 1892 the Populists received 8.5 percent of the total vote in the presidential election; after the election of 1908 they ceased to exist after having supported that year's Democratic nominee.[34] The Socialist Labor Party was organized in 1877 and was built on the remnants of the earlier Working Men's Party. The Party "blossomed under the leadership of De Leon" in the 1890s and began entering slates of candidates for office on a local, state, and national level.[35] A number of important labor leaders (as well as a host of influential reformers) were influenced by socialist thought, and the bulk of support for Socialist Party influence came in 1912 when Eugene V. Debs received 5.9 percent of the popular vote.[36]

The Populists hoped to undertake basic economic reform with the expectation that they could thus raise prices paid to farmers, although their concern was not solely with the farmer. The agrarian base of support on which they depended, however, caused them to focus in the main on

[33] Henry George, *Progress and Poverty* (New York: Robert Schalkenbach Foundation, 1948), p. 328.
[34] Hofstadter, *op. cit.*, p. 98.
[35] David A. Shannon, *The Socialist Party of America* (New York: Macmillan Co., 1955), p. 2.
[36] Hofstadter, *op. cit.*, p. 98.

agricultural problems. Competing in world markets subject to fluctuations beyond his control, the farmer was aware that control of the machinery of politics was gravitating toward the city and away from his hands. Legislation to protect farmers had been the concern of politicians earlier in the century; primary concern had now shifted to protection for the new industrial empire. With a rhetoric more radical than their actions, the Populists were alternately ridiculed and feared by the middle classes.[37]

The Socialists, espousing reform through such measures as a graduated income tax, public ownership of railroads and public utilities, and woman suffrage, were plagued by schisms and stigmatized as an immigrant political movement.[38] These factors, along with the fact that it was anti-technological and represented a point of view that was a rather radical departure from traditional American political thought, made socialism unacceptable to the majority of Americans.

At the opposite end of the political spectrum from the Populists and the Socialists were the deeply traditional and conservative members of the Democratic and Republican parties. As was the case with those seeking reforms in American society, conservative associations such as the Daughters of the American Revolution and the National Association of Manufacturers developed. Concerned with preserving existing institutions and fearful of the encroachments that a militant political Left might make, conservatives hastened to defend the *status quo*. That they did not develop a third political force themselves is testimony to the fact that they were generally content with the existing political parties. Effective political control rested with the well-to-do, who pragmatically accepted the fact of machine politics in the cities and states and occasional acts of chicanery at the federal level. The middle classes, unable to accept either Populism or Socialism, in the main voted for the *status quo* because of the lack of an acceptable alternative. After 1900 the Progressive movement within the Republican Party presented a suitable alternative and vehicle for action.

In many respects the vehicle of Progressive Republicanism was a middle ground between the Right and Left politically. Acceptable to the majority of Americans, the movement suited those who did not countenance unbridled capitalism but who also wished to avoid drastic innovations in American institutions. Adherents of the new political movement were in favor of reform, not revolution.

The Progressives included in their numbers advocates of prohibition, prison reform, labor legislation, regulation of working hours for women, women's suffrage, and so on. Although any given Progressive may have

[37] *Ibid.*, p. 99.
[38] Theodore Draper, *The Roots of American Communism* (New York: Viking Press, 1957), pp. 11–35.

supported only one kind of reform, initially the differences did not seem so important as the particular cause advanced and the possibility of gaining support and political action. The distinguishing mark of the Progressive was his belief in social progress and his conviction that positive government intervention should be used to advance society.[39] Consistency and uniformity of goals was not a hallmark of the movement.

The Progressive's attitude toward government's right to regulate was in opposition to the conservative belief that progress through time and nature was inevitable; it denied the radical leftist thesis of class conflict. Seeing the farmer as exploited by the railroad and unrewarded for his toil, the worker underpaid and in poverty in the slums, children denied an education and imprisoned in the factory, politics debased in the city, state, and nation by the privileged, Progressives looked to exposure, militancy, and the ballot as guideposts on the path to reform. In many respects they reaffirmed American faith in democracy and the free individual and ushered in a renewal of the political system. The new consensus position lay between the conservative laissez-faire view of government power that had prevailed and the aggressively interventionist state espoused by the political Left.

NEW SOCIAL WELFARE AGENCIES AND THE NEW PHILANTHROPY

As the nation was altered by the many changes taking place after the Civil War, social welfare programs and agencies were changed to accommodate to new conditions. New services were developed, and a new philanthropy that stressed the need for scientific giving and that went beyond the earlier idea of meliorative alms to the poor emerged.

In response to what seemed to be serious threats to community stability and the inadequacy of the almshouse in handling massive need in time of depression, many cities developed a Charity Organization Society as a way of helping the "truly needy." Originating in England, the Charity Organization Society was similar in many ways to the pre-Civil War Society for the Prevention of Pauperism, which had flourished in New York City, and the more widespread Association for Improving the Condition of the Poor which had begun in the 1840s. Like the earlier groups, the COS stressed the individual nature of poverty, the investigation of need by volunteers, the giving of advice through "friendly visiting," and the careful distribution of funds to the eligible. Unlike the earlier groups, however, the COS made widespread use of women for visiting, did not usually dispense charity itself, and eventually moved into the use of paid

[39] Richard Hofstadter, *The Progressive Movement, 1900–1915* (Englewood Cliffs, N.J.: Prentice-Hall, 1963), pp. 4–5.

agents and organizers. Of seminal importance to professionalism, the COS workers increasingly desired training and education to equip them for working with the poor.[40]

The first COS was set up in 1877 by the Reverend F. H. Gurteen in Buffalo, New York. Just 5 years later, there were 25 cities with such societies. The movement of women into the work of the organization reflects their increased emancipation and the presence of some in society who had enough income to permit individual work with the needy. With the aim of using local resources for rehabilitation, volunteers were asked to keep records in order to prevent duplication of effort. Record-keeping was also important in preventing persons from "shopping around" and receiving help from more than one relief-giving society. The COS provided a clearinghouse for agencies which developed into social service exchanges, a program still in operation in many cities.

In time the keeping of records led to the realization that people and their needs must be individualized and that people became needy for reasons unrelated to moral flaws. It also became apparent to some agents while visiting and giving advice that the nature of the problems presented often required more than suggestions and good will. Agents began to ask for training to help individuals and sociological information so they could better understand their clients. Many recognized that the destitution of a family might as easily be caused by an impersonal society that could not provide work for the unemployed as by drunkenness or vice.

By the turn of the century more and more paid visitors were employed by the societies and, in time, leaders who developed out of the COS led the way in professional education in the new field of social work. Most of the visitors, however, did not lose their disdain for any kind of public welfare program; perhaps the majority felt, as did Josephine Shaw Lowell, that public help should be given only in an institution. Mrs. Lowell, a leader in the New York COS, outlined the deficiencies thus:

> Out-door relief . . . fails to provide that no one shall starve or suffer for the common necessaries of life. . . . Unless self-restraint and providence be conferred upon those who receive it, all that is bestowed will often be wasted by them in riotous living. . . . It fails to save the recipient of relief and the community from moral harm, because human nature is so constituted that no man can receive as a gift what he should earn by his own labor without a moral deterioration, and the presence in the community of certain persons living on public relief has the tendency to tempt others to

[40] It should be noted that many services such as free milk, family summer camps, well-baby clinics, etc., were pioneered by the New York Association for Improving the Condition of the Poor. As the title suggests, the AICP also gave more emphasis to the environmental causes of poverty than did the later COS in most cities.

sink to their degraded level. . . . The tax payers are the losers by out-door relief, because, although the amount given to each individual is, undoubtedly, smaller than would be required for that individual in an institution, yet out-door relief is so infectious, and, once obtained is so easy a way of getting a living, that far larger numbers demand and receive it than could be induced to enter an institution, and thus the total cost of public relief is always increased by giving it outside of the workhouse or almshouse. . . . Out-door relief, in fact, can not be defended; it has none of the redeeming features of private charity, because there is nothing personal or softening in it, nor has it the advantages which might, perhaps, be derived from an acknowledged and openly advocated communism, for the principle underlying it is not that the proceeds of all men's labor is to be fairly divided among all, but that the idle, improvident and even vicious man has the right to live in idleness and vice upon the proceeds of the labor of his industrious and virtuous fellow-citizen.[41]

Another movement growing out of the unsettled conditions in the second half of the nineteenth century that has been of utmost importance to the development of social welfare programs was the settlement house movement. Like the COS, the settlement was of English origin and started in East London, where students from Cambridge University "settled" in Toynbee Hall in 1884. The motivation was social and religious, and the idea behind the movement was that the classes could mutually benefit from close association. Students living in the slums could learn how to help the downtrodden, and the deprived segments of society would harbor less resentment of the upper classes and be more willing to accept the help they wished to give.

The first American settlement, Neighborhood House, was organized by Stanton Coit in New York in 1887. However, Hull House, established by Ellen Gates Starr and Jane Addams in Chicago two years later, became the most famous. Miss Addams, recipient of the Nobel Peace Prize in the 1930s, became the best-known social worker in America.

The programs offered in the settlements varied and were developed to meet the identified needs of the communities they served. In a period when the slums were the urban way stations for immigrants rather than repositories for internal aliens, many settlements offered Americanization classes to help newcomers become citizens. Some operated day camps and nursery shools for children of working mothers, and most had social clubs for young people. Men's groups developed into political forums, and many of the "settlers" lived in the slum neighborhoods to gain experience or to do research on social problems. Much of the research work was used

[41] Josephine Shaw Lowell, *Public Relief and Private Charity* (New York: G. P. Putnam's Sons, 1884), p. 66–67.

to support requests to state legislatures for corrective legislation. Thus the settlement houses attempted to establish that a need existed, frequently demonstrated how a service such as juvenile probation could be provided, pushed for society's assumption of responsibility for the needed service, and then moved on to new social problems.

It is worth noting that many, if not most, of the settlements were under the direction of college-trained and religiously inspired young people. The percentage of men working in the settlements was higher than that found in the COS. The settlement offered a way for the person of middle-class standing to help the needy and at the same time achieve a measure of recognition for humanitarianism. The settlement, and indeed all of the areas of social work, offered a more stimulating and challenging profession for women than school teaching, which was generally the lot of the career woman in the nineteenth century. Hundreds of small-town and suburban girls went from college into social work. "Social work in the slums was to the girl at the beginning of the twentieth century what the support of missionary work abroad had been to her grandmother." [42]

Most settlements were not affiliated with a political ideology or a particular religious denomination. But most settlement house workers were Protestant and, after the turn of the century, Progressive Republicans with a generous admixture of Socialists. The strength of the settlement house movement lay in its close contacts with the increasingly competent American universities, the workers' receptivity to new ideas, and their willingness to be instructed by the people who were their neighbors. As a whole, workers in the settlement houses were more understanding of the social causes of poverty than the COS agents. The latter made only occasional sorties into the neighborhoods of the poor and were slower to give up preconceived ideas of *why* people might be deprived. Intimately acquainted with the effects a poor environment might have on families, settlement house workers looked to state and national legislative remedies and became more politically active than their COS counterparts.

Social action became an important part of the work of the settlement houses. The 1892 Illinois statute prohibiting employment of children under the age of 14 and the employment of women for more than eight hours a day is an example of the way in which social legislation was achieved

---

[42] Andrew Sinclair, *The Emancipation of the American Woman* (New York: Harper & Row, 1965), p. 245. A survey made of 1076 college graduates who received the Bachelor of Arts from Bryn Mawr College between 1888 and 1910 showed that, of those employed, teaching remained the overwhelming occupational choice, with social work next in line. Nearly 27 percent were teachers; 4.6 percent held paid or unpaid jobs in social work. Only 1.2 percent were secretaries, and the same percentage were physicians. Scott Nearing and Nellie M. S. Nearing, *Woman and Social Progress* (New York: Macmillan Co., 1914), p. 237.

by settlement action. The law was placed on the books as the result of studies made of working conditions by residents of Hull House, especially Florence Kelley. Mrs. Kelley was subsequently named to head up the Factory Inspection Department that was created to carry out the law. Although later declared unconstitutional on the basis that the law impaired the right of contract, the legislation was the result of settlement house lobbying.

The distinctions between the COS and the settlement should not be drawn too finely. Mrs. Kelley's affiliations and her career illustrate the way in which people of different political persuasions moved back and forth between the two. Mrs. Kelley, a Socialist, moved from factory inspection in Illinois to directorship of the National Consumers' League in 1899. This organization was founded in 1891 by Josephine Shaw Lowell and was one of the most effective middle-class women's groups, through the use of the boycott, in opposing products made in sweatshops or by child labor. In New York Mrs. Kelley took up residence at the Henry Street Settlement, which was headed by a nurse, Lillian Wald, who originated the Visiting Nurses' services. Mrs. Kelley's relationship with Mrs. Lowell, a lifetime opponent of "outdoor relief," was apparently congenial even though Mrs. Kelley and Miss Wald were instrumental in advancing the idea of the White House Conference on Children and Youth, which promoted the development of "mothers' pensions."

Perhaps the most striking differences in opinion between settlement house workers and COS agents existed in their attitudes toward education for social work and toward public welfare. Settlement house workers were more likely to be found in the ranks of the supporters of social security programs such as unemployment insurance. In respect to education, the settlements were regarded as being laboratories in which students in the social sciences or the ministry could find practical experience; in many places they were an extension of the university. COS agents became increasingly concerned with the treatment of the individual and saw a need for being better equipped for such work. As will be seen, it was from the COS that the first schools of social work and many leaders in the move toward professionalization developed.

During the years in which the COS and the settlement house were evolving to meet the challenge of massive change, a new spirit of philanthropy quickened. Although there had been some with the means and the interest in "doing good" by setting up charitable trusts before the Civil War, the giant foundation is a twentieth-century phenomenon; its point of origin was the late nineteenth century.

Pre-Sumter beneficence was characterized by bequests measured in thousands rather than in millions of dollars and was sectional rather than national in scope. Most early foundations were set up to help certain classes of needy, such as the Mullanphy Fund, established in 1851 in St. Louis to assist pioneers who were moving to the West. Said funds were not only limited in purpose but, as in the case of Girard College, which was created to educate poor white male orphans, they typically made no provision for change and led to litigation over "the dead hand of charity." [43] Religious conditions or moral judgments were frequently included in early bequests—for example, the Association for the Relief of Respectable Aged and Indigent Females, which benefited from the contributions of the penurious John Jacob Astor.

By contrast the new philanthropy that emerged toward the end of the nineteenth century reflected the tremendous affluence of some men of wealth and a new philosophy of giving. A bequest of $508,000 led to the creation in 1846 of the Smithsonian Institution, the first significant foundation in America.[44] The Peabody Education Fund, established in 1867 to promote free public education and teacher training in the South, was endowed with $3.5 million by its founder.[45] The increasing wealth of philanthropists such as Andrew Carnegie and John D. Rockefeller was reflected in the increasing size of their philanthropies. In 1914 the Rockefeller Foundation was chartered with assets of $235 million and with a charge to do good throughout the world.[46] Thus did the size and scope of the foundations increase.

The philosophy behind giving also changed, and the ancient religious concept of a "stewardship of wealth" underwent a permutation. The secular version that emerged was best expressed by Andrew Carnegie in an article in the *North American Review*. Carnegie outlined "The Gospel of Wealth" as a new moral code that required the wealthy to

> consider all surplus revenues which come to him simply as trust funds, which he is called upon to administer, and strictly bound as a matter of duty to administer in the manner which, in his judgment, is best calculated to produce the most beneficial results for the community—the man of wealth thus becoming the mere agent and trustee for his poorer brethren, bringing to their service his superior wisdom, experience, and ability to

[43] This phrase relates to the practice of setting up charitable trusts with a specific social goal or target population rigidly defined. Changing times and social advancement may make the original bequest restrictions anachronistic, but "the dead hand of charity" ties the present to the needs and conditions of the past.

[44] Joseph C. Kiger, *Operating Principles of the Larger Foundations* (New York: Russell Sage Foundation, 1954), p. 22.

[45] Geoffrey T. Hellman, "The First Great Cheerful Giver," *American Heritage*, Vol. 17, no. 4 (June 1966), p. 33.

[46] Abraham Flexner, *Funds and Foundations* (New York: Harper & Row, 1952), pp. 57–58.

administer, doing for them better than they would or could do for themselves.[47]

The new spirit of philanthropy required that the giver be careful of the consequences of his gifts and be scientific in his approach lest he do more harm than good. In many instances, grants from the new foundations required the recipients to raise matching funds, and the business of giving began to approach the level of business acumen practiced by the large corporation.

SOCIAL DARWINISM AND THE SOCIAL GOSPEL

The philosophy of Social Darwinism and the humanitarian doctrines of the Social Gospel are reflected in the kind of society America has produced. The one was secular and the other religious; both addressed themselves to rationalizing man and modern society. Neither succeeded although they both left a residue of ideas about man's responsibility to his fellow men.

Social Darwinism developed from the writings of Herbert Spencer, the first of which predated Charles Darwin's findings by six years. Influenced by the early writings of Thomas Malthus, the core of Spencer's ideas in all of his writings was "the generalization that social or institutional evolution is part and parcel of cosmic evolution as a whole, and hence cannot be successfully controlled by artificial human intervention and guidance." [48] Although Darwin's findings were generalized to the entire animal world and not man in particular, the scientific aura surrounding his work gave an unwarranted luster to Spencer's views.

Social Darwinism found favor in America, although it was little discussed elsewhere. The popularity of Spencer here has been attributed to the following factors:

It was scientific in derivation and comprehensive in scope. It had a reassuring theory of progress based upon biology and physics. . . . It offered a comprehensive world-view, uniting under one generalization everything in nature from protozoa to politics. . . . Presented in language that tyros in philosophy could understand, it made Spencer the metaphysician of the homemade intellectual, and the prophet of the cracker-barrel agnostic.[49]

[47] Andrew Carnegie, "The Gospel of Wealth," *North American Review*, Vol. 183, No. 599 (September 21, 1906), p. 534.
[48] Howard Becker and Harry Elmer Barnes, *Social Thought From Lore to Science*, Vol. 3 (New York: Dover Publications, 1961), p. 799.
[49] Richard Hofstadter, *Social Darwinism in American Thought* (Boston: Beacon Press, 1955), pp. 31–32.

It was above all a suitable philosophy for rationalizing opposition to federal or state regulation in social or economic matters. Conservatives were justified in opposing regulation because it represented man's interference with the natural order. Spencer's notion of "survival of the fittest," a phrase he coined, seemed to fit well with the prevailing practices of industry and to vindicate the practice of combining small companies into monopolistic combinations.[50]

One of the more unattractive corollaries of Spencerian logic was the idea that the "unsuitable" individual, like the inefficient small company, would die off in human evolution. To interfere in the process by too liberal a dole, society ran the risk of interfering in the "law of nature" through futile and misguided altruism. Unionization, the regulation of wages and hours for women and children, or the threat of control of industry through such things as the 1890 Sherman Anti-Trust Act represented perilous tamperings with nature's laws.

The ideas Spencer brought from England to America appealed to many people as a rational and scientific explanation for the sometimes inhumane social conditions that developed in the process of industrialization. Working weeks of 60 to 80 hours were not uncommon, and the employment of children actually increased in factories and mines. Men and women employed in industry were unprotected in the event of industrial accidents because of the common law theory that they had a right to refuse work if they considered the job hazardous. Although Social Darwinists accepted the idea of voluntary giving to the needy because of its elevating effect on the donor, state-sponsored programs of welfare were considered subversive to nature's plan for the universe. The undifferentiated almshouse remained the basic institution, although certainly suspect, for the care of the indigent. In these places epileptics, the aged, abandoned children, pregnant women, the insane, the blind, the deaf, and others were "all dumped together into some old farmhouse that has been bought by the authorities, and put to this use." [51] Children over the age of 7 were treated as adults before the law; it was not until 1899 that the first juvenile court was established in Chicago. Adult offenders were incarcerated to exact society's retribution; few prisons followed the example of the Elmira Re-

[50] John D. Rockefeller, Jr., applied the theory to the practice of the Standard Oil Company in an address he gave to his Sunday school class: "The growth of a large business is merely a survival of the fittest. . . . The American-Beauty rose can be produced in the splendor and fragrance which bring cheer to its beholder only by sacrificing the early buds which grow around it. This is not an evil tendency in business. It is merely the working out of a law of nature and a law of God." Quoted in Richard Hofstadter, William Miller, and Daniel Aaron, *The United States* (Englewood Cliffs, N.J.: Prentice-Hall, 1957), p. 413.

[51] Amos G. Warner, *American Charities* (New York: Thomas Y. Crowell & Co., 1894), p. 141.

formatory in New York, which in 1877 adopted a parole system. In matters of law, the courts usually decided on the basis of common law precedent. A notable exception was the U.S. Supreme Court's acceptance of the concept of "sociological jurisprudence" in cases such as *Muller* v. *Oregon*, which in 1908 upheld the right of the state to establish a maximum 10-hour working day for women.[52]

Major opposition to Spencer's theories came from reformers who were shocked by social conditions and unimpressed by the application of ideas of biological evolution to human institutions. Reform Darwinists argued that true acceptance of Darwinian thought would make it necessary for society to accept regulation as the only way the fittest could be assured an opportunity to survive. The religious leaders who were involved in the movement known as the Social Gospel argued against Social Darwinism on moral and ecclesiastical grounds. Finding their Judeo-Christian ethics offended by some of the excesses in the economic, political, and social systems, the leaders in the Social Gospel revived equalitarian ideas inherent in Christian theology and argued:

> If it is in any sense true that social good and evil is collective in nature, . . . not simply a sum total of the good and evil of individuals, then men are obliged to act directly upon the social order and work for its reconstruction, as a part of their religious responsibility to their fellow men.[53]

Taking an activist approach in religious matters, the Social Gospel was 'a reaction against the exaggerated spiritualism and the pietistic individualism that had been so largely responsible for the churches' removal from the field of social action." [54] Challenging the ideas of evangelical Protestantism, the Social Gospel found adherents in the upper-class churches, which, aside from the Unitarian, had been relatively untouched by transcendentalist ideas. Social Gospel ministers occupied pulpits in Congregational, Episcopal, Presbyterian, and Methodist churches, and the new emphasis on religion in secular life stirred the consciences of many in the upper and middle classes.

Few of the exponents of the reform-minded gospel were as radical as the Baptist Walter Rauschenbusch, who felt communism was "more in harmony with the genius of Christianity and with the classical precedents of . . . early social life." [55] Most were uncomfortable in movements such as the Society of Christian Socialists, founded in 1889. Probably most

---

[52] *Curt Muller* v. *State of Oregon*, 208 U.S. 412 (1908).

[53] Paul A. Carter, *The Decline and Revival of the Social Gospel* (Ithaca, N.Y.: Cornell University Press, 1954), p. 5.

[54] Bernard J. Coughlin, *Church and State in Social Welfare* (New York: Columbia University Press, 1964), p. 21.

[55] Henry Steele Commager, *The American Mind* (New York: Macmillan Co., 1955), p. 176.

lay somewhere in the middle ground occupied by Graham Taylor, Washington Gladden, and Herbert H. Jacobs. Most of the leaders came from the "old-stock and Protestant establishment" and sought reform within the established systems rather than revolution from without.[56]

In addition to the ministers, the Social Gospel found a number of prominent supporters in secular life, especially in the universities. Men such as the sociologists Edward A. Ross and Lester Ward helped found the American Sociological Society as an instrument of the New Social Science, which was closely akin in outlook to the Social Gospel view of man. Another important academician, Richard T. Ely, hoped to involve more people in the Social Gospel movement and wrote:

> The Church has, for the most part, contented herself with repeating platitudes and . . . has allowed the leadership in social science to slip away from her. It can, then, scarcely excite surprise that communism has become infidel, and socialism materalistic.[57]

Ely, an economics professor at the University of Wisconsin, helped found the American Economic Association in 1885. In drawing up the original platform he declared:

> We hold that the conflict of labor and capital has brought into prominence a vast number of social problems, whose solution requires the united efforts, each in its own sphere, of the church, of the state, and of science.[58]

The trilogy he described sums up the areas of interest of the Social Gospel leaders, both lay and clerical. The intertwining of the three was characteristic of the movement.

Despite the important part the Social Gospel movement played in awakening citizens to the religious side of social questions, it never enjoyed majority support in the churches. The bulk of the Protestants were unconvinced by either the Social Gospel or the New Social Science; Roman Catholics were perhaps more influenced by the 1891 Encyclical that held that the State had an obligation to the poor and the disadvantaged workers.[59]

---

[56] E. Digby Baltzell, *The Protestant Establishment* (New York: Random House, 1964), p. 163.

[57] Richard T. Ely, "Social Aspects of Christianity" (Boston: W. L. Green & Co., 1888).

[58] Quoted in E. Digby Baltzell, *op. cit.*, p. 162. Ely and Ross helped found the Wisconsin University Settlement House in Milwaukee, and Ely was a pioneer in social work education. He attempted to interest Edward T. Devine of the New York COS in a three-year course of study for students interested in working in charity organization societies, prisons, and reformatories.

[59] *Five Great Encyclicals* (New York: Paulist Press, 1939), pp. 1–30. Rerum Novarum.

Perhaps the bulk of America's churchgoers, Protestants and Catholics, held to the teachings of the past and believed in the gospel of individualism in religion and in things temporal. One of the most cogent statements of this faith was that delivered over 6000 times by Russell Conwell, founder of Temple University in Philadelphia and pastor of the Temple Baptist Church. Eloquently describing the traditional view of man and his relationship to the state, the nature of poverty and its cure, Conwell believed:

> To sympathize with a man whom God has punished for his sins, thus to help him when God would still continue a just punishment, is to do wrong, no doubt about it, and we do that more than we help those who are deserving. While we should sympathize with God's poor—that is, those who cannot help themselves—let us remember there is not a poor person in the United States who was not made poor by his own shortcomings, or by the shortcomings of some one else. It is all wrong to be poor when it is so easy to get rich.[60]

THE GROWTH OF GOVERNMENTAL RESPONSIBILITY FOR THE NEEDY

The growth of voluntary services and private philanthropy was the nation's response to social problems accompanying changes taking place in the nation after the Civil War. Reliance on private efforts was increasingly supplemented by governmental activity. Slowly at first, more rapidly later on, the Social Darwinist's attitude about the proper role of government began to give way to what social reformers considered a more positive view of governmental intervention.

A harbinger of this evolution of attitude was the assumption of responsibility by the states for the supervision of local institutions caring for the needy and for institutions created by the legislatures. Massachusetts in 1863 had created the first Board of State Charities to act in an advisory capacity to institutions and to the legislature. In succeeding years states such as Wisconsin and Rhode Island developed boards having the power of administration and control. Such boards were increasingly staffed with full-time salaried workers responsible for maintaining and directing charitable agencies throughout the state.

Early in the twentieth century, in the climate of political Progressivism, a number of states began to enact programs of categorical assistance to be given to the needy in their own homes. This kind of outdoor relief was to be available to all who fit into the categories established. The new programs were set up with the categorical feature to overcome constitutional hazards; the goal was to make public income maintenance programs more humane and more democratically available. Although the use of

[60] Russell Conwell, *Acres of Diamonds* (New York: Harper & Bros., 1915), p. 21.

categories of need was hardly new, the placing of a financial floor under some of the eligible poor through "outdoor relief" was a departure from the spirit of the almshouse.

In 1903 Illinois enacted the first statewide program of aid to the needy blind. As is true today, assistance for the blind led the way in the development of aid for other categories of dependent persons. By 1934, 24 states had begun their programs of aid to the blind.

As early as 1914 Arizona passed a law providing for pensions for the aged, but this was declared unconstitutional by that state's supreme court. In 1915 Alaska established the first old age assistance program, but it was not until eight years later that Montana became the first state to pass legislation that survived the challenge of constitutionality in the courts. As in the case of aid to the blind, the principal advocate of old age assistance programs was the Fraternal Order of the Eagles. By 1934, 34 states had been persuaded to pass laws providing for aged residents.

In 1911 Missouri passed the first "mother's pension" program, but it was applicable only in Jackson County (Kansas City). In the same year, however, Illinois adopted a program of aid for mothers that was statewide in coverage. By 1934 all states except Georgia and South Carolina had some form of aid to mothers of dependent children.

Along with the developing state leadership in providing for the categorically needy, programs of social insurance began to attract attention. The federal government under the leadership of Theodore Roosevelt took one of the first steps in this direction. In 1908 a workmen's compensation law was enacted by Congress, which applied to all artisans and laborers employed by the national government. Thereafter individual states followed the example of the federal government and passed laws based on the principle of "liability without fault" where industrial accidents were concerned.

In this movement toward government intervention on behalf of the citizens, the United States proceeded at a much slower pace than the industrial nations of Europe. Although state governments and on occasion the federal government took some responsibility for meeting need, the nation lagged far behind such countries as England. There, during the time the United States was making piecemeal attempts to come to grips with the new society, the modern welfare state had its genesis as an institutional program designed to ameliorate the effects of industrialization. In England in the first part of the twentieth century, old age pensions were developed, health and unemployment insurance programs were begun, and minimum wage legislation was passed. In America, programs of unemployment insurance, social insurance, and other social security measures were not enacted until the Depression era of the 1930s.

THE DEVELOPMENT OF NATIONAL ASSOCIATIONS FOR WELFARE GOALS

Along with the increase in governmental concern about social welfare problems, a renascence of national leadership and concern for problems confronting the nation developed toward the end of the century. Although during the Civil War the North had a high degree of interstate cooperation for meeting social needs connected with the war, this was less characteristic of the immediate postwar period. It was not until the last quarter of the century that significant moves were taken to overcome this lack of coordination and to recognize the fact that social problems were national in scope.

One of the first examples of this recognition was the creation in 1874 of the National Conference of Charities and Correction.[61] This organization was made up of individuals interested in improving man's lot and was designed to act as a clearinghouse for ideas and services. The Conference helped promote leadership and interstate cooperation and provided a pattern and an impetus for later professional organizations.

In the same period the American Red Cross had its beginnings as a national social agency concerned with problems of health and national disasters. This agency was the creature of Clara Barton, who became interested in the work of the International Red Cross following her work as a nurse during the Civil War. Her campaign for ratification of the Geneva Convention lasted from 1869 until 1882, when President Chester A. Arthur acceded to her persistent demands. The Red Cross pioneered in national fund-raising for benevolent purposes not connected solely with military problems or religious bodies. The giving of funds for helping fellow citizens in all states, as well as abroad, contributed to national unity in welfare concerns.

Other national organizations were created after the turn of the century, many of which were devoted to advancing a particular program or service. The National Tuberculosis Association had its beginnings in 1904; the American Child Health Association was organized in 1909; the National Committee for Mental Hygiene was created in 1908. The mental hygiene movement, although typical of many of the associations that developed to promote specific institutional reforms, was unusual because of the circumstances that led to the development of a national organization.[62]

The movement in mental hygiene, a cause advanced earlier by various

---

[61] This organization is now known as the National Conference on Social Welfare.
[62] Albert Deutsch, *The Mentally Ill in America* (New York: Columbia University Press, 1949), pp. 300–331.

people, was crystallized by the appearance in 1908 of a book entitled *A Mind That Found Itself*. The author, Clifford W. Beers, had graduated from Yale in 1897; from 1900 to 1903 he was hospitalized for mental illness in private and public institutions, where he was exposed to conditions that had changed but little since Dorothea Dix's time. Having recovered in spite of the treatment he received, Beers went on to write his book. Like other "muckraking" writings of the time, the mass circulation of his description of personal experiences led to the creation of public sentiment in favor of changes. The mental health movement was promoted by prominent doctors, psychologists, social workers, and interested citizens. The efforts of the national association led to the development of child guidance clinics and community mental health services.

Other national organizations were developed early in the twentieth century to focus on specific social health problems. Illustrative of this trend were the National Child Labor Committee, Goodwill Industries, and the National Association for the Advancement of Colored People.[63] The latter has been of particular significance in the history of the nation, and it indicated a renewed concern about the plight of the Negro.

Not since Radical Reconstruction had the white majority been involved in the problems that grew up in its wake. It is significant that the new impetus came from individuals acting voluntarily in concert and it is worth noting that some of the leaders in developing civil rights organizations were social workers.

Between 1866 and 1875 Congress enacted eleven civil rights acts and three amendments were added to the Constitution to enable Negroes to participate as citizens of the democracy. But before the end of the century most of the legal protection was vitiated and the race problem was relegated to the local communities or the states. Race riots in Springfield, Illinois, in 1908 prompted a number of journalists to write muckraking articles about the plight of the Negro. A number of middle-class Negroes and whites, including W. E. B. Du Bois, William E. Walling, Mary White Ovington, and Oswald Garrison Villard, editor of *The Nation*, worked together to start the National Association for the Advancement of Colored People. Du Bois was named first national executive of the organization. Groups such as the NAACP and the National Urban League provided a way in which legal remedies could be sought for a deprived group. They also were important in fostering interracial cooperation by working for legal redress for violations of civil rights and called attention to another kind of inequality that existed in the post-Civil War Period: in the case of the Negro the indignity of racial discrimination was added to the problem of economic exploitation that confronted many white Americans.

[63] Robert H. Bremner, *American Philanthropy* (Chicago: University of Chicago Press, 1960), p. 123.

Summary

The approach of the Civil War caused reformers to coalesce around the single issue of slavery. With the advent of hostilities, they and their supporters turned their attention to the fighting men and the freed slaves. New agencies and services were created to handle problems that arose in the course of the war.

The America built on the ruins of ante-bellum institutions was the scene of considerable conflict. The individual became increasingly lost in an impersonal society, and the locus of political power began an inexorable shift from the countryside to the city. Immigrants streamed in from southern and eastern Europe, in contrast to the earlier Anglo-American immigration pattern. The cultural differences that the new immigrants introduced added to the stresses of American life.

In the rush to industrialize, life in America and the philosophy of its citizens was challenged and changed. Old symbols and beliefs were confronted by new economic forces and scientific advances. The urban and industrial society that was being created required that accommodations be made through the altering of society's institutions. The churches, the legal system, the legislatures, and the political parties were affected by change. At the same time these institutions resisted change and sought to conserve so far as possible the older ways of doing things.

In the time between the Civil War and World War I, two social movements developed that were important at that time and that ultimately led to the creation of the profession of social work: the Charity Organization Society and the settlement houses which were voluntary groups that attempted to handle problems of massive poverty and urban misery. Intellectually and politically the leaders in both movements were progressive but not radical. They, like many other concerned citizens of the day, came to believe that the government should act as a positive force in society by making some effort to control change. The belief of the social workers that poverty could be eliminated through the efforts of voluntary agencies and government programs was to be of continuing importance in the years ahead.

Selected Bibliography

Addams, Jane. *Twenty Years at Hull House.* New York: Macmillan Co., 1910.
Altschule, Mark D. *Roots of Modern Psychiatry.* New York: Grune & Stratton, Inc., 1957.
Baltzell, E. Digby. *The Protestant Establishment.* New York: Random House, 1964.

Becker, Howard, and Barnes, Harry Elmer. *Social Thought From Lore to Science*, Vol. 3. New York: Dover Publications, 1961.

Beers, Clifford W. *A Mind That Found Itself*. New York: Longmans Green, 1908.

Bellamy, Edward. *Looking Backward*. New York: Houghton Mifflin Co., 1926.

Bentley, George R. *A History of the Freedmen's Bureau*. Philadelphia: University of Pennsylvania Press, 1955.

Blumberg, Dorothy Rose. *Florence Kelley*. New York: Augustus M. Kelley, 1966.

Bremner, Robert H. *American Philanthropy*. Chicago: University of Chicago Press, 1960.

Bremner, Robert H. *From the Depths*. New York: New York University Press, 1956.

Carnegie, Andrew. "The Gospel of Wealth." *North American Review*, Vol. 183, no. 599 (September 21, 1906), pp. 526–37.

Carter, Paul A. *The Decline and Revival of the Social Gospel*. Ithaca, N.Y.: Cornell University Press, 1954.

Cash, Wilbur J. *The Mind of the South*. Anchor Books. Garden City, N.Y.: Doubleday & Co., Inc., 1956.

Clarke, Helen I. *Social Legislation*. New York: Appleton-Century-Crofts, 1957.

Cochran, Thomas C., and Miller, William. *The Age of Enterprise*. New York: Harper & Row, 1961.

Commager, Henry Steele. *The American Mind*. New York: Macmillan Co., 1955.

Conwell, Russell. *Acres of Diamonds*. New York: Harper & Bros., 1915.

Coughlin, Bernard J. *Church and State in Social Welfare*. New York: Columbia University Press, 1964.

Croffut, William A. *The Vanderbilts and the Story of Their Fortune*. Chicago: Belford, Clark & Co., 1886.

Curt Muller v. *State of Oregon*, 208 U.S. (1908).

Curti, Merle. *The Growth of American Thought*. New York: Harper & Bros., 1951.

Deutsch, Albert. *The Mentally Ill in America*. New York: Columbia University Press, 1949.

Drake, Richard B. "Freedman's Aid Societies and Sectional Compromise." *Journal of Southern History*, Vol. 29, no. 2 (May 1963), pp. 175–86.

Draper, Theodore. *The Roots of American Communism*. New York: Viking Press, 1957.

Dulles, Foster Rhea. *The American Red Cross*. New York: Harper & Bros., 1950.

Eaton, Clement. *The Mind of the Old South*. Baton Rouge: Louisiana State University Press, 1967.

Ely, Richard T. *Ground Under Our Feet*. New York: Macmillan Co., 1938.

Ely, Richard T. "Social Aspects of Christianity." Boston: W. L. Green & Co., 1888. (Pamphlet).

Fishlow, Albert. *American Railroads and the Transformation of the Ante-Bellum Economy.* Cambridge: Harvard University Press, 1964.
Five Great Encyclicals. New York: Paulist Press, 1939.
Flexner, Abraham. *Funds and Foundations.* New York: Harper & Bros., 1952.
Fogel, Robert William. *Railroads and American Economic Growth.* Baltimore: Johns Hopkins Press, 1964.
Frost, S. E., Jr. *Historical and Philosophical Foundations of Western Education.* Columbus, Ohio: Charles E. Merrill Books, 1966.
Fuller, Louis. *Crusaders for American Liberalism.* New York: Collier Books, 1961.
Gabriel, Ralph Henry. *The Course of American Democratic Thought.* New York: Ronald Press, 1956.
George, Henry. *Progress and Poverty.* New York: Robert Schalkenbach Foundation, 1948.
Green, Fletcher M. "Cycles of American Democracy." *The Mississippi Valley Historical Review,* Vol. 48, no. 1 (June 1961), pp. 3–23.
Hays, Samuel P. *The Response to Industrialism, 1885–1914.* Chicago: University of Chicago Press, 1957.
Hellman, Geoffrey T. "The First Great Cheerful Giver." *American Heritage,* Vol. 17, no. 4 (June 1966), pp. 29–33 and 76–77.
Hicks, John D. *The Populist Revolt.* Minneapolis: University of Minnesota Press, 1931.
Hofstadter, Richard. *The Age of Reform.* New York: Alfred A. Knopf, 1956.
Hofstadter, Richard. *The Progressive Movement, 1900–1915.* Englewood Cliffs, N.J.: Prentice-Hall, 1963.
Hofstadter, Richard. *Social Darwinism in American Thought.* Boston: Beacon Press, 1955.
Hofstadter, Richard, Miller, William, and Aaron, Daniel. *The United States.* Englewood Cliffs, N.J.: Prentice-Hall, 1957.
Holbrook, Stewart H. *The Age of the Moguls.* New York: Doubleday & Co., 1954.
Holden, Arthur C. *The Settlement Idea.* New York: Macmillan Co., 1922.
Johnson, Guion Griffis. *Ante-Bellum North Carolina.* Chapel Hill: University of North Carolina Press, 1937.
Josephson, Matthew. *The Robber Barons.* New York: Harcourt, Brace & Co., 1934.
Kellogg, Charles Flint. *NAACP.* Baltimore: Johns Hopkins Press, 1967.
Kiger, Joseph C. *Operating Principles of the Larger Foundations.* New York: Russell Sage Foundation, 1954.
Kohn, Hans. *American Nationalism.* New York: Collier Books, 1961.
Leech, Margaret. *In the Days of McKinley.* New York: Harper & Bros., 1959.
Link, Arthur S. *Woodrow Wilson and the Progressive Era: 1910–1917.* New York: Harper & Row, 1954.
Lowell, Josephine Shaw. *Public Relief and Private Charity.* New York: G. P. Putnam's Sons, 1884.

Maxwell, William Quentin. *Lincoln's Fifth Wheel*. New York: Longmans, Green & Co., 1956.
Mencher, Samuel. *Poor Law to Poverty Program*. Pittsburgh: University of Pittsburgh Press, 1967.
Mowat, Charles Loch. *The Charity Organization Society 1869–1913*. London: Methuen & Co., 1961.
Mumford, Lewis. *The Story of Utopias*. New York: Harcourt, Brace & Co., 1945.
Myrdal, Gunnar, Sterner, Richard, and Rose, Arnold. *An American Dilemma*. New York: Harper & Row, 1944.
Nearing, Scott, and Nearing, Nellie M. S. *Woman and Social Progress*. New York: Macmillan Co., 1914.
New York Association for Improving the Condition of the Poor. *The 92d Annual Report of the AICP, 1934–1935*. New York: New York Association for Improving the Condition of the Poor.
Norris, Frank. *The Octopus*. New York: New American Library, 1964.
North, Douglass C. *Growth and Welfare in the American Past*. Englewood Cliffs, N.J.: Prentice-Hall, 1966.
Olds, Victoria. "The Freedmen's Bureau: A Nineteenth-Century Federal Welfare Agency. *Social Casework*, Vol. 44, no. 5 (May 1963), pp. 247–54.
Pelling, Henry. *American Labor*. Chicago: University of Chicago Press, 1960.
Rayback, Joseph G. *A History of American Labor*. New York: Macmillan Co., 1959.
Roper, Laura Wood. "Frederick Law Olmsted and the Port Royal Experiment." *Journal of Southern History*, Vol. 31, no. 3 (August 1965), pp. 272–84.
Schlesinger, Arthur, Jr., and Israel, Fred L. *The Chief Executive*. New York: Crown Publishers, 1965.
Shannon, David A. *The Socialist Party of America*. New York: Macmillan Co., 1955.
Sinclair, Andrew. *The Emancipation of the American Woman*. New York: Harper & Row, 1965.
Sinclair, Upton. *The Jungle*. New York: Collier Books, 1958.
Taylor, Alrutheus Ambush. *The Negro in the Reconstruction of Virginia*. Washington, D.C.: Association for the Study of Negro Life and History, 1926.
U.S. Department of Commerce. *Historical Statistics of the United States, Colonial Times to 1957*. Washington, D.C.: Government Printing Office, 1961.
U.S. Commissioner of Education. *Report of the Commissioner of Education, 1870*. Washington, D.C.: Government Printing Office, 1870.
Warner, Amos G. *American Charities*. New York: Thomas Y. Crowell & Co., 1894.
Weinberg, Arthur, and Weinberg, Lila. *The Muckrakers*. New York: Simon & Schuster, 1961.

Woodward, C. Vann. *The Strange Career of Jim Crow*. New York: Oxford University Press, 1966.

Wyllie, Irvin G. *The Self-Made Man in America*. New Brunswick, N.J.: Rutgers University Press, 1954.

Zilboorg, Gregory, and Henry, George W. *A History of Medical Psychology*. New York: W. W. Norton & Co., 1941.

Chapter Three

The Growth of Governmental
Responsibility for Social Welfare

Aᴍᴇʀɪᴄᴀ's ɪɴᴠᴏʟᴠᴇᴍᴇɴᴛ in World War I brought to a close the second major era of social reform; the advent of World War II brought the end of a third. Before World War I, voluntary services were created to help humanize and rationalize an expanding industrial system. States, and increasingly the federal government, produced legislation aimed at protecting society from the excesses of industrialization. The diverting of interest and resources to meet a challenge overseas meant that less attention was to be paid to domestic needs, and stresses in social institutions were glossed over for the sake of unity around a common purpose.

Wartime controls imposed by the government went far beyond measures that had been employed before. Intervention in business, commerce, labor, civil liberties, social services, and virtually every other phase of American life was accepted by the majority of the nation's citizens. The aftermath of the intervention was not the continuation of governmental regulation, which many social workers espoused, but rather a rejection of it and a return to laissez-faire. Disillusionment with the peace and fear of subversion from abroad contributed to the yearning for "normalcy," which meant decreased governmental activity.

The period of the 1920's was a time when many people were doing well—and were less interested in doing good. Belief in American institutions, as they were, formed a cardinal tenet in the democratic faith, and to challenge or to question was unpopular if not un-American. Existing economic institutions seemed capable of producing a good life for all, and reform appeared unnecessary. Individualism, defined as freedom from government control or regulation, was seen as the touchstone of the American economic miracle. Should the individual, through some failing of his own, be unable to participate fully in society, voluntary philanthropy existed to minister to the failures and rejects.

The vision of the perfect society grew increasingly dim in the 1930s. A major industrial depression, first considered as a temporary situation required to adjust supply to demand, brought a revival of the attitude that government should act positively in behalf of the people. As the formerly prosperous were submerged into the greatly enlarged majority poor, demands for insurance against future want and pressure for ameliorative action brought about a resurgence in governmental activity. Waging a war against want, which was as important for the survival of the nation as any military campaign, the New Deal inaugurated numerous programs that had their roots in the political progressivism of the century's earlier years.

In many respects the social welfare programs initiated by the New Deal were the triumphs of Progressivism.[1] Many were unrelated to then current

---

[1] Progressives who were social workers were more sympathetic to the New Deal than other Progressives because they welcomed federal minima in relief, public works,

realities, and a number of the programs initiated in the name of social welfare reform were regressive so far as the economy was concerned. They were all, however, pragmatic attempts to provide a foundation under the citizens so that dire want and crippling poverty could be eliminated in America.

The political success of New Deal programs can be measured by the continuation of many of them past the time of the depression crisis. The economic success of the New Deal was assured by World War II. Demands on the economy that were made by the need for war material required deficit spending by government that far exceeded any social spending programs of the New Deal. Unemployment became academic as factories worked overtime to produce guns and tanks. Government regulation of society's basic institutions was again permitted on a scale prohibited during the war against economic depression. Basic civil rights were denied to many citizens, notably the Japanese on the West Coast, in the name of national solidarity and defense. Once again, social reform was shunted aside as interest and activity were necessarily directed beyond the nation's shores.

THE CONSENSUS FOR REFORM

In the years between Theodore Roosevelt's assumption of the presidency in 1901 and the first stirrings of conflict in Europe in 1914, the political consensus in America was progressive and reformist. Municipal and state governments came under the scrutiny of muckraking writers in magazines such as *McClure's* and *Collier's*. Economic problems such as monopolies and social questions exemplified by a reawakened interest in the plight of the Negro were brought to public attention. In the federal government, no less than in the states, attempts were made to improve and make more humane social institutions affected by radically changed economic and demographic patterns. Congress wrote into law measures designed to safeguard the individual and to regulate industry and commerce. Laws such as the Hepburn Act, passed in 1906, delegated to independent commissions the power to regulate industries. Commerce was brought under the purview of federal authorities by legislation such as the Pure Food and Drug Act of 1906, which protected the public from contaminated foods and unscrupulous patent medicine vendors. In addition to congressional action, President Roosevelt expanded the power of his office by intervening in questions of national concern. Illustrative of

---

public housing, social security, and other programs espoused by the New Dealers. Otis L. Graham, Jr., *An Encore for Reform* (New York: Oxford University Press, 1967), p. 103.

this was his appointment in 1903 of an arbitration board of experts to settle differences between labor and management in a long and bitter coal strike. This kind of presidential intervention was in marked contrast to that of President Grover Cleveland, who had in 1892 sent federal troops into Pennsylvania to break a strike at the Homestead steel plant.

While the federal government sought to provide increased protection for the people, state legislatures acted to promote individual welfare. Beginning in 1908 with the landmark case of *Muller* v. *Oregon*, which held Oregon's law establishing a 10-hour working day for women constitutional, states increasingly legislated to correct social ills. New or improved maximum-hour laws for women were passed by 41 states between 1909 and 1917. Minimum wages for women were established in 12 states in the same period, and 30 states added workmen's compensation insurance to their statutes.

Economic conditions generally improved between 1900 and 1914. Private beneficence, supplemented by some state and local programs of income maintenance, appeared to be a suitable policy for meeting need in America. Orderly and progressive development was being made to meet the needs of new immigrants, and, with only occasional setbacks, industrial development provided employment for most of those seeking it. The mood in America was profoundly optimistic because of the belief that changes could be made without revolution and that rational dedication to principle would produce the best kind of free, though regulated, society. Walter E. Weyl in 1912 epitomized the hopeful spirit of the times in his writing about the progressive democracy. Rejecting the Marxian "class struggle" thesis as well as the elitist ideas of those he designated as plutocrats, Weyl answered affirmatively his question of whether or not a democracy could endure by stating the following:

We are now beginning to realize that our present acute social unrest is not due to an attempt to return to the conditions and principles of the eighteenth century, but is merely a symptom of a painfully evolving democracy, at once industrial, political, and social. We are beginning to realize that our stumbling progress towards this democracy of to-morrow results from the efforts, not of a single class, but of the general community; that the movement is not primarily a class war, but, because it has behind it forces potentially so overwhelming, has rather the character of a national adjustment; that the movement does not proceed from an impoverished people, nor from the most impoverished among the people, nor from a people growing, or doomed to grow, continually poorer, but proceeds, on the contrary, from a population growing in wealth, intelligence, political power, and solidarity. We are awakening to the fact that this movement, because of the heterogeneous character of those who further it, is tentative, conciliatory, compromising, evolutionary, and legal, proceeding with a minimum of friction through a series of partial victories; that the movement is influenced and colored by American conditions and traditions, proceeding, with but few violent breaks, out of our previous industrial, political, and intellectual development and out of our material and moral accumulations, and utilizing, even while reforming and reconstituting, our economic and legal machinery.[2]

The picture of orderly progress, supported by all segments of society, was slightly disrupted in 1914 by a business recession touched off by the coming of war in Europe. The effects on financial institutions were mitigated somewhat by the existence of the new Federal Reserve System, which had been set up the previous year.[3] A number of workers, however, were without employment as the supply of money available for plant expansion dwindled and as marketing patterns overseas were disrupted. The picture was further marred by continuing labor unrest resulting from a lack of improvement in real wages paid to workers and continuing changes in industrial organization.[4] One of the severest examples of labor trouble occurred in 1914 at Ludlow, Colorado, where a long-standing battle between miners affiliated with the United Mine Workers and operators culminated in the "Ludlow Massacre." Baldwin-Felts agency guards attacked the miners and their camps, slaying 4 adults and 12 children. The camp had been set up when families were evicted from the company town maintained by the Rockefeller-owned Colorado Fuel and Iron Company. West Virginia, the Pacific Northwest, and other areas of the country were also scenes of conflict.

Despite the evidences of internal problems, the process of reformation seemed to many to be proceeding in a much more rapid and orderly fashion than ever before in history. Most citizens shared the dominant attitude held by social workers that progress was inevitable and perfection of

---

[2] Walter E. Weyl, *The New Democracy* (New York: Harper & Row, 1964), pp. 348–49.

[3] M. W. Sprague, "The Crises of 1914 in the United States," *The American Economic Review*, Vol. 5, no. 3 (September 1915), pp. 499–533.

[4] The stages of industrial organization have been delineated by a government committee concerned with today's automating society: "Automation is the third phase in the development of technology that began with the industrial revolution of the eighteenth century. First came mechanization, which created the factory system and separated labor and management in production. In the early twentieth century mass production brought the assembly line and other machinery so expensive that the ownership of industry had to be divorced from management and atomized into millions of separate shareholdings." *Impact of Automation on Employment* (Washington, D.C.: Subcommittee on Unemployment and the Impact of Automation of the Committee on Education and Labor, 87th Congress, 1st Session, June 1961), p. 3.

social institutions achievable. The need for relief-giving had been success-fully met by voluntary and public efforts at the local level, and the revival of the economy, occasioned by the European demand for war materials, eased the strain on philanthropic resources. Federated fund-raising, adopted on a community-wide scale in Cleveland in 1913, offered promise as a more rational system of raising money. For the first time in a depression, na-tional groups such as the Charity Organization Department of the Russell Sage Foundation and the American Association for Labor Legislation helped social workers and agencies throughout the country to coordinate relief-giving.[5] Local public relief began to emerge from the earlier stigma placed on it by those interested in scientific giving, and increased use was made of the granting of tax money to private charities by states and municipalities.[6] A reversal of the latter procedure occurred in Colorado, where the Rockefeller Foundation granted $100,000 to the state for the administration of work relief through road construction. Never before had there been such concerted efforts on behalf of the needy or such a degreee of cooperation among voluntary agencies, public relief services, state government, and private philanthropic foundations.

WORLD WAR I AND SOCIAL REFORM

Four years of war in Europe brought profound changes in America's social institutions. Wartime prosperity reduced internal economic pres-sure, and reform zeal was diverted as world problems captured the atten-tion of the citizenry. Government controls and intervention increased in magnitude at home, and charity overseas claimed the attention of many agencies and individuals. As the nation was drawn into the conflict, those who had urged such a domestic battle for social justice reasoned that when peace came the wartime commitments and energies could be di-rected toward social problems.

America's first involvement in the war came in the form of loans to the warring nations and the supplying of goods and services to both sides. Various social welfare organizations, notably the American Red Cross, the YMCA, and the Salvation Army, collected vast amounts of money for war relief. The American Red Cross's War Council, consisting of top figures from business and financial circles, increased in membership from

[5] Leah Hannah Feder, *Unemployment Relief in Periods of Depression* (New York: Russell Sage Foundation, 1936).
[6] Jeffrey R. Brackett, "Public Outdoor Relief in the United States," and Robert D. Dripps, "The Policy of State Aid to Private Charities," in *Proceedings of the National Conference of Charities and Correction at the Forty-Second Annual Session* (Chicago: Hildmann Printing Co., 1915), pp. 446–73 *et passim*.

about 250,000 in 1917 to 21 million at the end of 1918. Contributions increased proportionally, and by the end of the immediate postwar years, the organization had collected some $400 million for relief purposes.[7] Notable efforts were also made by other informal agencies such as the Commission for Relief in Belgium headed by Herbert C. Hoover; he effectively organized food and clothing distribution to ward off famine in that country.[8]

In the United States a number of social workers and reformers were in conflict about their proper roles in time of war. In 1914 prominent individuals such as Jane Addams, Paul Kellogg, and Lillian Wald organized the "Henry Street Group" to denounce the war. As America moved close to war, the organization became interested in the problems of pacifism in general and conscientious objection to military service in particular. Eventually, under the direction of social worker Roger Nash Baldwin, the association developed into the American Civil Liberties Union.[9] Many social workers felt, as did Miss Addams, that social reform was impossible during the war and considered the conflict infinitely more immoral than such things as high infant mortality or poor working conditions for women.[10] Miss Addams's opposition to the war, her help in organizing the Women's Peace Party in 1915, which called for a "League of Neutral Nations," and a lifetime of work for the cause of international peace, led to her receiving the Nobel Peace Prize in 1931. She and others who opposed American participation in the war, however, met increasing hostility at home for their views and decreasing support for the agencies they headed.

The majority of persons interested in social reform and social welfare problems eventually accepted the fact of war and even American participation in the struggle. Florence Kelley, who found her social work ethics and her socialist political beliefs violated by the war, overcame both in order to press for better industrial conditions. During the war years Mrs. Kelley's services were utilized by the War Department for factory inspection and for studies and recommendations for changes in working conditions in war-contract factories.[11] The decline in immigration, improved working conditions, and new learning and involvement in settings connected with war work contributed to a decline in the need for some social work services and the achievement of certain reforms.

[7] Robert H. Bremner, *American Philanthropy* (Chicago: University of Chicago Press, 1960), p. 131.

[8] *Ibid.*, p. 127.

[9] Donald Johnson, *The Challenge to American Freedoms* (Frankfort: University of Kentucky Press, 1963), pp. 1–25.

[10] John C. Farrell, *Beloved Lady* (Baltimore: Johns Hopkins Press, 1967), pp. 140–70.

[11] Frances Perkins, *The Roosevelt I Knew* (New York: Viking Press, 1946), p. 21.

During the years before the war, and especially during the time of American involvement in 1917 and 1918, a number of changes took place that profoundly affected American life. Agencies were set up to control the supply and distribution of food and fuel, and railroads were brought under the unified control of the federal Railroad Administration. Industry was brought under the scrutiny of the War Industries Board, and a War Labor Conference Board was created in 1918 to govern the relationships between capital and labor. Dissidents and pacifists were jailed under the 1918 Sedition Act, and civil liberties adumbrated with the consent of the Supreme Court, which held that free speech could be suspended while men were fighting. By the end of the war most workers enjoyed an eight-hour day, income had steadily increased, membership in the American Federation of Labor had increased by nearly a million members, and farm commodities were selling at record prices.

Acting on the belief that there could be a peacetime counterpart to the war effort, a National Conference on Social Agencies and Reconstruction met in 1918 to press for a continuation of some wartime programs after peace was achieved. Composed of outstanding social workers and educators, the group called for federal aid to education, public works in time of unemployment crises, minimum wages and an 8-hour day, equality for minority groups, and extensive programs of social insurance.[12] Joining them in their pleas for social action were other groups such as the American Federation of Labor, the Federal Council of Churches of Christ in America, and the National Catholic Welfare Council. For those who supported the war effort, the time seemed propitious for action to achieve equality, democracy, and social justice. Actual achievements were to be somewhat less ambitious than what these groups sought.

THE AFTERMATH OF THE WAR

Speaking in 1921 with considerable insight and foresight, Supreme Court Justice Louis D. Brandeis observed that "Europe was devastated by war, we by the aftermath."[13] Many of the excesses had their foundations in legislation passed during the war—notably the Volstead Act, which implemented the Eighteenth Amendment and the Sedition Act of 1918. The stifling of dissent and the prohibition of intemperance were popular in a society that felt threatened from abroad, weary of governmental controls within the country, and optimistic about the chances

[12] Clarke A. Chambers, *Seedtime of Reform* (Minneapolis: University of Minnesota Press, 1963), p. 22.

[13] Alpheus T. Mason, *Brandeis: A Free Man's Life* (New York: Viking Press, 1946), p. 530.

of the individual to make good economically. Although the average construction worker earned but $1924 a year and the average public school teacher only $936, most people faced the future with confidence. As one writer described the situation of that time:

> Everyone felt qualified to win, or at least that his children were going to. It made for an air of extremity; extreme hope, extreme despair, a teetering upon possibilities. If it was to be success, what fun; if failure, how black and unimaginable. This was the mood of the beginning of the postwar period. For some this pitch was maintained for the decade. The success fever infected every kind of endeavor.[14]

A mixture of cynicism and optimism led to the election of Presidents Harding, Coolidge, and Hoover. Harding debased the office, Coolidge diminished it, and Hoover inherited the wreckage that his two predecessors had produced in keeping with the attitudes of their constituents. When Warren G. Harding took office in 1921 the event signaled the end of even moderate reform concern on a national level. It was also the beginning of a reversion to pre-progressive philosophies of political laissez-faire and denigration of the idea of government as a positive force in society.

The idea of prohibiting the sale or manufacture of alcoholic beverages was popular with the majority of people and found considerable support in the social work community. Alcoholism had long been considered a principal cause of poverty, and many believed prohibition would produce an "amazing economic and moral transformation."[15] The success of the movement reflected the attitude that the individual was responsible for his problems but that the force of the state could be directed at protecting him from himself. The continuing failure of a proposed constitutional amendment to prohibit child labor emphasized the fact that environmental conditions were considered to be of less importance in character building than individual weaknesses. Overlooked too was the fact that prohibition applied to all classes and had ramifications for people other than the poor. The unwillingness of the more affluent to abide by the law contributed to a toleration of lawlessness during the decade and an unequal application of the law between the classes.

The Volstead Act was passed during the war over the veto of President Woodrow Wilson, with a large measure of support from southern congressmen who feared the effects of alcohol on Negroes. This fear of Negroes, however, was hardly confined to the South. Testimony to the

[14] Elizabeth Stevenson, *Babbits and Bohemians* (New York: Macmillan Co., 1967), p. 74.
[15] Robert A. Woods, "Winning the Other Half," *The Survey*, Vol. 37, no. 13 (December 30, 1916), p. 352.

fear of economic competition from the Negro is supplied by the Chicago race riot of 1919 in which, during a 3-day outbreak, 36 persons were killed. Gangsterism flourished as Americans cheerfully broke the law and in the area of racial problems found a counterpart in the resurrection of the Ku Klux Klan. The migration to the North, promoted by industry so that the Negro could replace the immigrant and draftee, did not have a corresponding movement to the South after the war. A postwar recession aggravated racial tensions, and the Ku Klux Klan became a potent political force throughout the nation. Although finally discredited at the end of the decade because of the sexual and financial peccadilloes of some of its leaders, the Klan claimed 4.5 million members in 1924. It also dominated the political machines in Arkansas, California, Indiana, Ohio, Texas, Oklahoma, and Oregon.[16]

Conflict, it should be noted, prevailed not only between black and white but between the native-born and the immigrant as well. To the distress of the settlement house workers who had worked to sustain the immigrant's respect for his older culture, the war had contributed to a resurgence of nativism and ethnic antagonisms.[17] Zionism and Black Nationalism flourished. As in the case of the strike against the U.S. Steel Company in 1919, racial feelings were sometimes purposely stirred up in order to defeat labor organization. Within the labor movement itself, demands were made for the closing of immigration to prevent strikebreaking and to diminish competition for jobs. Threats to Protestant dominance contributed to the passage of restrictive immigration acts in 1921 and 1924 which limited the numbers admitted and, through the use of quotas based on the 1890 census, decreased the numbers of some nationalities and excluded others entirely. The immigration of Germans, Scandinavians, and the English was encouraged, while southern and eastern Europeans were severely restricted in numbers. Orientals were excluded.

The desire to uplift the morals of the people by denying access to alcohol and the distrust of the foreign-born produced specific legislation to handle the problems. The wartime Sedition Act and the 1917 Espionage Act remained on the books, available for use during the "Red Scare" of the early postwar years. Perhaps no other single event abroad in this century had as much impact on American life, excepting perhaps the two world wars, as the Russian Revolution. The radical reordering of society in Soviet Russia led many to accept the Communist dialectic that revolution was exportable and inevitable.

[16] Quincy Howe, *The World Between the Wars* (New York: Simon & Schuster, 1953), p. 119.
[17] John Higham, *Strangers in the Land* (New Brunswick, N.J.: Rutgers University Press, 1955), p. 236.

The fact of the revolution led some reformers, such as Mary K. Simkhovitch, President of the National Federation of Settlements, to lend support to the war effort. In a letter to the New York *Evening Post* Mrs. Simkhovitch declared that before the revolution the situation was "sullied" and the proper course of action unclear. However, she declared:

> The Russian Revolution, following the increased ruthlessness of Germany, resolved that doubt, and made it possible, and, yes, imperative for many of us to hesitate no longer. . . . Not for aggression, and not even for defence, but for world democracy, is America justified at this hour no longer to stand apart, but rather to die that the world may live.[18]

The Bolshevik success in Russia culminated in 1919 and 1920 in "red hunts" in the United States which brought wholesale deportations of aliens suspected of radical tendencies. Beginning modestly in 1919 when 249 persons were put on the military transport ship *Buford*, popularly called the "Red Ark," and sent to Russia, in the following year perhaps as many as 10,000 aliens and citizens were rounded up and detained. Anthony Caminetti, Commissioner-General of Immigration, described the deportees as "insane or otherwise public charges," with a few political agitators in their midst. Although he stated that "all of the cases have been handled in strict conformity with the law and due process has been obtained in every instance," it appeared that this was not the truth.[19] Investigation by the American Civil Liberties Union and a congressional committee of inquiry revealed that citizens had been imprisoned without charges being filed and arrests made without warrants being issued. This pogrom "against humorless idealists" was described in 1920 by H. L. Mencken, the scourge of *all* causes:

> The machinery brought to bear upon these feeble and scattered fanatics would have almost suffered to repel an invasion by the united powers of Europe. They were hunted out of their sweatshops and coffee-houses as if they were so many Carranzas or Ludendorffs, dragged to jail to the tooting of horns, arraigned before quaking judges on unintelligible charges, condemned to deportation without the slightest chance to defend themselves, torn from their dependent families, herded into prison-ships, and then finally dumped in a snow waste to be rescued and fed by the Bolsheviks. And what was the theory at the bottom of all these astounding proceedings? So far as it can be reduced to comprehensible terms, it was much less a theory than a fear—a shivering, idiotic, discreditable fear of a mere banshee—an overpowering, paralyzing dread that some extra-eloquent Red, permitted to emit his balderdash unwhipped, might eventually con-

---

[18] "Social Settlements and the War," *The Survey*, Vol. 38, no. 1 (April 7, 1917), p. 30.
[19] "The Deportations," *The Survey*, Vol. 41, no. 21 (February 22, 1919), pp. 722–24.

vert a couple of courageous men, and that the courageous men, filled with indignation against the plutocracy, might take to the highroad, burn down a nail-factory or two, and slit the throat of some virtuous profiteer. In order to lay this fear . . . all the constitutional guarantees of the citizen were suspended, the statute books were burdened with laws that surpass anything heard of in the Austria of Maria Theresa, the country was handed over to a frensied mob of detectives, informers and *agents provocateurs*— and the Reds departed laughing loudly, and were hailed by the Bolsheviks as innocents escaped from an asylum for the criminally insane.[20]

The fear of anything resembling dissent and the equating of demands for reform with desire for revolution, made it virtually impossible to achieve orderly change. Services were dismantled rather than improved, as in the instance of the federal Employment Service which had been created during the war and allowed to atrophy in peacetime.[21] Critics of social welfare services, believing "the problem of human difficulty is largely one of faulty character," argued that less voluntary philanthropy was needed than before the war.[22] The settlement houses were especially vulnerable, and Lillian Wald of the Nurses' Settlement in New York wrote her friend Lavinia Dock: "Confidentially, my political attitude is making some of our generous friends uneasy and one of our largest givers—nearly $15,000 a year—has withdrawn because I am 'socialistically inclined.' Poor things; I am sorry for them—they are so scared." [23]

The nadir of social reform influence politically was reached in the 1920s. The automobile increased the flight to suburbia, and new legislation restricted immigration; both contributed to the decline in settlement house vitality. It was alleged that for social workers in the 1924 presidential election, "a single vote for LaFollette, without undue publicity or public activity, has been known to produce injurious effects." [24] Little wonder that most of the estimated 25,000 social workers in the United States increasingly defined the profession as "the art of adjusting human relations," or that this theme came to dominate professional conferences and school of social work curriculums during the 1920s. The net effect of the "Red Scare" on social workers, and perhaps society as a whole, was the emphasizing of conformity and the stressing of functional roles rather

[20] Henry L. Mencken, *The Vintage Mencken*, Alistair Cooke, ed. (New York: Vintage Books, 1955), pp. 102–3.

[21] "The Shell of the Employment Service," *The Survey*, Vol. 46, no. 3 (April 16, 1921), p. 78.

[22] Cornelia J. Cannon, "Philanthropic Doubts," *Atlantic Monthly*, Vol. 128, no. 3 (September 1921), pp. 289–300.

[23] Quoted in Chambers, *op. cit.*, p. 25.

[24] William Hodson, "Social Workers and Politics," *The Survey*, Vol. 63, no. 4 (November 15, 1929), pp. 199–200.

than causes. Babbitt, the anti-hero of Sinclair Lewis's novel about the small-town businessman of the 1920s, advised his daughter: "The first thing you got to understand is that all this uplift and flipflop and settlement-work and recreation is nothing in God's world but the entering wedge for socialism. The sooner a man learns he isn't going to be coddled, and he needn't expect a lot of free grub . . . the sooner he'll get on the job and produce—produce—produce.' " [25] In such a climate it was difficult to achieve social reform objectives.

Politically, the fear of internal and external subversion divorced from reform the ideas and challenges of the moderate Left and placed the consensus of American political thought somewhere between the old middle ground and the extreme Right. In the new consensus area in which operational policy making occurred leaders of business and industry were accorded a new status. President Harding, in his Inaugural Address, described his political philosophy for the country:

> I speak for administrative efficiency, for lightened tax burdens, for sound commercial practices, for adequate credit facilities, for sympathetic concern for all agricultural problems, for the omission of unnecessary interference of Government with business, for an end to Government's experiment in business, and for more efficient business in Government administration.[26]

The return to laissez-faire was pursued vigorously by President Calvin Coolidge, who believed that "the chief business of the American people is business" and said that "the man who builds a factory builds a temple . . . the man who works there worships there." [27]

THE TEMPO OF THE TWENTIES

The religious overtones in Coolidge's remarks emphasized the way in which the Social Gospel was replaced in religious institutions by the gospel of "getting ahead." The dominant theme in religion was conservative and individualistic, and reformers such as Washington Gladden and Walter Rauschenbusch were followed by the evangelists Dwight Moody and Billy Sunday. Church governing bodies came to be dominated by conservative businessmen while the clergy continued to lose prestige and social standing. The decline in reform leadership by religious leaders also

[25] Sinclair Lewis, *Babbitt* (New York: Grosset & Dunlap, 1922), p. 17.
[26] Arthur M. Schlesinger, Jr., and Fred L. Israel, *The Chief Executive* (New York: Crown Publishers, 1965), p. 236.
[27] Quoted in Arthur M. Schlesinger, Jr., *The Crisis of the Old Order* (Boston: Houghton Mifflin Co., 1957), p. 57.

resulted from the disillusionment of many liberals with the church's stand on the war and dismay at the "undercutting of the Church by secularism." [28]

The process of secularization was especially evident in some of the popular writing of the time. The most complete synthesis of the religious and business ethic was accomplished in 1925 in the tremendously popular book, *The Man Nobody Knows*. The author, Bruce Barton, was a founder of the advertising firm of Batten, Barton, Durstine, and Osborn. In the introduction to the book, Barton, in an exegesis of Christ's statement "Wist ye not that I must be about my Father's business," remarked that Christ had "picked up twelve men from the bottom ranks of business and forged them into an organization that conquered the world." [29] The book, it should be noted, differed in tone but not in method from the end of the nineteenth century writing that had pointed to corruption and asked what might happen *If Christ Came to Chicago*.[30] The symbol remained the same, but the use made of the symbol had changed with the times.

The exalting of wealth, the belief that all could become prosperous through individual effort, and the secularization of the "stewardship of wealth" predominated in the 1920s. President Coolidge's 1925 Inaugural Address summarized the orthodoxy:

> We can not finance the country, we can not improve social conditions, through any system of injustice, even if we attempt to inflict it upon the rich. Those who suffer the most harm will be the poor. This country believes in prosperity. It is absurd to suppose that it is envious of those who are already prosperous. The wise and correct course to follow in taxation and all other economic legislation is not to destroy those who have already secured success but to create conditions under which every one will have a better chance to be successful. . . . All owners of property are charged with a service. These rights and duties have been revealed, through the conscience of society, to have a divine sanction. The very stability of our society rests upon production and conservation.[31]

The picture Coolidge painted was one of inactivity in the public sphere and made social progress an act of faith in the ultimate rightness of private decisions affecting the citizenry. That all were not participating in the system could be discounted so long as it was assumed that all might par-

[28] Paul A. Carter, *The Decline and Revival of the Social Gospel* (Ithaca, N.Y.: Cornell University Press, 1954), pp. 85–95.
[29] Bruce Barton, *The Man Nobody Knows* (Indianapolis: Bobbs-Merrill Co., 1925).
[30] William T. Stead, *If Christ Came to Chicago* (New York: Living Books, Inc. 1964).
[31] Schlesinger and Israel, *op. cit.*, p. 246.

ticipate at some point in the future. Given this frame of reference, unions were considered damaging to progress by many and strikes a conspiracy against those responsible for prosperity.

Between 1920 and 1924, membership in unions declined by 1.5 million, and wages went down from wartime highs. Strikes, and especially the steel strike of 1919, were broken, and the recession of 1920–1922 made workers afraid to organize lest they find themselves blacklisted by employers. Many in the labor movement, especially the followers of Eugene V. Debs, leader of the Socialist Party and the American Railway Union, were considered un-American because socialist beliefs had frequently led to opposition to the war.

The erosion of union gains made during the progressive period and during the war was compounded by adverse legal decisions such as *Hammer* v. *Dagenhart,* which in 1918 struck down the Owen-Keatings act.[32] This legislation attempted to correct abuses of child labor and the white-slave traffic. Further attempts to use the taxing power, rather than the power to regulate interstate commerce, to limit child labor were equally futile. In 1920 more than 1.5 million children were gainfully employed. Even the hard-won gains in the states were frequently clouded by adverse legal decisions. Illustrative of the latter was the decision in the 1923 District of Columbia case, *Adkins* v. *Children's Hospital.*[33] A minimum wage law for women which also limited the hours of employment was declared unconstitutional, and state laws which had appeared to be constitutionally safe after the Oregon Ten Hour test were placed under a shadow. Florence Kelley of the National Consumers' League commented on the "progress backward" of social legislation and voiced the despair felt by many reformers during the 1920s:

> Under the Fifth and Fourteenth Amendments of the federal Constitution as now interpreted by the court, it is idle to seek to assure by orderly processes of legislation, to wage-earning men, women or children, life, liberty or the pursuit of happiness. . . . Under the pressure of competition in American industry at this time, [the *Adkins* v. *Children's Hospital* decision] establishes in the practical experience of the unorganized, the unskilled, the illiterate, the alien, and the industrially sub-normal women wage-earners, the constitutional right to starve.[34]

Court decisions made during the decade reflected a strict construction attitude on the part of the judiciary and local control was emphasized in

[32] *Hammer* v. *Dagenhart,* 247 U.S. 529–35 (1918).
[33] *Adkins* v. *Children's Hospital,* 261 U.S. 394–406 (1923).
[34] Florence Kelley, "Progress of Labor Legislation for Women," *Proceedings of the National Conference of Social Work at the Fiftieth Anniversary Session* (Chicago: University of Chicago Press, 1923), p. 114.

government. During Coolidge's administration the size and power of the federal government actually diminished—a reversal of a long-range trend. Tentative steps toward viewing problems of relief and unemployment as national problems were taken in 1921. In that year President Harding had called a nationwide Conference on Unemployment with semiofficial status to act as a clearinghouse for employment data. With the end of the recession the following year the committee went out of existence. Significantly, local public relief did expand throughout the period and at least 70 percent of the cost of relief was borne by public agencies [35] despite the fact that voluntary agencies were still considered the mainstay for meeting want.

Reliance on state and local government for the services to be provided enabled the federal government to progressively reduce the national debt. Concurrently, taxes were reduced for the wealthy from a 65 percent surtax on high incomes in 1920 to only 20 percent in 1926. Only in the latter year did the lower income groups receive tax relief.[36] The effect of such a monetary policy was to place in the hands of the well-to-do surplus funds for stock speculation while most citizens turned to installment buying to absorb the products of an increasingly productive industrial complex.

Corporation profits increased 80 percent, and the profits of financial institutions went up 150 percent. Part of the increase in wealth represented the expansion of the economy to meet increased consumer demand for mass-produced items such as automobiles and electric appliances. Part of the expansion, however, represented the manipulation of "paper wealth" as more than a million Americans began to participate speculatively in the growth of corporate structures. The price of stock bore little or no relationship to dividends paid and prices fluctuated wildly. The Radio Corporation of America stock demonstrated the irrational nature of the market: in November of 1928 the stock sold for 400, fell 72 points in a single day, and reached a low of 94.5 in March 1929, before climbing to 505 in September. With only $1000 a speculator could have bought 100 shares at the low of 94.5 and borrowed on the margin some $8450 from his broker, who would become indebted for that amount to his bank. By selling in September the $1000 investment would have yielded $50,500 less broker's fees and interest.[37]

Despite the apparent health of the economy and the constant reassur-

[35] Linton B. Swift, "Private Agencies and Public Welfare," *This Business of Relief, Proceedings of the Delegate Conference, American Association of Social Workers* (New York: Columbia University Press, 1936), p. 84.
[36] Howe, *op. cit.*, p. 201.
[37] *Ibid.*, p. 202.

ances of those in positions of influence and power in business and government, the last years of the 1920s were the beginning of stagnation. Business was unable to insure high levels of employment after 1925, and stock speculation resulted not only from short-sighted monetary policies but from the lack of attractive areas for investment. Capital equipment became increasingly productive as mechanization proceeded toward a technological plateau, where no major innovation required great new capital investment.[38] Throughout the period at least one-third of the population had received incomes below the $2000 level considered necessary for a decent standard of living, and mechanization produced less new demand for workers. In some industries, wages were progressively lowered. Farmers were slow to recover from readjustment to peacetime and the competition from overseas producers; consequently farm prices remained at extremely low levels during the decade. When the depression began at the end of the 1920s, many Americans were only peripherally affected because they were already living in poverty.

THE BEGINNING OF THE
DEPRESSION YEARS

The election of 1928 was a bitterly fought contest between Herbert C. Hoover and Alfred E. Smith. Hoover, a Quaker, epitomized the American ideal of the self-made man who rose from poverty to become wealthy and influential as Secretary of Commerce during the Coolidge administration. Smith on the other hand was the son of Catholic immigrants who had made his way up to the governorship of New York with the assistance of Tammany Hall. After a campaign in which the main issues were the continuation of prosperity, enforcement and retention of prohibition, and the election of a Catholic to the presidency, the nation elected Hoover by an electoral vote of 444 to 87.

Shortly after Hoover took office Congress enacted into law his recommendations for stabilizing farm prices through the Agricultural Marketing Act. Under this act federal funds were available for loans to cooperatives and for the voluntary handling of crop surpluses. Shortly thereafter Hoover signed into law the Hawley-Smoot Tariff, with its extremely high rates that raised the protection level for industry by at least 7 percent. Although more than a thousand American economists signed a petition warning of the consequences for the economy, and despite the fact that Hoover himself opposed the measure, it was signed into law. These two pieces of legislation illustrate two of Hoover's characteristics. He was genuinely concerned about falling farm prices, but his solution

[38] Thomas C. Cochran, *The American Business System* (Cambridge: Harvard University Press, 1957), pp. 49–50.

was voluntary controls with a minimum of federal supervision. As a mining engineer he had seen much of the world and had administered relief programs in Belgium, Russia, and other countries and was aware of the interaction among national economies. When faced with an issue involving business interests in America, however, he ignored the advice of experts and his own knowledge derived from experience and accepted a program he considered unwise.

Hoover's background and experience as an administrator in the government persuaded him that his predecessor's policies were intrinsically correct. His philosophy of government was simplistic and centered on the belief that there should be as little interference as possible with the operations of the private sphere of economic life.[39] His attitude toward welfare measures was that of the class to which he had risen and included the belief that voluntary efforts were the backbone of charity. Like most Americans of the time, Hoover believed that the nation had entered upon a permanent plateau of prosperity and that only minor changes in social institutions were needed.

Signs that the plateau was ending were evident in the summer of 1929. Building contracts, generally a good indicator of economic progress, declined by $1 billion in a year's time. Consumer spending declined from a 7.4 percent rate in 1927–1928 to 1.5 percent the following year. Business inventories trebled as consumers were unable to purchase the products industry turned out.[40] During the previous eight years the number employed in factories decreased by nearly 1 million while the unemployment rate stood at a high 9 percent.[41] In the summer of 1929 the unemployment figures rose rapidly as manufacturers cut back production in order to reduce inventories.

The end of prosperity began on Black Thursday, October 24, 1929, when orders to sell flooded the New York Stock Exchange. Although the market was temporarily shored up by the purchase of deflated steel securities by the House of Morgan, the market was inundated the following week. On October 29 over 16 million shares changed hands as brokers tried to protect themselves by calling in their loans to customers who had bought on margin. Within a few weeeks the value of common stocks dropped $30 billion, almost double the amount of the national debt.[42]

Repercussions from the stock market crash were felt throughout the

[39] Herbert Hoover, *American Individualism* (Garden City, N.Y.: Doubleday Page & Co., 1923), pp. 1–13.

[40] Schlesinger, *op. cit.*, p. 157.

[41] Agnes Nestor, "Current Problems of Unemployment," *Proceedings of the National Conference of Social Work at the Fifty-Seventh Annual Session* (Chicago: University of Chicago Press, 1930), p. 315.

[42] An interesting documentary account is given in David A. Shannon, *The Great Depression* (New York: Prentice-Hall, a Spectrum Book, 1960).

economic system as the stock market continued to decline. By March 1930 unemployment had risen to nearly 4 million. A year later this figure had climbed to 7.5 million, and by 1932 some 12 million were seeking work. Profits retained by business for expansion or to guard against market fluctuations fell to $2.6 billion in 1933 from the record high of $11.5 billion in 1929.[43]

The initial reaction of business and government leaders was one of surprise and then optimism as the depression was altered in official terminology to a recession. Ernest G. Draper, vice president of the Hills Brothers Company, addressed the National Conference of Social Work in Boston in June 1930. Expressing the sentiment of many of the nation's leaders, Mr. Draper believed that "in spite of the setback in 1929 it is reasonable to assume that the era of industrial prosperity will continue for some time to come, even if in modified form."[44] Social workers at the conference were rather distressed by the increased demands on funds needed for income maintenance. Remembering the experience of 1920–22, however, most believed that voluntary efforts were equal to the challenge of the time.

President Hoover, as well as many influential business leaders, considered the stock market crash to have been an adjustment that was necessary to drive out speculators. Believing the economy basically sound, Hoover nevertheless called together leading bankers and industrialists to a conference the month after the break in stock prices. Pledges made that wages would not be cut and promises of $2 billion worth of new construction in 1930 "left the nation gasping at the titanic proportions of the work planned for the twelve-month."[45] The pledges and promises could not be honored, however, and the crisis deepened amid periodic predictions from Washington that the corner had been turned and recovery was imminent. By October 1930 President Hoover moved from words to action and sponsored the creation of the Emergency Committee for Employment under the direction of Colonel Arthur Woods. When the committee recommended a public works program that would have included slum clearance, rural electrification, and a national employment service, Hoover rejected the report. According to the President:

This is not an issue as to whether people shall go hungry or cold. It is solely a question of the best method by which hunger and cold shall be prevented.

[43] John Kenneth Galbraith, *The New Industrial State* (Boston: Houghton-Mifflin Co., 1967), p. 44.
[44] Ernest G. Draper, "What Employers are Doing," *Proceedings of the National Conference of Social Work at the Fifty-Seventh Annual Session* (Chicago: University of Chicago Press, 1930), p. 323.
[45] "A Plan to Promote Economic Balance," *Business Week* (January 8, 1930), p. 22.

It is a question of whether the American people will maintain the spirit of charity and mutual self-help through voluntary giving and the responsibility of local government, as distinguished from appropriations from the Federal Treasury.[46]

The remedies proposed for the difficult employment situation included "block aid" plans whereby each block in a community cared for its own. The principal defect in the plan was that the majority on a given block might well be seeking work to no avail. Another plan that gained some currency was the sharing of work through the reduction of work hours. Although this helped the unemployment situation slightly, it was pointed out that such a system forced the workingman to bear the brunt of the relief problem. During the first quarter of 1930, payments in wages declined over $300 million from the third quarter of 1929. In the same period dividend payments to stockholders increased by $360 million from reserve profits.[47] In such a situation, workers were reluctant to share their meager earnings with fellow workers.

The major burden for caring for the destitute as the situation worsened was shouldered by local public welfare agencies which typically gave food orders and used clothing to the needy. Bank closings (439 in 1929 and 934 in 1930) liquidated the savings of many in the middle class and forced them to seek public assistance as further constrictions in employment occurred.[48] In some cases state governments found it necessary to step in and make financial contributions to counties. Where drought added to the woes of farmers, the American Red Cross stepped in.[49] Local committees were set up to collect clothing and food in accordance with the advice of the President, and voluntary agencies were deluged with requests for help.

By 1932 it was apparent that the economic decline was more serious than most Americans had assumed. The depression had assumed worldwide proportions and it became apparent that, in the United States, the old methods of handling the consequences of business decline were inadequate. As early as 1930 President Hoover asked Congress for appropriations to improve roads and rivers and for the construction of public buildings. Building of the Boulder Dam on the Colorado River (later renamed Hoover Dam) was begun, and during Hoover's administration more than $2.25 billion was used to provide indirect aid for the unem-

[46] Quoted in Quincy Howe, *op. cit.*, p. 348.
[47] Agnes Nestor, *op. cit.*, p. 317.
[48] John Paul Jones, "Middle-Class Misery," *The Survey*, Vol. 48, no. 11 (September 1, 1932), pp. 402–4.
[49] Wilma Walker, "Distress in a Southern Illinois County," *Social Service Review*, Vol. 5, no. 4 (December 1931), pp. 558–81.

ployed. By 1932 fears of a further collapse of business led to the creation of the Reconstruction Finance Corporation to provide loans to banks, life insurance companies, railroads, and other organizations. Subsequently the RFC was permitted to make loans to voluntary social agencies, to states for relief, and to potential purchasers of farm commodities.[50] The RFC had lent nearly $2 billion before Hoover left office. In addition to these measures designed to stimulate the economy, the government established a series of Home Loan Banks to enable homeowners to keep their property. Although many had already suffered from mortgage foreclosures, the agency cut down on the loss of homes and in a minor way stimulated new building.

None of the measures taken to shore up the economy had a significant impact on an economy characterized by overproduction and underconsumption. Classical economy theory, predicated on theories revolving around a scarcity of goods, had no bearing in an age of abundance. If the economy were out of balance, traditional economic wisdom argued for the raising of taxes and the reduction of government spending in order to balance the budget. However, as John Maynard Keynes later argued in *The General Theory of Employment, Interest, and Money* published in 1935, supply and demand were in a state of equilibrium; consumption and production were balanced.[51] But the level was unacceptable to society, and Keynes suggested that aggregate demand could be increased by tax cuts, reduced interest rates, and stimulation of the economy by government spending. Keynes proposed to turn classical theory around by recommending increased governmental activity during recessions rather than a contraction as was generally proposed. Perhaps earlier economic theories had served well during the days of scarce goods. In an economy that appeared to have solved the problem of mass production, new theories might be needed to deal with the revolutionary fact of inadequate consumption. Although Hoover, by unbalancing the budget to provide for public employment, began the practice of deficit financing, it remained for later administrations to consciously pursue the policy of spending our way out of depression.

THE NEW DEAL BEGINS

Franklin D. Roosevelt's election to the presidency in 1932 capped a political career that began in 1910, with his election to the New York legislature. He served as Assistant Secretary of the Navy under Woodrow

[50] Grace Abbott, *From Relief to Social Security* (Chicago: University of Chicago Press, 1941), p. 26 *et passim*.
[51] John Maynard Keynes, *The General Theory of Employment, Interest, and Money* (New York: Harcourt Brace & World, a Harbinger Book, 1964).

Wilson and in 1920 was the unsuccessful Democratic vice-presidential candidate. Following a crippling attack of infantile paralysis in 1921, Roosevelt re-entered politics in 1928, when he was elected Governor of New York. According to his friend and biographer, Frances Perkins, "Franklin Roosevelt underwent a spiritual transformation during the years of his illness." [52] Although moderately interested in reform before, by 1928 he had deepened his interest in social problems and had become familiar with programs advanced by reformers to correct social injustice. Through his wife he became acquainted with individuals such as Rose Schneiderman and Maude Schwartz of the Women's Trade Union League and, later, Harry Hopkins, who had begun his career as a social worker at Christodora House, a settlement in New York City. In 1928 Hopkins was planning work projects for the Association for Improving the Condition of the Poor in New York City.[53]

As Governor of New York Roosevelt appointed a Commission on Stabilization of Employment to study ways of meeting the employment crisis and to educate the people about causes and possible cures. Acting on his belief that government had a responsibility to take positive steps toward relieving the distress that flowed from unemployment, he made state funds available to local communities for relief. A new agency, the Temporary Emergency Relief Administration, under the direction of Harry Hopkins, was created. In the first year of its existence as an employer of last resort, TERA administered a fund of about $30 million— the same amount as the RFC had loaned for relief purposes in its first year of existence.[54]

In the election of 1932 Hoover was defeated by Roosevelt by an electoral vote of 472 to 59, and he carried only 6 states. Both houses of Congress were overwhelmingly Democratic, and the new president was able to implement on a national level some of the programs he had inaugurated in New York State. Relying on the advice of a brain trust and various study commissions and committees, Roosevelt followed his previous pattern of bold experimentation based on information gleaned from experts in the field of immediate concern.

The first session of Congress to meet after Roosevelt's inauguration passed legislation intended to shore up financial institutions, provide work for one-fourth of the labor force needing jobs, give relief to homeowners and farmers, and effect economies in government. Much legislation was regulatory in nature, some was intended to be permanent, some relied

[52] Perkins, *op. cit.*, p. 31.
[53] Robert E. Sherwood, *Roosevelt and Hopkins* (New York: Harper & Bros., 1948), p. 30.
[54] Shannon, *op. cit.*, p. 35.

on voluntary participation, and most of the relief legislation was considered to be temporary. Roosevelt, like his predecessor, placed great faith in the viability of the American economic system, disliked the idea of an unbalanced budget, and considered the provision of relief by the federal government to be an expedient that should be soon returned to the local community for financing and administration. Betraying the conventional view that economic wisdom required a balanced budget, Roosevelt began his administration by cutting federal payrolls and salaries and reducing payments to veterans.

EARLY PROGRAMS FOR SOCIAL RECOVERY

In addition to cutting the federal payroll by $100 million, other deflationary measures were taken in the first "hundred days" of the new administration. A bank holiday was declared the day after Roosevelt's inauguration on March 4, 1933. Those found solvent by government examiners were permitted to reopen after March 13; in the interim $4 billion was tied up before federal guarantees to depositors restored confidence in the banking system. New revenue was sought through taxes on alcohol rather than on the rich or on business. The Agricultural Adjustment Act of May 12, 1933, sought to take land out of production and curb surpluses at the same time that many people were hungry. In these programs, as well as in taking the country off the gold standard to engage in domestic price-raising ventures, Roosevelt pursued a deflationary monetary policy more ruthless than anything Hoover would have dared.

At the same time that the administration took steps to curb production and government expenses, other social measures aimed at social reconstruction were passed in contradiction to the initial phase of fiscal conservatism. Perhaps the most revolutionary piece of legislation enacted during the New Deal was the National Industrial Recovery Act of June 1933, which created the National Recovery Administration. This legislation consisted of three titles, two dealing with public works, relief, and voluntary control of industry, and the third with taxing measures to finance the programs. The goals of the legislation were the promotion of cooperative action within industry, the elimination of unfair business practices, expansion of production and purchasing power, and the conservation of natural resources.[55] Under the act industrial groupings such as textile manufacturers, automobile producers, and steelmakers were to draw up codes of fair competition to standardize hours of work, establish minimum wages, and limit production. Codes were to include guarantees of the right of labor to organize and bargain collectively as well as pro-

[55] Ellis W. Hawley, *The New Deal and the Problem of Monopoly* (Princeton: Princeton University Press, 1966), p. 32.

visions outlawing child labor. In return for the concessions made by business, this experiment in employer law-making exempted participants from antitrust laws and made government, through the courts, responsible for enforcing code restrictions.[56]

Three disparate groups supported the NRA for different reasons, and, although the conflict in goals was not immediately apparent in time all three became disenchanted with what amounted to legal cartelization. The first group, those imbued with a faith in a cooperative, collectivist democracy, saw the NRA as a resurrection of the World War I Industries Board. Hoping for an organized and rationalized planned industrial order, they were heartened by the appointment of retired General Hugh S. Johnson as administrator of the codes. The second group was composed of men who favored classical economic theories and saw in the legislation one way of enforcing competition through regulation. By eliminating price-cutting, a technique of monopolization, a competitive system could be preserved, since discrimination against small enterprises was specifically prohibited by law. The third group supporting the NRA looked toward the creation of a "business commonwealth." Industrial self-government to this group "meant that business leaders should be entrusted with governmental powers and the making of economic decisions should be the exclusive prerogative of the managerial group." [57]

By February 1, 1935, there were 546 codes, drawn up cooperatively by deputy administrators, representatives of industry, and labor delegations. More than two and one-half million firms employing some 22 million workers were covered by the codes. Some 125,000 children under age 16 had been removed from the labor market, wage rates in coded industries had increased 20 percent above the average, and the average work week had declined.[58] Those not covered by an industry were brought under the Act by a presidential order that abolished child labor and fixed a 35-hour week for ordinary labor and a 40-hour week for white-collar employment. Minimum wages were also established, again by presidential decree. Recovery seemed assured.

Initially, the NRA, with its Blue Eagle emblem of compliance, seemed eminently successful. After less than 6 months of operations, production had increased by 50 percent, and the unemployment figure of 9 million was cut by 2.5 million. Unionization had increased as well, and in the American Federation of Labor, one-third of the locals increased membership and one-fourth doubled their rolls. The United Mine Workers, with

[56] "Fair Competition," *Business Week* (May 24, 1933), p. 1.
[57] Hawley, *op. cit.*, p. 39.
[58] M. D. Vincent and Beulah Amidon, "NRA: A Trial Balance," *Survey Graphic*, Vol. 24, no. 7 (July 1935), pp. 333–37, 363–64.

only 60,000 members in 1932, added 300,000 within a few months after enactment of the National Industrial Recovery Act.[59] By 1935 the Gross National Product, the value of the goods and services produced during the year, was about the same as it had been in 1924.

Nevertheless by May 1935, when the act was declared unconstitutional, neither labor nor industry supported its revival in modified form. Unions were frustrated by the growth of company unions (some 400 by 1935), and exemptions from hour and wage regulations had frequently been granted to some industries. The National Labor Board, which had been created to mediate grievances and secure unionization agreements, was ineffective because it had no power to enforce its decisions. Industry grew disenchanted as strikes multiplied; industrial conflict grew as the Committee for Industrial Organization, precursor of the Congress of Industrial Organizations (CIO), attempted to unionize industrial workers. Business was further alienated as the voluntary cooperation of those covered by the various codes was frequently refused. Because the Act contained no provisions for punishing the recalcitrant and because the courts responded to complaints inconsistently, "chiselers" could gain the edge on their competitors by price-cutting and by decreasing the cost of wages. In December 1935 the National Association of Manufacturers polled their membership on the question: "Do you favor legislation continuing in any form the principles and policies of the NIRA?" In reply, 82 percent answered no.[60]

Although the NRA was allowed to die a constitutional death, several provisions of the act had sufficient congressional support to win passage as separate pieces of legislation. The controversial Section 7 (a), enacted in 1935 as the Wagner-Connery Labor Relations Act to deal with unionization, greatly strengthened the National Labor Relations Board. In 1938 the Wages and Hours Act reinstituted minimum wages, maximum hours, and prohibitions against child labor in the manufacture of goods moving in interstate commerce.

Title II of the NIRA provided for the expenditure of $3.3 billion dollars for "job-making projects ranging from slum clearance to naval construction. . . ."[61] With responsibility lodged in the Department of the Interior, careful attention was given to the development of sound public work projects. Construction projects stimulated industry, although the slowness with which the Public Works Administration moved did not

[59] Joseph G. Rayback, A History of American Labor (New York: Macmillan Co., 1959), p. 328.

[60] "The Voice of Industry," Business Week (December 14, 1935), p. 44.

[61] "Public Works," Business Week (May 24, 1933), p. 2.

answer the immediate need for relief. This need had been dramatically revealed in hearings of the LaFollette-Costigan Senate committee prior to Roosevelt's inauguration. Held to publicize the unemployment problem and the inability of the voluntary agencies and local relief machinery to deal with it, the hearings helped obtain congressional approval of the Federal Emergency Relief Act in May 1933. With an initial appropriation of $500 million, the Federal Emergency Relief Administration created by the legislation moved quickly under the direction of Harry Hopkins to provide relief to an estimated 18 million needy persons.

Moving rapidly to assume functions previously performed by the Reconstruction Finance Corporation, Hopkins brought to his agency prominent social workers and administrators from throughout the country. By August 1933 FERA had decided on some methods of operation. These included the giving of funds to states, under FERA supervision, with the requirement that public agencies would administer funds given either on a matching basis to the states or as direct grants in those instances when a state's governor proved that funds were not available. Although the use of FERA funds for building rental or for salaries of workers not directly under supervision from unemployment relief authorities was prohibited, FERA money was made available to the unemployable unemployed.[62] It was also decided that medical and dental care and supplies would be provided to recipients of relief. Cash grants, rather than the customary "in-kind" issuing of food or grocery orders specifying what might be obtained, was the preferred system of giving relief.[63] The policies thus established by FERA were a significant break with the past and represented a changed philosophy about the responsibility of government for helping needy citizens.

Not content with supplementing state and local relief-giving agencies, Harry Hopkins proposed the creation of 4 million jobs during the winter of 1933–34. There was considerable support for such programs, and many local communities had already instituted projects, generally as work-for-

[62] Searle F. Charles, *Minister of Relief* (Syracuse, N.Y.: Syracuse University Press, 1963), p. 32.

[63] Harry L. Hopkins, *Spending to Save* (New York: W. W. Norton & Co., 1936), pp. 104–5. The giving of "relief in-kind" means the actual issuing of food or clothing to recipients. This was a general practice before the depression and FERA funded some state controlled commissaries. Surplus food commodities were also given to supplement cash payments, which Hopkins viewed as "the most acceptable form of giving assistance to those who could not be put on work relief." Grocery orders were not usually used by FERA and, because rent was usually not paid by relief administrators, rent orders were infrequently given. The latter practice led to the formation of welfare client groups to protest the practice.

relief measures.[64] As early as 1931 Monsignor John A. Ryan, author (in 1906) of *A Living Wage*, a sometimes Progressive and later a confirmed New Dealer, had urged the creation of a $5 billion public works program.[65] In 1932 a joint statement issued by the Federal Council of Churches, the National Catholic Welfare Conference, and the Central Conference of American Rabbis called for government to finance work relief projects as well as unemployment and old age insurance.[66] Businessmen also supported the idea because many considered work a more suitable way of helping people than the dole.

On November 9, 1933, President Roosevelt created the Civil Works Administration under the authority of Title II of the National Industrial Recovery Act. Funds for the program were transferred from the Public Works Administration and FERA, and many on the staff of the latter agency were used to set up work projects. Over $3½ million was appropriated by Congress for the program. State and local governments contributed approximately 10 percent of costs; before the dissolution of the CWA in May 1934, costs had reached slightly over $900 million.[67]

Projects involving a minimum of equipment were preferred, and local communities as well as federal authorities made recommendations for jobs to be performed. Administration of the program, including decisions about projects, were made at the federal level, in contrast to FERA, which involved a sharing of administrative responsibility among local, state, and federal bodies. The most popular among the 400,000 projects in operation during the winter was the building or repairing of roads. The next most popular form of work relief was the building or renovation of schools. Airports were built and improved, playgrounds constructed, and parks and swimming pools created in many communities. In addition some 50,000 teachers had their salaries paid through the CWA, and writers and artists were eligible for subsidization.[68] Whenever possible, the CWA attempted to develop jobs around the skills of those needing employment. Other agencies of government were used to supplement or support the work of the CWA when advisable; for example, the U.S. Public Health

[64] Properly designated, work relief means wages paid to employees on government sponsored projects irrespective of eligibility for other relief programs. Work-for-relief involves certification for work by a public agency and is frequently limited to the number of hours required at a given level of compensation to earn whatever is supplied.

[65] Francis L. Broderick, *Right Reverend New Dealer: John A. Ryan* (New York: Macmillan Co., 1963), p. 196.

[66] *New York Times*, January 5, 1932, p. 4.

[67] Charles, *op. cit.*, p. 50.

[68] Arthur M. Schlesinger, Jr., *The Coming of the New Deal.* (Boston: Houghton Mifflin Co., 1959), p. 270.

Service supervised the construction of 150,000 sanitary privies in rural areas; the Veterans Administration acted as paymaster for the projects.[69] There were a few charges of graft, and some projects were derided as "leaf-raking" or "make-work." Considering the magnitude of the undertaking, the actual defects were negligible.

The greatest opposition to the CWA was generated by wage policies rather than the quality of projects or their administration. Following Hopkins's prejudices and the policies of the Public Works Administration, wages paid were not based on the concept of "less eligibility." [70] Minimum hourly rates were those recommended by the NRA, and they varied from $1.00 an hour in the Southern Zone to $1.20 in the Northern Zone; the rates for unskilled workers in the same areas were 40 cents and 50 cents respectively. Wages paid by CWA frequently exceeded the prevailing scale in some communities, and workers naturally left private employment to work on government projects. This was especially true in rural areas and in the South. Farmers in the South in 1932 and 1933 paid 5 cents an hour for hired help (women receiving less), and private employers increasingly opposed the CWA's continuation.[71]

Despite the success of the CWA, its popularity among the unemployed, and the urging of the American Association of Social Workers, who had in February 1934 adopted resolutions opposing the program's termination, projects came to an end shortly after May 1, 1934.[72] The program had, for the first time, demonstrated the efficacy of work relief—a program that had long been advocated by Progressives and reformers. It also provided financial and psychological support to many unemployed persons, who would later find work with the slower moving but more thoughtfully planned Public Works Administration.

The end of the CWA meant full attention could be devoted to FERA. In addition to other activities, FERA administrators, in June 1933, established policies and created programs of some significance. For relief purposes, settlement was defined as one year of continuous residence in a state. For those not eligible for federally assisted programs of relief, State Transient Bureaus, financed entirely by federal funds, were created. Housing and financial grants were provided, and relief standards

[69] Hopkins, op. cit., pp. 120–21.
[70] The ancient doctrine of "less eligibility" holds that those receiving assistance or working on projects involving the government as the employer of last resort should not receive assistance or wages below the level of the lowest-paid person in the community who is otherwise employed.
[71] Charles, op. cit., pp. 51–53.
[72] Harry Greenstein, "Work Programs and Relief Measures," This Business of Relief (New York: American Association of Social Workers, 1936), p. 70.

were frequently higher than those of the relief administration in the same city or county.[73]

With the cooperation of the Department of Agriculture, FERA also developed the Federal Surplus Relief Corporation to distribute surplus commodities to the needy. School lunch programs were later inaugurated by the Works Progress Administration and concern with agricultural surpluses led to other relief-giving projects. Cotton, for example, was purchased from government warehouses and turned into mattresses by the unemployed for distribution to the needy; this venture that led to complaints that such projects were in competition with private enterprise. Proposals to purchase cattle through FERA and turn them into shoes and canned beef for persons on relief brought much adverse reaction. As a consequence the surplus commodity program was removed from the jurisdiction of FERA and lodged exclusively in the Department of Agriculture.

Community redevelopment was also undertaken, and the Rural Rehabilitation Division of FERA provided work projects for the rural needy. Men were engaged in cleaning up small towns, the customary FERA wage scale being 30 cents an hour. Loans were made to farm families for seed, fertilizer, and essential equipment. Attempts were made to relocate some stricken rural dwellers in planned communities such as Cherry Lake in Florida and in the Matanuska Valley of Alaska. The sensational reporting of this planned development in the press and the resistance most Americans had to planned relocation led to the abandonment of these radical projects.

Such innovative programs were overshadowed by the principal function of FERA, which simply stated, was to prevent the poor from bankrupting the states. When FERA was dismantled in 1935, more than $4 billion had been spent for all projects, the largest portion having been granted to the states for relief.[74] Under FERA rules, the more affluent states received a smaller percentage of funds from the federal government, a ratio of three local dollars to each federal dollar being a customary arrangement. By contrast the poorer states received almost total subsidization for relief programs. Experience dictated that in future matching programs, more equitable systems of reimbursement would need to be worked out.

FERA introduced federal supervision into local and state programs and made considerable impact on the way in which help was given. Harry Hopkins described his philosophy and existing conditions this way:

[73] Josephine C. Brown, *Public Relief 1929–1939* (New York: Henry Holt & Co., 1940), p. 260.
[74] Perkins, *op. cit.*, p. 185.

From the beginning we strove to make methods of emergency relief differ deeply from practices of local poor relief, which still held a heavy hand over many local agencies. Under the philosophy of this ancient practice, the applicant was in some way morally deficient. He must be made to feel his pauperism. Every help which was given him was to be given in a way to intensify his sense of shame. Usually he was forced to plead his destitution in an offensively dreary room. We asked for the establishment of respectable light quarters conveniently placed in the neighborhoods of those who had to use them. We tried to have the applicant received by an intelligent and sympathetic human being who did not, in his own mind, put a stigma upon the unfortunate person before him. We tried to see that relief officials were people who understood that the predicament of the worker without a job is in an economic predicament not of his own making; that his religion, race or party is irrelevant. His need was the only thing that had to be established.[75]

Supplementing the work done in conservation by the CWA and FERA were the various projects of the Civilian Conservation Corps. Proposals for such a program had been made early in the century by such men as Gifford Pinchot, first head of the Department of Agriculture's Forestry Service and governor of Pennsylvania during the depression. By 1932 the problem of the young male transient had led California to establish forestry camps, and Edith Abbott, chief of the Children's Bureau, recommended federal aid for similar programs.[76] President Roosevelt's great interest in conservation and his conviction that land should be rescued and restored led him to place special emphasis on the program. Consequently the Civilian Conservation Corps was one of the first programs enacted in the famous first "hundred days" of the New Deal.

The intent of the CCC was to place carefully selected young men between the ages of 18 and 25, who were either without families or whose families were on relief, at work in forestry camps throughout the nation. The focus was as much on reforestation and conservation as on employment, and by the time the program expired in 1942 much work had been accomplished and an aggregate of 450,000 youths were provided for annually. As the program was set up, young men of good character who were physically fit were recruited by the U.S. Department of Labor through a hastily resurrected National Re-employment Service. Those selected were assigned to projects by the Forestry Service and went to live in camps operated by the Army.

One of the most significant aspects of the CCC was the statement in the Act that "in employment of citizens . . . no discrimination shall be

[75] Hopkins, op. cit., pp. 100–101.
[76] A. Wayne McMillen, "An Army of Boys on the Loose," The Survey, Vol. 68, no. 11 (September 1, 1932), p. 393.

made on account of race, color, and creed." The depression had compounded the problem of employment for all minorities, and in 1933 unemployment rates for Negroes were double the national average. Discrimination in selecting young men for the CCC did occur although Frank Persons, former organizer for the American Red Cross and director of the Re-employment Service, took vigorous action to prevent it. In a few camps Negroes were integrated, although in general practice black enrollees were usually assigned to all-Negro camps with white administrators in charge. In time Negro pressure groups protested the practice, and Negro officers and supervisory personnel were used in some camps. During the 9 years the CCC existed some 2.5 million men had been enrolled, and almost 200,000 of these were Negroes. Although original ideals were compromised, the CCC policies with respect to recruitment and training of Negroes represented a hopeful experiment in racial integration.[77]

Another early New Deal program aimed at the conservation of natural resources, as well as the economic stimulation of a depressed region, was the Tennessee Valley Authority. The TVA had its origins in the early part of the century. Under the provisions of the National Defense Act of 1916, Wilson Dam near Muscle Shoals in Alabama had been constructed along with two nitrate plants built to produce nitrogen fertilizer for agricultural use and explosives. Incomplete when the war ended, the property fell into economic limbo during the 1920s. Efforts were made by men such as Senator George Norris, a Progressive Republican from Nebraska, to have the government operate Muscle Shoals to produce cheap power. Congress consistently refused to appropriate money to operate the installation, however, and was equally unwilling to sell the facility to private enterprise at distress prices.

On May 18, 1933, Congress approved legislation specifying that the Tennessee Valley Authority would have as its aims "not the limited objectives of producing and distributing power and producing and selling fertilizer, but the physical, economic, and social development and improvement of the whole area." [78] Thus the legislation enabled the Authority to transcend state boundaries and plan regionally for an economically submerged area. The corporation was charged with responsibility for improving navigation, instituting flood control, generating and selling power, and at the same time developing the social and economic resources of the region. Outstanding features of social planning included attention

[77] John A. Salmond, *The Civilian Conservation Corps 1933-1942* (Durham, N.C.: Duke University Press, 1967), pp. 88-101.

[78] Roscoe C. Martin, ed., *TVA The First Twenty Years* (Knoxville: University of Tennessee Press, 1956), p. 25 *et seq.*

to malaria control and public health, the construction of homes in planned communities, the development of public education facilities, and the creation of recreation resources. After only a few years in operation, the project demonstrated the viability of regional planning and the way in which massive federal intervention could transform the entire life style of the people in an area.

Other early New Deal programs aimed at speeding recovery and improving the lives of the people included the Securities and Exchange Act of 1933. This legislation reflected a Brandeisian philosophy of regulation and created a Federal Trade Commission to supervise the issues of new stocks. Homeowners were assisted through the Home Owners' Loan Corporation, through building projects of the PWA and NIRA, and through the Federal Housing Administration, which was established in 1934. Both public and private housing efforts were assisted by the various programs.[79]

To replace FERA, which ended in 1935, the Works Progress Administration was created by the Emergency Relief Act in April of the same year. Roosevelt had announced that the government would "quit this business of relief" and returned to the states the responsibility to care for the 1.5 million unemployables helped through FERA. Bitterly opposed by many professional social workers, the new work program required that 90 percent of the workers be certified by public agencies as being in need. A work-for-relief scheme that persisted until 1942, when war brought massive government intervention into the economy, the WPA paid unskilled laborers an average of $50 a month, with whitecollar workers earning somewhat more. During its existence the WPA engaged in the construction of public buildings, roads, dams, and playgrounds. Artists were given work on such things as painting murals in WPA-constructed post offices, while actors and playwrights brought the theater to communities that had previously been ignored by professional companies.

Later legislation provided a supplementary work program for students, who earned an average of more than $15 a month while remaining in school. The National Youth Administration rescued many colleges and universities from financial collapse and encouraged young people, for whom there were no jobs anyway, to continue their education. For those who were not in school, part-time jobs were made available so that the young people would be an asset rather than a burden to their families.

While these varied programs, along with many other New Deal measures, attempted to solve the problems of industrial stagnation and recov-

[79] Timothy L. McDonnell, S.J., *The Wagner Housing Act* (Chicago: Loyola University Press, 1957), pp. 29–50.

ery, increasing criticism was leveled at the national administration. The national debt was increasing rapidly from the 1933 level of over $22 billion and at least 20 percent of the labor force was still unemployed. Opposed by men as diverse as former Governor Alfred E. Smith of New York and Senator Huey P. Long of Louisiana within his own political party, Roosevelt also was under pressure from various groups for more vigorous action to meet the problems of economic security. Noteworthy in this regard were the followers of Dr. Francis E. Townsend, who were increasingly successful in electing sympathetic representatives to Congress. The Townsend Plan provided that all citizens 60 years and over would receive $200 per month, the only requirement being that the money must be spent within 30 days.[80]

Business had become increasingly restive under the impact of increasing bureaucratic control and resentful of what was considered the administration's pro-labor bias. Viewed by some as a "traitor to his class," Roosevelt found himself increasingly attacked personally and his policies widely assailed. It is also significant that the policies of the New Deal, after 1934, frequently were found unconstitutional in cases brought before the Supreme Court. In May 1935 the National Industrial Recovery Act was so declared on the grounds that it constituted an unwarranted delegation of legislative power to the executive branch. Shortly thereafter the Agricultural Adjustment Act, a major New Deal program for reducing surpluses, was found unconstitutional on the grounds that it was a usurpation by the federal government of power that was properly reserved to the states. Although TVA was narrowly upheld in the same term of Court, other major New Deal recovery legislation went down in, typically, 5-to-4 decisions. After an overwhelming victory at the polls in 1936, Roosevelt proposed a major overhaul of the judiciary. The Supreme Court alteration proposed was the retirement of justices at the age of 70, or, if they chose not to retire, a "counterpart" would be named to the bench, with 15 Justices being the maximum. Public opinion, marshaled by a press campaign that labeled the plan a court-packing scheme, opposed Roosevelt's reorganization effort, and Congress refused to change the number although it had the authority and had done so in the past. However, Roosevelt "lost the battle and won the war" for in coming sessions the Supreme Court changed and found New Deal programs, such as the Social Security Act, constitutional.[81]

[80] Arthur J. Altmeyer, *The Formative Years of Social Security*, (Madison: University of Wisconsin Press, 1966), p. 10.
[81] Fred Rodell, *Nine Men* (New York: Random House, a Vintage Book, 1955), pp. 213–54.

THE PROVISION OF SOCIAL SECURITY

When President Roosevelt and his advisers began to consider creating a program for social security, there was a political need to placate the radical Right and Left. At the same time any bill written would have to be carefully drawn in order to stand the test of constitutionality. The idea for a system of social insurances had been considered as early as the summer of 1934, when President Roosevelt appointed a cabinet Committee on Economic Security. Members included Frances Perkins, the first woman cabinet member and former social worker, Henry A. Wallace, Secretary of Agriculture, and Harry Hopkins. This committee was established to make recommendations for programs that would be more comprehensive than the ones Congress was then considering. Believing that "reconstruction and recovery must go hand in hand," President Roosevelt looked to something more than the piecemeal provision of such things as unemployment compensation or old age benefits.[82]

Advisory and technical committees were created to study various programs of social insurance, all functioning under the general direction of Edwin E. Witte. Witte became Executive Director of the Committee on Economic Security after heading the Wisconsin program of unemployment insurance, the first in the nation. Working intimately with Witte was his colleague from Wisconsin Arthur J. Altmeyer, who was to become the first chairman of the Social Security Board. In setting up programs for the nation the planning groups drew not only on the experience of the states with various programs but the way in which foreign nations had met similar situations. Germany, England, and the Scandinavian countries in particular had had considerable experience with social security measures; as the last major industrial nation to develop such programs, the United States could benefit from their experiments.

In the deliberations of the committees and study groups, three major systems for providing social security were considered. First among them was a program that used a means test and varied benefits to meet individual needs. Generally known as public assistance, such programs were noncontributory and payments were made from general revenues. A second system made payments as a matter of right rather than of need. Frequently restricted to occupational groups below a certain income level, benefits could be financed from general revenues, employer or employee contributions, or a combination of the two. The third system provided

---

[82] Edwin E. Witte, *The Development of the Social Security Act* (Madison: University of Wisconsin Press, 1962), p. 6.

benefits to all members of society regardless of status or income, and payments were typically uniform. Such programs were financed by ordinary revenues or through special taxes although contributory insurance could be used to pay variable benefits.[83] As a result of the study process, the planners for social security in America used a combination of the first two systems.

As passed by Congress on August 14, 1935, the Social Security Act for the first time committed the nation to a program of unemployment insurance and an old-age insurance system. The program for the aged was to be financed through taxes on payrolls that would be borne equally by the employer and employee. Subsequently broadened to pay benefits to survivors (1939) and to those workers who become disabled (1956), the original legislation gave coverage to approximately half of the nation's workers. Medical coverage was not extended to recipients because of the hostility of physicians' associations. Some of the most needy, such as the farm workers, were denied coverage in order to win approval for the bill from congressmen representing farm bloc states. Payments were to be made as a matter of right, and benefits were to be determined by the duration of coverage and wages received, although in general the program was designed to pay a higher percentage of benefits to those lowest on the income scale.

The second departure from the past was represented by the federal-state program for unemployment insurance included in the Social Security Act. Americans had become accustomed to the idea of pensions for the aged as states adopted public assistance programs. Also, the Fraternal Order of Eagles and the American Association for Old Age Security, under the direction of Abraham Epstein, agitated for a national system. Unemployment insurance legislation, however, had not been attempted in the states until 1916, and was successfully gained only in Wisconsin before 1935. Opposed by business and organized labor, it is probable that the program would not have been initiated had it not been included in the bill for old age benefits.[84] As it was passed, the states were encouraged to develop programs in order to receive tax offsets from revenues collected through payroll taxes. States establishing programs that were approved by the federal government received payments for benefits and for covering the costs of operating state employment offices. States were free to choose a particular combination of employer-employee contribution system, and benefits, later extended, were initially limited to 16 weeks. Unrelated to family size and based on duration of employment and wage level, unem-

[83] J. Henry Richardson, *Economic and Financial Aspects of Social Security* (Toronto: University of Toronto Press, 1960), pp. 40–41.
[84] Witte, *op. cit.*, pp. 78–79.

ployment insurance was designed to sustain purchasing power during periods of "frictional" unemployment.[85] Insurance is most successful in meeting the problem of frictional unemployment and of limited utility with respect to business recessions or structural and technological change. It is apparent that in the 1930s structural and technological developments, combined with the cyclical nature of the unemployment during the period, made the program established somewhat irrelevant to existing conditions. Nevertheless by 1937 all states had adopted some kind of unemployment insurance program entitling unemployed persons to payments varying from $5 to $15 per week.

The limited coverage of the old age insurance scheme and the fact that payments would not be made until the 1940s made it necessary to make additional provision for the aged. The limitations of the unemployment insurance scheme required that something else be done to provide family security and to help the unemployed and the unemployable. To meet the immediate needs, the "omnibus" social security bill was broadened to include a program of federal subvention to the states that was reminiscent of FERA.[86]

Under the program federal tax moneys from current revenues were allocated to states to assist in paying for benefits to the aged, the dependent child, and the blind.[87] Benefits were to be paid to those who fit into categories, making status rather than need alone the determinant of eligibility. States might elect to operate their programs of categorical assistances directly or could delegate them, under state supervision, to counties for administration. Such principles as the requirement that grants be made

[85] Generally, three kinds of unemployment occur in industrial societies. Frictional unemployment is short-term and is expected in a dynamic economy. It consists of people who are entering or leaving the labor market, changing jobs, or temporarily dislocated through changes in consumer demand, inclement weather, or retooling for model changeovers. A second type of unemployment is caused by business recessions and is of grave national concern when it occurs. It is of import to all classes since unemployment may affect individuals in white-collar employments and managerial positions as well as the blue-collar worker. A third kind of unemployment is due to structural and technological developments. Changes in defense policies, depletion of national resources, or the automating of industrial processes can require changes in skills or alter product demand and the location of factories. William Haber and Merrill G. Murray, *Unemployment Insurance in the American Economy* (Homewood, Ill.: Richard D. Irwin, 1966), pp. 10–25.

[86] An omnibus bill contains more than one title and, although usually directed toward a single objective, creates several programs. With the addition in 1965 of medical care to some social security programs, the Social Security Act was increased to contain 19 titles.

[87] Amendments in 1950 added disability as a category, although the program was not funded until sometime later.

by public welfare offices and cash grants to recipients were established by FERA and revived in the Act. The idea of settlement in a locality was rejected in favor of a policy of residence within a state, with boundaries established for durational requirements.

The public welfare programs of categorical public assistance built on the experience of the states, most of which had had similar programs in operation prior to 1935. Many state programs were permissive rather than mandatory, however, and during the depression many communities and counties with categorical aids suspended operations. Federal law required that all subdivisions have public assistance, that all have a right to apply, and that a system of appeals be established to handle disputes. By the time World War II began, most states had established federally subvented categories of public assistance.

The program of public welfare, like the other programs included in the Social Security Act, has undergone a series of amendments to perfect the programs, broaden coverage, and liberalize benefits. The amendments of 1939 corrected flaws in the original legislation, flaws that had led to political use of the rolls in some states and individual mistreatment in some situations. In that year Congress decreed that information given by clients was to be kept confidential, and employing agencies were required to select employees through merit systems.

Other social welfare programs which, like the categorical assistances, antedated the Social Security Act were included in the 1935 legislation. Some were to be administered by the Social Security Board; others came under the jurisdiction of the Department of Labor, the U.S. Public Health Service, and various other federal and state administrative agencies. Additional funds were made available to the Public Health Service, whose inception dates back to 1799. New responsibilities and additional money were provided to agencies administering programs under the Vocational Rehabilitation Act of 1920. The Children's Bureau, a part of the Department of Labor until 1946, initiated programs for crippled children and revived grants to the states for promoting maternal and child health.[88] Similar programs had been in operation from 1922 to 1929 under the provisions of the Maternity and Infancy Act, customarily called the Sheppard-Towner Act. All of these programs operated as federal-state cooperative ventures; only the insurance program for the aged was designed as a strictly federal system to be administered by district offices irrespective of state boundaries.[89]

[88] U.S. Social Security Administration, *Annual Report of the Federal Security Agency*, 1948 (Washington: Government Printing Office, 1949), p. v.
[89] Altmeyer, *op. cit.*, pp. v–vi.

Summary

The passage of the Social Security Act of 1935 was the high point of social welfare legislation during the New Deal. Important programs such as the National Housing Act of 1937, the Wagner-Connery Act, and the National Youth Act were subsequently passed, but they did not deal in a comprehensive way with problems of social security. Other domestic programs, such as a revised Agricultural Adjustment Act, were initiated, but the threat to peace arising in Europe and Asia took attention away from the New Deal tasks of reform, relief, and recovery. After 1938, when Roosevelt asked Congress to appropriate $1 billion for naval defense, international problems of peace increasingly claimed the attention of the administration. As World War II approached, increased appropriations spurred industrial recovery, and the production of war materials, combined with conscription, temporarily solved most of the problems of relief. On balance one might question how well the New Deal had met the problems of reforming society, providing for social needs, and bringing industrial democracy nearer to realization.

The period between the two world conflicts began with a hope for society's improvement that was shattered by the increasing complacency of the people. Despite the fact that significant improvements were made during this time in some areas, notably in child welfare services, the overall attitude toward reform was hostile. Earlier reform leadership by academicians and intellectuals was replace by critics and pedants with little concern for democratic society. H. L. Mencken wrote, "If I am convinced of anything it is that Doing Good is in Bad Taste." The author James Branch Cabell spoke for many of his contemporaries when he said, "I burn with generous indignation over this world's pig-headedness and injustice at no time whatever." [90] As with most of their contemporaries, the literati concluded that the business system had solved problems of production permanently and could only decry the social consequences flowing from the system.

Reform leaders of the earlier period and social workers in the emerging profession were disappointed by the diminishing commitment to the improvement of society. Aware that not all shared equally in the expanding economy, programs advocated earlier in the century were deferred until the internal crisis of the 1930s made possible the enactment of necessary social legislation. Grace Abbott summed up the situation in 1936 when she addressed her colleagues in the American Association of Social Workers:

[90] Quoted in Schlesinger, *The Crisis of the Old Order, op. cit.,* pp. 145–46.

The war postponed for two decades the development of what was in 1912, a promising social reform movement. In the hard and brittle days after the war we were not very much concerned with problems of this sort and it took the great catastrophe of 1929 to bring again to public attention the problems that we had hoped to solve twenty years earlier.[91]

Disillusionment with Prohibition, fear of the Russian experiment, and the need to incorporate new learning about individual behavior and its treatment led increasingly to an identification of social work as social casework. Lamenting the concentration on means to ends rather than on goals of social reform, Abraham Epstein in 1928 wrote:

No longer are the voices of the early Isaiahs heard in the demand of justice. Vital social reforms are left to languish and social workers as a group take but little interest in them. Except for campaign purposes social work no longer proclaims itself as pure altruism. . . . It has lost its spiritual equilibrium and it has become too practical to be passionate. . . . It speaks with the polished tongue of the financier through expert press agents and high-pressure publicity. Instead of denouncing wrongs it has become merely amiable. Its only crusades are community chest drives which it conducts with the zip-zip of a successful team's cheer leader.[92]

The opportunity soon arose for something more dynamic than fund drives and amiability, and social workers and public officials were caught up in attempting to meet a constantly growing need for income maintenance. Leaders in the field of social work, many of whom had continued throughout the 1920s to push for social changes, were involved in designing and administering programs on a scale never before approached in America. A changed attitude in society and a government committed to positive action made possible the beginning of institutional programs on a federal level that many had sought for virtually a lifetime.

The most radical program of the New Deal, carried out by the National Industrial Recovery Administration, was experimented with and rejected. Less revolutionary programs of social insurance were written into law, and federal subvention provided for categorical aid programs that were considered to be temporary measures, useful during the interim before other programs could be implemented and expanded. Programs of work-for-relief replaced earlier, more radical, programs and provided employment for one-fourth of all families in the United States at one time or

[91] Grace Abbott, "Social Workers and Public Welfare Developments," *This Business of Relief* (New York: American Association of Social Workers, 1936), p. 18.
[92] Abraham Epstein, "The Soullessness of Presentday Social Work," *Current History*, Vol. 28, no. 3 (June 1928), pp. 391–92.

another. At the same time the WPA, CCC, CWA, and TVA contributed to the physical beauty of the nation as well as to the arts and sciences.

Economically the New Deal, perhaps because of the sometimes conflicting goals of recovery, reform, and relief, is difficult to assess. Such programs as NIRA undoubtedly contributed to business recovery. Regulatory legislation helped restore confidence in banks and securities. Labor reform led to a more equitable division of industrial profits as well as improved working conditions in factories. However, investments, income, employment, and profits never returned to predepression levels until the advent of World War II assured recovery by an expansion of government involvement in the private sector. Some programs, such as old-age and unemployment insurance, worked against recovery because money was withdrawn by taxation for the creation of trust funds that generally made payments after the worst of the crisis had passed.

Perhaps the most significant achievements of the New Deal lay in the change in attitudes toward the functions of government. The creation of a foundation of social insurance was laid, and areas previously considered the exclusive province of the private sector were brought under the scrutiny of a democratic government. In contrast to the experience of some other industrial nations, the New Deal enabled the people to feel that industrial justice could be achieved without abandoning democratic paths on the road to social reform.

Selected Bibliography

Abbott, Grace. *From Relief to Social Security*. Chicago: University of Chicago Press, 1941.

Abbott, Grace. "Social Workers and Public Welfare Developments." *This Business of Relief*. New York: American Association of Social Workers, 1936.

Adkins v. Children's Hospital, 261 U.S. (1923).

Altmeyer, Arthur J. *The Formative Years of Social Security*. Madison: University of Wisconsin Press, 1966.

Angoff, Charles. *The Tone of the Twenties*. New York: A. S. Barnes & Co., 1966.

Barton, Bruce. *The Man Nobody Knows*. Indianapolis: Bobbs-Merrill Co., 1925.

Bossard, James H. S., ed. "Social Welfare in the National Recovery Program." *Annals of the American Academy of Political and Social Science*, Vol. 176 (November 1934), pp. 1–183.

Brackett, Jeffrey R. "Public Outdoor Relief in the United States." *Proceedings of the National Conference of Charities and Correction at the Forty-*

Second Annual Session. Chicago: Hildmann Printing Co., 1915, pp. 446–73.

Bremner, Robert H. *American Philanthropy.* Chicago: University of Chicago Press, 1960.

Broderick, Francis L. *Right Reverend New Dealer: John A. Ryan.* New York: Macmillan Co., 1963.

Brown, Josephine C. *Public Relief 1929–1939.* New York: Henry Holt & Co., 1940.

Burns, Eveline M. *The American Social Security System.* Boston: Houghton Mifflin Co., 1949.

Cannon, Cornelia J. "Philanthropic Doubts." *Atlantic Monthly,* Vol. 128, no. 3 (September 1921), pp. 289–300.

Carter, Paul A. *The Decline and Revival of the Social Gospel.* Ithaca, N.Y.: Cornell University Press, 1954.

Chamberlain, John. *The Enterprising Americans.* New York: Harper & Row, 1961.

Chambers, Clarke A. *Seedtime of Reform.* Minneapolis: University of Minnesota Press, 1963.

Charles, Searle F. *Minister of Relief.* Syracuse, N.Y.: Syracuse University Press, 1963.

Cochran, Thomas C. *The American Business System.* Cambridge: Harvard University Press, 1957.

Cohen, Nathan Edward. *Social Work In The American Tradition.* New York: Holt, Rinehart & Winston, 1958.

Commager, Henry Steele. *The American Mind.* New Haven: Yale University Press, 1950.

"The Deportations." *The Survey,* Vol. 41, no. 21 (February 22, 1919), pp.

Cowley, Malcolm. *Exiles Return.* New York: Viking Press, 1951.
722–24.

Draper, Ernest G. "What Employers are Doing." *Proceedings of the National Conference of Social Work at the Fifty-Seventh Annual Session.* Chicago: University of Chicago Press, 1930, pp. 320–24.

Dripps, Robert D. "The Policy of State Aid to Private Charities." *Proceedings of the National Conference of Charities and Correction at the Forty-Second Annual Session.* Chicago: Hildmann Printing Co., 1915, pp. 446–73.

Epstein, Abraham. "The Soullessness of Presentday Social Work." *Current History,* Vol. 28, no 3 (June 1928), pp. 390–95.

"Fair Competition," *Business Week* (May 24, 1933), pp. 1–2.

Farrell, John C. *Beloved Lady.* Baltimore: Johns Hopkins Press, 1967.

Feder, Leah Hannah. *Unemployment Relief in Periods of Depression.* New York: Russell Sage Foundation, 1936.

Galbraith, John Kenneth. *The New Industrial State.* Boston: Houghton Mifflin Co., 1967.

Gittler, Joseph B., ed. *Understanding Minority Groups.* New York: John Wiley & Sons, 1956.

Graham, Otis L., Jr. *An Encore for Reform*. New York: Oxford University Press, 1967.

Greenstein, Harry. "Work Programs and Relief Measures." *This Business of Relief*. New York: American Association of Social Workers, 1936, pp. 69–77.

Haber, William, and Murray, Merrill G. *Unemployment Insurance in the American Economy*. Homewood, Ill.: Richard D. Irwin, 1966.

Hammer v. Dagenhart, 247 U.S. (1918).

Hawley, Ellis W. *The New Deal and the Problem of Monopoly*. Princeton, N.J.: Princeton University Press, 1966.

Higham, John. *Strangers in the Land*. New Brunswick, N.J.: Rutgers University Press, 1955.

Hodson, William. "Social Workers and Politics." *The Survey*, Vol. 63, no. 4 (November 15, 1929), pp. 199–201.

Hoover, Herbert. *American Individualism*. Garden City, N.Y.: Doubleday Page & Co., 1923.

Hopkins, Harry L. *Spending to Save*. New York: W. W. Norton & Co., 1936.

Howe, Quincy. *The World Between the Wars*. New York: Simon & Schuster, 1953.

Johnson, Donald. *The Challenge to American Freedoms*. Frankfort: University of Kentucky Press, 1963.

Jones, John Paul. "Middle-class Misery." *The Survey*, Vol. 68, no. 11 (September 1, 1932), pp. 402–4.

Kelley, Florence. "Progress of Labor Legislation for Women." *Proceedings of the National Conference of Social Work at the Fiftieth Anniversary Session*. Chicago: University of Chicago Press, 1923, pp. 112–16.

Keynes, John Maynard. *The General Theory of Employment, Interest, and Money*. New York: Harcourt, Brace & Co., a Harbinger Book, 1936.

Kitagawa, Daisuke. *Issei and Nisei: The Internment Years*. New York: Seabury Press, 1967.

Lekachman, Robert. *The Age of Keynes*. New York: Random House, 1966.

Lewis, Sinclair. *Babbitt*. New York: Grosset & Dunlap, 1922.

McDonnell, Timothy L., S.J. *The Wagner Housing Act*. Chicago: Loyola University Press, 1957.

McMillen, A. Wayne. "An Army of Boys on the Loose." *The Survey*, Vol. 68, no. 11 (September 1, 1932), pp. 389–93.

McWilliams, Carey. *Prejudice; Japanese-Americans: Symbol of Racial Intolerance*. Boston: Little, Brown & Co., 1944.

Martin, Roscoe C., ed. *TVA The First Twenty Years*. Knoxville: University of Tennessee Press, 1956.

Mason, Alpheus T. *Brandeis: A Free Man's Life*. New York: Viking Press, 1946.

Mencken, Henry L. *The Vintage Mencken*. Edited by Alistair Cooke. New York: Vintage Books, 1955.

Miller, Robert Moats. *American Protestantism and Social Issues, 1919–1939*. Chapel Hill: University of North Carolina Press, 1958.

Nestor, Agnes. "Current Problems of Unemployment." *Proceedings of the*

National Conference of Social Work at the Fifty-Seventh Annual Session. Chicago: University of Chicago Press, 1930, pp. 315–319.

Perkins, Frances. *The Roosevelt I Knew.* New York: Viking Press, 1946.

"A Plan to Promote Economic Balance." *Business Week.* January 8, 1930, pp. 22–24.

"Public Works," *Business Week* (May 24, 1933), p. 2.

Rayback, Joseph G. *A History of American Labor.* New York: Macmillan Co., 1959.

Reynolds, Bertha C. *An Uncharted Journey.* New York: Citadel Press, 1963.

Richardson, J. Henry. *Economic and Financial Aspects of Social Security.* Toronto: University of Toronto Press, 1960.

Rodell, Fred. *Nine Men.* New York: Random House, a Vintage Book, 1955.

Salmond, John A. *The Civilian Conservation Corps, 1933–1942.* Durham, N.C.: Duke University Press, 1967.

Schlesinger, Arthur M., Jr. *The Coming of the New Deal.* Boston: Houghton Mifflin Co., 1959.

Schlesinger, Arthur M., Jr. *The Crisis of the Old Order.* Boston: Houghton Mifflin Co., 1957.

Schlesinger, Arthur M., Jr., and Israel, Fred L. *The Chief Executive.* New York: Crown Publishers, 1965.

Shannon, David A. *The Great Depression.* New York: Prentice-Hall, a Spectrum Book, 1960.

"The Shell of the Employment Service." *The Survey,* Vol. 46, no. 3 (April 16, 1921), pp. 78–79.

Sherwood, Robert E. *Roosevelt and Hopkins.* New York: Harper & Bros., 1948.

"Social Settlements and the War." *The Survey,* Vol. 38, no. 1 (April 7, 1917), pp. 29–30.

Sprague, O. M. W. "The Crisis of 1914 in the United States." *American Economic Review,* Vol. 5, no. 3 (September 1915), pp. 499–533.

Stead, William T. *If Christ Came to Chicago.* New York: Living Books, Inc., 1964.

Stevenson, Elizabeth. *Babbits and Bohemians.* New York: Macmillan Co., 1967.

Swift, Linton B. "Private Agencies and Public Welfare." *This Business of Relief, Proceedings of the Delegate Conference, American Association of Social Workers.* New York: Columbia University Press, 1936, pp. 83–89.

U.S. Congress. Subcommittee on Unemployment and the Impact of Automation of the Committee on Education and Labor. *Impact of Automation on Employment.* 87th Cong., 1st sess., 1961.

U.S. Department of the Interior, War Relocation Authority. *Impounded People: Japanese Americans in the Relocation Centers.* Washington, D.C.: Government Printing Office, 1946.

U.S. Department of the Interior, War Relocation Authority. *Legal and Constitutional Phases of the War Relocation Authority Program.* Washington, D.C.: Government Printing Office, 1946.

U.S. Social Security Administration. *Annual Report of the Federal Security Agency,* 1948. Washington: Government Printing Office, 1949.

Vincent, M. D., and Amidon, Beulah. "NRA: A Trial Balance." *Survey Graphic,* Vol. 24, no. 7 (July 1935), pp. 333–37, and 363–64.

"The Voice of Industry." *Business Week.* December 14, 1935, p. 44.

Walker, Wilma. "Distress in a Southern Illinois County." *Social Service Review,* Vol. 5, no. 4 (December 1931), pp. 558–81.

Weyl, Walter E. *The New Democracy.* New York: Harper & Row, 1964.

Witte, Edwin E. *The Development of the Social Security Act.* Madison: University of Wisconsin Press, 1962.

Woods, Robert A. "Winning the Other Half." *The Survey,* Vol. 37, no. 13 (December 30, 1916), pp. 349–52.

Chapter Four

Perfecting the Welfare State

$\mathbf{T}$HE ROAD of social change from Franklin D. Roosevelt's third inauguration in 1940 until the election of President John F. Kennedy in 1960 was
circuitous at best and impassable at times. Concern with winning World
War II, reaction to the programs and philosophy of the New Deal, fear
of internal subversion and threats from abroad, and ineffectual presidential leadership made improvement of or innovation within social welfare
institutions difficult.

Many voluntary social service agencies, as well as public services,
were necessarily concerned for much of the time with providing for
the needs of men and women in military service and their dependents.
Notable among these were the quasi-public American Red Cross and the
agencies affiliated with the National Travelers Aid Association.

As was the case during World War I, those interested in improving
social welfare services were hopeful about the prospects for the postwar
period. Writing in 1943 in the *Journal of the American Association of
Social Workers,* the chairman of the department of economics at Vassar
made a cautious prediction: "If popular interest in full employment, an
expanded social security program, housing and other measures benefitting
the general public continues, the next postwar period should offer opportunity for advancing both the quality and quantity of the public welfare
program." [1]

The idea that further reforms would be necessary was sparked by the
widespread conviction of both the experts and the general public that a
postwar economic slump was inevitable. In 1943, the midpoint of the war,
over 63 million persons were in the labor force, and the war accounted
for the employment of approximately 28 million of these. The armed
services stood at 10 million and was rising, while more than 17 million
worked at jobs connected with the war effort.[2] The end of hostilities
would mean the demobilization of the bulk of the military force and
conversion to peaceful occupation for civilians. Among the latter were
many aged, handicapped, and young people who would have difficulty
in getting or keeping work.[3] It was widely held that individuals who had
been able to find jobs in wartime (consequently reducing the numbers
needing public assistance) would be reluctant to return to the welfare
rolls. The likelihood of an unemployment level of 5 or 6 million did
not seem unreasonable.[4]

[1] Mabel Newcomer, "The Social Workers' Stake in the Program of War Finance,"
The Compass, Vol. 24, no. 3 (March 1943), p.7.
[2] A. D. H. Kaplan, *Liquidation of War Production.* Report by the Committee for
Economic Development (York, Pa.: Maple Press Co., 1944), p. 15.
[3] "Social Security in Review," *Social Security Bulletin,* Vol. 8, no. 2 (February
1945), p. 1.
[4] William Haber, "Economic and Social Readjustments in the Reconversion Period,"
Proceedings of the National Conference of Social Work, 1945 (New York: Columbia
University Press, 1945), p. 36.

Although unemployment rates went as high as 7 percent, the immediate postwar years brought less severe economic constriction than anticipated—due in large measure to the crises of the cold war and continuing defense expenditures. Many social insurance measures and programs involving social spending were defeated in a rising tide of reaction against social legislation and a virulent anti-Communist hysteria that convulsed the nation at midcentury. Although revisions in the social security programs were made during both the Truman and Eisenhower administrations, radical innovations were rejected.

Foreign policy concerns and ideological questions dominated the scene in the 1940s and 1950s. A fear of economic collapse was replaced by a fear of subversion. Television sets came to be standard equipment in most homes during the 1950s. With nearly one-third of the working force of roughly 64 million being women in 1955, it was likely that two incomes per family helped to buy them. Television became another of the mass media and surpassed radio, newspapers, and magazines as an agent for stimulating consumer desires. At least one critic pointed out that the affluent society was being dominated by artificially stimulated consumer wants while public needs languished.[5]

A revived interest in religion occurred to the delight of some religious leaders and the despair of others. Young people, concerned with "getting ahead," were regarded as having forsaken adventure in favor of pension plans and economic security. The way in which they moved into a suburban world by way of the corporation was described, half satirically, in The Organization Man, and the gray flannel suit described a way of life as much as an item of apparel.[6] The American of the 1950s found himself described as an "other-directed" person taking his cues for his behavior from his peers and forsaking his individualism.[7] The "silent generation" differed significantly from that which preceded it and that which was to come later. It typified a nation wanting peace when there was no peace and isolation in a world that would not permit it. A later writer described the era in these terms:

> A time-capsule representative of the generation reaching adulthood during the 1950's would have consisted of a subpoena, a blacklist, a television tube, a gray flannel suit, a copy of Time magazine with Herman Wouk on the cover, a Lawrence Welk album, an "I like Ike" button, and a blank sheet of paper.[8]

[5] John Kenneth Galbraith, The Affluent Society. (Boston: Houghton Mifflin Co., 1958).

[6] William Hollingsworth Whyte, The Organization Man (Garden City, N.Y.: Doubleday & Co., 1956).

[7] David Riesman, The Lonely Crowd (New Haven: Yale University Press, 1950).

[8] Jack Newfield, A Prophetic Minority (New York: New American Library, 1966), p. 37.

Despite the misgivings of observers and critics, significant changes took place in what was a crucial period of American history. Social welfare institutions created during the New Deal were at least left intact and, in some instances, improved. If institutional change did not occur rapidly enough to meet changed conditions, it is equally true that they probably never have. The foundations for change were laid in many areas of national life, and in no respect was this more true than in the realm of race relations and civil rights. It is perhaps paradoxical that in a time when civil liberties and rights were most severely challenged, the seeds were sown for an enlargement of these democratic guarantees of the Constitution.

The executive branch of the government had increasingly dominated the legislative branch during the 1930s. In the next two decades neither dominated the other, either because of inability or unwillingness to act on both parts. Most actions were the result of compromises between Democratic Congresses and a Republican president or vice versa. In this milieu the Supreme Court became increasingly active (some would say activist) as an agent of social change. Although the judiciary has traditionally been neither far behind nor far in front of the national mood, the Warren Court from 1954 until 1969 was an exception. Only the Marshall Court of the early days of the republic so profoundly affected the nature of the American social and political system. In a time when the young seemed cautious before their years and their parents affluent and apathetic, the Supreme Court moved ahead of the nation by requiring that the promise of American life be a reality for all.

AMERICA AND WORLD WAR II

Events in various parts of the world in the late 1930s increased President Roosevelt's concern about peace. Congressional sentiment reflected the opinion of the electorate toward Roosevelt's declaration in October 1937 that aggressors should be "quarantined." Although Americans were involved in the Spanish Civil War at the time and aware of Japan's attack on China in 1937, most were more concerned with an economic decline that hit the nation that year. The isolationist mood of the country was expressed in 1935, 1936, and 1937 when Congress passed successive Neutrality Acts to prevent the selling of arms or munitions to warring powers. Certainly few would argue that the problem of industrial depression had been solved.

In November 1938 employment through the Works Project Administration reached a peak of 3.33 million.[9] The numbers receiving public

[9] Ruth White, "The Effect of Liquidation of the WPA on Need for Assistance," *Social Security Bulletin*, Vol. 6, no. 6 (June 1943), p. 4.

assistance benefits increased rapidly as the states took advantage of federal subvention. In an effort to encourage retirement of older workers and to provide a stimulus for the economy, Congress in 1939 passed the first series of amendments to the Social Security Act. Under these, the date of payment of benefits was advanced to January 1, 1940, for social insurance, and eligibility and benefit provisions were liberalized. Federal payments for recipients of aid in the adult categories of public assistance were increased, and alterations were made to protect the individual rights of clients. The original Act had made no mention of the confidentiality of transactions between the agencies and recipients. During the 1938 congressional elections there were many instances of misuse of the names of persons receiving public assistance. Some of the most flagrant abuses occurred in Ohio, where social workers were required to actively solicit votes for the governor, and form letters were sent out to new recipients and those receiving increases in their grants implying that aid would be cut off or reduced should the incumbent be defeated. Protection was provided in 1939 when states were required, as part of their plan of operation, to restrict the use of information about recipients to purposes directly connected with the administration of welfare assistance. The amendments of 1939 also required that the federal and state governments select all personnel administering any aspect of the act through a merit system.

In the year in which the Social Security Act was first amended, expenditures for social welfare totalled over $9.5 million. This represented 10.9 percent of the Gross National Product (GNP) and 54.6 percent of all government expenditures.[10]

Concern with federal budgets of $8 billion or $9 billion and attempts to improve social welfare institutions were pushed to the background as the nation moved toward war. Planning for economic recovery was overshadowed by defense planning, and a National Defense Advisory Commission was created in May 1940. The Reconstruction Finance Corporation was given authority to assist in the construction of defense plants. The stimulus of Lend-Lease to the Soviet Union and the provision of supplies to England created new employment opportunities. The supply of workers to fill the new jobs began to contract following passage, in 1940, of the Selective Training and Service Act.

Total involvement in the war followed the attack on Pearl Harbor, Hawaii, on December 7, 1941. The effect of participation in the war was evident as federal budgets climbed to $34 billion in 1942, to $79 billion in 1943, and a wartime high of $98 billion in 1945. The national debt,

[10] U.S. Department of Commerce, Bureau of the Census, *Historical Statistics of the United States, Colonial Times to 1957* (Washington, D.C.: Government Printing Office, 1960), p. 193.

which had climbed from $19 billion in Hoover's last year in office to $40 billion in 1939, by 1946 stood in excess of $269 billion.[11]

Within two years after Pearl Harbor, unemployment had practically disappeared, and the value of goods and services produced had increased by more than 60 percent.[12] By the end of the war in 1945 the GNP stood at $215 billion—over twice that of 1939. This was accomplished without a corresponding increase in the labor force, a fact that reflected in large measure the increased productivity of American industry. Output per man had increased by 41 percent from 1930 to 1940, when pressure for efficiency and economy led to the maximum utilization of manpower and the adoption of many technological improvements. By contrast, from 1920 to 1930 output per man hour had increased by only 21 percent.[13]

Productivity and technological advances increased as the industrial system met the demands imposed by the war. In the process the characteristics of the working force were altered significantly, as was the well-being of the workers. Between 1939 and 1945 the average weekly earnings of manufacturing workers went up by 86 percent, the cost of living by only 29 percent. Higher salaries and a scarcity of labor created unheard of opportunities for the aged, the handicapped, adolescents, and mothers with small children. The result was to bring into productive employment many who had retired or who had been considered marginal as employees. Attention was paid to structuring production to the needs of employees, and many communities provided services such as day nurseries to assist the war effort. The need for public welfare assistance declined each year during the war, as did the payment of unemployment benefits.[14] In California the legislature gave some thought to abolishing the Aid to Needy Children program (ADC in other states), as mothers found work at high enough wages to make employment economically feasible. In that state the funds for unemployment insurance accumulated to the point that surplus funds were used to create a sickness and disability program to cover nonindustrial accidents and illness.[15]

Wartime full employment proportionally benefitted the lowest income groups the most. But as a group, Negro Americans were the last to feel

[11] Frederick Lewis Allen, *The Big Change* (New York: Harper & Bros. Publishers, 1952), p. 166.

[12] George E. Mowry, *The Urban Nation 1920–1960* (New York: Hill & Wang, 1965), p. 196.

[13] Allen, *op. cit.*, p. 165.

[14] "Social Security in Review," *op. cit.*

[15] In addition New York, New Jersey, and Rhode Island have benefit programs of insurance against illness and disabilities not having a work-connected origin. In 1942 Rhode Island led the way in providing this kind of social insurance, a kind of insurance consistently advocated by administrators of the national social security system.

the effects—except, of course, for Americans of Japanese descent, who were scattered in a modern Diaspora or herded into concentration camps. From 1939 to 1942, while the need for WPA employment declined for most men, the percentage of Negroes on the rolls increased from 14.2 percent to 17.5 percent. Surveys of industries converting to wartime production revealed that at least 51 percent of the prospective new jobs would not be open to Negroes.[16]

Economic discrimination created a movement among Negro pressure groups, churches, newspapers, and community associations to actively protest the fate of black Americans. Led by A. Philip Randolph of the Pullman Porters' Union, the movement adopted a "nonviolent yet coercive program" to secure equality in defense hiring. Plans were made to stage mass meetings in the major cities throughout the nation and, as a last resort, to march on Washington, D.C., on July 1, 1941. The prospect of having perhaps as many as 100,000 Negroes converging on the nation's capital at a time when the country was fighting a war for democracy's preservation led to the issuing of Executive Order 8803 by President Roosevelt. This forbade discrimination in hiring by companies holding defense contracts and established the President's Committees on Fair Employment Practice to deal with violations.[17] The need for workers and pressure by the government led to some improvement in employment, although the armed forces were untouched by antisegregation policies.

PLANNING FOR PEACETIME

Increasing optimism about the outcome of the war led to a renewed interest in social planning during the course of the war. Although congressional action had, by 1943, eliminated the WPA, the CCC, and the NYA, President Roosevelt warned Congress in a message of March 10, 1943, "We must not return to the inequities, insecurity, and fears of the past, but ought to move forward toward the promise of the future." [18] Congressional response was the elimination of funds for the National Resources Planning Board. This group, a staff agency in the White House, had never received strong support from Congress. The submission of their report in 1943 calling for a drastic reorganization of American industries, a federal system of unemployment insurance, a governmental guarantee

[16] Louis C. Kesselman, "The Fair Employment Practice Commission Movement in Perspective," *Journal of Negro History*, Vol. 31, no. 1 (January 1946), pp. 30–46.
[17] *Ibid.*
[18] "Message From the President of the United States," *Congressional Record*, Vol. 89, Part I, January 6, 1943 to April 5, 1943 (Washington, D.C.: Government Printing Office, 1943), p. 1792.

of a right to a job, and improved health services (among other things), was the immediate cause of the board's demise. The data collected and the recommendations for improvements in social security progress formed the basis, however, for a number of proposals that captured the attention of the people in the postwar period.

Liberal magazines, labor journals, and many academic publications supported the idea of national planning to avert economic dislocations. Social workers generally supported the proposals for improving programs of social security. Some saw in the proposals and the factual material collected the basis for immediate improvement when taxes could be channeled into constructive programs. One social worker remarked: "These data demonstrate beyond question the extent of insecurity or, shall we say, plain poverty in this most generous of nations, which happens, for the moment, to be enjoying an employment boom in certain places." [19]

Acting on some of the recommendations of the National Resources Planning Board, President Roosevelt in 1944 asked Congress to pass a law to limit incomes to $25,000 net a year.[20] In his annual message to Congress in January 1944, he called for a postwar bill of economic rights that would include the right to a job, a decent home, a good education, adequate medical care, and a complete program of social insurance. In regard to the latter, the Social Security Board in its *Annual Report* for the fiscal year 1942–43 reflected the thinking of the National Resources Planning Board. Among the recommendations were proposals for a federalized system of unemployment benefits, the inclusion of disability as a basis for claims in social insurance, cash benefits for temporary sickness not connected with industrial causes, and medical insurance under an expanded social security system to cover all workers.[21]

Social welfare measures to benefit the larger population were eschewed by Congress. However, many of the recommendations were implemented for returning veterans. In 1944 Congress passed the Servicemen's Readjustment Act without a single dissenting vote in either House. The law provided for enlarged and improved hospital facilities, tuition, books, and maintenance allowances for training and education; loans for purchasing homes; assistance in finding work through the then federalized

---

[19] Dorothy C. Kahn, "The Real Crisis in Social Work," *The Compass*, Vol. 24, no. 5 (June 1943), p. 3.

[20] This request found little congressional support. A 1942 executive order placing such a limit on personal incomes had been countermanded by act of Congress.

[21] U.S. Social Security Commission, *Eighth Annual Report* of the Social Security Board for the Fiscal year 1942–43 (Washington, D.C.: Government Printing Office, 1944), pp. 31–45.

U.S. Employment Services; and readjustment compensation at the rate of $20 per week to be paid for a maximum of 52 weeks in a two-year period.[22] Within 10 years, 8 million veterans had been helped in obtaining an advanced education, 196,000 were assisted in starting their own businesses, and 64,000 received help in buying farms. In addition, the government had helped during the same period to finance 3 million privately constructed homes through loans guaranteed by the Veterans Administration.[23]

In later years opponents of such benefits saw in the provisions for education the danger of "free government-paid scholarships for everyone." The possibility of federal control of education was, by some, considered inherent in such schemes.[24]

On the other hand advocates of federal assistance to education pointed to the GI Bill as an example of intelligent social spending. The educational program had operated without federal intervention into curriculums or policies. It had a "pump-priming" effect by putting money into the hands of individuals who would spend rather than save and contributed to economic stability after the war by delaying the entry of returning veterans into the labor market. In addition to cultural gains for society, tax revenues were probably increased as the result of the higher earning power of beneficiaries, and colleges and universities expanded facilities while upgrading the skills of workers needed by an automating industrial complex.[25]

Congress did not exhibit the same attitude toward workers who would be displaced by conversion to peacetime industrial production. Proposals that workers in war industries be given federal unemployment compensation, transportation allowances for resettlement, and additional education to acquire new skills received little support. Neither was Congress willing to extend some of the benefits available to veterans to the public at large. In the immediate postwar period attempts to provide a guarantee of a job and medical care for all citizens were the occasion for heated congressional battles. Failure to accomplish either, during a time when Canada and many European nations were establishing programs of national medical care, children's allowances, and income insurance plans for workers, reflected an increasing conservatism of the people and their political rep-

[22] "The G.I. Bill of Rights: An Analysis of the Servicemen's Readjustment Act of 1944," *Social Security Bulletin*, Vol. 7, no. 7 (July 1944), pp. 3–13.

[23] Louis Filler, ed., *The President Speaks: From William McKinley to Lyndon B. Johnson* (New York: G. P. Putnam's Sons, 1964), pp. 3–13.

[24] Raymond Moley, *How to Keep Our Liberty* (New York: Alfred A. Knopf, 1952), p. 176.

[25] Michael Harrington, *The Accidental Century* (New York: Macmillan Co., 1965), pp. 282–85.

resentatives.[26] Increasing rejection of the ideology of the New Deal illustrated the fact that those who have been helped by government intervention are prone to be less esthusiastic about continued help to the disadvantaged.

THE FIGHT FOR FULL EMPLOYMENT LEGISLATION

One of the most revolutionary ideas in the last report of the National Resources Planning Board was the concept of full peacetime employment.[27] Supported by specialists in social security, among others, such a plan would have involved governmentally financed work programs that would not be based on need and that would pay wages parallel to private employment. The debt owed to the early New Deal CWA program was obvious.

In his message to Congress on January 6, 1945, President Roosevelt called for legislation to insure full employment for over 60 million workers. A few weeks later Senator James Murray of Montana introduced a bill that would "establish a national policy and program for assuring continuing full employment to a free competitive economy through the concerted efforts of industry, agriculture, labor, State and local governments, and the Federal Government." [28] Specifically, the legislation proposed would have required the president to transmit to Congress at each regular session a national production and employment budget. In the event that nongovernmental investment and expenditure would not produce a gross national product of sufficient magnitude to assure full employment, the act contemplated further action and planning. Work projects were to be initiated as "a general program for Federal invest-

---

[26] In using the terms "liberal" and "conservative" one enters into a world of historical ambiguity and contemporary imprecision. In the United States, "conservatism" is generally used to describe a position that defends the value of existing institutions and is opposed to those who seek to transform them. Included is the notion of freedom in the market place and the sanctity of free enterprise. The idea of limited government with a strict line drawn between the rights of states and local governments, as opposed to the power of the federal government, is a cornerstone of the philosophy. The ideas of individual freedom from interference from governmental notions, now considered part of conservative belief, was equated with liberalism in the nineteenth century. Liberalism in this century has centered on the belief that the individuality of the citizen can best be assured by positive action by his government. Man's reason is considered sufficient to guide him in making social innovations and whenever private enterprise and initiative fail, government on some level is seen as a reasonable institution to provide equality of opportunity.

[27] J. Raymond Walsh, "Action for Postwar Planning," *Antioch Review*, Vol. 3, no. 2 (Summer 1943), p. 154.

[28] Anne Scitovszky, "The Employment Act of 1946," *Social Security Bulletin*, Vol. 9, no. 3 (March 1946), p. 26.

ment and expenditure which would bring the aggregate volume of private and Government investment and expenditure up to the necessary level." [29] As proposed, the measure would have adopted as national policy the concept of national planning and intervention to prevent economic recession.

Over a year after the introduction of the first act, the Employment Act of 1946 emerged from Congress significantly changed from the original. The statement of the original legislation that "all Americans able to work and seeking work have the right to useful, remunerative, regular, and full-time employment" was deleted. Removed also was the requirement that the federal government act as the employer of last resort in times of economic crisis. Instead the bill affirmed that it was "the continuing policy and responsibility of the Federal Government . . . to coordinate and utilize all its plans, functions, and resources for the purpose of creating and maintaining . . . conditions under which there will be afforded useful employment opportunities, including self-employment for those able, willing, and seeking to work, and to promote maximum employment, production, and purchasing power." [30] As passed into law, the bill made full employment a goal of national policy but provided no machinery for insuring realization of the goal. Perhaps the only way in which the final measure was superior to the original as a piece of action legislation was the modification of the section dealing with the creation of a Council of Economic Advisers. Originally a similar group of economic experts were to be appointed by the president and were to serve at his pleasure. In the final bill the council was to be appointed by the president with the consent of the Senate, thus making them a part of the congressional apparatus as much as an appendage of the executive branch.[31] Through the years the council, consisting of three specialists in economics and a small staff, has had considerable impact on national planning and legislation. *The Annual Report of the Council of Economic Advisers* is included in the *Economic Report of the President* to Congress, and a Joint Economic Committee in Congress holds hearings on the findings of the Council of Economic Advisers.

The effect of the Employment Act of 1946 has been less profound than what would have been the case had the original bill survived intact. Nonetheless, the legislation has been cited by some as a commitment to the idea of full employment and the acceptance of the notion that government has a role to play in the national economy. The failure of the initial measure can be attributed to congressional hostility toward expansion of

[29] *Ibid.*

[30] *Ibid.*, p. 25.

[31] Carl Landauer, *Theory of National Economic Planning* (Berkeley: University of California Press, 1947), p. 222.

the New Deal, the change of leadership after President Roosevelt's death in 1945, and impatience with wartime regulations and controls. Combined with these factors, rejection of a guaranteed "right to work" probably reflected the antipathy the American people have customarily shown toward national planning proposals.[32]

THE TRUMAN ADMINISTRATION AND MEDICAL CARE LEGISLATION

In 1920 the House of Delegates of the American Medical Association adopted a resolution that has ever since expressed the organization's position on compulsory health insurance:

The American Medical Association declares its opposition to any plan embodying the system of compulsory contributory insurance against illness, or any other plan of compulsory insurance which provides for medical service to be rendered contributors or their dependents, provided, controlled, or regulated by any state or Federal government.[33]

Fear that the inclusion of medical care might jeopardize the entire program of the Social Security Act of 1935 caused elimination of such consideration. However, it was generally felt by social insurance advocates that medical coverage could be included later as modifications of a more restricted initial Act.

In July 1938 a National Health Conference was held in Washington, D.C., to commemorate the 141st anniversary of the U.S. Public Health Service. Called by the President's Committee to Coordinate Health and Welfare Activities, the Conference made recommendations that looked toward a national health program. The final statement of its report called for expansion of public health and maternal and child health services, expansion of hospital facilities, medical care for the medically needy, a general program of medical care, and insurance against loss of wages during sickness. The report was supported by most groups represented including the American Federation of Labor, which had previously opposed the extension of health services under government auspices. The only opposition came from representatives of the American Medical Association.[34]

[32] Stephen Kemp Bailey, *Congress Makes A Law* (New York: Random House, a Vintage Book, 1950).
[33] Quoted in Odin W. Anderson, "Compulsory Medical Care Insurance, 1900–1950," *Annals of the American Academy of Political and Social Science*, Vol. 273 (January 1951), p. 108.
[34] Monte Poen, "The Truman Administration and National Health Insurance" (Unpublished Ph.D. dissertation, University of Missouri, 1967), pp. 25–26.

As a result of this meeting a new organization, the American Association for Social Security, came into being under the direction of Abraham Epstein. Created to push for enactment of medical care legislation, this voluntary group made its major effort at the state level. The recommendations were translated nationally into an omnibus health bill introduced by Senator Robert A. Wagner of New York in February 1939. The first legislation thus proposed languished because of the world situation and the lack of presidential support.

Interest is expanded medical care services revived when the government was required to take care of servicemen and their dependents. A high rate of rejection for Selective Service also contributed a sense of urgency to national planning for health. The hope that national action would be forthcoming was given a boost from abroad when the government of England endorsed the 1942 report of Sir William Beveridge. This report recommended the extension of health services to the entire population of Great Britain. Nearer to home, the Canadian government passed a law to give grants to provinces that established health insurance systems.[35]

Early in 1943 Senators Wagner and Murray, along with Congressman John Dingell of Michigan introduced the first of a series of Wagner-Murray-Dingell bills designed to assure all citizens of adequate medical care. Portions of the bill were drafted by Isidore Falk and the staff of the Social Security Board's Bureau of Research. In succeeding years the Social Security Board replaced the American Association for Social Security as the chief architect and advocate of health legislation.[36]

On November 19, 1945, President Harry S Truman recommended the passage of a National Health Program to Congress. Included in his plan were grants for the construction of hospitals and other health facilities, grants for research programs and medical education, and a dual system of social insurance. The last would have been composed of a program to cover the loss of wages due to sickness and disability and a second program to provide workers and their dependents with a comprehensive program of medical services prepaid by social security taxes.[37]

Following the advice of Arthur J. Altmeyer, chairman of the Social Security Administration, Truman stressed that he was not asking for "socialized medicine" but rather for a "system of prepayment of the cost of medical care through contributory social insurance."[38] In requesting

[35] *Ibid.*, p. 35.
[36] *Ibid.*, p. 38.
[37] *Ibid.*, p. 67.
[38] Letter from Arthur J. Altmeyer to Samuel Rosenman, May 28, 1945, Harry S. Truman Library, Rosenman Papers, Box 3, Social Security Folder.

medical care legislation President Truman was advocating a national program that had been successfully opposed on the state level by organized professional medical groups. Five months before his message to Congress, the California legislature had turned down a compulsory health insurance program. The California Medical Association and its public relations firm had given the scheme the pejorative label "socialized medicine" and had warned against the introduction of "politics" into the doctor-patient relationship.[39] Despite Altmeyer's and Truman's protests to the contrary, the term socialized medicine soon became the recognized euphemism for health insurance in social security and was used by friend and foe alike.

Within the administration there was considerable difference of opinion about pressing for medical care as part of a broadened program of social security. The Department of Labor, which at that time included the Children's Bureau, considered proposals for general medical care to be "desirable but postponable" and sought instead an improvement of existing programs and retention of categories of need.[40] The Veterans Administration actively opposed the program of national medical insurance, which it, like the Children's Bureau, felt would have an adverse effect on the agency's stature. It is also possible that the Children's Bureau and the Department of Labor considered a program of children's allowances easier of achievement and more beneficial to the welfare of children.[41] As early as 1945 Grace M. Marcus, a consultant to the Bureau of Public Assistance and an authority in public welfare matters, suggested the desirability of such allowances as one alternative to the restrictive program of categorical Aid to Dependent Children.[42]

The medical bill introduced in 1945 received support from the National Medical Association, which was composed of 4000 Negro physicians, organized labor, and the liberal National Farmer's Union. Voluntary social welfare organizations and professional associations gave qualified support to the concept of making medical care generally available.

Affirmative action on the 1945 legislation was impossible, and in 1946 President Truman, in his State of the Union Address and budget message, again called for national health insurance. In the interim the provisions for promoting hospital construction were removed from the Wagner-Murray-Dingell bill and enacted as the Hospital Survey and Construction Act,

[39] John D. Weaver, *Warren: The Man, The Court, The Era* (Boston: Little, Brown & Co., 1967), pp. 137–40.
[40] Letter from Frances Perkins to President Harry Truman, May 25, 1945, Harry S Truman Library, Rosenman Papers, Box 3, Social Security Folder.
[41] See Chapter 6 for a discussion of children's allowances.
[42] Grace M. Marcus, "Reappraising Aid to Dependent Children as a Category," *Social Security Bulletin*, Vol. 8, no. 2 (February 1945), pp. 3–5.

popularly known as the Hill-Burton Act. The 1946 version of the health care bill also dropped the provision calling for a federal system of unemployment insurance. What remained were proposals to give grants to the states for expanded health services for the general public, for the needy, and for mothers and children. General medical care, including outpatient, hospital, and dental services, would be provided for workers paying social security taxes and their dependents, as well as businessmen and farmers not covered by social security.

On July 9, 1946, Senator Murray advised the press that he was abandoning efforts for the bill because of the lack of support the measure received. Political opposition crystallized around Senator Robert Taft, the spokesman for Senate conservatives, who described the Wagner-Murray-Dingell bill as "the most socialistic measure that this Congress has ever had before it." [43] In 1946, for the first time since the beginning of the New Deal, Republicans took over both houses of Congress, and the National Health Program began to recede as a viable political issue. Although Oscar Ewing, administrator of the Federal Security Agency in 1947, advocated a national health insurance system, the Democratic platform of 1948 did not pledge the party to enactment of "health insurance." Truman's surprise victory at the polls in 1948 revived interest in health insurance. The following year, however, the American Medical Association assessed each member $25 to build a "war chest," and the public relations firm of Whitaker and Baxter, which had helped defeat the California medical plan, helped spend more than $1.5 million during the year to defeat the legislation. When the Wagner-Murray-Dingell bill was reintroduced in 1949 the major welfare organizations of the Catholic Church, the 5 million-member General Federation of Women's Clubs, the American Legion, and other important groups announced their opposition to compulsory insurance programs in favor of voluntary health insurance. By the end of the year the proposal for compulsory health insurance had become a political liability. In future years the National Health Insurance scheme, like other New Deal programs, "was linked to the welfare state, the welfare state to socialism, and socialism to Communism." [44]

AN AMERICA CHANGING

The period during which the questions of a right to work and a comprehensive medical care program were debated and, at least temporarily,

[43] Poen, *op. cit.*, p. 103.
[44] Richard Hofstadter, *Anti-Intellectualism in American Life* (New York: Alfred A. Knopf, 1963), p. 41.

resolved, was a time of rapid change in America. The nation became increasingly urbanized, continuing a long-standing trend. The characteristics of the new urban dwellers, however, were changed by war and immigration policies as well as internal developments. The increasing mechanization of southern agriculture and the lure of better jobs and living conditions led, between 1940 and 1960, to the migration of approximately 3 million Negroes to the North and West. Although a congressional Joint Committee on the Economic Report found one family in 10 living on less than $1000 a year, one-third of America's families had an income between $3000 and $5000.[45] Although large numbers of individuals and families were doing poorly, other factors helped create an optimistic view of the future and satisfaction with things as they were. The birthrate, which had declined in the 1930s to 17 or 18 per thousand of population, had climbed throughout the 1940s to a level of 23.5 in 1950. The percentage of unemployment was not significantly different from the 1920s in the immediate postwar period, and the savings accumulated during the war were used to purchase newly available consumer goods such as automobiles, appliances, and the new addition to the mass media—television.

The sense of well-being was fostered by the widespread use of miracle drugs, which helped to lower the death rate and virtually eliminated pneumonia, typhoid, and influenza as epidemic scourges. The widespread use of tranquilizing drugs in the treatment of mental illness led to the hope that mental hospitals could be emptied through further advances in chemotherapy.

The image, and necessarily the status, of labor changed significantly during the postwar period. During the war labor unions had accepted a formula limiting increases in salaries to the percentage increase of the cost of living, using the months between January 1, 1941, and May 3 1942 as the base period. After the war a succession of strikes took place as unions moved to increase the salaries of their members. Disruption caused by labor unrest occasionally threatened the smooth operation of the economy. A national railroad strike was narrowly avoided, and only by seizing the coal mines in 1946 did the federal government avert an industrial catastrophy. The picture of an oppressed labor force seeking just remuneration was replaced by the image of the powerful labor leader who could bring the economic activity of the nation to a halt through strikes. Further distrust of union activities was occasioned by the revelation that some constituent groups, especially affiliates of the CIO, were dominated by Communists. The 1947 Labor-Management Relations Act,

[45] Allen, *op. cit.*, p. 210.

popularly known as the Taft-Hartley Act, developed out of the feeling that labor unions were becoming too powerful and prone to act against the best interests of the community at large. This legislation outlawed the closed shop, made unions liable for damages if they failed to live up to contracts, forbade political contributions by unions, required a 60-day cooling-off period before a strike, and required that elected union officials take an oath that they were not Communists.[46] Section 14(b) of the Act made possible the passage of state right to work laws, which added to the confusion in terminology and prohibited, in the 19 states that eventually passed such laws, the requirement of mandatory union membership in negotiated contracts.

Despite the passage of this Act (over the veto of President Truman), labor shared in the postwar economic boom, and new contracts with rather radical innovations were secured. The steelworkers had sought a guaranteed annual wage in postwar negotiations. A government report, generally known as the Latimer Report, recommended against such a concession but considered such a plan a possibility for the future. Before 1947 not more than 3 percent of all the firms in the United States had provided some kind of guarantee of wages or employment.[47]

Such a goal became accepted by much of union leadership, however, and in 1955 the Ford Motor Company agreed to an unemployment insurance supplementary plan whereby an employee could receive 65 percent of his wages while laid off. Shortly thereafter the United Steelworkers and workers in the glass industry received similar benefits that moved blue-collar workers nearer to the pay patterns of management and white-collar employment.[48]

In addition to changes that had occurred in the labor movement, some observers noted in the industrial system significant departures from the past. By midcentury some 45 percent of the industrial assets of the United States were owned by 135 giant corporations. The idea of the critical role of the entrepreneur and his sources of financial backing, expounded forcefully by Schumpeter and incorporated into many American textbooks on elementary economics, had to be reexamined.[49]

One of the most cogent statements about the new industrial system was made by Adolf A. Berle, Jr., a former New Dealer. According to

---

[46] Samuel Eliot Morison, *The Oxford History of the American People* (New York: Oxford University Press, 1965), p. 1053.

[47] Valdemar Carlson, *Economic Security in the United States* (New York: McGraw-Hill Book Co., 1962), p. 151.

[48] *Ibid.*, p. 154.

[49] Joseph Schumpeter, *The Theory of Economic Development* (Cambridge: Harvard University Press, 1934).

Berle, the ability of the large corporations to concentrate economic power in themselves was matched by their ability to increase both production and distribution prodigiously. These he saw as the "most notable achievements of the twentieth-century corporation." Capitalism and capital remained, but the capitalist had been replaced by a board of directors and hired managers. "For the fact seems to be that the really great corporation managements have reached a position for the first time in their history in which they must consciously take account of philosophical considerations." [50] Berle was also one of the first to note that corporations engaged in sophisticated planning (although they might oppose it for government) and that such planning was not necessarily dependent on existing markets.

Changes in demographic patterns, the economic system, and moral values perhaps contributed to what one writer described as a surge of piety in America.[51] Whatever the reasons, it was evident that Americans as never before were involved in one way or another with institutional religion. In 1940, 49 percent of the population claimed church membership; by 1960 the percentage had reached 63.6 before beginning a relative decline.[52] Although the Federal Council of Churches had, among other actions reminiscent of the Social Gospel, called in 1946 for "an integrated church in an integrated society," few of the congregations allied with the Council were ardently concerned with social questions.[53] The dominant concern of most religious groups was with individual problems. Positive thinking and success were stressed by the most popular religious leaders of the period. Dr. Norman Vincent Peale, Bishop Fulton J. Sheen, and Dr. Billy Graham all stressed the importance of individual responsibility as the starting point for social change. Perhaps none went quite so far as Dr. Peale, who offered the following preachment on improving race relations:

A Negro boy said to me glumly, "I can never amount to much in this country."
"Why not?" I asked.
"You ought to know," he answered.
"You are healthy, aren't you?" I asked. "And smart?"
He grinned and agreed.
"You have a good mother? A good father?"

[50] Adolph A. Berle, Jr., *The 20th Century Capitalist Revolution* (New York: Harcourt, Brace and Co., 1954), p. 166.

[51] A. Roy Eckardt, *The Surge of Piety in America* (New York: Association Press, 1958).

[52] Benson Y. Landis, ed., *Yearbook of American Churches* (New York: National Council of the Churches of Christ in the U.S.A., 1965), p. 280.

[53] Charles S. McCoy, "The Churches and Protest Movements for Social Justice," in Robert Lee and Martin E. Marty, eds., *Religion and Social Conflict* (New York: Oxford University Press, 1964), p. 39.

He nodded.

"Let me feel your muscle."

He rolled up his sleeves and grinned again when I congratulated him on his well-developed muscles.

"And you have a wonderful smile." I added this item to his assets.

"But I am colored," he objected.

"So is Ralph Bunche, who used to be a janitor," I reminded him. "So is Jackie Robinson. So is the President of the Borough of Manhattan, Hulan Jack." And I went on to mention others. "Your thinking is twenty-five years behind the times, son. Then it was more difficult for Negro men and women, but some of them did mighty well, all the same.[54]

Although some repeated the bromide that Sunday morning was America's most segregated time of the week, others decided that if people were to spend time anywhere, church might not be the worst place.

An America that was changed and that was continuing to change seemed to some to be coming apart at the seams. One writer described the impact on the average man in these terms:

The man who was middle-aged in 1949 had lived through transformations of life within the United States more swift and sweeping than any previous generation of Americans had known. He grew up in a land where free economic enterprise was the normal way; white, Protestant, old-stock families dominated the community; and the whole of everyday activities moved within a basically fixed pattern. In 1949 this American made his living in a crazy-quilt system of free enterprise, the welfare state, welfare capitalism, and the patches of socialism represented by public power. Negroes, Catholics, Jews, and the sons of recent immigrants jostled the one-time elite for jobs and status. Wherever the American turned, whether to the details of the home or the mores of the Presidency, nothing seemed unchanged except change.[55]

THE REACTION TO CHANGE

The Korean War began in the summer of 1950. In the same year Senator Joseph R. McCarthy of Wisconsin began a crusade that resembled in many ways the "Red Scare" that followed World War I. In a nation troubled by Communist successes in Czechoslovakia and China, accusations of treason against high government officials, and frightening reports of collusion by American citizens in the Russian achievement of nuclear power status, McCarthy's charges of internal subversion made sense to many. Problems ranging from increasing juvenile delinquency to a chang-

[54] Norman Vincent Peale, *Stay Alive All Your Life* (Englewood Cliffs, N.J.: Prentice-Hall, 1957), pp. 95–96.

[55] Eric F. Goldman, *The Crucial Decade—And After* (New York: Alfred A. Knopf, 1966), p. 121.

ing moral code were attributed to Communist infiltration by the more extreme. Although many claimed not to like the tactics employed, they frequently voiced the opinion that something obviously needed to be done.

The fear of internal subversion had led in 1947 to the issuing of Executive Order 9835, which authorized the dismissal of civil servants suspected of disloyalty and authorized the nonhiring of those who were suspect. This has been described as the beginning of "a crisis in political freedom" from which later antidemocratic acts were to flow. Professor Franz L. Neumann of Columbia University, in the midst of the anti-Communist frenzy, described two integrating alternatives that could unite a democracy. Opposed to the moral alternative of freedom or justice was the "fear of an enemy." [56] From 1950, when McCarthy first accused the State Department of harboring large numbers of subversives, until 1955, when he was censured by the Senate, the nation chose the latter.

Although the phenomenon of McCarthyism was undoubtedly strengthened by the Korean War, which lasted from 1951 to 1953, the focus was as much on internal conspiracy as external threats. Congressional committees investigated Hollywood, Protestant churches, the armed forces, and educational institutions with a frequently callous disregard of democratic processes. Accusations of disloyalty were recklessly made, and "guilt by association" became a commonplace phrase. The televising of hearings assured political figures an eager audience if the revelations were sufficiently breathtaking, and it sometimes appeared that truth was treated almost casually. Although the news media undoubtedly contributed to the hysteria, the televised hearings of the Army-McCarthy confrontation were responsible for restoring national equilibrium. In 1954, in a controversy between Senator McCarthy and the Secretary of the Army, the nation was repelled by blatant attempts by the Senator to malign all who opposed him. The spectacle was the beginning of the end. Senator McCarthy, who had intimated most of his colleagues and two presidents as well, began to fade into oblivion.

McCarthy's frequent use of past associations or the championing of causes subsequently found to be sponsored by Communist front organizations had a profound effect on the nation's youth. Many became convinced that it was better not to get involved in social issues if future disclosures might prove damaging to careers. In an era when intellectualism was attributed to the egghead and became a term of public derision, a deeper meaning was attributed to McCarthyism than the imperative of non-involvement. The eminent social historian Richard Hofstadter described

[56] Franz L. Neumann, "The Concept of Political Freedom," *Columbia Law Review*, Vol. 53, no. 7 (November 1953), p. 935.

the "Great Inquisition of the 1950s" as a release of pent-up emotions that enabled the participants "to discharge resentments and frustrations, to punish, to satisfy enmities whose roots lay elsewhere than in the Communist issue itself." [57] According to this theory, the exposing of Communists was secondary to settling political accounts from the New Deal and, "Communism was not the target but the weapon." [58]

Internal developments necessarily had repercussions abroad. *The Christian Century*, a liberal religious journal, described the reaction to the removal of books by such authors as Paul B. Anderson, secretary for Europe for the YMCA and Walter White, secretary of the NAACP, from government libraries: "Had some malign force set out to convince the rest of the world that the United States is being reduced to neurotic irresponsibility by its fears, it could not have found any quicker means than the current uproar over purging our government's overseas libraries." [59]

The effect of McCarthyism on social welfare programs was perhaps less dramatic than some of its other manifestations. As creatures of the New Deal, however, federally supported social welfare programs and persons connected with them were frequently suspect. One time New Dealer Raymond Moley had progressively moved away from the ideology of liberalism and by the 1950s saw federally supported programs as a threat to social welfare institutions:

> The vast social security setup is gradually shaping the policies and methods of all private social welfare work. Inevitably, the notable professional associations, schools, and agencies of social work which have hitherto built up technical standards and ideals will be dominated by government workers who can scarcely be uninfected by the bureaucratic virus of statism. The ideal of the welfare state is, of course, to absorb all private charity except perhaps a few cases protected by powerful religious groups. [60]

The 1953 meeting of the National Conference of Social Work considered the problem of civil liberties and the freedom of speech. One of the principal speakers pointed out that, although the Conference was not devoted to social action, social workers in their communities should be involved in political issues. [61] Another participant described how a member

---

[57] Hofstadter, *op. cit.*, p. 41.

[58] *Ibid.*

[59] "Libraries, Book-Burning and the Toll of Fear," *Christian Century*, Vol. 70, no. 28 (July 15, 1953), p. 812.

[60] Moley, *How to Keep Our Liberty, op. cit.*, p. 176.

[61] Charles I. Schottland, "Social Work Issues in the Political Arena," *The Social Welfare Forum, 1953*, Official Proceedings, 80th Annual Meeting, National Conference of Social Work (New York: Columbia University Press, 1953), pp. 18–33.

of an agency board had objected to an informational pamphlet, which was described as "pink" because it used such phrases as "civil rights," "fair employment practices," and "insight, understanding, and skill." [62] A representative from the American Civil Liberties Union urged social workers to preserve their freedom of speech and stated:

> Intolerance and fear are producing the demand that our schools and our social work agencies should be staffed by people who are noncontroversial. . . . The boards and top administrators of social work agencies are constantly having to decide whether to hire or retain people who in one way or another are counted in their respective communities to be controversial.[63]

SOCIAL WELFARE PROGRAMS AT MIDCENTURY

Despite the farrago of McCarthyism, differences in political allegiances between presidents and Congresses, and the preeminence of foreign policy concerns, refinements were made in social welfare programs. In the year following the end of the war Congress debated and passed the National Mental Health Act. This legislation provided for a broad program of mental health services to be conducted by the Public Health Service. It authorized research by the PHS and made funds available for grants to support research, training, and community mental health services throughout the country.[64] In 1949 these programs were designated the National Institute of Mental Health, and through the years NIMH has provided leadership for local programs. Grants to the state have encouraged the creation of an expanding network of community mental health facilities. Funds given to institutions of higher learning and mental health facilities have contributed to the training of psychiatrists, psychologists, psychiatric social workers, and psychiatric nurses.

Other legislation amended the U.S. Housing Act of 1937 to encourage private enterprise to build housing for low-income families and to stimulate slum clearance in urban areas. In 1947 a permanent Housing and Home Finance Agency was created to coordinate the activities of various housing programs. The Act of 1949, one of the most important in a series of amendments, authorized cities to use federal funds to purchase slum

[62] Donald S. Howard, "Civil Liberties and Social Work," *ibid.*, p. 43.
[63] Patrick Murphy Malin, "Civil Liberties and Social Responsibilities in Social Work," *ibid.*, pp. 34–40.
[64] James V. Lowry, "Public Mental Health Agencies, State and National," *Annals of the American Academy of Political and Social Science*, Vol. 286 (March 1953), p. 103.

property, relocate the occupants of substandard dwellings, and sell the land to private developers for the erection of dwellings and commercial buildings. Land obtained was to be sold at discount prices, with the federal government providing two-thirds to three-fourths of the loss.[65] Senator Robert Taft estimated in 1949 that 810,000 new units of low-cost housing would be needed by 1953. Although that number was authorized by the 1949 housing law, nothing near that figure had been constructed by the end of the five-year period. Under conditions of the law, local housing authorities could construct federally aided low-rent housing but only if it could be demonstrated that "these needs are not being met through reliance solely upon private enterprise, and without such aid. . . ." [66]

In 1954 a new housing act was passed to prevent urban decline and to promote slum redevelopment. Under the law the concept of urban renewal was introduced, and communities seeking funds were required to develop plans to combat blight. Such programs required that housing and building codes be enforced, that families displaced by slum clearance or neighborhood rehabilitation be assisted in finding new housing, and that there be citizen participation in renewal programs. Amendments in later years continued to involve the federal government in housing programs and standard-setting so that the 1949 emphasis on private enterprise was successively modified.

The Social Security Act had been amended in 1939 to prevent abuses in public assistance and to make survivors and dependents of insured workers eligible for benefits. Amendments made in 1946 and 1948 placed the Children's Bureau in the Federal Security Agency, increased the federal share of public assistance benefits, and raised the payment maximum of Old Age and Survivor's Insurance. Substantive charges in the programs of social insurance and public assistance were not made in these amendments, however.

Acting on long-standing recommendations of the Social Security Ad-

[65] Charles Abrams, *Man's Struggle for Shelter in an Urbanizing World* (Cambridge, Mass.: M.I.T. Press, 1964), p. 118. Important second order effects were to flow from these Acts and from the government sponsored housing for veterans. Large numbers of the poor in central cities, typically black and aged citizens, were displaced and dispersed. Also, the promoting of ownership of private homes, typically in suburbs, created tax problems for central city services and led to the creation in later years of vast new programs of highway building. Concentration on private ownership of homes and automobiles caused a decline in mass transit systems, pollution of the environment became a serious concern, and much agricultural land was removed from production for home sites.

[66] "Selected Provisions of the Housing Act of 1949," *Urban Affairs Reporter*, Vol. 1 (New York: Commerce Clearing House, 1969), pp. 6186–235.

ministration, Congress in 1950 extended the system of federal grants-in-aid to the totally and permanently disabled. Thus the new category of Aid to the Disabled was created, although Congress refused to add disability as a reason for entitlement to social insurance benefits. The Aid to Dependent Children program was broadened to include needy relatives in the computing of grants. In the Old Age Assistance category federal funds were made available to the states for payments to vendors of medical care, including doctors, hospitals, druggists, and nursing homes. Institutions receiving payments for providing care were required to meet federally determined standards. To reduce the number requiring Old Age Assistance, some 10 million workers were brought into the insurance system, including self-employed persons, farm laborers with regular employment, household workers; state and local government employees could participate in the insurance program if they elected to do so.[67] Payments under social insurance were increased by about 77 percent, and the time required for eligibility to maximum benefits was shortened. The objective was to change a situation in which outlays for public assistance payments exceeded social insurance benefits, and many aged persons were obliged to receive funds from both.[68]

In 1953 Congress acted to reorganize the welfare structure and to elevate the Social Security Agency to cabinet status, a plan unsuccessfully attempted in 1946 by President Truman. The new U. S. Department of Health, Education, and Welfare was composed of some 37,000 employees from the Social Security Administration, the Public Health Service, the Food and Drug Administration, the Office of Education, and the Office of Vocational Rehabilitation. Under the new organization it was hoped that administrative efficiency could be improved and that more coordinated planning for meeting problems of dependency would be possible.[69]

In 1954 and 1956 further modifications were made to bring into the social insurance system most of the members of the labor force left out of the original act. Disability was added as a basis for eligibility to social security benefits. In one of the most important changes, as far as the social work profession was concerned, funds were made available for the training of public assistance workers. The giving of social work service was, for the first time, recognized in law as an integral part of public assistance, essential to rehabilitation. The concept of public welfare as a rehabilitative program was further underlined by the granting of research funds for investigation of ways to reduce and prevent dependency. Dramatic in-

[67] Letter from Donald B. MacPhail to William J. Hopkins, August 24, 1950, Harry S Truman Library, Bill File, H.R. 6000, Folder 1.
[68] Carlson, *op. cit.*, pp. 79–81.
[69] Schottland, *op. cit.*, pp. 22–24.

creases in the number receiving help through the Aid to Dependent Children program caused concern throughout society. It was hoped that better training for social workers, an emphasis on rehabilitative casework, and social research could provide solutions for some of the problems.

In 1960, by amendment of the Social Security Act, a fifth category of assistance was initiated: Medical Aid to the Aged. This program, established by the Kerr-Mills bill, authorized medical assistance for older citizens, including those who were not receiving Old Age Assistance. The intent of the program was to forestall medical care for the aged through the social insurance program. Available to those who could meet normal living expenses but who had insufficient income or resources to meet the costs of medical care, the range of services to be provided was left to the discretion of participating states. Although the legislation received support from organized medicine and the insurance industry, it was greeted with something less than enthusiasm by the aged needing medical care.

THE MOVEMENT FOR EQUALITY

Although the changes made in the basic social welfare institutions between 1940 and 1960 were unspectacular, advances in assuring civil rights and liberties to all citizens were more dramatic. Action to assure equality to black Americans was taken by all three branches of government to meet rising Negro demands for justice. Of the three, the Supreme Court undoubtedly played the largest part in creating conditions favorable to a revolution in rights.

In 1944 the Swedish economist Gunnar Myrdal had described institutionalized segregation as an American dilemma. The central thesis of Myrdal's massive study was that the nation's dedication to the ideals of democracy was strained by the perpetuation of the undemocratic phenomenon of racial discrimination. After the end of the war A. Philip Randolph renewed his attempts to achieve racial integration in the armed forces. Assisted by Grant Reynolds, a leader in the Young Republicans living in New York, Randolph organized the Committee Against Jimcrow in Military Service and Training. During 1948 testimony was given before congressional committees, the White House was picketed, and Randolph made speeches urging Negroes and whites to refuse conscription.[70]

Pressure from Negro leaders and President Truman's own convictions led to the issuing in 1948 of Executive Order 9981, which called for

[70] L. D. Reddick, "The Negro Policy of the American Army Since World War II," *Journal of Negro History,* Vol. 38, no. 2 (April 1953), pp. 194–215.

equal treatment in military service. Despite the order, integration was not achieved in the armed forces until the late 1950s. In other areas of American society, segregation of the races remained the established way of life. The relative economic condition of the Negro worsened after the full-employment days of World War II. An unemployment rate more than twice that of whites confirmed the truism that Negroes were the last to be hired and the first to be fired. The median Negro family income in 1950 was estimated to be 50 percent less than that of whites, and the greatest percentage increase on Aid to Dependent Children rolls was found among Negro Americans. In terms of infant and maternity mortality, life expectancy, level of education achieved, and virtually all other statistical measurements, it was abundantly clear that the Negro occupied a social position inferior to that of white Americans.[71]

Impatient with an inferior status that was enforced by laws and legal decisions, the Negro in the 1950s began a march toward equality; the end is not yet in sight. By insisting that the promise of democracy be fulfilled for all Americans, virtually every social institution in the nation came to be affected by the revolution in human rights that began in 1954. In overturning the "separate but equal" doctrine, approved in 1896 in *Plessy* v. *Ferguson*, the Supreme Court entered a phase of activism that gave new meaning to sociological jurisprudence.

Before President Eisenhower's inauguration in 1952, the Reverend Oliver Brown of Topeka had challenged an 1867 Kansas statute permitting cities with more than 15,000 in population to maintain segregated schools. With the help of the NAACP, the case of *Brown* v. *Board of Education of Topeka* reached the Supreme Court; the case of the plaintiff was presented by Thurgood Marshall.[72] While the Army-McCarthy hearings were occupying the attention of most Americans, the Court issued, in 1954, what was one of the most significant decisions in its history. Holding that "separate educational facilities are inherently unequal,"[73] the Court "restated the spirit of America and lighted a beacon of hope for Negroes at a time when other governmental voices were silent."[74]

---

[71] Although the Negro most dramatically illustrates the plight of the minority-group person in America, others also suffered the indignity of racial discrimination. For example a 1955 study of an Indian Reservation in the Dakotas revealed an unemployment rate of 59 percent, and nearly 30 percent of all families were receiving over half of their income from welfare benefits. William A. Brophy and Sophie D. Aberle, *The Indian: America's Unfinished Business* (Norman: University of Oklahoma Press, 1966), p. 68.

[72] Weaver, *op. cit.*, pp. 210–18.

[73] *Brown* v. *Board of Education of Topeka*, 347 U.S. 686–92 (1954).

[74] Archibald Cox, *The Warren Court* (Cambridge: Harvard University Press, 1968), p. 27.

In rejecting the doctrine of separate but equal, the Supreme Court had struck at the idea that a democratic society could exist with widely differing degrees of freedom. But it remained for the promise to be actualized. The tocsin was sounded on December 1, 1955, when Mrs. Rosa Parks boarded a bus in Montgomery, Alabama. Refusing to move to the rear of the Jim Crow vehicle, Mrs. Parks was arrested for violating a city ordinance and was subsequently fined $10 and required to pay $4 in court costs. Her arrest led to the boycott of the public transportation system and its eventual desegregation. The Southern Christian Leadership Conference developed out of this successful, nonviolent use of economic power, and the Reverend Martin Luther King, Jr., achieved prominence as a leader of the black community. By the time of his assassination in Memphis, Tennessee, in April 1968, Dr. King had led countless battles for racial justice in the United States. As the recipient of the 1964 Nobel Peace Prize he was recognized internationally for his contributions to human rights.

For the remainder of the 1950s, the civil rights struggle was primarily a legal and legislative battle, punctuated by the passage of the Civil Rights Acts of 1957 and 1960, the first civil rights legislation since Reconstruction; both bills were signed by President Eisenhower. The 1957 law, passed after 63 days of filibuster and debate, authorized the Justice Department to bring suit in federal courts against discrimination in voting cases. The 1960 act improved on the earlier legislation by making legal action against state and local officials possible. Neither act made much of an impact, and only a few cases were brought into the courts. Much more profound action was being pushed in the schools, even though the integration of elementary and secondary schools was to remain agonizingly slow. Not until the end of 1969, in the case of *Alexander* v. *Holmes County Board of Education*, did the Supreme Court decide that "all deliberate speed" was no longer constitutionally permissible. In a unanimous decision, a recommendation of the Secretary of Health, Education, and Welfare that desegregation in some districts in the South be delayed was reversed. The Court required that "school districts operating dual school systems based on race or color must begin immediately to operate unitary school systems within which no person would be effectively excluded from any school because of race or color." [75]

One of the most dramatic instances of confrontation between federal intent and local practice took place in 1957 in Little Rock, Arkansas. The entry of nine black youths into Central High School in Little Rock was accomplished only after President Eisenhower sent federal troops to the

[75] *Alexander* v. *Holmes County Board of Education*, 90 U.S. 29–632 (1969).

city to assure their personal safety. In succeeding years, school districts throughout the South and universities and colleges yielded reluctantly to the force of court action and occasionally to federal troops and U.S. marshals.

Summary

Although Franklin D. Roosevelt remained President until 1945, the main thrust of the New Deal ended during his second term in office. Even before 1940 the principal concern of the administration had shifted from domestic issues to problems arising abroad. The Fair Deal was conceived of as the ideological successor to the New Deal, but the times, like many of the people involved, had changed. Continuing prosperity at home for most people removed any sense of urgency for altering basic institutions. Although many did not share at all, and some only slightly, in society's affluence, it is probably true that those who have been helped are frequently disinclined to extend a hand to those who remain submerged.

The nation rejected a program of national planning to prevent unemployment in 1946. But in 1949, when unemployment claims increased by nearly 1 million because of a recession, a housing program frankly aimed at creating jobs received congressional approval. Medical care for all was repeatedly turned down, but help for the mentally ill was given, and a committee of experts to study the problem was appointed by President Eisenhower. Care for the medically indigent was accepted as a proper governmental responsibility.

National attention was also given to the needs of the veteran, and in 1958 the National Education Act increased the involvement of the federal government in the area of education. Although social welfare institutions changed little in focus, the scope of coverage and extent of benefits were broadened. In 1960 Sidney Hook declared that the debate over the welfare state had ceased to be a suitable argument since it existed in fact in the United States.[76] Although the analysis was perceptive, the topic remained a subject for disputation.

World War II and its aftermath brought challenges to fundamental democratic ideals and a reaffirmation of the nation's dedication to those ideals. As the Supreme Court moved to the forefront in reasserting that all men were indeed created equal, the nation was required to seek solutions for the consequences of years of discrimination and racial prejudice.

[76] Sidney Hook, " 'Welfare State'—A Debate That Isn't," *New York Times Magazine* (November 27, 1960), pp. 27 and 118-19.

Some of the more subtle changes that had occurred in America during the 1940s and 1950s were less striking than the Negro's quest for justice. Although religious affiliation increased significantly, the impact of the church on social issues diminished. Political questions were increasingly resolved on the advice and recommendations of experts, and "the end of ideology" was proclaimed.[77] The economic system had undoubtedly been transformed, and the corporation had assumed new functions in rationalizing and ordering production and consumption. Both the economic and political systems were effected by a technological revolution that had been taking place; if that revolution contained promise for a better future, it had in it also the possibility of social disruptions. Whatever the future held, it was quite clear that more radical changes were likely. Adaptations to scientific and technological institutions were to become as important to social welfare as the defense of an imperfect welfare state.

Selected Bibliography

Abrams, Charles. *Man's Struggle for Shelter in an Urbanizing World*. Cambridge: M.I.T. Press, 1964.

Allen, Frederick Lewis. *The Big Change*. New York: Harper & Bros., 1952.

Alexander v. Holmes County Board of Education, 90 U.S. (1969).

Anderson, Odin W. "Compulsory Medical Care Insurance, 1900–1950." *Annals of the American Academy of Political and Social Science*, Vol. 273, (January 1951), pp. 106–113.

Ascoli, Max, ed. *Our Times*. New York: Farrar, Straus & Cudahy, 1960.

Bailey, Stephen Kemp. *Congress Makes a Law*. New York: Random House, a Vintage Book, 1950.

Bell, Daniel. *The End of Ideology*. New York: Free Press of Glencoe, 1960.

Berle, Adolph A., Jr. *The 20th Century Capitalist Revolution*. New York: Harcourt, Brace & Co., 1954.

Beveridge, William H. *Full Employment in a Free Society*. New York: W. W. Norton & Co., 1945.

Brophy, William A., and Aberle, Sophie D. *The Indian: America's Unfinished Business*. Norman: University of Oklahoma Press, 1966.

Brown v. Board of Education of Topeka, 347 U.S. (1954).

Buckley, William F., Jr. *God and Man at Yale*. Chicago: Henry Regnery Co., 1951.

Buckley, William F., and Bozell, L. Brent. *McCarthy and His Enemies*. Chicago: Henry Regnery Co., 1954.

Carlson, Valdemar. *Economic Security in the United States*. New York: McGraw-Hill Book Co., 1962.

[77] Daniel Bell, *The End of Ideology* (New York: Free Press of Glencoe, 1960).

Cox, Archibald. *The Warren Court.* Cambridge: Harvard University Press, 1968.

Eckardt, A. Roy. *The Surge of Piety in America.* New York: Association Press, 1958.

Eisenhower, Dwight D. *Mandate for Change, 1953–1956.* Garden City, N.Y.: Doubleday & Co., 1963.

Filler, Louis, ed. *The President Speaks: From William McKinley to Lyndon B. Johnson.* New York: G. P. Putnam's Sons, 1964.

Fisher, Robert Moore. *20 Years of Public Housing.* New York: Harper & Bros., 1959.

Friedman, Lawrence M. *Government and Slum Housing, A Century of Frustration.* Chicago: Rand McNalley & Co., 1968.

Galbraith, John Kenneth. *The Affluent Society.* Boston: Houghton Mifflin Co., 1958.

"The G.I. Bill of Rights: An Analysis of the Servicemen's Readjustment Act of 1944." *Social Security Bulletin,* Vol. 7, no. 7 (July 1944), pp. 3–13.

Goldman, Eric F. *The Crucial Decade—And After.* New York: Alfred A. Knopf, 1966.

Haber, William. "Economic and Social Readjustments in the Reconversion Period." *Proceedings of the National Conference of Social Work, 1945.* New York: Columbia University Press, 1945, pp. 26–44.

Harrington, Michael. *The Accidental Century.* New York: Macmillan Co., 1965.

Harry S Truman Library, Rosenman Papers.

Hayek, Friedrich. *The Road to Serfdom.* Chicago: University of Chicago Press, 1944.

Hazlitt, Henry. *Economics in One Lesson.* New York: Harper & Bros., 1946.

Hofstadter, Richard. *Anti-Intellectualism in American Life.* New York: Alfred A. Knopf, 1963.

Hook, Sidney. " 'Welfare State'—A Debate That Isn't." *New York Times Magazine,* November 27, 1960, pp. 27 and 118–19.

Howard, Donald S. "Civil Liberties and Social Work." *The Social Welfare Forum, 1953.* Official Proceedings, 80th Annual Meeting, National Conference of Social Work. New York: Columbia University Press, 1953.

Howe, Quincy, and Schlesinger, Arthur M., Jr., eds. *Guide to Politics 1954.* New York: Dial Press, 1954.

Jacobs, Jane. *The Death and Life of Great American Cities.* New York: Random House, 1961.

Kahn, Dorothy C. "The Real Crisis in Social Work." *The Compass,* Vol. 24, no. 5 (June 1943).

Kaplan, A. D. H. *Liquidation of War Production.* Report by the Committee for Economic Development. York, Pa.: Maple Press, 1944.

Kesselman, Louis C. "The Fair Employment Practice Commission Movement in Perspective." *Journal of Negro History,* Vol. 31, no. 1 (January 1946), pp. 30–46.

Landauer, Carl. *Theory of National Economic Planning*. Berkeley: University of California Press, 1947.

Landis, Benson Y., ed. *Yearbook of American Churches*. New York: National Council of the Churches of Christ in the U.S.A., 1965.

"Libraries, Book-Burning and the Toll of Fear." *Christian Century*, Vol. 70, no. 28 (July 15, 1953), pp. 812.

Lowry, James V. "Public Mental Health Agencies, State and National." *Annals of the American Academy of Political and Social Science*, Vol. 286 (March 1953), pp. 100–106.

Lubell, Samuel. *Revolt of the Moderates*. New York: Harper & Bros., 1956.

McCoy, Charles S. "The Churches and Protest Movements for Social Justice." *Religion and Social Conflict*. Edited by Robert Lee and Martin E. Marty. New York: Oxford University Press, 1964.

Malin, Patrick Murphy. "Civil Liberties and Social Responsibilities in Social Work." *The Social Welfare Forum, 1953*. Official Proceedings, 80th Annual Meeting, National Conference of Social Work. New York: Columbia University Press, 1953.

Marcus, Grace M. "Reappraising Aid to Dependent Children as a Category." *Social Security Bulletin*, Vol. 8, no. 2 (February 1945), pp. 3–5.

Millis, Harry A., and Brown, Emily Clark. *From the Wagner Act to Taft-Hartley*. Chicago: University of Chicago Press, 1950.

Moley, Raymond. *How to Keep Our Liberty*. New York: Alfred A. Knopf, 1952.

Morison, Samuel Eliot. *The Oxford History of the American People*. New York: Oxford University Press, 1965.

Mowry, George E. *The Urban Nation 1920–1960*. New York: Hill & Wang, 1965.

Neumann, Franz L. "The Concept of Political Freedom." *Columbia Law Review*, Vol. 53, no. 7 (November 1953), pp. 901–35.

Newcomer, Mabel. "The Social Workers' Stake in the Program of War Finance." *The Compass*, Vol. 24, no. 3 (March 1943), pp. 3–7.

Newfield, Jack. *A Prophetic Minority*. New York: New American Library, 1966.

Peale, Norman Vincent. *Stay Alive All Your Life*. Englewood Cliffs, N.J.: Prentice-Hall, 1957.

Poen, Monte. "The Truman Administration and National Health Insurance." Unpublished Ph.D. dissertation, University of Missouri, 1967.

Reddick, L. D. "The Negro Policy of the American Army Since World War II." *Journal of Negro History*, Vol. 38, no. 2 (April 1953), pp. 194–215.

Riesman, David. *The Lonely Crowd*. New Haven: Yale University Press, 1950.

Rovere, Richard. *Senator Joe McCarthy*. New York: Harcourt, Brace & Co., 1959.

Schottland, Charles I. "Social Work Issues in the Political Arena." *The Social Welfare Forum, 1953*. Official Proceedings, 80th Annual Meeting, National Conference of Social Work. New York: Columbia University Press, 1953.

Schumpeter, Joseph. *The Theory of Economic Development*. Cambridge: Harvard University Press, 1934.

Scitovszky, Anne. "The Employment Act of 1946." *Social Security Bulletin*, Vol. 9, no. 3 (March 1946), pp. 25–29.

"Selected Provisions of the Housing Act of 1949." *Urban Affairs Reporter*, Vol. 1. New York: Commerce Clearing House, 1969, pp. 6186–235.

"Social Security in Review." *Social Security Bulletin*, Vol. 8, no. 2 (February 1945), pp. 1–3.

Truman, Harry S *Memoirs*. Vol. 1: *Year of Decisions*. Garden City, N.Y.: Doubleday & Co., 1955.

Truman, Harry S *Memoirs*. Vol. 2: *Years of Trial and Hope*. Garden City, N.Y.: Doubleday & Co., 1956.

U.S. Department of Commerce. Bureau of the Census. *Historical Statistics of the United State, Colonial Times to 1957*. Washington, D.C.: Government Printing Office, 1960.

U.S. Social Security Administration. *Annual Report of the Social Security Board for the Fiscal Year 1942–1943*. Washington, D.C.: Government Printing Office, 1944.

Voorhis, Jerry. *Confessions of a Congressman*. Garden City, N.Y.: Doubleday & Co., 1947.

Walsh, J. Raymond. "Action for Postwar Planning." *Antioch Review*, Vol. 3, no. 2 (Summer 1943), pp. 153–161.

Weaver, John D. *Warren: The Man, The Court, The Era*. Boston: Little, Brown & Co., 1967.

White, Ruth. "The Effect of Liquidation of the WPA on Need for Assistance." *Social Security Bulletin*, Vol. 6, no. 6 (June 1943), pp. 4–7.

Whyte, William Hollingsworth. *The Organization Man*. Garden City, N.Y.: Doubleday & Co., 1956.

Chapter Five

The Age of the Great Society

I N THE ELECTION of 1960 the nation was faced with a choice between two men whose ideological differences were not so great as their dissimilarities in personality and background. Both were committed to a federal presence in the economic life of the nation and, avowedly, to the assurance of equal rights to all citizens. Richard M. Nixon as well as John F. Kennedy promised improvement in social welfare programs and showed concern for the quality of American life. Both had had experience in Congress, and neither was in basic disagreement with the foreign policy of the Eisenhower decade. Nixon was Protestant, middle-class, a Westerner, and ran as the political protégé of Eisenhower; Kennedy projected a Rooseveltian image and was Catholic, upper-class, and an Easterner. What came to be called the Kennedy "style" probably made possible his election, but the small margin of victory was consonant with the absence of substantive disagreement on most issues. Receiving less than half of the 67 million votes cast, Kennedy's margin of victory of 112,000 ballots was hardly an overwhelming mandate for change. In a nation that was more or less at peace and generally enjoying prosperity, a sense of urgency in handling social problems was missing.

Kennedy—the youngest man to be elected president—entered the White House believing that Eisenhower had managed to escape without taking action on some domestic situations of critical importance. Criticizing both foreign and domestic policies, Kennedy promised top priority for action in housing, education, extension of minimum wages, and relief for depressed areas. Along with these tangible problems Kennedy also sought to make use of technological advances for their solution and enlisted the creative abilities of the intellectual community. Not since the brain trust days of the New Deal had Harvard scholars been so much a part of the political landscape of Washington.

President Eisenhower, in his parting address to Congress on January 17, 1961, warned against the peril of a military-industrial complex with great influence on government and of a scientific-technological elite creating public policies.[1] Having done little to control or understand the forces he spoke against, Eisenhower's warning showed a distrust of experts as policy-makers and a vague yearning for a time when American life was less complex and answers to problems more simplistic. Both his distrust and his yearning did not mark him as essentially different from most of the people. His fear of the future, his recognition of new dimensions in social institutions, and his dislike of change formed an integral part of his appeal to the electorate.

During the Eisenhower administration, sophisticated weaponry and the military establishment had required a high level of expenditures. At least

[1] Louis Filler, ed., *The President Speaks: From William McKinley to Lyndon B. Johnson* (New York: G. P. Putnam's Sons, 1964), pp. 365–69.

9 percent of the Gross National Product throughout the 1950s was devoted to defense requirements, and in 1960 the cost to the nation for this single item was in excess of $76 billion.[2] Technological change came to the forefront of public consciousness with the development in 1951 of Univac, the first electronic computer capable of handling literal information. The rapid expansion during the 1950s of machine solution of general data-handling problems raised the specter of replacing human hands with mechanical ones. Problems inherent in expanding technologies were pointed out by some, but not until the 1960s did the intellectual and political leadership of the nation seriously attempt to come to grips with these problems.

Having promised priority action on social problems, Kennedy faced a need to arouse a people not anxious to be aroused. The complacent decade of the 1950s was barely over when, in his inaugural address on January 20, 1961, Kennedy challenged his fellow Americans to "ask not what your country can do for you: ask what you can do for your country." As the writer Richard Rovere pointed out, Kennedy was "attempting to meet a challenge whose existence he and his associates are almost alone in perceiving."[3] Part of the Kennedy style then was to bring forcefully to the attention of the people the fact that there were issues to be resolved and that not all problems of poverty and misery had been dealt with in the 1930s.

Kennedy's assassination in November 1963 brought to the White House a man skilled in politics and destined to perfect and even resurrect parts of the New Deal. Kennedy had provided the vision of a New Frontier; Johnson worked to improve the quality of the welfare state in the Great Society. Less abstract than the New Frontier, the Great Society, characterized by massive federal reform, accomplished what might have been impossible in the climate of public opinion existing during Kennedy's incumbency. Legislation dealing with civil rights, tax reform, support for education, conservation measures, new structures to handle urban problems, and new programs to eliminate poverty poured forth in the early Johnson years. For the first time since the 1930s domestic policies and programs rivaled foreign policy concerns. A more conservative Congress, elected in 1966, and escalation of what many considered to be an unjust as well as unending war in Vietnam slowed down intensive social reform. Internal discord reached new heights as black citizens frequently took to the streets to press for equality in this generation. Student groups

[2] *The U.S. Book of Facts Statistics & Information* (New York: Essandess Special Edition, 1967).

[3] Quoted in Arthur M. Schlesinger, Jr., *A Thousand Days* (Boston: Houghton Mifflin Co., 1965), p. 720.

on campuses throughout the nation, dissatisfied with the quality of life in the Great Society, sought through radical means to change norms and values.

For the profession of social work the 1960s were a time of momentous change as welfare institutions, as well as all other spheres of American life, were challenged to prove their relevance to the times. A new emphasis on social reform and renewed recognition of the importance of environmental factors on individual lives led to changes in the profession and in social welfare programs. The explosion of knowledge and the rapidly accelerating pace of change created a crisis of identity for social workers of unprecedented proportions. Despite a historic commitment to change, social welfare institutions were scarcely prepared for the variety or the depth of the changes that were to be faced in the age of the Great Society.

Toward the end of the decade, despite the election of Richard M. Nixon to the presidency and less vigorous leadership from Washington, it appeared doubtful that the pace could be much slowed. An increased reliance on local efforts and the promotion of private-sector involvement in problem solution did, however, give promise of bringing a better balance in the reformation of social institutions.

THE THRESHOLD OF A NEW FRONTIER

Before the election of 1960, the President's Commission on National Goals submitted a report outlining programs of action for the next decade and an assessment of the condition of the American nation. The report recommended that the unemployment level be kept below 4 percent and that the federal government promote community mental health services, make medical services for the aged available through social security, increase social services in the categorical aid programs, eliminate slums, and promote technological change without threatening the individual.[4] All of these goals were laudable, but the specifics for attaining them and a national dedication for reaching the goals were missing. Perhaps the significance of the document lay in the official recognition that such problems existed even though they had been scarcely approached for solution by the administration that created the Commission.

A more critical assessment of the state of the Union was made the following year when the Rockefeller Brothers Fund published a case study of America's social institutions. Expert opinion on the problems in society and recommendations for change were made. While recognizing that private philanthropic contributions aggregated at least $6.7 billion an-

[4] *Goals for Americans*, Report of the President's Commission on National Goals (New York: Prentice-Hall, 1960).

nually, the bulk of the recommendations called for increased federal involvement in areas such as welfare, education, employment, and medical care. Panel reports advocated the extension of unemployment insurance benefits to the 12 million not covered by the program and an extension of time of coverage. Public works to employ those dislocated through technological change or unable to gain entry to the job market were recommended. It was also noted that social welfare needed increased commitments, both public and private, and a more adequate standard of living for welfare recipients was proposed. Vocational education, urban redevelopment, medical care for the indigent through federal subvention, and federal aid to education were considered essential.[5]

If the Rockefeller Brothers Fund recommendations were more specific and more critical than the earlier presidential committee's view of the American nation, the difference may be attributable to renascent social criticism. In the repressive atmosphere that characterized much of the 1950s (and, it should be noted, the 1920s), criticism of social ills was frequently equated with Communist Party sympathies. It would seem that by 1961 America had once again become safe for democracy, and the welfare state, which had been at least left intact and somewhat improved, was critically examined to determine what changes were needed.[6] Although the welfare state had in practice (if not in the mind of the citizenry) become a reality, doubts were expressed about the efficacy of the structure and the viability of welfare state ideology for a culture engulfed by change.[7] In no sector of society was there more evidence of a need for change and of the discrepancies between promise and reality than the social welfare institution, save perhaps for the related area of civil rights.

Although the term civil rights is broader than the single question of minority rights, much of the social upheaval of the 1960s stemmed from the Negro's insistence on equal treatment economically, socially, and politically. Although, as will later be shown, the problem of civil rights and

[5] *Prospect for America*, The Rockefeller Panel Reports (Garden City, N.Y.: Doubleday & Co., 1961).

[6] Emmet John Hughes, *The Ordeal of Power: A Political Memoir of the Eisenhower Years* (New York: Atheneum, 1963), p. 333.

[7] Sidney Hook, while pointing out that the substance, if not the terminology of the welfare state has been accepted in America, considers it an incoherent philosophy because programs are improvised to meet evils rather than planning programs to prevent social problems. Hook, a philosopher, describes the welfare state as "The complex proposition that it is the responsibility of the government to adopt measures that tend to produce and sustain full employment and, in its absence, to offer some insurance against unemployment; to coordinate policies to strengthen the economy . . . and to foster, wherever private enterprise fails, the social, economic and educational conditions that make for equality of opportunity." Sidney Hook, " 'Welfare State'—A Debate That Isn't," *New York Times Magazine* (November 27, 1960), p. 27.

civil liberties was equally a concern in areas such as criminal justice, the racial question became the focal point for unrest and the stimulus to other ferment. Notable as an outgrowth of the racial tension and disquiet was the student protest against the educational system and traditional politics and an unusual degree of involvement of youth in social questions.

In the milieu of unrest and change, the institution of social welfare was profoundly altered by the development of the 1960s. In the first part of the decade the profession and welfare programs were criticized on the one hand for being too generous and, later, for being unrelated and unconcerned with the problems of the poor. Older programs were altered to try to better meet the needs of the people, and new programs were initiated in an effort to handle contemporary social problems. The rediscovery of the problem of poverty was one of the most profound occurrences in the 1960s, and social workers as a professional group were perhaps the most challenged to justify their activities. By necessity the profession became reinvigorated in seeking new solutions for both old and new problems, and as a result society became more sympathetic to professional goals. Higher salaries and an improvement in professional status took place as improved results in solving problems challenged professionalism and methodological refinements as the first concern of social workers. Although relating to the poor as the primary obligation of the profession was resisted in many quarters (and not without justification), a new and perhaps more healthy professional balance was struck. Working with communities and groups began to attract more attention in social work, and individual therapy assumed a less dominant role in the structure of the profession.

Associated with the revolution in rights and responsibilities was a new way of regarding man's responsibilities to his fellow man. The effect on the church as an institution was profound, the consequences uncertain. A new morality, deriving perhaps from an existential view of humanistic responsibility for the welfare of others, emerged to challenge the more conventional ideas of individualism and self-reliance. The secular nature of much of the moral leadership, especially in the area of civil rights, spurred religious institutions to a new concern about human rights.[8] Whether the moral reawakening took place within the churches or without reference to an organized system, the objectives and the devotion to man's dignity and equality had some striking similarities.

The economy of the nation, shakey in some areas in the 1950s became an area of special concern during the 1960s as the unemployment rate remained at a high level. With a commitment to full employment, the

[8] Harvey Cox, *The Secular City* (New York: Macmillan Co., 1967).

nation was in a situation in which high unemployment co-existed with high levels of consumption and majority prosperity. Arguments about monetary, fiscal, and structural policies were important areas of conflict and debate at times other than election years.[9]

THE PROBLEM OF THE ECONOMY

One of the most important issues in the election campaign of 1960 was the question of what government ought to do in order to alleviate unemployment. In 1960 there was little question that the majority of the people were working and enjoying prosperity on a level higher than ever before. Neither could it be denied that large areas of poverty existed and that cases of individual want existed side by side with prosperity. Areas tied to traditionally dominant products prospered or declined in relation to the fate of the commodity. As in the case of West Virginia, where coal mining was a key element in the state's economy, new technology or new power sources could act to render the industry obsolete or decrease manpower needs. Other parts of Appalachia, as well as such places as the Ozarks and portions of the Southwest, were perennially distressed—perhaps because of geographical isolation or lack of natural resources. The national view of the people living in such areas as "happy peasants" who could, if they chose, join the mainstream of the affluent society changed in the decade to a more realistic appraisal of their situation.[10]

Individual-case poverty existed in rural and urban areas, where problems of health, age, education, race, or ethnic background led to want in the midst of plenty. Although the slums of the great cities were the most dramatic locales for the tableau of destitution, a greater percentage of the poor were to be found in rural areas. Among none was the problem

[9] Structural remedies for unemployment include education for those obsoleted by new products or perhaps automation, vocational training for the young and manpower retraining for the older worker, as well as area redevelopment, new careers, and massive federal presence in the creation of new job opportunities. Fiscal policy is related to the use of tax funds to stimulate production and consumption as well as such measures as tax cuts or increased taxes to stimulate or depress the economy. Monetary policy refers to "the money-supply function of the economy and the political institutions and power system related to it." Interest rates and the availability of money for capital investment are dependent, for example, on the monetary policy followed by the government, especially the Federal Reserve Board. John M. Culbertson, *Macroeconomic Theory and Stabilization Policy* (New York: McGraw-Hill Book Co., 1968), p. 420.

[10] The special case of Appalachia has been brilliantly delineated in the book written by a member of the Kentucky House of Representatives. See Harry M. Caudill, *Night Comes to the Cumberlands* (Boston: Little, Brown and Co., 1962).

more severe than among the migrant workers; usually Mexican-Americans and Negroes made up the majority. Poor in part because of their exclusion from minimum-wage legislation and denied the right to organize into unions under the protection of the National Labor Relations Act, migrant workers were an especially deprived group. Although they might earn less than $1500 a year, even with entire families working in the fields, most were ineligible for institutional welfare assistance because of state residence requirements.[11]

For the nation as a whole between the years 1950 and 1960 unemployment averaged about 4.5 percent, and at the time of Kennedy's inauguration it stood at 8.1 percent.[12] A percentage growth rate of 2.5 percent in the Gross National Product in the 1950s had made possible the employment of 9 million more people during the decade, while increased productivity led to nearly a 40 percent increase in the production of goods and services.[13] Despite these accomplishments, the level of unemployment was intolerably high and the growth rate less than that of other industrialized nations. Kennedy pledged his administration to take steps to stimulate the economy to a 5 percent growth rate. Even the more conservative economists felt that something between a 3 and 4 percent growth rate in the economic system was necessary if the nation was to approach the full employment policy expressed in the 1946 legislation.

Perhaps as significant as the lagging economy and the high rate of unemployment was the changing nature of employment. Continuing a long-term trend, employment patterns were changing significantly. The demand for professional, technical, and managerial skills increased while the need for unskilled and semiskilled workers declined. By the middle of the 1950s the demand for workers in service occupations exceeded the number required for the production of goods.

Another interesting characteristic of the unemployment situation in the 1960s was the age of those seeking work. Of some 5 million unemployed persons in 1960, 3 out of 10 were under the age of 25, and during the decade an estimated 26 million new job-seekers were entering the labor pool. Of these, 30 percent would not have finished high school, and a full 2.5 million would not have graduated from elementary school.[14] Thus the youth of the nation, during a time of rising aspirations, would also be the ones most likely to be confronted by a job market that was

[11] *Farm Labor Organizing 1905–1967* (New York: National Advisory Committee on Farm Labor, 1967).

[12] Schlesinger, *A Thousand Days, op. cit.*, p. 626.

[13] *Goals for Americans, op. cit.*, p. 194.

[14] Sylvia Porter, "The Jobless—II: Untrained Youth," *New York Post* (January 24, 1961).

declining in relative terms although not in absolute numbers. For the minority young the problem was even more severe; in some ghetto areas of large cities youths who also suffered the indignities of racial discrimination faced unemployment rates as high as 45 percent.

Economic problems facing the nation were multifaceted, but many of the difficulties had had their genesis in the preceding decade. A minority poor existed within a prosperous majority, and their political power was insufficient to force the government to become the employer of last resort. A minimum wage of $1 an hour for those engaged in interstate commerce provided less than an adequate standard of living; for the young, access to any job was difficult. Discrimination led to at least double rates of unemployment for groups such as Mexican-Americans, Negroes, and Puerto Ricans. In some instances social customs enforced patterns of poor education, poor housing, and other social handicaps. In 1961 a modest beginning was made in confronting some pressing social and economic problems. In succeeding years new legislation, new programs, new legal interpretations of constitutional rights, and a new moral-humanist revival produced incredible stresses on the nation's social institutions.

ECONOMIC POLICIES IN THE 1960S

In the early days of Kennedy's administration, action was taken to try to implement measures promised during the campaign. Eschewing civil rights legislation because of congressional hostility, Kennedy concentrated on structural economic programs aimed at reducing economic distress and fiscal policies designed to stimulate the economy.[15] In a message to Congress on February 2, 1961, Kennedy proposed the granting of federal funds to enable states to pay unemployment insurance for a maximum of 39 rather than 26 weeks. He had lowered Federal Housing Authority interest rates to stimulate private construction and asked for a Distressed Area Development Program that would give massive assistance to islands of poverty in the country. He also proposed an increase in the minimum wage to $1.15 and to $1.25 within two years and authorized the secretary of agriculture to speed up the distribution of surplus foods through direct issuance and through food-stamp programs. Also recommended was the granting of categorical assistance to families in which the head of the household was unemployed and liberalization of social scuerity insurance benefits. Specifically, it was suggested that men be made eligible for reduced benefits at age 62, that the quarters needed for qualifying be reduced, that widow's benefits be increased along with the basic minimum

[15] Helen Fuller, *Year of Trial* (New York: Harcourt, Brace & World, 1962), p. 72.

payments, and that disability be broadened from the total and permanent requirement then in effect.[16] Later in the month, before Democratic congressional leaders, Kennedy repeated some of his earlier requests and added his hope for a program of federal aid to education, Medicare, federal support for expanding community health facilities, and assistance to communities to encourage new industries and increased vitality outside urban metropolitan areas.[17] In the next six months Congress proved responsive to a structural approach to economic recovery. "Within six months it passed an area redevelopment bill, an omnibus housing bill, a farm bill, a rise in the minimum wage, the liberalization of social security, temporary unemployment benefits, benefits for dependent children of unemployed parents and a program to combat water pollution— a record of action on the domestic front unmatched in any single sitting since 1935." [18] In 1962 Congress made further structural adjustments by establishing, through the Manpower Development and Training Act, a modest program of education and retraining, ostensibly to attack what was called a "manpower drag"; that is, the lack of qualified workers for jobs created by newer technology and new kinds of jobs at the same time many were thought to be unemployed by virtue of job elimination.[19] In addition, Congress in 1962 made changes in the Social Security Act in an attempt to liberalize the categorical aid programs and to provide more intensive social worker service to clients.

One of Kennedy's most enduring achievements in the area of economics was his education of the American people to the fundamentals of Keynesian economics. The first consciously Keynesian president, Kennedy adopted many of the fiscal policy ideas espoused by Walter W. Heller,

[16] "Message From the President of the United States," *Congressional Record*, Vol. 107, Part I, January 30, 1961 to February 24, 1961, (Washington, D.C.: Government Printing Office, 1961), pp. 1677–81.

[17] "Presidential Message to Congress," *Congressional Quarterly*, Vol. 19, Part I, February 24, 1961 (Washington, D.C.: Congressional Quarterly, Inc., 1961), pp. 307–21.

[18] Schlesinger, *A Thousand Days, op. cit.*, p. 629.

[19] U.S. Department of Health, Education, and Welfare, *Education and Training, Third Annual Report of the Secretary of Health, Education, and Welfare to the Congress on Training Activities Under the Manpower Development and Training Act*, (Washington, D.C.: Government Printing Office, 1965). It is interesting to note that by 1967, when over 900,000 individuals had received assistance through MDTA, the bulk of the training was for traditional employments such as clerical and sales, operating drill presses, and secretarial skills. U.S. Department of Health, Education, and Welfare, *Education and Training, Sixth Annual Report to the Department of Health, Education, and Welfare to the Congress on Training Activities Under the Manpower Development and Training Act* (Washington, D.C.: Government Printing Office, 1968).

chairman of the Council of Economic Advisers.[20] Acting on the recommendations of Heller, Kennedy approached budgeting on a long-term basis and persuaded the people and Congress that a budgetary deficit could be an acceptable alternative in fiscal planning. Heller's theory of "fiscal drag" described a situation wherein high tax rates drained purchasing power and prevented full employment by a constriction of economic expansion. Acting on his acceptance of some of Heller's ideas (as well as some of those of John Kenneth Galbraith) Kennedy sought to stimulate business expansion through a 7 percent investment tax credit in his first year in office. Subsequently he proposed planned deficits at the crest of the recovery cycle to stimulate the rate of economic growth to approach the 5 percent rate he had set as a target. Part of this was the reducing of taxes in a time of prosperity in order to stimulate consumption—a scheme realized after his death in November, 1963.[21] Such a proposal ran contrary to conventional economic ideas, but the acceptance of the idea by Senator Barry Goldwater in the 1964 election campaign made deficit budgeting both a conservative and a liberal policy.

The elevation of Vice-President Lyndon B. Johnson to the presidency in 1963 brought an increased emphasis on structural remedies to produce what Johnson believed could be a "Great Society." Acting with some counsel from the chairman of the Council of Economic Advisers, at that time Gardney Ackley, a wave of structural programs were enacted; most were more reminiscent of the New Deal than the New Frontier. Economic recovery, begun perhaps even before Kennedy took office, accelerated during Johnson's term in office, 1963–68.

The sustained acceleration was evident in the growth of the Gross National Product. Rising from slightly more than $500 billion in 1960 to nearly $600 billion in 1963, by 1968 the total of goods and services produced exceeded $800 billion. By 1968 unemployment was less than 4 percent, and the growth rate of the economy during the Johnson years exceeded the 5 percent that Kennedy had desired.[22] Minority unemployment, still double the rate for white Anglo-Saxons, improved significantly as the need for war materials for the conflict in Vietnam increased. The largest percentage increase in employments for this chronically underhired group was found in war related industries.

[20] E. Ray Canterbury, *Economics on a New Frontier* (Belmont, Calif.: Wadsworth Publishing Co., 1968), pp. 8–16.

[21] William Greenleaf, ed., *American Economic Growth Since 1860* (Columbia, S.C.: University of South Carolina Press, 1968), pp. 292–93.

[22] U.S. President, *Economic Report of the President* (Washington, D.C.: Government Printing Office, 1967).

By 1968, when the sense of prosperity was felt by most Americans and even the poor had more reason to be hopeful, problem areas were still evident in the economy. Although Keynesian fiscal policies could demonstrably lower the unemployment rate and stimulate the growth rate, doing so without increasing the rate of inflation simultaneously, eluded the planners. Increases in prices that accompanied the increases in employment led, in 1968, to congressional demands for decreased domestic spending in return for passing a presidential request for a surtax to remove some of the purchasing power from the hands of consumers. Those genuinely concerned about inflation were joined in the endeavor by congressmen eager to trim the social programs spawned by the Great Society.

Another nagging question that was still unanswered as the decade drew to an end was the degree of dependence of the economic advance of the late 1960s on the war in Southeast Asia. Although the military might be the perfect consuming unit, producing nothing and consuming goods and services, it could not be known what the economic consequences would be of an "outbreak of peace." In 1968, 43 cents of each tax dollar was devoted to defense needs, and a decrease would probably have consequences for the economy unless other ways of stimulating it were found. In addition the release of part of the 4 million men from military service, a disproportionate number of whom were black, would present new challenges as they were reabsorbed into civilian life. If, as in the past, the cessation of hostilities would mean the loss of jobs for minority groups, economic distress might produce civil unrest on an unprecedented scale.

THE POLITICS OF THE PERIOD

If Kennedy was the first president to consciously embrace Keynesianism in economics, he was also the first to proclaim an end of ideology. The term ideology has been defined as "a comprehensive, passionately believed, self-activating view of society, usually organized as a social movement, rather than a latent half-conscious belief system." [23] Believing that the traditional dichotomy of liberalism and conservatism was the politics of the 1930s, Kennedy felt that future ideas for social progress would be developed differently (and more rationally) than in the past. Speaking in 1962, he remarked:

The fact of the matter is that most of the problems, or at least many of them, that we now face are technical problems, are administrative problems. They are very sophisticated judgments which do not lend themselves

[23] Robert E. Lane, "The Decline of Politics and Ideology in a Knowledgeable Society," *American Sociological Review*, Vol. 31, no. 5 (October 1966), p. 660.

to the great sort of "passionate movements" which have stirred this country so often in the past.[24]

Inherent in this view of politics is the notion that we need not have in
this nation great chasms of misunderstanding on political or ideological
grounds. According to this way of viewing American society, abundance
makes it possible, for example, for union leaders and management to sit
down and decide what is right in light of predictable consequences and
to avoid serious and damaging confrontations. The political problem
associated with this is the discovery of the best, rather than the most
doctrinaire, solution for social ills. In keeping with this philosophy
Kennedy brought into his administration bipartisan cadres of experts to
advise on policies, and he attempted, not always successfully, to promote
understanding between such groups as business and labor. Not since the
New Deal had economists, historians, social critics, and others from the
intellectual and educational community been accorded as much a voice
in national decision-making.

Associated with this enhancement of the status of the intellectual (a
reversal of the attitude prevalent in the Eisenhower years) was the revival
of the literature of protest as a genre. Writers during the New Deal had
poked into every facet of American life and had written much about the
deficiencies of a system that could produce such massive want amid the
basis for general prosperity. The fact of the Great Depression, however,
had forcefully brought to the citizenry's attention the fact that something
was wrong and had instilled a willingness to accept structural changes to
achieve a better society. In the literature of the 1960s, there was no
corresponding sense of urgency abroad in the land. In many respects,
the protest of the decade was more nearly like that of the muckraking
era around the turn of the century. During that period of journalistic
social awakening the description of evils was intended to be and func-
tioned as a way of bringing attention to the existence of widespread
poverty and to the fact that remedies could be found to eliminate social ills.

In the 1960s a similar need for arousal existed because of the prevalence
of affluence and the belief that the programs and policies of the 1930s
had solved the worst social problems, perhaps for all time. The fact that
the institutions of the 1960s were not those of the 1930s was evident in
the vast array of protest writings that began to proliferate during the
Kennedy administration and that increased in quaniity as the decade wore
on. The automotive industry, television, pesticides and pollution, taxation,
racism, and even *The American Way of Death*[25] became the subjects of

[24] Quoted in Schlesinger, *A Thousand Days, op. cit.*, p. 644.
[25] Jessica Mitford, *The American Way of Death* (New York: Simon & Schuster,
1963).

authors' concern. Periodicals such as *Harper's Magazine* and *Atlantic Monthly* became vehicles for wide circulation of articles dealing with a host of social problems in a way that was reminiscent of the earlier *McClure's* and *Colliers*. For the field of social work, Michael Harrington's *The Other America*,[26] Edgar May's *The Wasted Americans*,[27] and articles by Ben H. Bagdikian in the *Saturday Evening Post* and Dwight MacDonald in the *New Yorker* were crucial.

In addition to the printed word as a means of acquainting the majority of the people to the problems of the poor minority, the medium of television contributed tremendously to the education of the people. Just as television helped to produce mass protest against a foreign war, it also made people acutely and intimately aware of the grinding poverty extant in America.[28] Programming in the 1960s may have included much that could justifiably be considered a "wasteland," but documentary reports on social problems and newscasts of police dogs attacking civil rights workers produced a sense of shock that the written word could not hope to duplicate. Illustrative of the impact that television was to have on public poilcy was the 1968 documentation of hunger in America. The claim that 10 million people were hungry in America led to a nationwide congressional investigation, an Administration sponsored conference on the subject in Washington, D.C., and some liberalization of government food programs. The Nixon administration, however, seemed disinclined to deal effectively with the facts produced and proposed less than a total assault on hunger in the nation.

In the 1960 presidential contest, the first television campaign, Kennedy's projection of idealism, vigor, and concern provided an impetus to the protest and reform movement of the decade. Although there was some upsurge in social criticism before he took office, Kennedy had a pervasive effect on the national mood.[29] In no quarter was this more true than among the young, who were challenged by the vision of excellence he held for the quality of American life. The climate of purposefulness and spirit of dedication that he inspired was in sharp contrast to the youthful apathy of the 1950s. By the end of the decade it seemed unlikely that anyone would describe college students of the 1960s the way Clark Kerr, chancellor of the University of California during the Berkeley "Free Speech Movement," described students of the 1950s:

[26] Michael Harrington, *The Other America* (New York: Macmillan Co., 1962).

[27] Edgar May, *The Wasted Americans* (New York: Harper & Row, 1964).

[28] Marshall McLuhan and Quentin Fiore, *War. and Peace in the Global Village* (New York: Bantam Books, Inc., 1968).

[29] Arthur M. Schlesinger, Jr., and Fred L. Israel, *The Chief Executive* (New York: Crown Publishers, 1965), p. 306.

The employers will love this generation. They aren't going to press many grievances. They are going to be easy to handle. There aren't going to be any riots.[30]

One of the most significant occurrences in the early 1960s was the elevation of domestic policy concerns above foreign policy matters. Although this was reversed toward the end of President Johnson's tenure in office (and the reversal became more pronounced under President Nixon) concern about changing domestic social institutions was preeminent under Kennedy. Programs such as the Peace Corps appealed to all ages as an instrument of peace and a tangible expression of idealism and dedication. Later, the idea of a war against poverty similarly inspired a feeling that it was as reasonable to fight inequity at home as it was to spend billions of dollars to advance the interests of the nation abroad through military expenditures.[31] In the international arena the government in the first part of the decade stressed economic assistance to underdeveloped nations, sometimes in preference to military aid. Kennedy initiated and Johnson supported an expanded Food-for-Peace program, a revamped Agency for International Development, and a new Alliance for Progress with South American nations that demonstrated a willingness to use governmental power to help all needing help.

Kennedy's assassination in November 1963 brought to the presidency a man less guided by theory than his predecessor, more familiar with the vagaries of congressional politics in matters of social legislation, and philosophically more akin to Populism and the New Deal than the New Frontier.[32] The choice of terms, Johnson's "Great Society" rather than Kennedy's "New Frontier," is perhaps instructive in understanding the difference between the administrations. In a Great Society it is possible to envision a perfectable society in which social justice can be created by the development of institutions to meet the needs of the citizens. A New Frontier is more descriptive of an attitude that places the participant on the edge of knowledge but still leaves much to be discovered.

After taking the oath of office, and especially after his overwhelming defeat of Senator Barry Goldwater, in 1964, President Johnson successfully pushed to fruition much of the legislation Kennedy had sought and he added his own programs and policies. His predecessor had sought regional solutions for structural unemployment through the Area Redevelopment Act of 1961; Johnson four years later signed the Appalachian

[30] Quoted by Jack Newfield, *A Prophetic Minority* (New York: New American Library, 1966), p. 37.
[31] Theodore C. Sorensen, *Kennedy* (New York: Harper & Row, 1965), pp. 530–37.
[32] Harry S. Ashmore, *The Man in the Middle* (Columbia: University of Missouri Press, 1966), p. 12.

Regional Development Act, which, although it was basically a roads and dams bill, did take a regional approach and transcended state boundaries. Kennedy had achieved passage of a Manpower Training and Development Act in 1962, but bills for vocational education and employment opportunities for the young had faced strong congressional resistance. By contrast, Johnson was able to achieve both, as well as more ambitious training programs for the unemployed with social or physical handicaps. Although Kennedy had argued for medical care for the aged during 1962 and 1963, opposition from most of the medical profession and public arguments about socialized medicine had made passage of such legislation impossible. In 1965 Johnson signed into law at the Truman Library in Independence, Missouri, a Medicare bill providing medical assistance not only for the aged but for the medically indigent of all ages as well. Acting on a family concern and interest, Kennedy had achieved passage of Public Law 88–164, which provided funds for the construction of research centers for the mentally retarded and for subventions to states for the construction of community mental health centers. During Johnson's administration the programs begun under Kennedy were expanded in such areas as the development of regional centers for service to crippled children, mentally retarded children with physical handicaps, expectant mothers, and more.

In tackling the problem of income maintenance, President Kennedy had achieved a revision of the Social Security Act in 1962 to promote the giving of social service and planned to initiate programs aimed at poverty eradication by 1964. The Economic Opportunity Act of 1964, passed during Johnson's tenure in office, included some programs he especially favored and incorporated some principles, such as participation of the poor, which Kennedy had espoused. Like Kennedy, who had been unable to get a program of federal aid to education because of the opposition of the Roman Catholic Church in 1963, Johnson saw educational opportunities as a key to promoting social well-being. He was able to get such a bill in the Elementary and Secondary Education Act of 1965. Because this legislation made economic aid available to both parochial and public schools, it was even more innovative than earlier proposals.

A Civil Rights Act, pressed for in 1963, was achieved in 1964; it prohibited discrimination in federally assisted programs. In 1965 Congress took action through the Voting Rights Law to protect and enfranchise citizens systematically excluded from suffrage. Johnson in 1965 also persuaded Congress to change its stance of 1963, and a major revision of the Housing Act created a cabinet-level Department of Housing and Urban Development.

This recitation of failures, compromises, and successes points up the fact that in terms of accomplishments the Johnson record exceeded that of his predecessor. Undoubtedly the sense of grief that was pervasive in society after the assassination contributed to Johnson's successes, as did the election of an overwhelmingly Democratic majority in both houses. It is probably also significant that Johnson, as Majority Leader in the Senate, had a better working knowledge of congressional politics. His success may also have derived in part from the sense of ease politicians felt around him—a feeling that the urbane and somewhat distant Kennedy did not instill. It is also likely that the process of educating the public to public needs, begun under Kennedy, reached fruition after his death and that the programs initiated, or at least discussed by the one, were achievable in time only under the other. It is possible that many of the programs Johnson pushed for had a familiar ring to an electorate that had grown up and perhaps had been a part of the consensus that made the New Deal possible. Furthermore the awakening of the Negro American to a feeling that equality before the law was achievable, and the civil unrest that accompanied it, no doubt acted as a coercive force in getting the majority of Americans to acquiesce to social reform. All of these factors, and perhaps others as well, acted to produce one of the most significant periods of political change in the history of the nation.

Amid all of the change some declared the pace was too rapid; for others the rate of change seemed incredibly slow for meeting the needs of society. It may be that Kennedy, whose "style" became almost a hackneyed adjective, would not have been able to escape the criticism later to be heaped on his vice-president. It may well be that the process of change and activism that began in the 1960s would have swept away the incumbent who could not control the forces of change. Involvement in Vietnam, which had begun under Eisenhower, increased during Kennedy's years in office, and greatly accelerated under Johnson, might have had a somewhat similar course no matter who held the office of president. Whatever the conjectures might be, it is inescapably true that the war, along with a backlash demand for law and order that was in part directed against black militancy, helped to produce a breakdown of consensus politics. The result was the candidacy in 1968 of George Wallace of Alabama—the champion of white, Anglo-Saxon, Protestant dominance—and the election of Richard M. Nixon with less than a majority mandate from the electorate.

The politics of the second half of the decade were clearly different from those of the first. New political alignments, emphasized by the emergence of the extreme Right and the New Left, gave some promise of upsetting the notion of an "end of ideology" in America.[33] Militant students

[33] Paul Jacobs and Saul Landau, *The New Radicals* (New York: Vintage Books, 1966).

striking and sitting-in at Columbia University, San Francisco State College, the University of Wisconsin, and a host of other institutions of higher learning large and small added a new element to the political configuration of the nation. Increased participation of youth in politics further added to the confusion of traditional politics. Assassination, first of President John F. Kennedy and then his brother Senator Robert F. Kennedy in June 1968, added a disturbing element to the political realignment of the nation and contributed to an increasing feeling of alienation on the part of youth.

SOCIAL WELFARE PROGRAMS IN THE 1960S

At the beginning of the Kennedy administration, concern about the condition of people living in poverty led to the development of legislative schemes aimed at liberalizing public welfare programs. Food-stamp programs, increased distribution of surplus foodstuffs, extended periods of eligibility for unemployment benefits, and higher public welfare grants combined with intensive service to clients were among the methods proposed for ending the problem of dependency.

The person not working and dependent on public support has always been an uncomfortable figure for Americans to accept because of traditional beliefs about individual responsibility for economic well-being.[34] Although there is more tolerance of dependency in times of general economic distress, when most people are working those who are not become the objects of general concern. Traditionally in America, consumption of goods and services lies at the other end of a continuum that begins with work, however it is defined. Increasing dependency in the 1960s, when more people were working than at any time in the past, brought a number of resentments to the fore. Some of the hostility to public welfare programs centered on the large percentage of minority persons receiving help; part of it was owing to apprehension about a changing moral code that was most conspicuously mirrored in a rising rate of illegitimacy. In many respects welfare programs were incorrectly viewed as the cause rather than the by-product of a changing society in which social institutions were in a state of flux.

The rising tide of criticism reached flood proportions in 1960 in the city of Newburgh, New York. Officials there brought national attention to focus on the community when recipients of welfare were fingerprinted, photographed, and interrogated. Reacting to the movement of Negroes to the city, the increasing fact of urban blight, and the growth of welfare rolls, 13 proposals were made for reducing welfare expenditures. Among

[34] Ralph H. Gabriel, *The Course of American Democratic Thought* (New York: Ronald Press, 1956), pp. 3–25.

these were the denial of aid to persons with multiple illegitimacies, limits on the amount of financial aid, refusal of assistance to persons moving to the city without definite employment commitments, and 40 hours per week of maintenance work for able-bodied males on relief. Although a subsequent court decision prohibited implementation of 12 of the 13 proposals, the community and perhaps a large number of citizens nationally were sympathetic to Newburgh's solution for cutting welfare costs. So prominent a citizen as Senator Barry Goldwater wrote the city manager saying: "The abuses in the welfare field are mounting. The only way to curtail them are the steps which you have already taken." [35] After much publicity, the fact that the number of people receiving welfare assistance who were able-bodied and available for work was miniscule led to the collapse of the "revolt." But the feeling grew that something was radically wrong when welfare rolls increased during prosperous times. One result in 1962 was a major revision of the Social Security Act.

President Kennedy had made the improvement of social welfare programs one of the major themes of his presidential campaign. The realization that some programs contributed to family disintegration while others were inadequate to the tasks they were supposed to perform had prompted him to espouse a number of revisions. Foremost was the desire to provide more comprehensive protection for the elderly through a government-sponsored medical care program. Concern that unemployed fathers might have to leave their families to make them eligible for aid led to his interest in making unemployment a basis for eligibility in the Aid to Dependent Children program. A belief that the focus of many welfare programs was something other than rehabilitation contributed to his interest in making social services more accessible to welfare recipients.

Shortly after his inauguration President Kennedy appointed a task force to make recommendations for temporary measures to assist those affected by the economic recession which obtained. Acting on this group's recommendation, Congress enacted temporary legislation that made unemployed parents eligible for Aid to Dependent Children grants and extend unemployment insurance to a maximum of 39 weeks. The need for the latter, financed through federal funds, was apparent in 1961 when nearly 2.5 million unemployed workers had exhausted their benefits and were still unable to find jobs.[36]

After enactment of these temporary programs, the secretary of Health, Education, and Welfare, Abraham Ribicoff, began a review and investi-

[35] Edgar May, *op. cit.*, p. 37. Also see pp. 27–45 for an excellent documentation of the Newburgh plan and its history.
[36] William Haber and Merrill G. Murray, *Unemployment Insurance in the American Economy* (Homewood, Ill.: Richard D. Irwin, 1966), p. 218.

gation of welfare programs to assess needed legislation. Depending heavily on recommendations from professionals and specialists within the Social Security Administration, Ribicoff and Kennedy in February 1962 urged Congress to make numerous revisions in the Social Security Act. In response to these recommendations, legislation in 1962 provided for 75 percent federal matching of funds for social services and limited to 60 the number of cases handled by social workers providing social services on an intensive level. In addition, training of social workers was funded at this higher rate, although other noneconomic services were to be reimbursed at the existing half federal and half state and local rate. Provisions made it possible for social services to be given to individuals or families not in economic distress; prevention of need and family breakdown was stressed, as was rehabilitation for those in financial need. Work relief, reminiscent of the Works Progress Administration, was revived, and unemployment was recognized as a valid basis for eligibility although acceptance was contingent on state enabling legislation. The new legislation also provided for funds to create day care centers to provide for an estimated 400,000 children under the age of 12 whose mothers were already working and for those whose ADC mothers were expected to find jobs because of the new emphasis on rehabilitation. Earnings of those receiving Old Age Assistance were exempt up to an amount of $30 per month, and 5 percent of an agency's caseload could be placed on a money management scheme of restricted payments.

In assessing the developments in 1962 and in judging the performance of the modified programs, it is apparent that the 1962 measures fell far short of congressional expectations. Although the number of clients served and the expenditures of funds showed a relative and sometimes actual decline in some programs, the retitled Aid to Families with Dependent Children (AFDC) program continued a seemingly inexorable climb. In 1960 AFDC had assisted 3,073,000 persons at a cost of slightly more than $1 billion. By 1965 the cost had nearly doubled, and the recipients numbered 4,396,000. If prevention of dependency and rehabilitation of families had been the intent, clearly the 1962 amendments hit wide of their mark.

The 1962 amendments had been hailed as innovative and as a change in the philosophy of welfare programs. In actuality they did not change the states' rights emphasis of the programs, and the potential for innovation in such things as day care or service to nonrecipients of cash grants was not realized.[37] Although the changes of 1962 were widely supported by professional social workers and highly touted by the bureaucracy in the federal agency, most of what was genuinely "new" in the so-called service

[37] Gilbert Y. Steiner, *Social Insecurity* (Chicago: Rand McNally & Co., 1966), pp. 18–47 *et passim*.

amendments was new paper work.[38] As Winifred Bell, an authority on public welfare programs, later pointed out, "unfortunately, the federal guidelines provided more clues to identifying and classifying problems than to operationalizing goal-directed social services, a process with which public welfare agencies seldom had much experience." [39] Furthermore the amendments of 1962 continued to approach the problem of public dependency as one that was generally amenable to individual casework treatment. Tacit approval was given to the idea prevalent among the general population that the cause of need invariably lay within the individual rather than sometimes in his being victimized by the social system. The 1962 amendments were not designed to promote group work and community organization approaches and were hardly meant to upset traditional lines of authority and power in neighborhoods and communities.[40]

A more radical departure from past practice was suggested in Kennedy's push for medical care to be provided through the social security structure. In 1962 the president carried his fight to the people in a rally of senior citizens at Madison Square Garden that was televised nationallly. This he deemed necessary because of the reluctance of Congress to pass medical care legislation and because of the well-financed lobbying campaign of the American Medical Association.[41] Documentation was increasingly available to show that private insurance companies could not adequately provide insurance for the aged, who constituted the group most likely to need expensive long-term care and hospitalization. Despite Kennedy's attempt to pressure Congress and increasing public sentiment in favor of such legislation, it was not until after his assassination that Medicare was passed. As it was enacted in 1965, the inclusion of the medically indigent as eligible for state-structured medical services, as well as the optional prepayment for physicians' services, made the act more comprehensive than Kennedy had dared to seek. Other medical care legislation was passed early in the decade dealing with drug safety, hospital construction, and the well-being of the mentally ill and retarded. In the first executive message on mental illness and mental retardation ever delivered to Congress, President Kennedy called for special legislation to help the nearly 1.5 million people who each year receive treatment in mental institutions. In response, Congress in 1963 passed the Mental Retardation

[38] Russell E. Smith, "In Defense of Public Welfare," *Social Work*, Vol. 11, no. 4 (October, 1966), pp. 90–97.

[39] Winifred Bell, *Aid to Dependent Children* (New York: Columbia University Press, 1965), p. 171.

[40] *Ibid.*, p. 172.

[41] Sorenson, *op. cit.*, pp. 342–44.

Facilities and Community Mental Health Centers Construction Act.[42] Although it initially provided for construction needs, subsequent amendments provided funds for staffing purposes as well.

During the months before President Kennedy's assassination, he became increasingly concerned about ways to improve the condition of the poor and was determined to accompany a tax reduction with a poverty program. After his death the program was enacted as the Economic Opportunity Act of 1964. This piece of legislation spawned a number of new programs designed "to eliminate the paradox of poverty in the midst of plenty in this Nation." [43] Many of the programs reinstituted and updated New Deal measures that had been allowed to lapse during World War II. Some were innovative and required much testing and refinement in the course of operation. Other parts were virtually inoperable or were so controversial that they were modified significantly or permitted to lie fallow.

Programs with New Deal antecedents included such things as the Job Corps and Training Centers designed to equip youth with educational opportunities not otherwise available in their home communities. A Work Study Program was instituted through institutions of higher learning to encourage disadvantaged young people to attend college. Students in secondary schools were encouraged to remain in school through the community work-training programs that were developed. Part of the program, administered by the Department of Health, Education, and Welfare through public assistance agencies, was aimed at work training for welfare recipients. Under this provision of the law, local and state agencies were given funds to offer work experience and training, adult education, and vocational training to clients.

A major innovation in the act was the creation of the Volunteers in Service to America which had the convenient acronym, VISTA. Akin to the earlier Peace Corps idea, volunteers were to be trained and then assigned to agencies and organizations working to eliminate poverty and its causes. Loans were also provided for persons in rural areas for home improvement or for the purchase of occupational equipment or supplies; urban dwellers were eligible for loans to start small businesses and could receive consultation from the Small Business Administration.

One of the most innovative and controversial ideas contained in the Economic Opportunity Act was the provision for urban and rural community action programs. Immediately traceable to the Ford Foundation's

[42] U.S. Congress, Senate, *Mental Retardation Facilities and Community Mental Health Act of 1963*, Pub. L. 88–164, 88th Cong., 1st sess., 1963, S. 1576.
[43] U.S. Congress, Senate, *The War on Poverty, The Economic Opportunity Act of 1964*, Pub. L. 88–452, 88th Cong., 2nd sess., 1964, S. 2642.

Gray Areas slum redevelopment programs of the 1950s, and New York City's Mobilization for Youth (MFY) in the early 1960s, local neighborhood councils were to be formed to include representation from those to be helped so that more effective measures for eliminating poverty could be found.[44]

The possibility that power might be exercised by a politically conscious group of the poor and the fact that organized attempts were made to change business practices in poor neighborhoods were but two objections raised to the concept of organization of the underprivileged.[45] Consumer protection, housing concerns, and legal problems of all kinds were the cause of local and regional agitation as community legal services were increasingly funded through War on Poverty funds.[46] New journals appeared to report on the many legal decisions affecting people in the culture of poverty, and the legal profession was challenged by the new interest in poor people and their rights. Organizations funded by the Office of Economic Opportunity, such as the Project on Social Welfare Law at the New York University School of Law, developed from the 1966 amendments to the Economic Opportunity Act, as did the unique California Rural Legal Assistance agency. New legal structures contributed to a number of court challenges to welfare practices. During 1967 and 1968 cases concerned with establishing the right to pretermination hearings for recipients being removed from welfare rolls were affirmatively decided in federal district courts and in state courts and were confirmed in 1970 by the Supreme Court. Notable in providing this right were *Williams v. Mississippi Department of Public Welfare* and the New York case *Kelley v. Wyman*.[47] In the case of *King v. Smith*, an Alabama regulation declaring that a man who cohabited with an AFDC mother was ipso facto a "substitute father" for any and all of her children was found unconstitutional. Between 1964 and 1967 Alabama had reduced the number of AFDC recipients by some 20,000 persons, of whom 16,000 were children, through this device.[48] Cases such as these proved the value of legal services for the poor, especially for public welfare clients.

[44] Sar A. Levitan, *The Design of Federal Antipoverty Strategy*. Policy Papers in Human Resources and Industrial Relations, No. 1 (Detroit: Wayne State University, 1967), pp. 18–21.

[45] "All Power to the Soviets," *National Review*, Vol. 17, no. 24 (June 15, 1965), pp. 492–94, and Paul Hencke, "Is War on Poverty Becoming War on Business?," *Nation's Business*, March 1966, pp. 41–61 are illustrative.

[46] Max Doverman, "Today's Legal Revolution," *Social Service Review*, Vol. 40, no. 2 June 1966), pp. 152–68.

[47] *Poverty Law Reporter* (New York: Commerce Clearing House, 1968), pp. 2457–61.

[48] *King v. Smith*, 392 U.S. 2128–44 (1968).

In addition to increased legal activity, a revived welfare rights movement using tactics of the civil rights movement, including picketing, protest marches, and sit-ins, added to the discomfiture of local officials. Some of those who picketed and helped organize local welfare rights organizations were social workers employed by public welfare agencies. The formation of a National Welfare Rights Organization in Washington, D.C., added to the effectiveness of the movement in challenging the adequacy of aid to families as well as certain social agency intervention techniques as applied to the poor.[49]

In 1968 the control of community action councils was placed more firmly under the agencies of local and state government; the requirement for "maximum feasible participation of the poor" was defined as a one-third representation on boards. So long as this phrase remained indefinite, it was not unusual for such boards to have a majority of poor people. Potentially controversial programs such as the provision of assistance to migrant workers and cooperative associations that could be set up through loan provisions were but little exploited.

The programs of the War on Poverty were set up in most instances to provide direct contact between the federal government and local communities. In things such as the Head Start program contacts between local school boards and other agencies bypassed the state machinery and frequently the local units of government. In a sense this was part of a trend, evident in the early 1960s, toward employing regional or local concepts of administration to the point of transcending traditional governmental patterns. It also reflected a dissatisfaction with state and local government and an impatience with getting help directly to the people needing assistance. Toward the end of the 1960s, at least in the areas of poverty abolition, control began to swing back toward more conventional lines of power and distribution partly because of rivalry between governors and big-city mayors. The election of President Nixon promised further movement toward more traditional approaches, as evidenced by the progressive stripping of the functions of the Office of Economic Opportunity and the parceling out of its programs to other bureaucracies. Although predictions of a demise of the War on Poverty might have been premature in the early days of the Nixon administration, it was quite apparent that the battle against want would be fought in a different and less socially abrasive way in the future.

Funding of War on Poverty projects was frequently without reference to local funds in the early days of the battle, and the ignoring of tradi-

[49] Joseph E. Paull, "Recipients Aroused: The New Welfare Rights Movement," *Social Work*, Vol. 12, no. 2 (April 1967), p. 102.

tional methods created further difficulties for the programs. Direct financing from Washington was considered justified, since some programs
such as Head Start might not have got off the ground if local investment
through a "matching grant" scheme had been insisted on. In those cases
for which a local contribution, typically 10 percent, was required, "in-
kind" contributions of buildings, volunteer time, and so on were used to
qualify for federal funds.

As important as the opposition of some local government officials was
in dissipating the War on Poverty, it is probable that the need for ever-
increasing funds to support the war in Vietnam was as important a factor.
Although President Johnson had maintained that the country was wealthy
enough to have both "guns and butter," congressional sentiment was for
a reduction in domestic programs. In 1968 concern about inflation led
to substantial cutbacks in social welfare programs and a tax surcharge
to finance the war. The cutbacks on some War on Poverty programs,
coupled with the structural changes, diminished the freedom of action in
local community action programs. Along with this was a feeling of dis-
couragement on the part of some who had viewed the poverty programs
as a mechanism for helping the poor help themselves.

During the same years in which the War on Poverty was being reined
in, Congress was also making further revisions in the Social Security Act.
Perhaps because of the disillusionment with the 1962 amendments, which
had fallen so short of promises made, in 1967 Congress passed what one
critic called "the first purposively punitive welfare legislation in the
history of the American national government." [50] Reorganization within
the Department of Health, Education, and Welfare brought together in
a new office of Social and Rehabilitation Service the Vocational Rehabilitation Administration, the Welfare Administration, the Administration on
Aging, and the Division of Mental Retardation of the Public Health Service.[51] The reorganization reflected a new emphasis on rehabalitation, and
important changes were made in the family programs. Employment and
job training programs were transferred to the Department of Labor;
AFDC was limited so far as federal matching funds were concerned to
cases in which fathers had employment for over a year in the three-year
period before assistance was granted. Caseloads were to be restricted after
June 30, 1968, to the percentage of the state's under-18 population receiving help as of January 1, 1968, although this provision was not enforced
and was later discarded. Families receiving benefits through unemploy-

[50] Daniel P. Moynihan, "Improving Social Welfare, The Bankrupt Welfare System,"
Current, No. 94 (April 1968), p. 40.
[51] U.S. General Services Administration, *United States Government Organization
Manual* 1968–69 (Washington, D.C.: Government Printing Office, 1968), pp. 374–382.

ment insurance could not receive supplementary help through AFDC-U, the unemployed parent program, although provisions for income earned by children and adult recipients receiving aid were liberalized. Child welfare services were to be made available in every community in the nation, and day care had to be provided for the children of parents required to seek jobs or training in Department of Labor projects. In the area of medical care, states such as New York, Massachusetts, and California were required to curtail their liberal programs. Income levels of 133.33 percent of the state's AFDC payment level were prescribed as maximums for eligibility to medical care.

The effect of the legislation was to curb expenditures for medical care for the indigent and to require work or training for parents. It also placed the computerized records of the Social Security Administration at the disposal of welfare departments seeking absent-parent support and funds from noncontribuing responsible relatives. Questions about the dangers to civil liberties inherent in such plans and restrictions troubled many, perhaps as much as the punitive nature of the amendments.[52] Congress was clearly taking responsibility for program development into its own hands.

Contrary to the trend in Congress for more punitive approaches to public dependency were several decisions of the Supreme Court regarding welfare restrictions. Court intervention in many jurisdictions promised the elimination of residence requirements for the recipt of welfare. The promise was actualized in the 1969 Supreme Court decision, *Shapiro v. Thompson*.[53] Professional social workers had long complained against such restrictions on aid, but the constitutional safeguard protecting the right of mobility proved to be a more fruitful approach to the goal than legislative action. The specter of residence requirements being eliminated led the governors of populous states, especially Nelson Rockefeller in New York, to propose a national and federalized program of public assistance payments.

Court action in 1969 challenging the legality of persons being required to take jobs at less than assistance standards also raised the possibility of the supplementation of families; this would, in effect, create a guaranteed annual income. Although such a scheme was not uncommon in industry, notably the automotive industry, a future Supreme Court ruling holding such supplementation necessary would give added impetus to the idea

[52] A valuable discussion of the concept of privacy may be found in Charles Fried, "Privacy," *The Yale Law Journal*, Vol. 77, no. 3 (January 1968), pp. 475–93. See also, "Privacy and Efficient Government," *Harvard Law Review*, Vol. 82, no. 2 (December 1968), pp. 400–417.

[53] *Shapiro v. Thompson*, 89 U.S. 1322 (1969).

of a guaranteed annual income. In addition to the legal changes the 1967 amendments also offered, through the requirement that services and income maintenance be separated, the promise of true community social services available to all regardless of income. This was a long-standing plea of the professional social worker.[54]

THE REVOLUTION IN HUMAN RIGHTS

During the late 1950s and throughout the succeeding decade, human rights became a paramount national issue. Not since the Civil War had the problems faced by a racial minority been the focus of such intense national concern. It was not that the problems or the minority group concerned had changed. Rather, social institutions—especially the law—became more agreeable to extending basic democratic freedoms to all Americans. The impact of the revolution in human rights in the 1960s rivaled that of the previous century as ideas and ideals became levers for social action. A new black militancy combined with a nonviolent insistence that Christian ethics be honored and that constitutional rights and liberties be extended to all people in America. In a relatively short time business and industry examined hiring practices, while educational institutions were sometimes forcefully reminded that the culture and history of minorities had been virtually ignored. Churches of all denominations were challenged by the recognition that large numbers of people had beeen systematically degraded and victimized by the majority in the democracy. The resulting upsurge in social consciousness on the part of both clergy and laity was reminiscent of the earlier Social Gospel.[55] Social workers and social agencies were brought up short with the charge that not only had they frequently lost contact with the problems of poverty, they had also in their practice helped to perpetuate racism in America.[56]

Although the plight of the Negro was perhaps the most dramatic, other minority groups, such as the Indians, the Mexican-Americans, and the Puerto Ricans, lived in conditions hardly less desperate. Because Negroes

[54] Eveline M. Burns, "What's Wrong with Public Welfare?" *Social Service Review*, Vol. 36, no. 2 (June 1962), pp. 111–22; Gordon Hamilton, "Editor's Page," *Social Work*, Vol. 7, no. 1 (January 1962), pp. 2 and 128.

[55] Harvey G. Cox, "The 'New Breed' in American Churches," *Daedalus*, Vol. 96, no. 1 (Winter 1967), pp. 135–150.

[56] Charles E. Silberman, *Crisis in Black and White* (New York: Random House, 1964), pp. 308–55. Also, *Report of the National Advisory Commission on Civil Disorders* (New York: Bantam Books), p. 460 and Joseph Golden, "Desegregation of Social Agencies in the South," *Social Work*, Vol. 10, no. 1 (January 1965), pp. 58–67. The pamphlet "Title VI . . . One Year After," *United States Commission on Civil Rights* (Washington, D.C.: Government Printing Office, 1966) is subtitled "A Survey of Desegregation of Health and Welfare Services in the South" and is especially revealing.

were most evident as the result of increasing migration to the urban North, and because they constituted more than 10 percent of the total population, much of the emphasis on minority rights in the 1960s was directed toward them. But as the thrust of black members of society began to achieve a modicum of success, Orientals, Indians, and the Spanish-speaking peoples also claimed their legitimate debts from society. As leaders such as Dr. Martin Luther King, Jr., and Malcolm X moved to positions of leadership in the Negro community, others such as Reies Tijerina in New Mexico and Cesar Chavez in California pressed their peoples' demands for justice.

Majority sympathy waxed and waned, and sometimes liberal advocates of institutional and attitudinal change voiced fears that change was coming too fast and that patience was called for. It was estimated, however, that even if the 1950–1960 rate of relative change prevailed, black citizens would achieve educational equality with whites in 60 years, occupational equality in 93 years, and parity in income in 219 years.[57] In the 1960s there was a growing impatience with any evolutionary process that would have meaning only for unborn generations. The emphasis was on equality now and for the living.

The 1954 Supreme Court decision in *Brown* v. *Topeka Board of Education* had destroyed the legal rationale for the curious doctrine that separate education systems based on skin color or national origins could be equal. The eradication of this as a legal basis for discrimination in education produced a reasonable expectation on the part of black citizens that separation of the races in other areas might also be swept away legislatively as well as judicially. Although most black citizens might have agreed with President Eisenhower and Senator Goldwater that laws alone could not change "the hearts of men" and stop them from being prejudiced, they nevertheless wanted laws and legal protection against discrimination.[58] As Martin Luther King, Jr., pointed out, "While it may be true that morality cannot be legislated, behavior *can* be regulated" and "the habits, if not the hearts," of people could be changed by government and legal action.[59] The battle to change the habits of the citizenry—black and white—brought forth new organizations to challenge the past, and various protest methods, some based on nonviolence and some on new ideas about how power could be redistributed in society, were developed to press the fight for equality.

[57] Morroe Berger, *Equality by Statute* (Garden City, N.Y.: Doubleday & Co., 1967), p. 43.
[58] Anthony Lewis, *The New York Times, Portrait of a Decade* (New York: Random House, 1964), pp. 105–13 and Barry Goldwater, *Where I Stand* (New York: McGraw-Hill Book Co., 1964), p. 39.
[59] Quoted in Berger, *op. cit.*, p. 49.

In 1960 the move toward desegregation entered a new phase as college students, both black and white, began a sit-in campaign to force the desegregation of dining facilities. Beginning on February 1, 1960, when four college students tried to get service at a downtown lunch counter in Greensboro, North Carolina, the movement soon spread to other areas. Meeting with success and perfecting techniques of demonstrating and confronting local authorities from an unassailable moral position, the participants in the sit-ins impressed the nation with their determination in the face of organzed white brutality and violence. Out of the sit-ins came the acceptance of black citizens in some public facilities and a new organization, the Student Non-violent Coordinating Committee (SNCC).[60]

In 1961 the Congress of Racial Equality (CORE) planned for the interracial movement of groups across the South to see if federal rulings requiring the desegregation of interstate travel facilities were being obeyed. Principally composed of students and clergymen, some 300 people in these groups were jailed for participating in freedom rides. In many instances riders were threatened or actually subjected to physical violence.

A. Philip Randolph, a persistent fighter in the cause for racial justice, in 1963 brought to fruition a plan he had proposed two decades earlier, a "March on Washington" to dramatize the Negro's plight. Supported by 10 national organizations, including labor unions and religious groups as well as civil rights organizations, the demonstration for "jobs and freedom" represented the largest public rally ever held in the nation's capital. In addition to exerting pressure on Congress, the peaceful march helped to gain support for civil justice among whites and a commitment from religious bodies.[61]

In 1964 and 1965 Congress passed two civil rights acts. The first was aimed at establishing legal restraints against discrimination in public schools, housing, employment, and areas of economic opportunity. The 1965 act, prompted by the march of some 20,000 people from Selma, Alabama, to that state's capital to dramatize the problems encountered by Negroes registering to vote, took cognizance of the problem. In a message to a joint session of Congress President Lyndon B. Johnson requested and got a bill authorizing federal examiners to intervene in communities in which Negroes were subjected to discriminatory literacy tests or otherwise harassed in attempting to vote in federal elections.[62]

In many respects 1964 was the high-water mark of the civil rights battle

[60] Howard Zinn, SNCC: The New Abolitionists (Boston: Beacon Press, 1964).

[61] Francis E. Kearns, "Marching for Justice," Commonweal, Vol. 78, no. 21 (September 20, 1963), pp. 551–54.

[62] Leslie H. Fishel, Jr., and Benjamin Quarles, eds., The Negro American (New York: William Morrow & Co., 1967), p. 492.

legislatively and the high point of the career of Dr. Martin Luther King, Jr., the apostle of nonviolent action for civil rights. Impatience with the slow rate of economic and social improvement for black citizens and disdain for traditional groups such as the NAACP and the Urban League led Negro leaders such as Stokeley Carmichael of SNCC to advocate far more militant methods to achieve full rights for all citizens. The militant, politically oriented Black Panthers eschewed nonviolence and became the object of police suppression in a number of cities. Influential writers such as LeRoi Jones and Malcolm X disdained the idea of being integrated into what they considered to be a morally bankrupt white society. Impatient with the progress achieved through nonviolence, Jones commented:

> The Negro must take an extreme stance, must attack the white man's system, using his own chains to help beat that system into submission and actual change. The black man is the only revolutionary force in American society today, if only by default. The supposed Christian ideal of Nonviolence is aimed at quieting even these most natural of insurrectionary elements. As an actual moral category all rational men are essentially nonviolent, except in defense of their lives. To ask that the black man not even defend himself . . . is to ask that black man to stay quiet in his chains while the most 'liberal' elements in this country saw away at those chains with make-believe saws. The Negro, again, in this instance, is asked to be what the white man makes of him. Not only does the white man oppress the Negro, but he is even going to tell him how to react under the oppression. Surely, however, the most patiently Christian man must realize that self-defense in any situation is honest and natural. It is also obligatory, otherwise there is no use in asking for any right since the asker will probably not be around to benefit by its granting.[63]

The concept of "black power" that began to replace the ideas of nonviolence sounded ominous to many white ears, and the exclusion of whites from organizations such as SNCC and CORE alienated some whites who had been sympathetic to Negro demands. Although later writers might point out that "such ideas as black power and self-determination, which seem to be heard now for the first time, have deep roots in our national life," events of 1965 and succeeding years began to produce a "white backlash."[64]

The most violent phase of the Negro's quest for social justice began in 1965 in Los Angeles, when Watts erupted. At the end of some five days of rioting 34 persons were dead, almost 4000 were arrested, and approxi-

[63] LeRoi Jones, *Home* (New York: William Morrow & Co., 1966), p. 151.
[64] Paul Jacobs and Saul Landau, "To Serve the Devil," *The Center Magazine*, Vol. 2, no. 2 (March 1969), p. 43.

mately $35 million in damage had been done in the ghetto area.[65] Previous
to Watts—except in the cases of New York and New Jersey, where less
severe and less prolonged rioting had occurred—most of the violence associated with the civil rights controversy had been perpetrated against
the persons of the rights advocates, primarily but not exclusively in the
South. After the disturbance in Watts, however, the succeeding summers
in New York City, Detroit, Cleveland, and other urban centers focused
on property. In some respects the riots represented the desire of ghetto
dwellers to drive white business owners out and to get back at society
for the slow progress in assuring equality of opportunity, especially in
jobs and housing. By 1968 violence in civil rights matters had almost come
to be a feature of what were termed the "long, hot summers." In April
of that year, while attempting to help a group of striking garbage workers in Memphis, Tennessee, Martin Luther King, Jr., was struck down by
James Earl Ray, an ex-convict who had grown up in the culture of poverty. Conscious that rioting within ghettos did more damage to the residents than to those considered to be white oppressors, the civil rights
movement began to develop into a separatist and pro-black phenomenon
which stressed white acceptance of Negro values and culture. The movement for equality progressed out of the slums and into the schools and
universities, where black was proclaimed to be beautiful and militant
youth took action to demand freedom as equals. The outcome of the
changed character of the movement was uncertain; what was certain was
the fact that in the future Negroes and other ethnic groups could not be
ignored as in the past.

White Americans, made aware of the discrepancies between democratic
ideals and social realities in personal testaments such as Claude Brown's
Manchild in the Promised Land [66] and James Baldwin's *Nobody Knows
My Name*,[67] were confronted with disturbing documentation in the Kerner Report. Named after Governor Otto Kerner of Illinois, chairman of
the National Advisory Commission on Civil Disorders, the report, issued
in 1968, described white racism as the underlying cause of the urban riots
of the 1960s. Widely discussed and generally accepted as a reliable com-
pendium of facts, the report on the riots was of questionable value in influencing further congressional action. Recommendations for improving
education, welfare, housing, employment, and so forth made little impact
on political figures concerned with white backlash and reelection.

The dissipation of the direct action–public protest phase of the civil
rights movement was signaled by the "Poor People's Campaign" of 1968.

[65] *Report of the National Advisory Commission on Civil Disorders, op. cit.,* p. 38.
[66] Claude Brown, *Manchild in the Promised Land* (New York: Macmillan Co., 1965).
[67] James Baldwin, *Nobody Knows My Name* (New York: Dial Press, 1961).

Planned initially by Dr. Martin Luther King, Jr. to call attention to the fact that the black and the poor of all races were still awaiting economic justice, the gathering of poor people in "Resurrection City" accomplished little. Housed in tents and shacks on public lands near the Capitol, adverse weather and press reactions together with poor leadership, insufficient funds, and confused goals produced little but apprehension among white Americans.[68] In Congress the demonstration produced even less sympathy. The poor turnout and fear of civil unrest led Congress to be more concerned about law and order than about hunger in the nation or racial injustice.

Despite the numerous contradictions in the civil rights campaign of the 1960s (perhaps they are inevitable in such mass movements), it was apparent that American society had been profoundly altered by what the black journalist Louis Lomax called in his book of that title, *The Negro Revolt*.[69] The Negro had impressed upon society the need for change and the deficiencies of American institutions. Imbued with an increased respect for black culture, black history, and black physical characteristics, Negro citizens began a transformation in outlook that affected not only the way they were viewed by whites but also by themselves. Fighting to overcome psychological scars of long duration, black men increasingly demanded and grudgingly received more equal treatment and increased respect as a race-conscious group. Acting as a goad to the American conscience, black unrest prompted others to question the relevance of social institutions, and many areas of America life were callled into question. The ferment of the black revolution had a meaning and a message that spread far beyond the problem of minority rights.

NATIONAL HOUSING POLICIES IN THE 1960S

During the 1960s the nation began to modify its housing policies and programs in three principal ways. First, and perhaps foremost, the national government established the Department of Housing and Urban Development. Second, housing programs were increasingly designed to consider the wishes of the target population, a reversal of actual practice under the urban renewal concept. Third, private-sector involvement was encouraged in an attempt to improve the quality of government-assisted

[68] "The Abernathy Show," *National Review*, Vol. 20, no. 22 (June 4, 1968), p. 534. See also Robert Terrell, "Poor People Goodbye: The Press Did You In," *Commonweal*, Vol. 88, no. 16, July 12, 1968, pp. 453–454 and "Poor People's Campaign, *New Republic*, Vol. 158, no. 23, June 15, 1968, p. 7.

[69] Louis E. Lomax, *The Negro Revolt* (New York: Harper & Row, 1962).

housing and to gain local community acceptance of federally subvented programs. Part of this involvement resulted from an increased interest in the concept of "new towns" development as a way of decreasing pressure on urban centers.

In 1961, consistent with President Kennedy's wish to provide housing assistance for minority people, the Housing Act gave primary attention to depressed areas development, a part of which was housing. Congressional acceptance of new housing legislation hinged on a desire to stimulate the economy; partly it was due to the disclosure in the 1960 Census of Housing that about 20 percent of renter-occupied housing was unsound.[70] In rural areas in 1960, one-fourth of rural nonfarm families were occupying substandard housing.[71] In the case of both urban and rural dwellers those living below the poverty line were the most severely affected by inadequate shelter.

In accordance with President Kennedy's belief that the urban situation demanded especial attention, he proposed in 1961 and 1962 the creation of a special cabinet post for Urban Affairs. Although Congress recognized the need for increasing attention to housing, clean air, and rapid transit, the expectation that Kennedy would appoint his housing administrator Dr. Robert C. Weaver to head the Department led to its defeat both years. Although Weaver was qualified in every way, he was opposed because of the color of his skin; creation of the proposed cabinet-level office was delayed until 1965. In that year the Department of Housing and Urban Development was set up, and President Johnson appointed Dr. Robert C. Weaver as its head; he was sworn into office in January 1966. The new department had as its responsibility the increasing list of urban ills and the coordination of federal programs that cut across several departmental areas of specialization. Included were such problems as substandard housing, deficient schools, increasing urban welfare caseloads, air and water pollution, insufficient recreational facilities, and a general deterioration of central cities.[72]

In a message to Congress in January 1966 President Johnson described the way in which the Federal Housing Administration and Veterans Administration had previously helped nearly 15 million middle-class citizens become homeowners. At the same time, however, federally subvented

[70] Leon H. Keyserling, ed., *Progress or Poverty, Conference on Economic Progress* (Washington, D.C.: Conference on Economic Progress, 1964), p. 127.

[71] U.S. Department of Housing and Urban Development, *Hearings Before the National Advisory Commission on Rural Poverty*, Testimony of Robert C. Weaver, Secretary, HUD (Washington, D.C.: Government Printing Office, 1967), p. 290.

[72] Dwight A. Ink, "The Department of Housing and Urban Development—Building a New Federal Department," *Law and Contemporary Problems*, Vol. 32, no. 3 (Summer 1967), pp. 375–84.

programs had provided housing for only 605,000 families from decayed and unsanitary dwellings, and all but 300,000 dwelling units had been constructed under urban renewal.[73] Commenting on the failure to provide housing for the poor and the way in which federal programs actually promoted the decay of central cities, Michael Harrington remarked:

> The well-to-do have generally fled to the suburbs, and enforced zoning and housing codes will exclude the typical public housing units from their retreats. Within the central city, public housing has had to compete for land with profitable slums and office buildings. The result has been the segregation of the poor in impersonal steel and concrete warrens or in the suppurating units of the ancient neighborhoods.[74]

In the Housing Act of 1966 Congress took steps to try to correct some of the problems that had arisen under prior legislation. Noteworthy among these were the fact that approximately 75 percent of the people displaced by urban renewal were black. The improvement of the physical appearance of cities had often been accompanied by severe relocation problems for the poor, especially the minority poor. Furthermore the destruction of neighborhoods had added to the sense of alienation from society of the lower class family; government had become the vehicle of oppression in the eyes of some. The building of luxury apartments in redeveloped areas led to the comment that American housing policies had produced "socialism for the rich and free enterprise for the poor."

The Demonstration Cities and Metropolitan Development Act of 1966 gave impetus to low-income groups to rehabilitate and conserve their homes rather than to remove to housing developments. Requiring local planning and coordination, the idea of "Model Cities" is the rehabilitation through planning of neighborhoods to include education, health, and recreation facilities as well as housing. Under the "turnkey" program initiated in 1966, the federal government embarked on a course intended to turn a part of the responsibility for public housing over to private developers. Housing authorities on a local level, with the concurrence of federal officials, contract with private developers for the construction of housing, which is turned over at its completion to the housing authority. In line with the trend toward less large-scale development and more local involvement, the federal government had in 1965 instituted a program of rent supplements. Under this scheme, first funded in 1966, housing is

[73] U.S. Congress, House, *Message from the President to the Congress, Transmitting Recommendations for City Demonstration Programs, January 26, 1966*, H.R. Doc. No. 368, 89th Cong., 2d sess., 1966.
[74] Michael Harrington, *The Accidental Century* (New York: Macmillan Co., 1965), pp. 287–88.

leased by housing authorities, and then rented to low-income families. The difference between the amount of the lease and the amount paid by the renter is paid by the housing authority. The benefit of such a program is that low-income persons can be dispersed throughout a community rather than isolated in a development. The latter, frequently poorly planned and the scene of abuse of individual privacy, are no longer considered the panacea for inadequate housing.

Under the Housing Act of 1968, reliance on the private sector increased significantly as the government sought to provide over a 10-year period, over 6 million new dwellings for the economically disadvantaged. Although it was unlikely that Congress would appropriate the sums needed to accomplish the aims of the Act, two new programs were introduced in the legislation. One was the provision of incentives to corporations in the building of new cities and involvement in extant urban centers alike. The second was the granting of an interest subsidy to private lenders for the provision of loans to prospective homeowners in the next to the lowest income groups.[75]

In the improvements in housing legislation, the movement was toward the rehabilitation of housing, preservation of neighborhoods, and involvement of local resources in a holistic approach to community planning. The question that remained was whether the commitment to eliminate poor housing would survive new political forces and realignments. None could deny that a need for improved housing existed or that housing could be an important economic force in America. There was disagreement about whether small programs such as Model Cities offered any real hope for the future in our massively blighted urban centers.

LAW AND THE SOCIAL ORDER

The Supreme Court decision in Brown v. Board of Education crystallized for the Negro the possibility of an improved society that could be changed by recourse to the law and through legislative enactments. Other actions by the Supreme Court during the 1960s were very nearly as revolutionary as that 1954 decision.

Throughout the 1960s the Supreme Court and its Chief Justice, Earl Warren, were the center of bitter controversy over decisions dealing with civil rights and civil liberties.[76] A public that had generally considered

[75] Walter F. Wagner, Jr., "The Housing Act: We Know What it Says, But What Does It Mean?" Architectural Record, Vol. 144, no. 4 (October 1968), p. 8.

[76] President Kennedy defined civil rights as "those claims which the citizen has to the affirmative assistance of government. In an age which insistently and properly demands that government secure the weak from needless dread and needless misery, the

Supreme Court decisions to be based on a discovery of natural law rather than a reinterpretation of the Constitution to fit the needs of the times was frequently outraged at some libertarian judgments. Cases such as *Engel v. Vitale* (1962) and *School District of Abington* v. *Schempp* (1963), which ruled against prayers and Bible reading in the public schools, created a storm of editorial and public protest.[77] Perhaps equally disquieting to politicians was the 1962 decision in the case of *Baker* v. *Carr*. In this instance the constitutionality of state elections based on clearly unequal representation of rural and urban areas was at issue. The refusal of the state of Tennessee to reapportion seats in both Houses of the General Assembly decennially as required by the state Constitution led to the decision that became known as the "one man—one vote" judgment.[78]

Some of the most disturbing judgments centered around criminal procedure, as the Bill of Rights was increasingly applied to state courts and amplified in federal jurisdictions. The resentment of some police officials and the generally hostile public reception to the Court's guarantee of due process to those accused of criminal behavior led to the pre-eminence of the issue of "law and order" in the 1968 presidential contest. Presidential task force reports showing an ever-increasing rate of juvenile and adult crime, which, coupled with the numerous outbreaks of urban riots and unrest, led to the feeling that the Court was shackling law-enforcement rather than protecting the rights of citizens.[79]

The first of the landmark cases, *Gideon* v. *Wainright* (1963), reversed the historical reluctance of the Court to apply criminal law guarantees of the Bill of Rights to the states.[80] Clarence Gideon had been convicted in Florida of breaking and entering a poolroom and was sentenced to five years in prison. Denied the right to counsel, Gideon sent to the

---

catalog of civil rights is never closed." Civil liberties he described as "an individual's immunity from governmental oppression. . . . The Bill of Rights, in the eyes of its framers, was a catalog of immunities, not a schedule of claims." Quoted in Edward Bennett Williams, *One Man's Freedom* (New York: Atheneum, 1962), p. 299.

[77] G. Theodore Mitau, *Decade of Decision* (New York: Charles Scribner's Sons, 1967), pp. 119-50.

[78] Wallace Mendelson, *The Supreme Court: Law and Discretion* (New York: Bobbs-Merrill Co., 1967), pp. 264-91.

[79] *Juvenile Delinquency and Youth Crime*, Task Force on Juvenile Delinquency, The President's Commission on Law Enforcement and Administration of Justice (Washington, D.C.: Government Printing Office, 1967). Also, *The Challenge of Crime in a Free Society*, Report by the President's Commission on Law Enforcement and Administration of Justice (Washington, D.C.: Government Printing Office, 1967). According to the Department of Justice Uniform Crime Reports, between 1960 and 1965 crimes of violence increased three times, and crimes against property, 36 percent per 100,000 people. Population during that time increased only 8 percent.

[80] *Gideon* v. *Wainwright*, 372 U.S. 792-801 (1963).

Supreme Court a handwritten petition asking for a review of his case under the Supreme Court's rules allowing such a procedure in *in forma pauperis* cases.[81] In a unanimous decision the Court reversed Gideon's conviction; Justice Hugo L. Black, writing the opinion, observed:

> Reason and reflection require us to recognize that in our adversary system of criminal justice, any person haled into court, who is too poor to hire a lawyer, cannot be assured a fair trial unless counsel is provided for him. This seems to us to be an obvious truth. Governments, both state and federal, quite properly spend vast sums of money to establish machinery to try defendants accused of crime. Lawyers to prosecute are everywhere deemed essential to protect the public's interest in an orderly society. Similarly, there are few defendants charged with crime, few indeed, who fail to hire the best lawyers they can get to prepare and present their defenses. That government hires lawyers to prosecute and defendants who have the money hire lawyers to defend are the strongest indications of the widespread belief that lawyers in criminal courts are necessities, not luxuries. The right of one charged with crime to counsel may not be deemed fundamental and essential to fair trials in some countries, but it is in ours.[82]

The Gideon decision, extending constitutional guarantees to include a right to counsel, in state court criminal proceedings was followed up by the case of *Escobedo* v. *State of Illinois* (1964). This reversed a conviction because an attorney had not been permitted to consult with his client, who was being interrogated by police.[83] Danny Escobedo, arrested on suspicion of shooting his brother-in-law in Chicago, had confessed to knowledge of the killing; the point at which a counsel's assistance became essential was at issue. In ruling in favor of Escobedo the Supreme Court established that the accused person must be warned of his rights as soon as the process shifted from the investigatory to the accusatory stage and that the right to counsel in criminal proceedings extended to the process of interrogation and not merely defense.[84]

In 1966 in the case of *Miranda* v. *State of Arizona* the Supreme Court again extended the right to counsel and the protections under the Fifth and Sixth Amendments to include the right of suspects to remain silent as well as to be protected during interrogations.[85] Ernesto Miranda, arrested for kidnapping and rape, had been identified by the victim and confessed to the crime. Without having been advised of his rights to coun-

[81] Anthony Lewis, *Gideon's Trumpet* (New York: Random House, a Vintage Book, 1964), p. 4.
[82] *Ibid.*, p. 189.
[83] *Escobedo* v. *State of Illinois*, 378 U.S. 1758–69 (1964).
[84] "The Supreme Court, 1963 Term," *Harvard Law Review*, Vol. 78, no. 1 (November 1964), pp. 217–23.
[85] *Miranda* v. *State of Arizona*, 384 U.S. 1602–65 (1966).

sel and his right to remain silent, Miranda was found guilty and the conviction was upheld by the Arizona Supreme Court. The finding of the U.S. Supreme Court in favor of Miranda required that, from the outset of interrogation, the defendant has an absolute right to counsel. Furthermore, the defendant must be apprised of his right to remain silent, and admissions of guilt might be inadmissable as evidence unless the prosecution could demonstrate that adequate procedural safeguards had been employed to protect the accused.[86]

Of perhaps even more significance for social workers was the 1967 decision that overturned lower court findings in *Application of Gault*.[87] In 1964 Gerald Francis Gault and a friend were taken into custody by the sheriff on the complaint of a neighbor about lewd and indecent phone calls. Gerald's parents had both been at work and were not notified that their son had been taken to the Children's Detention Home. At a subsequent court hearing in the matter, Gerald was at the age of 15, committed to the State Industrial School for a possible period of detention that could extend to age 21, this despite the fact that he denied making the calls, had never confronted his accuser, and had been denied legal counsel. Acting under the doctrine of *parens patriae*, the Supreme Court of Arizona held that the state did not deprive the child of rights but gave him protection by taking custody through civil rather than criminal proceedings. In reversing the decision, the U.S. Supreme Court affirmed that minors should enjoy the same protections of the Constitution that citizens over 21 have traditionallly enjoyed.

Although the outcry against the Supreme Court produced several nearly successful movements to amend the Constitution to nullify Court decisions, by the end of the decade the Court was still engaged in forcing readjustments in many social institutions. Holding against practices ranging from wiretapping to obtain criminal convictions to conditions of eligibility for welfare, the Court took cognizance of sociological information with a vengeance. Sensitive as ever to public criticism of its actions, and especially to complaints of some members of the legal profession that the Court had failed to explain and justify its actions, change in the future is to be expected.[88]

The resignation of Justice Abe Fortas and of Chief Justice Earl Warren as well as the age and health of other members provided Nixon the opportunity to name Warren E. Burger as new Chief Justice and several

[86] "The Supreme Court, 1965 Term," *Harvard Law Review*, Vol. 80 no. 1 (November 1966), pp. 208–13.
[87] *Application of Gault*, 387 U.S. 1428–72 (1967).
[88] Robert H. Bork, "The Supreme Court Needs a New Philosophy," *Fortune*, Vol. 78, no. 7 (December 1968), pp. 138–41, 167–70, 174, and 177–78.

new justices during his term in office. This gives further support to the idea that the Supreme Court will become relatively more conservative in the future despite the Senate's refusal to confirm Clement Haynsworth or G. Harrold Carswell to the bench.

Summary

Problems associated with human rights and poverty consumed much of the energy of individuals concerned with social reform during the 1960s. Poverty, defined early in the decade as an income of less than $3000 for a nonfarm family of 4 and half that amount for a single individual, declined.[89] The Census Bureau in 1970 reported that between 1959 and 1969 the number of poor people had decreased from 39.5 million to 25.4 million. The threshold of poverty had, in the intervening years, moved from $3000 to $3553. During these years the number living in poverty in metropolitan areas increased from 44 percent to 51 percent; there was a 42 percent drop in the number of white families below the poverty level while the decline for black families was but 27 percent. The high incidence of poverty among black citizens, half of whom were living in families headed by women, was also apt to be more severe poverty than that of whites. Incomes of white poor families averaged $900 below the poverty line in 1968; the average deficit was $1250 for black poor people.[90]

Politics during the decade were marked by an increasing sense of the importance of technology in rational decision-making, although there were indications that both a reinvigorated Left and Right were emerging. Assassination of important political and moral leaders was one of the uglier features of the decade and contributed much to the sense of alienation from social processes on the part of youth. Extreme movements such as the Hippies and the Yippies, concerned either with withdrawal from society and rejection of its values or revolution, became the style for some youth. A renascent conservatism collided with a revived radicalism. Liberalism was accused of "maintaining economic growth through arms spending, of containing revolution through a series of limited police actions, and of buying off domestic discontent by building superhighways and cars."[91] By the end of the decade political liberalism was in a state of genuine disarray.

[89] David Hamilton, *A Primer on the Economics of Poverty* (New York: Random House, 1968), p. 29.

[90] "Poverty Declined in 1960s But Millions Remain Poor," *Sacramento Bee* (Sacramento, California), January 10, 1970, pp. 1 and 16.

[91] Christopher Lasch, "Where Do We Go From Here?," *New York Review of Books*, Vol. 11, no. 6 (October 10, 1968), p. 4.

National policies in social welfare programs were more distinguished for change as a reaction to legal decisions than for revolutionary change resulting from legislative actions. The field of correctional services, especially juvenile probation, was challenged for practices related historically to the idea of protecting a child from criminal proceedings. Local efforts to involve indigenous groups in planning had a counterpart in such things as community treatment of mental illness and a de-emphasis on institutionalization for groups such as the mentally retarded.

Social work, like other professions, was stimulated and reinvigorated by new programs and new methods designed to help people out of poverty. Internally, many agencies were forced to make adjustments to the increased militancy of clients and the new configurations among workers in the agencies themselves. A revival of unionism led to strikes among public employees in New York City, Chicago, Sacramento, and other cities. Workers in many public agencies worked after hours with community groups and gave support to welfare rights organizations. In some instances, legal cases resulted from workers' refusals to engage in activities violating professional ethics and the constitutional rights of clients. Noteworthy in this respect was the case of *Parrish* v. *Civil Service Commission of County of Alameda*. In early 1963 the social workers in the Alameda County, California, public welfare agency were ordered to take part in early Sunday morning calls on recipients to determine whether "unauthorized males" were present. Bennie Max Parrish refused to participate because he felt it would violate the dignity and constitutional rights of his clients. He was discharged but brought suit, which in 1967 resulted in his reinstatement with back pay dating from 1963.[92]

On the federal level the government's focus in poverty problems was more and more on education than on welfare programs and measures. Education and rehabilitation emerged as the primary weapons (for the time being) for elimination of want. Voter resistance to increased taxes and expenditures for military needs threatened even the modest improvements of the 1960s. In addition technology became a threat to, among other things, job stability and traditional ideas about work.

Perhaps the most momentous occurrences of the decade were those connected with attitudes. Assumptions about the inevitability of progress were changed significantly, and major revisions in attitude were made necessary as virtually every idea that Americans cherished was challenged for its validity and utility. Rooted in the decade were some problems and some changes that were, perhaps, even more significant for the future than for the present. It is to these that we now turn.

[92] *West's California Reporter*, Vol. 57 (St. Paul: West Publishing Co., 1967), pp. 623–34.

Selected Bibliography

Abell, Aaron I., ed. *American Catholic Thought on Social Questions.* New York: Bobbs-Merrill Co., Inc., 1968.

"The Abernathy Show." *National Review,* Vol. 20, no. 22 (June 4, 1968), p. 534.

"All Power to the Soviets!" *National Review,* Vol. 17, no. 24 (June 15, 1965), pp. 492–94.

Application of Gault, 387 U.S. (1967).

Ashmore, Harry S. *The Man in the Middle.* Columbia: University of Missouri Press, 1966.

Baldwin, James. *Nobody Knows My Name.* New York: Dial Press, 1961.

Bazelon, David T. *Power in America.* New York: New American Library, 1967.

Bell, Winifred. *Aid to Dependent Children.* New York: Columbia University Press, 1965.

Berger, Morroe. *Equality by Statute.* Garden City, N.Y.: Doubleday & Co., 1967.

Bork, Robert H. "The Supreme Court Needs a New Philosophy." *Fortune,* Vol. 78, no. 7 (December 1968), pp. 138–41, 167–70, 174, 177–78.

Brown, Claude. *Manchild in the Promised Land.* New York: Macmillan Co., 1965.

Burns, Eveline M. "What's Wrong with Public Welfare?" *Social Service Review,* Vol. 36, no. 2 (June 1962), pp. 111–12.

Canterbury, E. Ray. *Economics on a New Frontier.* Belmont, Calif.: Wadsworth Publishing Co., 1968.

Caudill, Harry M. *Night Comes to the Cumberlands.* Boston: Little, Brown & Co., 1962.

The Challenge of Crime in a Free Society. A Report by the President's Commission on Law Enforcement and Administration of Justice. Washington, D.C.: Government Printing Office, 1967.

Cox, Harvey G. "The 'New Breed' in American Churches." *Daedalus,* Vol. 96, no. 1 (Winter 1967), pp. 135–150.

Cox, Harvey G. *The Secular City.* New York: Macmillan Co., 1967.

Culbertson, John M. *Macroeconomic Theory and Stabilization Policy.* New York: McGraw-Hill Book Co., 1968.

Donald, Aida Dipace, ed. *John F. Kennedy and the New Frontier.* New York: Hill & Wang, 1966.

Doverman, Max. "Today's Legal Revolution." *Social Service Review,* Vol. 40, no. 2 (June 1966), pp. 152–68.

Escobedo v. State of Illinois, 378 U.S. (1964).

Everett, Robinson O., ed. *Anti-Poverty Programs.* Dobbs Ferry, N.Y.: Oceana Publications, 1966.

Farm Labor Organizing 1905–1967. New York: National Advisory Committee on Farm Labor, 1967.

Filler, Louis, ed. *The President Speaks: From William McKinley to Lyndon B. Johnson*. New York: G. P. Putnam's Sons, 1964.

Fishel, Leslie H., Jr., and Quarles, Benjamin, eds. *The Negro American*. New York: William Morrow & Co., 1967.

Editors of *Fortune. Markets of the Sixties*. New York: Harper & Bros., 1960.

Freidel, Frank, and Pollack, Norman, eds. *American Issues in the Twentieth Century*. Chicago: Rand McNally & Co., 1966.

Fried, Charles. "Privacy." *Yale Law Journal*, Vol. 77, no. 3 (January 1968), pp. 475–93.

Friedman, Leon, ed. *The Civil Rights Reader*. New York: Walker & Co., 1968.

Fuller, Helen. *Year of Trial*. New York: Harcourt, Brace & World, 1962.

Gabriel, Ralph H. *The Course of American Democratic Thought*. New York: Ronald Press, 1956.

Gideon v. Wainwright, 372 U.S. (1963).

Gleeson, Patrick, ed. *America, Changing. . . .* Columbus, Ohio: Charles E. Merrill Publishing Co., 1968.

Goals for Americans. The Report of the President's Commission on National Goals. New York: Prentice-Hall, 1960.

Golden, Joseph. "Desegregation of Social Agencies in the South." *Social Work*, Vol. 10, no. 1 (January 1968), pp. 58–67.

Goldwater, Barry. *Where I Stand*. New York: McGraw-Hill Book Co., 1964.

Goldwin, Robert A., ed. *A Nation of Cities: Essays on America's Urban Problems*. Chicago: Rand McNally & Co., 1968.

Greenleaf, William, ed. *American Economic Growth Since 1860*. Columbia, S.C.: University of South Carolina Press, 1968.

Gross, Bertram M. *A Great Society?* New York: Basic Books, 1968.

Haber, William, and Murray, Merrill G. *Unemployment Insurance in the American Economy*. Homewood, Ill.: Richard D. Irwin, 1966.

Hamilton, David. *A Primer on the Economics of Poverty*. New York: Random House, 1968.

Hamilton, Gordon. "Editor's Page." *Social Work*, Vol. 7, no. 1 (January 1962), pp. 2 and 128.

Harrington, Michael. *The Accidental Century*. New York: Macmillan Co., 1965.

Harrington, Michael. *The Other America*. New York: Macmillan Co., 1962.

Heller, Walter W. *Perspectives on Economic Growth*. New York: Random House, 1968.

Hencke, Paul. "Is War on Poverty Becoming War on Business?" *Nation's Business*, Vol. 54, no. 3 (March 1966), pp. 41 and 58–61.

Hook, Sidney. " 'Welfare State'—A Debate That Isn't." *New York Times Magazine*, November 27, 1960, pp. 27 and 118–19.

Hughes, Emmet John. *The Ordeal of Power: A Political Memoir of the Eisenhower Years*. New York: Atheneum, 1963.

Ink, Dwight A. "The Department of Housing and Urban Development—Building a New Federal Department." *Law and Contemporary Problems*, Vol. 32, no. 3 (Summer 1967), pp. 375–84.

Jacobs, Paul, and Landau, Saul. *The New Radicals*. New York: Random House, a Vintage Book, 1966.
Jacobs, Paul, and Landau, Saul. "To Serve the Devil." *The Center Magazine*, Vol. 2, no. 2 (March 1969).
Jencks, Christopher, and Riesman, David. *The Academic Revolution*. Garden City, N.Y.: Doubleday & Co., 1968.
Jones, LeRoi. *Home*. New York: William Morrow & Co., 1966.
Juvenile Delinquency and Youth Crime. Task Force on Juvenile Delinquency, The President's Commission on Law Enforcement and Administration of Justice. Washington, D.C.: Government Printing Office, 1967.
Kearns, Francis E. "Marching for Justice." *Commonweal*, Vol. 78, no. 21 (September 20, 1963), pp. 551–54.
Keyserling, Leon H., ed. *Progress or Poverty, Conference on Economic Progress*. Washington, D.C.: Conference on Economic Progress, 1964.
King v. Smith, 392 U.S. (1968).
Krislov, Samuel. *The Supreme Court and Political Freedom*. New York: Free Press, 1968.
Lane, Robert E. "The Decline of Politics and Ideology in a Knowledgeable Society." *American Sociological Review*, Vol. 31, no. 5 (October 1966), pp. 649–62.
Lasch, Christopher. "Where Do We Go From Here?" *New York Review of Books*, Vol. 11, no. 6 (October 10, 1968), pp. 4–5.
Lasky, Victor. *J.F.K.: The Man and the Myth*. New York: Macmillan Co., 1963.
Lekachman, Robert. *The Age of Keynes*. New York: Random House, 1966.
Levitan, Sar A. *The Design of Federal Antipoverty Strategy*. Policy Papers in Human Resources and Industrial Relations, No. 1. Detroit: Wayne State University, 1967.
Lewis, Anthony. *Gideon's Trumpet*. New York: Vintage Books, 1964.
Lewis, Anthony. *The New York Times, Portrait of a Decade*. New York: Random House, 1964.
Lomax, Louis E. *The Negro Revolt*. New York: Harper & Row, 1962.
McLuhan, Marshall, and Fiore, Quentin. *War and Peace in the Global Village*. New York: Bantam Books, 1968.
Marris, Peter and Rein, Martin. *Dilemmas of Social Reform*. New York: Atherton Press, 1967.
May, Edgar. *The Wasted Americans*. New York: Harper & Row, 1964.
Menashe, Louis, and Radosh, Ronald, eds. *Teach-ins: U.S.A.* New York: Frederick A. Praeger, 1967.
Mendelson, Wallace. *The Supreme Court: Law and Discretion*. New York: Bobbs-Merrill Co., 1967.
"Message From the President of the United States," *Congressional Record*, Part I, Vol. 89 January 6, 1943 to April 5, 1943. (Washington, D.C.: Government Printing Office, 1943), pp. 1792–93.
"Message From the President of the United States," *Congressional Record*, Vol. 107, Part I, January 30, 1961 to February 24, 1961. Washington, D.C.: Government Printing Office, 1961, pp. 1677–81.

Miller, Herman P. *Poverty American Style.* Belmont, Calif.: Wadsworth Publishing Co., 1966.

Miranda v. State of Arizona, 384 U.S. (1966).

Mitau, Theodore G. *Decade of Decision.* New York: Charles Scribner's Sons, 1967.

Mitford, Jessica. *The American Way of Death.* New York: Simon & Schuster, 1963.

Moynihan, Daniel P. "Improving Social Welfare, The Bankrupt Welfare System." *Current,* No. 94 (April 1968), pp. 40–51.

Moynihan, Daniel P. *Maximum Feasible Misunderstanding.* New York: The Free Press, 1969.

Myrdal, Gunnar. *Challenge to Affluence.* New York: Vintage Books, 1965.

Newfield, Jack. *A Prophetic Minority.* New York: New American Library, 1966.

Paull, Joseph E. "Recipients Aroused: The New Welfare Rights Movement." *Social Work,* Vol. 12, no. 2 (April 1967), pp. 101–6.

"Poor People's Campaign." *New Republic,* Vol. 158, no. 23 (June 15, 1968), p. 7.

Porter, Sylvia. "The Jobless—II: Untrained Youth." *New York Post,* January 24, 1961.

"Poverty Declined in 1960s But Millions Remain Poor," *Sacramento Bee* (Sacramento, California), January 10, 1970, pp. 1 and 16.

"Poverty—Fading Problem in U.S." *U.S. News & World Report,* Vol. 65, no. 14 (September 30, 1968), pp. 62–63.

Poverty Law Reporter. New York: Commerce Clearing House, 1968.

"Privacy and Efficient Government." *Harvard Law Review,* Vol. 82, no. 2 (December 1968), pp. 400–417.

"Presidential Message to Congress," *Congressional Quarterly,* Vol. 19, Part I, February 24, 1961. Washington, D.C.: Congressional Quarterly, Inc., 1961, pp. 307–21.

Prospect for America. The Rockefeller Panel Reports. Garden City, N.Y.: Doubleday & Co., 1961.

Rand, Ayn. *Capitalism: The Unknown Ideal.* New York: New American Library, 1966.

Report to the National Advisory Commission on Civil Disorders. New York: Bantam Books, 1968.

Salinger, Pierre. *With Kennedy.* Garden City, N.Y.: Doubleday & Co., 1966.

Schlesinger, Arthur M., Jr. *A Thousand Days.* Boston: Houghton Mifflin Co., 1965.

Shapiro v. Thompson, 89 U.S. (1969).

Silberman, Charles E. *Crisis in Black and White.* New York: Random House, 1964.

Simon, Arthur R. *Faces of Poverty.* St. Louis: Concordia Publishing House, 1966.

Smith, Russell E. "In Defense of Public Welfare." *Social Work,* Vol. 11, no. 4 (October 1966), pp. 90–97.

Sorensen, Theodore C. *Kennedy.* New York: Harper & Row, 1965.

Steiner, Gilbert Y. *Social Insecurity*. Chicago: Rand McNally & Co., 1966.
Sundquist, James L., ed. *On Fighting Poverty*. New York: Basic Books, Inc., 1969.
"The Supreme Court, 1963 Term," *Harvard Law Review*, Vol. 78, no. 1 (November 1964), pp. 179–312.
"The Supreme Court, 1965 Term," *Harvard Law Review*, Vol. 80, no. 1 (November 1966), pp. 125–272.
Terrell, Robert. "Poor People Goodbye: The Press Did You In." *Commonweal*, Vol. 88, no. 16 (July 12, 1968), pp. 453–54.
The U.S. Book of Facts, Statistics & Information. New York: Essandess Special Edition, 1967.
U.S. Commission on Civil Rights. "*Title VI ... One Year After*." Washington, D.C.: Government Printing Office, 1966. (Pamphlet).
U.S. Congress. House. *Message from the President to the Congress, Transmitting Recommendations for City Demonstration Programs, January 26, 1966*. H. R. Doc. No. 368, 89th Cong., 2d sess., 1966.
U.S. Congress. Senate. *Mental Retardation Facilities and Community Mental Health Act of 1963*. Pub. L. 88–164, 88th Cong., 1st sess., S. 1576. 1963.
U.S. Congress. Senate. *The War on Poverty, The Economic Opportunity Act of 1964*. Pub. L. 88–452, 88th Cong., 2d sess., S. 2642. 1964.
U.S. Department of Health, Education, and Welfare. *Education and Training, Third Annual Report of the Secretary of Health, Education, and Welfare to the Congress on Training Activities Under the Manpower Development and Training Act*. Washington, D.C.: Government Printing Office, 1965.
U.S. Department of Health, Education, and Welfare. *Education and Training, Sixth Annual Report to the Department of Health, Education, and Welfare to the Congress on Training Activities Under the Manpower Development and Training Act*. Washington, D.C.: Government Printing Office, 1968.
U.S. Department of Housing and Urban Development. *Hearings Before the National Advisory Commission on Rural Poverty*. Testimony of Robert C. Weaver, Secretary, HUD. Washington, D.C.: Government Printing Office, 1967.
U.S. General Services Administration. *United States Government Organization Manual 1968–69*. Washington, D.C.: Government Printing Office, 1968.
U.S. President. *Economic Report of the President*. Washington, D.C.: Government Printing Office, 1967.
Wagner, Walter F., Jr. "The Housing Act: We Know What it Says, But What Does it Mean?" *Architectural Record*, Vol. 144, no. 4 (October 1968), p. 8.
West's California Reporter, Vol. 57. St. Paul: West Publishing Co., 1967, pp. 623–34.
Wicker, Tom. *JFK and LBJ*. New York: William Morrow & Co., 1968.
Williams, Edward Bennett. *One Man's Freedom*. New York: Atheneum, 1962.

Winter, Gibson. *The Suburban Captivity of the Churches.* Garden City, N.Y.: Doubleday & Co., 1961.
Zimmerman, Stanley, ed. *Housing for the Poor: Rights and Remedies.* New York: Project on Social Welfare Law, New York University School of Law, 1967.
Zinn, Howard. *SNCC: The New Abolitionists.* Boston: Beacon Press, 1964.

Chapter Six

American Social Welfare Institutions:
Prospects for the Future

CONCERN ABOUT THE FUTURE has been a continuing theme in the history of mankind. Making projections about the future of social institutions has been a literary genre in the Western world, and Sir Thomas More's *Utopia*, published in 1516, gave us not only a word but a structure that was to be followed by later writers. Dissatisfied with their contemporary social systems, such writers as Edward Bellamy in the 1880s sought to describe an ideal society to replace the harsh realities of a changing social order. More recent writings, for example George Orwell's *1984*, have centered more on the threat to personal liberties that a technologically sophisticated future might pose rather than the rational reorganizing of the social and economic system. In either case the novels and treatises of the past have been typically polemics or prescriptions, subjective in nature, and of limited use in planning for the future.

In the 1960s the study of the future assumed a somewhat different character as the result of increasingly sophisticated technologies and increased awareness that present planning would help to determine the shape of tomorrow's social institutions. Daniel Bell, chairman if the Commission on the Year 2000 of the American Academy of Arts and Sciences, has described the changes that have taken place in the nature of studies now being made and the reason for being concerned about the future.

> Every society today is consciously committed to economic growth, to raising the standard of living of its people, and therefore to the planning, direction, and control of social change. What makes the present studies, therefore, so completely different from those of the past is that they are oriented to specific social-policy purposes; and along with this new dimension, they are fashioned, self-consciously, by a new methodology that gives the promise of providing a more reliable foundation for realistic alternatives and choices, if not for exact prediction.[1]

In addition to the scholarly study of the future, other institutions of society in the 1960s evidenced a profound interest in the years ahead. At the White House the Office of Science and Technology was created, and a new documentary form—the technical report—became an important tool in assessing future production needs. One such report, dealing with future requirements in the textile industry, predicted for the 1970s an increased use of machinery and man-made fibers, with high rates of unemployment and a need for retraining workers to provide them with new skills.[2] Apart from governmental concern about the future, companies such as General Electric commissioned independent studies in order to make decisions about future markets for products and the social environ-

---

[1] Herman Kahn and Anthony J. Wiener, *The Year 2000* (New York: Macmillan Co., 1967), p. xxv.

[2] U.S. Department of Labor, *Technology and Manpower in the Textile Industry of the 1970's* (Washington, D.C.: Government Printing Office, 1968), p. 3.

185

ment that would have an influence on consumption patterns.[3] Society, which was in part transformed by what Marshall McLuhan described as the "message" of television, was further informed of the continuing change process by the same medium. The National Broadcasting Company, in a 2½-hour documentary, described the possible avenues and areas of change that might occur "From Here to the Seventies."

Organizations customarily identified with defense needs, such as the RAND Corporation, developed studies and made recommendations for planned change.[4] At the Center for the Study of Democratic Institutions in Santa Barbara, California (a "think tank" like the RAND Corporation) scholars examined proposals ranging from ways to improve the public school system to schemes for rewriting the Constitution to accommodate and control technology. Ad hoc groups also came into being to calll attention to possible problems of the future. One group, the Ad Hoc Committee on the Triple Revolution, outlined three separate but mutually reinforcing revolutions they felt were taking place with grave implications for the future: a weaponry revolution, a human rights revolution, and a cybernation revolution. The latter was defined as follows:

A new era of production has begun. Its principles of organization are as different from those of the industrial era were different from the agricultural. The cybernation revolution has been brought about by the combination of the computer and the automated self-regulating machine. This results in a system of almost unlimited productive capacity which requires progressively less human labor. Cybernation is already reorganizing the economic and social system to meet its own needs.[5]

Within the social work profession a number of new plans for restructuring social services were advanced and alternate methods of income maintenance debated. One of the most heated debates of the decade took place between advocates of children's allowances and supporters of the guaranteed annual income. Increasingly, the two schemes were being actually tried out or planned for experimentation under the auspices of the federal government. At the same time a number of proposals were made for the improvement of the extant public welfare system. In part this was required by changes in the Social Security Act or by administrative decisions of the Department of Health, Education, and Welfare. Such

---

[3] "Our Future Business Environment," A Progress Report on a Continuing General Electric Study of Informed Opinion Outside the Company on Social, Political and Economic Trends of the Next Decade (New York: General Electric, April 1968).

[4] Richard R. Nelson, Merton J. Peck, and Edward D. Kalachek, *Technology, Economic Growth and Public Policy* (Washington, D.C.: Brookings Institution, 1967).

[5] "The Triple Revolution," Ad Hoc Committee on The Triple Revolution (Santa Barbara, Calif., 1964).

was the mandatory separation of income maintenance from the provision of social services, which may well be the precursor of an automated system of income maintenance and community social services.

At least a part of the desire for more equality in income maintenance resulted from Supreme Court decisions such as the one throwing out residence requirements in federally subvented categories of aid. The fact that states such as New York, Wisconsin, and California had far higher standards of assistance than states such as Mississippi and Georgia caused fears that no residence requirements would lead to an acceleration of the exodus from the South. Although informed opinion held that the yearly migration of 100,000 people to the North was more the result of technological displacements in southern agriculture, discrimination, and other factors and that people rarely moved for higher welfare benefits, the fear persisted.[6] Although some families or individuals might possibly move to get higher grants, it was doubtful that the number would justify the political capital some politicians, notably Governor Ronald Reagan of California, tried to make of it. Others, such as Governor Nelson Rockefeller of New York, believed the solution to the problem of unequal grants lay in a federally mandated level of assistance; some urged full assumption of costs by the federal government.

Criticism of the profession and the delivery of services forced social workers and the schools of social work to seek ways of becoming more relevant (to use one of the more crashing cliches of the period) to the technological society. Pressure from student groups served as a catalyst throughout society; in social work schools and in agencies new student-institutional relationships emerged.[7] An increased interest in how to influence policy-making and to participate in its creation, coupled with a renewed interest in the democratic organizing of communities for genuine self-help led to a questioning of the idea of social work as a generic discipline. With an eye to the future, schools of social work and the accrediting body, the Council on Social Work Eduction, began to critically explore the necessity for developing programs to provide for the demands for more sophisticated levels of expertise. Throughout the profession the dichotomy between individual therapists and social interventionists deepened. The trained nonprofessional developed as a new factor in the delivery of social services, while undergraduate programs began to receive increased attention as an entry level to professional practice. For the future, even more than in the past, it appeared true that

[6] Roger Beardwood, "The Southern Roots of Urban Crisis," *Fortune*, Vol. 78, no. 2 (August 1968), p. 81.
[7] David Wineman and Adrienne James, "The Advocacy Challenge to Schools of Social Work," *Social Work*, Vol. 14, no. 2 (April 1969), pp. 23–32.

recognition of and accommodation to change would be the greatest challenge to all the professions, including social work.

With the advent of new scientific solutions to old problems, such as that of population control, the need for new social and philosophical formulations appeared. Changes were evident in ideas about traditional morals and morality; social institutions were changing and simultaneously creating a need for other institutions to change. Discussing the changed moral system, Henry D. Aiken commented on factors surrounding the development of situational ethics:

> Moral principles now become first-personal precepts for the guidance of one's own conduct through the maze of one's life. It is no longer possible to talk of something called *"the* moral point of view"; the question is not what "one" should do, but what "I" should do, not what are "the rights of man," but what, man or no man, "my" commitments and loyalties are to be.[8]

Such things as individual privacy, ethics, and sexual relationships became the subject of much concern in an incredibly fluid society. The quest for what was called a "new politics" reflected, as did the search for a "new economics" and a "new morality," the pervasive nature of change confronting the nation. The paramount concern to some was not whether rapid change would or should occur, but rather whether social institutions could change rapidly enough to somehow accommodate the transformations being wrought by some of the consequences of technological change. The first youth to grow up in the shadow of nuclear war and with the instantaneous transmission of the face of war were impatient for ever more radical change. As one New Left leader allegedly put it, "When you've booked passage on the Titanic, why go steerage?"

TECHNOLOGY AND SOCIAL INSTITUTIONS

Aristotle, in *The Politics,* attributed the development of the political state to man's need to fashion an instrument to make life possible, and its continued existence was justified in order to promote a good life for all men. Aristotle considered the existence of masters and slaves essential and saw only one condition under which managers and subordinates would not be required by society and the state. This would so be if

> every tool we had could perform its function, either at our bidding or itself perceiving the need, like the statues made by Daedalus or the wheeled

[8] Henry David Aiken, "The New Morals," *Harper's Magazine,* Vol. 236, no. 1413 (February 1968), p. 68.

tripods of Hephaestus, of which the poet says that "self-moved they enter the assembly of the gods"—and suppose that shuttles in a loom could fly to and fro and a plucker play on a lyre all self-moved, then manufacturers would have no need of workers nor masters of slaves.[9]

The idea of self-actuating and self-correcting machines of production, relieving man of much inhuman labor, seemed a farfetched idea throughout most of man's history. In our time, however, it has become a reality, and the possibility of the emergence of a post-industrial society raises numerous questions about man and his social relationships.[10] Some of these questions that deal with such things as the nature of "work," technology as a social institution, and the necessity for other institutions to make rapid accommodations to technology, impinge in a very important way on social welfare systems.

The concept of the post-industrial society rests on an assessment of the major sources of employment and innovation in society. It is an important factor in assessing the source of values and the determinants of the way of life of the people. In a post-industrial society it is to be expected that industry as a prime motive force would decline in importance. From roughly 1620 to 1870 the United States was an agricultural society; for the next 90 years industry was the most important factor in determining the life-style of Americans. What is now postulated is the emergence of a society "in which the organization of theoretical knowledge becomes paramount for innovation in the society, and in which intellectual institutions become central in the social structure." [11]

Although there were many other reasons for radical student action to reform higher education, at least part of the focus on the university may have been due to an awareness that it was there that the life-style might be influenced. Because it was projected that some 80 percent of the population would be attending colleges and universities by the end of the century, the educational establishment was perhaps a natural place to make demands for the reform of society.[12]

The likelihood of a post-industrial society arose because of improved technologies and the ability of American industry to exploit them to produce an ever more abundant consumer society.[13] Anxiety about the future

[9] Aristotle, The Politics (Baltimore: Penguin Books, 1962), p. 31.
[10] The writer is indebted for this insight into the past and present to material included in Michael Harrington, The Accidental Century (New York: Macmillian Company, 1965), pp. 241–74.
[11] Kahn and Wiener, op. cit., p. vii. See also John Kenneth Galbraith, The New Industrial State (Boston: Houghton Mifflin Co., 1967), pp. 370–78.
[12] Ivor Kraft, "There is No Panacea," The Nation, Vol. 208, no. 3 (January 20, 1969), pp. 71–73.
[13] J. J. Servan-Schreiber, The American Challenge (New York: Atheneum, 1968).

of the technological society was due to an increasing awareness that technology had itself become a social institution. It was, like the family or religion, a "recognized solution" for problems that emerged.[14] As one writer, urging the control of technology, pointed out:

> Technology is not just another historical development taking its place with political parties, religious establishments, mass communications, household economy, and other chapters of the human story. Unlike the growth of those institutions, its growth has been quick and recent, attaining in many cases exponential velocities.[15]

The exponential nature of technological improvement was evident in computer technology itself. In the 1950s the first-generation computers were capable of handling 2000 words in 2.5 microseconds. The second generation, developed in the early 1960s, could handle 185,000 words in 15 megaseconds; the third generation can manage 16 million words in only 1.5 megaseconds.

The explosion of knowledge and the changes wrought in production methods by new technologies brought new methods of work organization and opened new possibilities for the future. Mechanization of industry earlier in the century, epitomized in the assembly line, was organized in lineal sequence. Workers in mechanized systems were literally "hands." But in a cybernated production process, a new centralization and new skills on the part of such operatives as were needed led to a decreased need for workers and new attitudes about the place of workers in the production process.

The decreased need to toil at making and growing things is reflected in the nature of employment, which has changed dramatically in the past few years. During the last 15 years employment in services has nearly doubled, but employment in manufacturing has shown virtually no increase. Today only one-third of our civilian labor force works in agriculture, mining, construction, and manufacturing.[16] Clearly the traditional definition of work as the production of "things" has been greatly broadened in reality.

The impact of mechanization (the substituting of mechanical processes for human muscle) is well illustrated in the case of farming, which, in the technological society, has become agribusiness. From 1950 to 1966,

[14] Robert A. Nisbet, "The Impact of Technology on Ethical Decision-Making," in Robert Lee and Martin E. Marty, eds., *Religion and Social Conflict* (New York: Oxford University Press, 1964), p. 10.
[15] Wilbur S. Ferry, "Must We Rewrite the Constitution to Control Technology?" *Saturday Review*, Vol. 51, (March 2, 1968), p. 50.
[16] J. B. McKitterick, "Planning the Existential Society," *Vital Speeches of the Day* (September 15, 1968), p. 731.

while agricultural output per man-hour increased 150% because of technological innovation, the number of job opportunities declined by two-thirds. Affected by this declining job market were some 6 million whites and over 12 million nonwhites. Helping to produce this declining job market were the extensive programs of research and development carried out by federal and state governments, frequently under the auspices of colleges and universities. In 1964 the Department of Agriculture spent over $178 million for research to eliminate jobs while in the same year the Welfare Administration and Department of Labor, combined, spent less than $12 million on research to find ways of helping people technologically displaced.[17]

In addition to the discrepancies in research between putting people out of jobs and finding ways to help people, there was also disagreement about the effects of technology on the employment of people.[18] Although it seemed true that in the long run people replaced by computers or machines did find other service or production employment, in the short run severe dislocations occurred. An example of the way technological advances in agriculture worked to the disadvantage of workers occurred in the Salinas Valley of California. Agricultural policies, technological developments, and political action and inaction, conspired to produce short-run misery. From 1930 to 1950 the harvesting and marketing of lettuce in the Salinas Valley was a twofold process. Fieldworkers harvested the crop and shed workers trimmed, packed, and iced the product for shipment. The shed workers, largely unionized Anglo-Americans, were direct employees of the growers. Covered by the provisions of the National Labor Relations Act, these employees earned in 1954 an average rate of $1.62½ per hour. Fieldworkers, who were generally migrant workers of various ethnic groups, were neither unionized nor covered by the National Labor Relations Act. They earned an average of 87½ cents an hour in 1954. Between 1950 and 1954 vacuum-cooling was introduced; this made it impossible to immediately truck lettuce to processing plants, thus eliminating the need for shed workers.[19] Technological innovation thus made possible the elimination of the higher-priced workers, and, although the number of jobs did not change appreciably, harvesting costs for the grower were greatly reduced. Federal legislation making possible the introduction of imported workers known as *braceros* during the same period contributed to the depression of wages for lettuce work-

[17] Nelson, Peck and Kalachek, *op. cit.*, pp. 152–53.
[18] A. J. Jaffe and Joseph Froomkin, *Technology and Jobs* (New York: Frederick A. Praeger, 1968), p. 69.
[19] Judith Chanin Glass, "Organization in Salinas," *Monthly Labor Review*, Vol. 98, no. 6 (Washington, D. C.: U. S. Department of Labor, June 1968), pp. 24–27.

ers and the replacement of native workers with foreign employees. By the late 1950s the use of foreign nationals had increased from 4 percent early in the decade to 70 percent at the end of the decade.[20] Thus did technology, inadequate planning, and public policy act together to produce short-run social misery.

Although technological advances first appeared as a threat in blue-collar employments, white-collar and middle-management jobs appear to be the next area of technological displacement. Not only will work be redefined by necessity, but it appears that other traditional institutions will be vastly changed by technology. In subtle ways, too, cybernation has affected and will continue to exert a deepening influence on human beings. The baking of bread is already cybernated and, as Jacques Ellul has pointed out, our taste in what *is* bread has undergone a radical change; methods of production have made it necessary to change the taste and texture of the product, and the new commodity has come to be preferred under the old name.

That technology would continue to produce new problems for other social institutions, at the same time it introduced entirely new and exciting possibilities for the future, was one of the principal concerns at the end of the 1960s. Clearly, it was not a question of whether there would be technological advances. Rather, it was a problem of how to plan for the changes and make the necessary adjustments in other social institutions affected by change. As one writer put it, the economic question of the technological future would not be who would own the means of production but "who will be in a position to support, absorb, and integrate progress and to furnish optimal conditions for its development." [21]

THE ECONOMICS OF A NEW ERA

Any discussion about the future of social welfare institutions must necessarily be concerned about the economic policies and problems that might be expected. By the end of the 1960s Keynesian ideas of manipulating tax, credit, and budget policies to produce economic stability were generally accepted as tools the government might use to produce stability. As Milton Friedman, the nation's leading conservative economist has stated, "We all use the Keynesian language and apparatus; none of us any longer accepts the initial Keynesian conclusions." [22] New ideas about ways of assuring

[20] *Farm Labor Organizing 1905–1967* (New York: National Advisory Committee on Farm Labor, July 1967), p. 43.

[21] Jacques Ellul, *The Technological Society* (New York: Alfred A. Knopf, 1964), p. 198.

[22] Milton Friedman, *Dollars and Deficits* (Englewood Cliffs, N. J.: Prentice-Hall, 1968), p. 15.

growth have been added to Keynesianism, and it is certain that new problems will arise that demand solutions for the "new economics." The intervention of government to compensate or correct for deficiencies in the private sector has now shifted to a discussion on what kind of compensation or correction and for what purposes.

The possibility of increasing productivity with less manpower requirements raises serious questions about the fate of an increasing labor force for whom traditional jobs may not be available. Conservative predictions that early in the 1970s the national economy will have passed the trillion dollar a year mark (in 1965 dollars) are accompanied by projections showing an employment decline in the "goods-producing sector, including agriculture" from 41 percent in 1964 to 36 percent in 1975.[23] Conservative predictions forecast a steadily rising labor market with 15 or 16 million additional persons seeking jobs during this period.[24]

Faced with the increasing size of the labor pool and the declining need of agriculture and industry for workers, it is apparent that new kinds of jobs must be created. The National Commission on Technology, Automation, and Economic Progress in 1965 recommended creation of some 5 million jobs in public service employment. Included were jobs in health services, educational programs, welfare and home care services, public protection, urban renewal, and national beautification.[25]

Embodied in the idea of job creation in public works is the requirement that middle- and upper-class taxpayers acquiesce in the redistribution of income by paying taxes for salaries. In the face of what is increasingly identified as a "taxpayer's revolt," generally a middle-class phenomenon expressed typically in a rejection of increased school taxes, such acquiescence seems doubtful. Economists concerned about the future growth potential of the economy point out that present governmental policies are hardly calculated to result in benefits to those most needing affirmative help. Tight money and higher interest rates to combat inflation, both undertaken early in the Nixon administration, were contraindicative of movement toward serious income redistribution. As Leon H. Keyserling pointed out, such policies serve to "inflate the fat and starve the lean" as money in transferred from those who borrow to those who lend.[26] Furthermore the Nixon administration's seeming preference for urban Job

[23] Howard R. Bowen and Garth L. Mangun, eds., *Automation and Economic Progress* (Englewood Cliffs, N.J.: Prentice-Hall, 1966), pp. 20–21.

[24] Editors of *Fortune, Markets of the Seventies* (New York: Viking Press, 1967), pp. 29–30.

[25] Bowen and Mangum, *op. cit.*, p. 24.

[26] Leon H. Keyserling, "The Problem of Problems: Economic Growth," in Robert Theobald, ed., *Social Policies for America in the Seventies: Nine Divergent Views*, (Garden City, N.Y.: Doubleday & Co., 1968), p. 17.

Corps Centers, frequently operated by private enterprise, over Job Corps Camps devoted to conservation work appears to diminish the possibility of expanding federally subvented public employment.

If it is true that in the future not everyone seeking work will be able to find it, what is to be the future for the unemployed? One writer has said:

> In a society nurtured by the Protestant ethic, which has yoked man's identity firmly to his work, what happens to the man who is permanently excluded from the productive enterprise? [27]

Economists such as John Kenneth Galbraith, one of the avant garde of the new economics, argues persuasively that ways of assuring income to all to insure comsumption in a highly productive technological society are essential. Galbraith also argues that new options to the 40-hour week and 50-week year of toil are now possible and should be available to workers who choose to forego some income in favor of more leisure.[28] Others have argued that the connection between work and consumption of goods must be severed and "non-market methods of providing incomes" found.[29] An alternative that would benefit underdeveloped nations was suggested by J. Herbert Holloman, a professional engineer and the president of the University of Oklahoma:

> Let's suppose we *would* decide in the next 10 years to decrease the amount of work we do, that is, not to decrease the work week or to advance the time at which people retire or to postpone the time at which they enter the work force. We have been putting a little less than one percent per year into decreased work. Now let us suppose we decide, instead, to keep everybody working at the same level and give that one percent away to the least developed countries. That would be the same as taking it in leisure. The first year we *could* give away seven billion dollars and not notice it, the next 14 billion, and the next 21 billion all without in the slightest affecting our own standard of living. I am not suggesting that as a national policy; I am simply illustrating the point that what we do with the fruits of technology is a social decision and has nothing to do with the technology itself.[30]

Whatever the alternatives might be, it is abundantly clear that some new alternatives will have to be found to replace traditional ideas about work.

[27] Myron B. Bloy, Jr., "The Christian Norm," in John Wilkinson, ed., *Technology and Human Values* (Santa Barbara, Calif.: Center for the Study of Democratic Institutions, 1966), p. 18.

[28] Galbraith, *The New Industrial State, op. cit.*, pp. 363–69.

[29] Robert Theobald, *Free Men and Free Markets* (Garden City, Anchor Books, N.Y.: Doubleday & Co., Anchor Books, 1965).

[30] J. Herbert Holloman, "Technology and Public Policy," *ASTME Vectors*, American Society of Tool Manufacturing Engineers, 1967, p. 17.

William A. Williams, a noted historian, has suggested that work should be defined in the future as "any act which manifested the individual's or the group's urge and need to express its creative powers, and to extend and strengthen its relationships with nature and with other human beings." In today's cybernating industrial system, according to Williams, "creative work is primarily defined as a job in the marketplace system. Hence the dehumanization of that job, or the outright loss of such employment, plays a central causative role in alienation." [31]

The future requires economic planning, and economists have become increasingly important in determining the course of society. The role of economists in post-Keynesian economic systems is well described by Kenneth Boulding who writes:

> Modern economists are not merely interested in predicting the business cycle but in controlling it, and in setting up social "thermostats" which will counteract the random and perverse processes which operate on the economy, just as a thermostatically controlled furnace counteracts changes in outside temperatures.[32]

An increasing acceptance of the need for planning and control appears likely in the years ahead. In the post-industrial society, conventional ideas about economics predicated on industrial norms appear to have limited social utility. The most challenging tasks in the economic sphere appear to be the sustaining of growth in the economy, providing full employment without inflation, and assuring income to those who may be idle or in new kinds of employment. Even a redefinition of work and worth might be possible.

THE FUTURE OF POLITICS

Viewing politics as "any activity involving human beings associated together in relationships of power and authority where conflict occurs," it is quite evident that the decade of the 1960s was a very political decade indeed.[33] Despite the persuasive case made for an "end of ideology," equally compelling evidence can be adduced for an upsurge in ideology with portents for the future. Polarization at the ends of the political spectrum around a New Left and a New Right are a fact of political life, and a resurgence of political consciousness and activity among youths was surely one of the most dramatic occurrences of the 1960s. The political rever-

[31] William Appleman Williams, *The Great Evasion* (Chicago: Quadrangle Books, 1964), p. 105.
[32] Kenneth E. Boulding, *Beyond Economics* (Ann Arbor: University of Michigan Press, 1968), p. 161.
[33] Robert A. Dahl, "What Is Political Science?" in Stephen K. Bailey, ed., *American Politics and Government* (New York: Basic Books, 1965), p. 8.

berations of the decade would surely shape the politics of the 1970s. Projections indicated that there would be 130 million citizens under the age of 35 by the time of the 1976 elections, and the bulk of the voters would have been shaped by the politics of the preceding decade.

The political demise of President Lyndon B. Johnson over the issue of involvement in Vietnam and increasing public criticism of that war resulted in large measure from the protest of youths. The facetiously and derisively labeled "Children's Crusade" for Senator Eugene McCarthy in the 1968 elections also gave evidence of the interest of youth in politics and their effectiveness in challenging the amorphous but identified enemy of change, "the Establishment." The movement in the 1960s toward political involvement has been characterized thus:

> In the past decade we have moved from criticism to protest, when the criticism was largely ignored; from protest to resistance, when the protest showed itself insufficient; and, currently, unsuccessful resistance appears repeatedly to break out into rebellion.[34]

A renascent conservatism in the 1950s was punctuated by the emergence of such populizers of conservative thought as William H. Buckley, founder and Editor of the *National Review* and sometime candidate for mayor of New York City. A resurgence of conservative negativism in social welfare, exemplified by the simplistic ideas of Barry Goldwater, was superceded by a more sophisticated conservative philosophy. Illustrative of the latter was the creation of organizations such as the Foundation for Voluntary Welfare and the renewed interest in what was termed the "independent sector" of society. Richard C. Cornuelle, mentor in welfare philosophy to Governors Reagan of California and Romney of Michigan, urged philanthropic institutions to abandon concepts of pioneering programs to have them assumed by government. Instead, he argued, the private sector should keep programs and compete with government.[35]

Some of the renewed vitality of conservative philosophy was the result of new ideas and programs that found wide appeal. It was also perhaps

[34] Kingsley Widmer, "Why Dissent Turns Violent," *The Nation*, Vol. 208 (April 7, 1969), p. 429.

[35] Richard C. Cornuelle, *Reclaiming the American Dream* (New York: Random House, 1965). Cornuelle's ideas appeared to be quite influential on Governor Romney, Nixon's first Secretary of the Department of Housing and Urban Development. Shortly after the new administration took office President Nixon announced a one million dollar program to establish a clearinghouse for information on where volunteers and voluntary programs are most needed. According to Romney, "Eventually we hope to enlist every American as a citizen volunteer." The irony of using public funds to foster voluntarism was apparently lost on the adminstration. It was hardly in line with Cornuelle's philosophy.

due to the decline of liberalism as a creative force in society and the realization that government might well encroach too much on individual liberties. Stephen C. Shadegg described conservatism as "revolutionary, not reactionary, in that it suggests liberating the individual and calls for a government which is benevolent but not a benefactor." [36]

Although the newer and more creative variety of conservative thought was more positive, it is questionable whether the word revolutionary was the correct one to apply. Perhaps only at the outer limits of the political spectrum could such conservative and alienated groups as the John Birch Society or the Minutemen be considered revolutionary. Certainly only within such groups was there radicalism in the sense of a desire to make root-and-branch changes and reforms, immediately and all together. [37]

More nearly revolutionary and certainly far more radical were the groups identified at the end of the 1960s as the New Left. The amorphous nature of the new political grouping has been thus described:

> The term "New Left" is vague. Since the New Left is, first, revolutionary activity and sentiment, you cannot point to one organization and say, "This is the New Left." There is no official "New Left International" or "New Left Party." There are only individuals, groups and organizations that in one or another degree express New Left sentiments and act along New Left lines. [38]

In describing the New and Old Left, *Time* magazine contrasted the two and also pointed toward one thing that united the numerous and sometimes ideologically incompatible groups:

> The Old Left had a program for the future; the New Left's program is mostly a cry of rage. The Old Left organized and proselytized, playing its part in bringing about the American welfare state. But it is big government, the benevolent Big Brother, that the New Left is rebelling against. [39]

Disagreements about the validity of the new political synthesis were as varied as the reasons advanced to explain its emergence and continued vitality. By the end of the decade the Students for a Democratic Society, founded at the convention at Port Huron, Michigan, in June 1962, had emerged as one of the most controversial of the New Left groups. The SDS also illustrated a pattern of development outlined by Eldridge

[36] Stephen C. Shadegg, "Conservatism and Political Action," in Robert A. Goldwin, ed., *Left, Right and Center* (Chicago: Rand McNally & Co., 1968), p. 131.

[37] William Montgomery McGovern and David S. Collier, *Radicals and Conservatives* (Chicago: Henry Regnery Co., 1958), p. 10.

[38] James Burnham, "The New Left and the Old," *National Review*, Vol. 20, no. 26 (July 2, 1968), p. 645.

[39] "The New Radicals," *Time*, Vol. 89, no. 17 (April 28, 1967), p. 27.

Cleaver. According to Cleaver, the politicization of youth went through four stages in the 1960s. First there was the rejection of conformity; second, the search for roles in changing society; third, the joining of Negro demonstrations in active work; and fourth, the taking of initiative to gain change "using techniques learned in the Negro struggle to attack problems in the general society." [40] Certainly the renascence in human rights associated with the Negro Revolution has had a decided influence in making the young aware of the discrepancies between the promise of American democratic ideals and the reality of social institutions. Mario Savio, leader of the Free Speech Movement at the University of California at Berkeley, where the first open insurrection on a college campus began in 1964, also ascribes to the Negro demand for equality much of the impetus for the new political involvement of youth. Added to this "external influence" Savio considered as causal factors the impersonal treatment of students and an increasing feeling that educational institutions had perpetuated un-American practices and had become irrelevant to American life.[41] Anent the idea of irrelevancy, one New Left leader commented, after leaving the movement, about the attitudes of the student radicals:

> One very important thing is that they feel that they are not able to have active control over the decisions and institutions that affect their lives. And they see this very clearly in their relationships with their parents, the school systems in their home towns, and their universities, and in society as a whole.[42]

Added to this sense of alienation and lack of participation was a belief that a spirit of militarism infected American life, and the draft and the war in Vietnam became prime targets of New Left militancy. Thomas Hayden, a leader in the SDS, scored American militarism, the failure of the welfare state to deal adequately with the problem of poverty, and the educational system's "stifling paternalism that infects the student's whole perception of what is real and possible and enforces a parent-child relationship." [43]

A psychologist and chronicler of the doings of the young radicals, Kenneth Keniston, added another dimension in attempting to explain the new political consciousness of youths. According to Keniston, the emerging post-industrial society and economic affluence is making possible a

[40] Eldridge Cleaver, *Soul on Ice* (New York: McGraw-Hill Book Co., 1968), pp. 71–75.
[41] Hal Draper, *Berkeley: The New Student Revolt.* (New York: Grove Press, Inc., An Evergreen Black Cat Book, 1965), pp. 1–7.
[42] Phillip Abbot Luce, *The New Left* (New York: David McKay Co., 1966), p. 9.
[43] Thomas Hayden, "A Letter to the New (Young) Left," in Mitchell Cohen and Dennis Hale, eds., *The New Student Left* (Boston: Beacon Press, 1967), pp. 2–3.

THE FUTURE OF POLITICS / 199

post-adolescent time called "youth" that ranges from around age 18 to 26. Physically and psychologically mature, but sociologically immature because of a lack of economic self-sufficiency, the labor of youths is not essential for production in an automating society. Supported financially by more affluent parents, the young have the luxury of having a time between adolescence and adulthood when they have the freedom to reflect and, if they choose, to act. The result of this new freedom is the reaction

> against the impersonality of technological society with personalism, against irrelevant tradition with generational identification, against technologism, and above all, against violence. [Positively, youth is searching for] new values, for institutional forms, and intellectual formulations that are adequate to life in the last third of the twentieth century.[44]

Whatever the precise factors might be in producing the new involvement of youth, there was little question that they were making a decided impact on American life. In a radical and profound way the New Left was upsetting traditional arrangements in institutional politics and in the educational system, to mention but two of the institutions affected. Composed of a mélange of people, organizations, and ideals, the new radicalism was dedicated to finding "a new politics and a new ideology that will permit them to link existential humanism with morally acceptable modes of achieving radical social changes."[45]

One of the institutions to bear much of the brunt of the demand for radical change was the educational system. Perhaps the reason lay in the alleged irrelevancy of the university to the society; perhaps it was because it was familiar and close at hand. Or it may have been a recognition that the university has increasingly become a paramount center for innovation in society and that "intellectuals are moving closer to the center of power" in the post-industrial United States.[46] In the 1960s, violent confrontations between university officials and students, police and strikers, and the seizure of buildings became an almost routine occurrence on American campuses. Colleges and universities such as San Francisco State, Howard, Stanford, Wisconsin, Columbia, and innumerable other institutions of varying size were affected. Demands for black studies programs, student representation (if not control) of curricula, an end to Defense Department subsidized research, elimination of Reserve Officer Training Corps

---

[44] Kenneth Keniston, *Young Radicals* (New York: Harcourt, Brace & World, 1968), p. 286.
[45] Paul Jacobs and Saul Landau, *The New Radicals* (New York: Vintage Books, 1966), p. 3.
[46] Noam Chomsky, "The Menace of Liberal Scholarship," *New York Review of Books*, Vol. 11, no. 12 (January 2, 1969), p. 30.

programs, and a voice in teacher selection were among the more common aims. The assertion that only a minority of students were involved in such activities, frequently made, was true in one sense and quite wrong in another. Although the SDS, the leading group in campus unrest, had but 250 chapters and perhaps 35,000 members in 1968, it could, depending on the issue, mobilize between 100,0000 and 300,000 supporters on campuses throughout the nation.[47] As one astute writer observed, "Mass activity is always prompted by a minority and the test of its validity is whether the less emotional are opposed." He noted that surveys of students and college newspaper editors indicated that this was not the case in the wave of student rebellions aimed at reforming higher education in the 1960s.[48]

Despite the calls for increased repression of student rebellion and the action of Congress to cut off federal funds to students participating in disruptions, there seemed little reason to believe that the new involvement of the young would decrease significantly in the near future. Along with the influence of technology, new systems of morality, and changing family patterns and functions, other forces contributed to the upsurge in activity. A worldwide revolution in rights and a resurgence in youthful political activity unquestionably influenced events in America. The fact of "the bomb" and the dominance of "the tube" made the frequently heard dichotomy of "over-30 and under-30" something different from previous generational conflict. The experiences of youth and the reality in which they grew up was far more significant than the differences separating their parents from their grandparents. The quality of conflict between the generations was of a much different nature in the 1960s than the raccoon coat and bathtub gin rebellion of the 1920s and 1030s. It was also far different from the minor resistances to the orderly processing through academia of the 1940s or the panty raids of the 1950s. The objects, objectives, and moral system of the protesting young in the 1960s were clearly of a different nature. Despite some anarchic and aberrant manifestations, such as the attachment to drugs as a means of involvement or a denial of free speech to others on occasion, the concern of the young with revivifying and reforming social institutions seems likely to continue.

In spite of reactions and overreactions to the new ferment caused by youth, the character of the future will be different because of the upsurge of interest and the commitment of youth to make a difference. One of the best statements about the continuing nature of the conflict and the goals sought was contained in a letter sent to President Nixon on May 1, 1969, endorsed by the majority of students, faculty, and administration of Am-

[47] Gene E. Bradley, "What Businessmen Need to Know About the Student Left," *Harvard Business Review*, Vol. 81, no. 46 (September 1968), p. 54.

[48] Felix Morley, "What's Behind the Student Demonstrations," *Nation's Business*, Vol. 54, no. 3 (March 1966), p. 25.

herst College in Amherst, Massachusetts. In the letter President Calvin H. Plimpton stated:

We believe that we must speak out to make clear that much of the turmoil among young people and among those who are dedicated to humane and reasoned change will continue. It will continue until you and the other political leaders of our country address more effectively, massively and persistently the major social and foreign problems of our society.

Plimpton also noted that unrest on campuses stemmed from "a shared sense that the nation has no plans for meeting the crises of our society." [49]

ALTERNATIVES IN INCOME MAINTENANCE

Disenchantment with some of the ameliorative measures of the welfare state was not limited to youth or the New Left. Increasingly it was recognized that such things as public income maintenance programs were inadequate to the task of eliminating poverty. It was also apparent that technology made possible new alternatives for assuring income; this has produced serious discussion about methods and has resulted in experimentation with different proposals. Chief among the alternatives are the idea of the government as the employer of last resort, the guaranteed annual income, and children's allowances. The profession of social work, as was the rest of society, was divided in respect to the alternatives, although there was general agreement that what existed was unsatisfactory. Illustrative of the profession's divided loyalties to the different approaches was the official position adopted in 1967 by the Delegate Assembly of the National Association of Social Workers. Meeting in Detroit, the Delegate Assembly adopted a position favoring any of the three alternatives that might be politically feasible. At the 1969 Delegate Assembly the inability to agree on a unified approach continued.

The idea of the government as the employer of last resort is inextricably tied to the nation's past experiments with work relief and work for relief. The Civil Works Administration and the Works Progress Administration of the New Deal are illustrative of both concepts respectively. Others have advocated work-sharing programs and flexible work periods as a way of guaranteeing to all seeking work an opportunity to toil.[50] Work programs developed as a result of the 1967 Amendments to the Social Security Act

[49] Letter from Calvin H. Plimpton, President of Amherst College, Amherst, Massachusetts, to President Richard M. Nixon, April 29, 1969.
[50] Benjamin Graham, *The Flexible Work Year: An Answer to Unemployment*, An Occasional Paper on the Role of the Economic Order in the Free Society (Santa Barbara, California: Center for the Study of Democratic Institutions, 1964). John Kenneth Galbraith, *The New Industrial State, op. cit.*, pp. 363–69.

by the Department of Labor are, in a way, part of this idea. So too are the private efforts of groups such as the National Alliance of Businessmen and various programs developed under the aegis of the War on Poverty. All are interested in taking action to provide jobs, either in private employments or, in lieu of that, government sponsored work. Involved in the government projects is the idea of defining as work some things that are not now so defined. Paraprofessional jobs such as welfare aides in welfare departments or teachers' aides in the schools are two examples of the new careers that have been developed to meet the problems of unemployment and underemployment. Among the problems involved in this approach to the need for assuring income is the fact that if work is meaningful, the machinery already exists for hiring on an open market. Historically, made work has been just that, and wages paid have generally been far less than that paid for jobs considered essential. Prohibitions against the creation of jobs that would compete with either public or private employment make it difficult to envision the kind of jobs that the government as employer of last resort could create. Public attitudes toward work relief and work-for-relief projects are very pejorative. It is unlikely that government in a democracy would ever, except in a time of national emergency, assign workers to private industry as an enforced guarantee of work for all. Such schemes also leave more or less intact the welter of programs designed to alleviate dire want. Such progressive adjustments as mailed affirmations of eligibility in the categorical aid programs do not get to basic needed reform of the system.

The modern family allowance system is the descendent of the Speenhamland system that was inaugurated in 1795 in England and eliminated in the Poor Law Amendment Act of 1834.[51] Economic conditions and a fear of revolutionary ideas led to this program of guaranteeing to each family, depending on its size, a minimum standard of living. Combined with a system of work relief, the allowance in support of wages was soon discredited and replaced by punitive workhouse legislation. The effect of the program was the lowering of the standard of wages by employers and the destroying of initiative on the part of the laborers.[52] Not until the present century were children's allowances adopted again, and today all industrial nations except the United States have as a part of their social insurance programs a system of children's allowances.

[51] U.S. Congress, Joint Economic Committee, Martin Schnitzer *Guaranteed Minimum Income Programs Used by Governments of Selected Countries,* Joint Committee Print, Study Paper 11 (Washington, D.C.: Government Printing Office, 1968), p. 9.

[52] Karl de Schweinitz, *England's Road to Social Security,* (New York: A. S. Barnes & Co., a Perpetua Book, 1943), pp. 69–78.

Under a children's allowance scheme a payment in cash is made to the parent for each child or for children above a specified number. The payment is made as a "demogrant," that is, to all in the population fitting the designation regardless of need or other conditions. Typically, however, children's allowance programs are limited by age or school attendance, and payments may be taxable and even related to occupational categories.[53] The source of funds may, as in Canada, which pays an allowance of $8 a month for children under 8 and $10 for those above that age, be the general tax revenue of the the government. It may also be financed, as in France, which pays the world's most substantial allowance, by a tax on employers.

Alvin L. Schorr, one of the leading advocates of the children's allowance in the United States, has proposed the payment of a benefit of fifty dollars a month for each child under 6 years of age, the cost to be paid from general tax revenues. Present income tax exemptions of $600 would be eliminated, and the benefit would be taxed in order to recover part of the costs from those more affluent families. An improved system of public assistance would assist children after age 6 as would a greatly expanded program of public services to be administered through the schools. Included would be health services, vocational aids, and cultural opportunities.[54]

The cost of such a proposal would be nearly $6 billion for children's allowances only; the extension of the most adequate foreign system, the French, would cost an estimated $30 billion if used in the United States.[55] In neither instance would the family allowance system abolish poverty, although it would be a decided help to large families living in impoverished circumstances. One of the most appealing things about the idea of the children's allowance is the fact that it does not differ substantially from other welfare state programs and has been tried in other countries. Militating against its adoption is the opposition of politically powerful groups such as the AFL-CIO, the cost of the proposals, and the fear that it might increase the birthrate.

The idea of a negative tax has historical antecedents in the proposal made by Lady Rhys-Williams of England in the 1940s for a transfer-by-taxation plan of income maintenance. In the United States the principle of a negative income tax was proposed in 1946 as an alternative to a minimum wage

[53] Eveline M. Burns, ed., *Children's Allowances and the Economic Welfare of Children* (New York: Citizens' Committee for Children of New York, 1968), p. 9.

[54] Alvin L. Schorr, *Poor Kids* (New York: Basic Books, 1966), pp. 146–65.

[55] *Guaranteed Minimum Income Programs Used by Governments of Selected Countries, op. cit.,* p. 86.

by economist George Stigler. He advocated the extension of "the personal income tax to the lowest income brackets with negative rates in these brackets."[56] Under such a plan payment of a cash grant is made to families or individuals whose incomes fall below a specified minimum level, the amount of payment depending on the amount of income and the negative tax rate.

Central in the idea of a negative tax is the establishment of the income level necessary for an individual or family. Above the established level, families and persons would pay "positive taxes," and below that level the present tax system would be reversed to pay a "negative tax." The difference between the present tax system and that proposed is that at present one either pays or does not pay taxes. Under a "negative tax" the government would make payments to those whose income and family size placed them in a category of having insufficient income to be taxpayers.

A number of different schemes have been advanced to guarantee an annual income to all. The scheme advocated by Milton Friedman of the University of Chicago would pay unused tax exemptions and deductions and a tax rate of 50 percent would provide an incentive to work. If the $3000 minimum level of the Council of Economic Advisers for the family of four were used and if a family had no income, $1500 would be paid as a "negative tax." Above $3000 a "positive tax" would be paid; with a tax rate of 14 percent and an income of $4000 a family of four would pay $140 tax and have $3860 left.[57]

A more ambitious proposal, advanced by Edward E. Schwartz of the School of Social Service Administration at the University of Chicago, includes the provision of a federally guaranteed minimum income. Designed to eliminate poverty, under the Schwartz plan persons would each year file income statements with reports of last year's needs and income along with estimates of their income for the coming year. The difference between the two would be paid by the federal government as a family security benefit, and persons with substantial assets might not be eligible. With a minimum income level of $5000, the Schwartz plan would cost perhaps $38 billion a year in contrast to a cost of perhaps $6 billion in the Friedman scheme.[58]

Other variations on the annual income guarantee theme include that of Robert J. Lampman, who favors a decreasing negative income taxation as income rises. James Tobin suggests a combination of the various schemes

[56] George J. Stigler, "The Economics of Minimum Wage Legislation," *American Economic Review*, Vol. 36, no. 3 (June 1946), p. 365.

[57] Friedman, *Capitalism and Freedom, op. cit.*

[58] Edward E. Schwartz, "A Way to End the Means Test," Social Work, Vol. 9, no. 3 (July 1964), pp. 3–12 and 97.

but makes modifications in basic allowances and tax rates to provide a generous family supplement.[59]

The guaranteed annual income is being tested by the government. Although President Nixon opposed the idea during the presidential campaign, after his election he supported continuation of pilot programs and, in October 1969, called on Congress to enact a nationwide assured income scheme.

The first test of the idea was inaugurated in New Jersey in 1968, to last for three years. *Mathematica, Inc.*, a private firm, under contract with the Office of Economic Opportunity, is testing seven separate negative tax schemes in that state. Poverty-stricken families receive payments with the amounts determined by family size and income; recipients file accurate monthly reports on earnings and number of dependents. With a 50 percent tax rate, a family with $2000 yearly income could increase earnings by $1000 and have payments cut by only one-half the amount earned. Under the most generous plan, a family can continue to receive a small payment even with earnings over $10,000 a year. Families are free to move as they choose without having payments disrupted, and the use of computers sharply cuts the cost of administration.[60]

The program of guaranteeing an annual income, recommended by the Office of the President in 1969 was intended to benefit all except single adults under age 65, married couples without dependent children, and able-bodied parents of needy families who refuse to accept jobs or job training. The aged, the blind, and the disabled would be guaranteed an income of $90 a month; in the 37 states that in 1969 paid more than that, supplementation by the states would be required. In the family program, $500 a year would be paid for the first two members of the family and $300 for each additional member. Aid would decline in proportion to earnings, and supplementation would cease when earnings and assured income exceeded $3920. As in the case of the adult programs, states would be required to maintain the previous level of program expenditures. Payments could be made to benefit families if the new Family Assistance Plan meant a decline in income from previous public assistance standards. Job training would be provided through an expanded Department of Labor Work Incentive program or through a revamped Manpower Training scheme consolidating the major manpower development programs.[61]

[59] *Guaranteed Minimum Income Programs Used by Governments of Selected Countries, op. cit.*, pp. 4–7.
[60] "Replacing Welfare," *Wall Street Journal* (October 11, 1968).
[61] U.S. National Archives and Records Service, Office of the Federal Register, *Weekly Compilation of Presidential Documents* (Washington, D.C.: Government Printing Office, August 18, 1969), p. 1138.

The Family Assistance Plan, as originally proposed, retained categories of need, was administratively complex, and involved continuing state and local financial participation. It did assure a slightly above poverty line income for adults but the family program was to remain sub-standard. Nevertheless, the FAP did represent a change in direction in income maintenance in the United States. This despite the president's pandering to American myths in presenting the proposal as a way "to become a working nation that properly cares for the dependent" rather than to become a "Welfare State that undermines the incentive of the working man." [62] Although the appeal was to the Protestant ethic of the past, it was manifestly clear that private sector jobs could not be generated to hire all seeking work and that the nation was on the threshold of a guaranteed annual income for all.

The greatest area of disagreement in the proposed Family Assistance Plan was the level at which income should be maintained. At a White House Conference on Hunger and Nutrition held the first week in December, 1969, the inadequacy of the proposed $1600 income guarantee for a family of four was spelled out by representatives of the poor. The average income for such a family was $9300 in 1969 and the Bureau of Labor Statistics estimated that a low cost budget for a family of four in the Northeast United States would be $6771. Therefore, the Conference recommended to the President a $5500 guarantee, much to the chagrin of the Conference's organizer, Presidential assistant Daniel P. Moynihan.

The three alternatives to the present system of income maintenance that have been discussed are, in actuality, designed to do different things and, therefore, in many respects are not competitive ideas. The concept of guaranteeing work, first on a private basis and then with the government as employer of last resort, is designed to give jobs to those willing and able to work. It can be fitted into the present social insurance and welfare programs, is in accord with American traditions, and is based on the recognition of work as a way "human beings develop and affirm their personality." [63] The idea of a children's allowance is a logical extension of the welfare state and is in the tradition of American liberalism. The guaranteed income through a negative tax and computerized income maintenance payments is nonideological and is seen by Milton Friedman, a conservative, and Paul Goodman, who lies at the other end of the political spectrum, as a way of protecting the individual from the encroachment of government on individual liberty.[64] The idea is also attractive to busi-

[62] *Ibid.*, p. 1125.
[63] Jacques Ellul, *op. cit.*, p. 399.
[64] Paul Goodman, "Two Issues in Planning," *Commentary*, Vol. 44, no. 2 (August 1967), p. 77.

nessmen interested in assurances that products produced can be consumed and the growth dimension of our market economy assured. Those interested in finding a more efficient system of making transfer payments, those who wish to protect and reinforce our present socio-economic system, and those who wish to modify the latter can all find areas of agreement in supporting a guaranteed annual income.

The greatest problem with the creating of jobs is that the economy cannot, except in wartime, apparently generate enough "traditional" jobs without being faced with the Keynesian dilemma—how to increase employment without inflation. In addition, jobs that need doing are created without public or private intervention and, to help the worker, the job must be meaningful to him and to society. A redefinition of work to include some jobs not now considered to be work involves serious attitudinal change on the part of the American people.

The children's allowance is essentially a plea for "more of the same" and the general consensus of the nation is that what we have had in the past has not worked very well. Concern about an increased birthrate is perhaps overdone and the experience of other countries would lead us to believe that, overall, money given would be wisely spent. However, the children's allowance is not a way of attacking either the problem of general poverty or the creation of jobs.

A guaranteed income appears to be the most suitable vehicle for eliminating poverty and, at the same time, accommodating technological changes that may force society to a reassessment of what work is. Two conflicting pressures, however, are operating in the case of the guaranteed annual income. The first is the need to raise the poor out of poverty through provision of an adequate income; the second is the desire to maintain an incentive to work. Experimentation with various proposals, study by the Presidential Commission on Income Maintenance Programs, and new legislation promise drastic changes in the nature of income maintenance programs.

Concern with the abolition of poverty through helping the unemployed and the underemployed might well lead to the use of technology in solving the problems that might well result, in part, from technological advances. In 1945 blue-collar workers outnumbered white-collar workers by 15 percent. In 1970 white-collar workers outnumbered blue-collar workers by 30 percent. By 1980, according to the National Industrial Conference Board, professional and technical workers will outnumber all other kinds of workers. Further projections into the future include estimates that by the year 2000 only half of the labor force would be working what we now define as a "normal" work year. Some would, in the "post-industrial and affluent society by half-time hobbyists, some would voluntarily be unemployed and others would work only long enough to achieve their individual goals.[65] If in fact fewer and fewer people are needed for production and service jobs, some new concepts and methods of income maintenance will have to be developed to avoid creation of a permanent underclass of the poor.

POPULATION GROWTH AND CONTROL

One of the most serious problems of the future, and of the present in some countries, is the control of population growth. The problem centers around the fact that in preindustrial and primitive countries science and technology have conspired to lower death rates without a corresponding increase in the ability of various nations, such as India and China, to keep food production advancing apace. The population of the world at the time of Christ has been estimated to have been 250 million. When Columbus discovered America it stood at some 400 million. In 1939 it was 2.2 billion and is, in 1970, more than 3.5 billion. According to projections made by the United Nations, by the year 2000 the world's population will stand at about 6 billion.[66]

The possibility of the world's population outstripping the ability of the land to support mankind was introduced into economic thought by Thomas R. Malthus in 1798, with the publication of a pamphlet entitled "An Essay on the Principle of Population."Subsequently expanded into a book, Malthus's interest in welfare economics led him to postulate the simple theory that population grew geometrically, food supplies arithmetically. Therefore in time the ability of the land to support its people would reach a point beyond which additional mouths could not be fed. Malthus described both "positive" and "preventive" checks on population. Included in the latter were delayed marriage and sexual abstinence; in the former were all unwholesome occupations, severe labour and exposure to the seasons, extreme poverty, bad nursing of children, great towns, excesses of all kinds, the whole train of common diseases and epidemics, wars, plague, and famine." [67]

Malthus's ideas were, during his lifetime and for centuries after, either ignored or considered to be the illogical notions of a man going beyond

---

[65] Kahn and Wiener, *op. cit.*, pp. 194–96.

[66] "World's No. 1 Worry—Too Many People," *U.S. News & World Report,* Vol. 66, no. 11 (March 17, 1969), p. 48.

[67] Thomas R. Malthus, *An Essay on the Principle of Population* (Homewood, Ill.: Richard D. Irwin, 1963), p. 8. Malthus, a minister, opposed charity since it might keep alive those who would propagate and for whom "at Nature's mighty feast there is no cover."

his competence in the area of economics. Until the scientific and technological explosions of recent times (90 percent of history's scientists are
now alive), the prospect of overpopulation seemed remote and not among
the most pressing of world problems. Increased knowledge of the world
and society's ability to make people safer from disease and the disabilities
of laboring, if not war, have led to serious reconsideration of the Malthusian thesis.

In the United States the rising concern about population pressure and
the gaining of scientific ability to control the number of births originally
ran counter to a number of practices and social conventions. Dating from
the nineteenth-century activities of Anthony Comstock, a moral and religious crusader, a number of states prohibited the use or dissemination of information about contraceptive devices. Comstock and his followers were
even able to persuade Congress to pass a law prohibiting use of the mails
to send information regarding birth control. Perhaps the most extreme and
most enduring of the state statutes was that of Connecticut. Passed in 1879,
the law forbade contraception by anyone, including married couples, and
prohibited information-giving on the subject. Such laws were passed in
the puritanical belief that knowledge of contraception methods or possession of devices would encourage sexual license.

The earliest assault on the state laws came in 1916 when Margaret
Sanger, a feminist rebel, was sentenced to jail in New York for giving information on birth control. The following year she founded what was to
become the Planned Parenthood Federation of America, the leading organization in the promotion of family planning in the United States. But not
until the 1950s when foundations such as Milbank, Ford, and Rockefeller
undertook essential research and training support in population problems,
did the nation become aroused about the potential problems of a "population explosion."

In 1959 the American Public Health Association declared population
problems to be a major health concern, and increasingly private and public agencies, notably the National Academy of Sciences, called for federal
and state action. Between 1960 and 1965 the number of local health departments providing family planning services increased from 7 to 27, an
indication of increased support of the concept.[68] The reluctance of public
welfare agencies to provide family planning services was related to a lack
of funds on the one hand and a fear of controversy, social and religious,
on the other. By the middle of the 1960s, however, the attitude of Congress, the Department of Health, Education, and Welfare, and the general
public had changed. In 1963 the Division of Indian Health, Education, and

[68] U.S. Congress, Senate, Committee on Government Operations, *Population Crisis*,
S. Rept. 1676, 89th Cong., 1st sesss., 1965, Part 2B, pp. 1203–12.

Welfare issued a policy statement that permitted physicians to give contraceptive information or devices on request. In 1965 the Secretary of Health, Education, and Welfare issued a policy statement pledging HEW support of health programs making family planning information available.[69] In those states that enacted medical care legislation to benefit the poor, contraceptive devices could be obtained or medication provided to facilitate family planning.

In 1965, too, came the Supreme Court decision in *Griswold* v. *State of Connecticut*, which finally laid to rest the spirit of Anthony Comstock.[70] Estelle T. Griswold, executive director of the Planned Parenthood League in New Haven, and the medical director of a Planned Parenthood clinic were arrested, in 1961, for giving birth control information to married couples. Found guilty in the state courts, they appealed to the Supreme Court: the statute forbidding dissemination of birth control information was found to violate at least four guarantees of personal liberty or privacy in the Bill of Rights.[71]

One of the greatest stumbling blocks in family planning or birth control has been the official position of the Roman Catholic Church. It has traditionally supported the control of fertility through abstinence or "rhythm," —abstinence in marriage during periods of fertility. In the 1960s American Catholics were suddenly faced with increasingly sophisticated methods of contraception that did not have the sanction of their church. Birth control pills and intrauterine devices were a reality; on the horizon were a single pill for a full menstrual cycle, oral contraceptives for men, and possibly a 20-year capsule that could be implanted under the skin to suppress fertility.[72]

In view of the fact that scientific discoveries made sophisticated family planning possible, coupled with a revolution in morals that made contraception respectable for most other religious bodies, Pope Paul VI commissioned a study and review of the traditional church stand on the matter. The encyclical *Humanae Vitae* (Of Human Life) issued in 1968 promised not a resolution to the problem but rather further discord. As one Catholic scholar stated, the prohibition of artifical contraception contributed significantly to "a crisis more serious than any it [the Church] has confronted since the mighty religious upheaval of the 16th century fragmented Christendom."[73] The resistance to the statement, which was not issued as an infallible document, and the fact that the majority of Catholic

[69] "Birth Control: U.S. Program Off to Slow Start," *Science*, Vol. 156, no. 3776 (May 12, 1967), pp. 765.

[70] *Griswold* v. *State of Connecticut*, 381 U.S. 1678–1707 (1965).

[71] *Ibid.*

[72] Editors of *Fortune, op. cit.,* pp. 27–28.

[73] John A. O'Brien, " 'Humanae Vitae': Reactions and Consequences," *Christian Century*, Vol. 76, no. 9 (February 26, 1969), p. 288.

and non-Catholic opinion was opposed to *Humanae Vitae* leads to the belief that future reversal of the position is likely. Although official public pronouncements were guarded and progress on population control, slow, in recent years there has been strong congressional support for birth control in the United States. Although the concern about food supplies being inadequate is not the major one in a nation that is restricting agricultural production, other reasons are advanced for the active promotion of population control. Prominent among these are the social consequences of uncontrolled fertility for the family in the areas of housing, education, employment, an improved standard of living in general, and the constitutional question raised by Women's Liberation leaders about women's rights to decide whether they will have children. The President's Commission on the Causes and Prevention of Violence, headed by Dr. Milton Eisenhower, in 1969, pointed to poverty as a cause of violence and family size was an important factor contributing to poverty. Nationally too, rapid population growth added to ecological problems of environmental pollution and complicated provision of such things as mass transportation, needed recreation facilities, and generally increased the stresses in urban living.[74]

There appears to be little question but that the control of man's fertility is a problem to be faced in the future, and the Malthusian thesis is again echoed in this generation. Neither is there serious disagreement that the 5.3 million American women living in poverty need and want family planning, whereas only 850,000 (1 in 16) are receiving it today. It must be recognized, however, that population pressure is a problem for the entire society and not simply the poor. Old and discredited ideas of "eugenics" have raised the false question whether the poor in procreating produce inferior children—a fallacious notion dating back at least to the nineteenth-century studies of the Jukes and Kallikaks. Such misguided ideas have led to the introduction of legislation in at least 8 states which makes sterilization compulsory for various classes of relief recipients.[75] In some jurisdictions judges have made sterilization a condition of probation or receipt of benefits from public programs. In some states, such as Louisiana, public welfare recipients with multiple illegitimacies were denied welfare benefits. These developments and the fact that oral contraceptives were tested in Puerto Rico (and the approval first of federally financed contraception for Indians) raised in the minds of many, especially black militants, the specter of race suicide.

[74] Richard N. Gardner and Max F. Millikan, eds., *The Global Partnership: International Agencies and Economic Development* (New York: F. A. Praeger, 1968).

[75] Frederick S. Jaffe and Steven Polgar, "Family Planning and Public Policy: Is the 'Culture of Poverty' the New Cop-Out?," *Journal of Marriage and the Family*, Vol. 30, no. 2 (May 1968), p. 235.

Despite the fear of coercive control and the admitted focusing on the poor, especially the nonwhite, as the cause of the "population explosion," future control is a problem for all segments of society. Population control is not the solution for the living who are faced with the fact of going hungry in this nation—a group that may number as many as 10 million.[76] Neither is it the solution to the problem of the many young children suffering from disease, a fact vividly reported by doctors who traveled in the South and recommended federally supported medical facilities and programs to provide emergency medical treatment.[77] Nor is it the solution to the problem of increasingly inadequate housing in the central cities, where the number living in substandard housing is probably increasing. For the future, the planning of numbers must be done if human aspirations and values are to be maintained, not to mention improved. Undeniably it is true that stabilization of numbers is essential. "Anybody capable of plugging values into the compound interest formula can easily demonstrate that this is a logical necessity." [78]

Summary

The most important internal problems facing the nation and demanding resolution include the opening of American society to enable all races, ethnic groups, and age groups to fully participate on equal terms. Ways of insuring economic well-being to all citizens either through employment or through income maintenance schemes designed to keep government from an intrusive role must be devised. The development of technology as an institution demands adjustments of other social institutions such as religion, the family, the legal system and politics. It is also imperative that some thought be given to controlling the effects of technology that have a deleterious effect on man's social institutions and his environment. Changes must be made in society to make institutions more relevant to the times if they are to continue to fill their proper roles. Recognition of population control as a priority item on the social agenda is essential in order to assure continued progress in the nation and, most certainly, in the world.

This generation has witnessed the greatest amount of change taking place in a shorter space of time than ever before. The synergistic nature of change in a technological society leads to the inevitable conclusion that

[76] Elizabeth B. Drew, "Going Hungry in America," *The Atlantic*, Vol. 222, no. 6 (December 1968), p. 61.

[77] Joseph Brenner, et. al., *Children in Mississippi: A Report to the Field Foundation* (Chicago: Field Foundation, 1967). (Mimeographed).

[78] Robert E. Neil, "The More the Merrier?," *Commonweal*, Vol. 87, no. 18 (February 9, 1968), p. 556.

the tempo of change will accelerate rather than diminish. To think otherwise is to court disaster in the highly complex society that now exists in
our nation. In the past the conventional explanation for periods of quies-
cence following times of rapid change have been explained as breathing
periods to allow society time to absorb new laws, new demands, and so
forth. A more reasonable explanation of the phenomenon might be that
society has delayed action on pressing problems and then acted in a rush
to bring social institutions up-to-date with social realities; for example,
much of the social legislation of the New Deal was concerned with problems that had been serious early in the century. Many of the programs
of the War on Poverty, such as the Job Corps, were needed in the 1950s
or perhaps earlier. It may well be that the luxury of time, or at least such
prolonged spells of inaction between our "wars" on poverty, may not be
possible in the future.

In our social welfare system, new ways of combatting man's historic
enemies—ignorance, sickness, and poverty—either exist now and await
implementation or will be found in the future. Technology may exist as a
"problem" to be dealt with institutionally, but it also offers some new
options for solving some of man's human problems. In a future in which
many things may be possible thinking must be heuristic rather than with
an eye in the rearview mirror solving the problems of "Bonanzaland." [79]
With sophisticated hardware available for prediction and in a society in
which miscalculations in one institution have immediate and profound
consequences for other institutions, the necessity for social planning
should be self-evident.

The profession of social work, wedded for many years to a welfare
state ideal that deals with problems when they become acute, will need to
accommodate to the fact that problems may become predictable and pre-
ventable. Although the rhetoric of the profession has been suffused with
ideas of the prevention of numerous ills, in reality social workers have
merely been picking up the pieces in an industrial society. In a post-
industrial society different problems can be expected, and the functions
of social workers will necessarily undergo permutations. Emphasis in the
profession, as promised at the 1969 Delegate Assembly of the National Association of Social Workers, must be given to social action without diminishing the importance of improving techniques of serving individuals and
groups. The recognition of undergraduate education as suitable preparation for professional practice is essential, and even more radical accommodation may have to be made for those involved in social welfare
tasks with less than a bachelor's degree. For the future two of the most
critical problems for professionals at all levels of education will be the

[79] Marshall McLuhan and Quentin Fiore, *The Medium Is the Massage* (New York:
Random House, 1967), p. 75.

assurance of a counterpart to academic freedom to agency employees who insist on ethical practices and serve as advocates for their clients. A second, and related, area of concern is the necessity for public service employees to identify as professionals rather than principally as civil servants. Along with this there is the necessity for developing objective criteria for determining professional status and some system of accountability and measure of effectiveness.

Within the educational system the 1960s witnessed an upsurge of student participation in their own education, and a drastic overhauling of the terms on which social work education is offered will have to occur. Because of the frequent guilt of a paternalistic domination rather than a democratic determination of educational goals between teachers and learners, the prospect of further educational reforms is almost a certainty. In practice settings the newer patterns of relationships will affect such things as traditional supervisor–social worker relations.

The return of peace (or at least some kind of détente) will not likely mean that the sums devoted to guns will then be allocated to social welfare butter. Certainly the experience of the past would hardly warrant such an optimistic view. When we consider that since the end of World War II this nation has spent more than $900 billion on military needs and less than $100 billion of the national budget on education, health, welfare, housing, and community development, some notion of our national priorities is evident. Knowledge of the experience in postwar periods, when social workers and reformers expected peacetime involvement of attention and money for social needs at a level of military expenditures of time and money, makes it unrealistic to expect that the present will be different from the past.

This does not mean that there ought be any lessening of social worker's efforts to bring forcefully to the attention of society the need for social justice and social security. Although the process of educating the public to social needs seems agonizingly slow, recent history gives some hope that it can be done. Progress and attitudinal change in the area of race relations has, in fact, been quite dramatic since 1954. Perhaps the educational task of the future for the profession is to convince society that social gains can be of benefit to everyone. As Robert Theobald describes this process of improvement:

Today we assume that somebody must lose what the other person gains— this is a zero-sum game: tomorrow, we will understand that the only activities worth carrying out are those where everybody gains.[80]

[80] Robert Theobald, "American Physical Abundance," *Vital Speeches of the Day* (May 1, 1968), p. 439.

Selected Bibliography

Aiken, Henry David. "The New Morals." *Harper's Magazine*, Vol. 236, no. 1413 (February 1968), pp. 58-72.

Aristotle, *The Politics*. Baltimore, Md.: Penguin Books, 1962.

Barrett, William. *Irrational Man: A Study in Existential Philosophy*. Garden City, N.Y.: Doubleday & Co., 1958.

Beardwood, Roger. "The Southern Roots of Urban Crisis." *Fortune*, Vol. 78, no. 2 (August 1968), pp. 80-87 and 151-56.

"Birth Control: U.S. Program Off to Slow Start." *Science*, Vol. 156, no. 3776 (May 12, 1967), pp. 765-67.

Bloy, Myron B., Jr. "The Christian Norm." *Technology and Human Values*. Edited by John Wilkinson. Santa Barbara, Calif.: Center for the Study of Democratic Institutions, 1966.

Boore, William F. and Murphy, Jerry R. *The Computer Sampler*. McGraw-Hill Book Co., 1968.

Boulding, Kenneth E. *Beyond Economics*. Ann Arbor: University of Michigan Press, 1968.

Bowen, Howard R. and Mangum, Garth L., eds. *Automation and Economic Progress*. Englewood Cliffs, N.J.: Prentice-Hall, 1966.

Bradley, Gene E. "What Businessmen Need to Know About the Student Left." *Harvard Business Review*, Vol. 81, no. 46 (September–October 1968), pp. 49-60.

Brenner, Joseph, *et. al., Children in Mississippi: A Report to the Field Foundation*. Chicago, June 1967 (Mimeographed).

Burnham, James. "The New Left and the Old." *National Review*, Vol. 20, no. 26 (July 2, 1968), p. 645.

Burns, Eveline M. ed. *Children's Allowances and the Economic Welfare of Children*. New York: Citizen's Committee for Children of New York, 1968.

Chomsky, Noam. "The Menace of Liberal Scholarship." *New York Review of Books*, Vol. 11, no. 12 (January 2, 1969), pp. 29-38.

Clark, Colin. *Population Growth and Land Use*. New York: St. Martin's Press, 1968.

Cleaver, Eldridge. *Soul on Ice*. New York: McGraw-Hill Book Co., 1968.

Cornuelle, Richard C. *Reclaiming the American Dream*. New York: Random House, 1965.

Dahl, Robert A. "What is Political Science?" *American Politics and Government*. Edited by Stephen K. Bailey. New York: Basic Books, 1965.

de Schweinitz, Karl. *England's Road to Social Security*. New York: A. S. Barnes & Co., a Perpetua Book, 1961.

Draper, Hal. *Berkeley: The New Student Revolt*. New York: Grove Press, Inc., An Evergreen Black Cat Book, 1965.

Drew, Elizabeth B. "Going Hungry in America." *The Atlantic*, Vol. 222, no. 6 (December 1968), pp. 53-61.

Ellul, Jacques. *The Technological Society*. New York: Alfred A. Knopf, 1964.

Fabry, Joseph B. *The Pursuit of Meaning.* Boston: Beacon Press, 1968.
Farm Labor Organizing 1905–1967. New York: National Advisory Committee on Farm Labor, July 1967.
Ferry, Wilbur S. "Must We Rewrite the Constitution to Control Technology?" *Saturday Review,* Vol. 51 (March 2, 1968), pp. 50–54.
Editors of *Fortune. Markets of the Seventies.* New York: Viking Press, 1968.
Friedman, Milton. *Capitalism and Freedom.* Chicago: University of Chicago Press, 1962.
Friedman, Milton. *Dollars and Deficits.* Englewood Cliffs, N.J.: Prentice-Hall, 1968.
Galbraith, John Kenneth. *The New Industrial State.* Boston: Houghton Mifflin Co., 1967.
Gardner, Richard N. and Millikan, Max F. (eds.). *The Global Partnership: International Agencies and Economic Development.* New York: F. A. Praeger, 1968.
Glass, Judith Chanin. "Organization in Salinas." *Monthly Labor Review,* U.S. Department of Labor, Vol. 91, no. 6 (June 1968), pp. 24–27.
Goodman, Paul. "Two Issues in Planning." *Commentary,* Vol. 44, no. 2 (August 1967), pp. 75–77.
Graham, Benjamin. *The Flexible Work-Year: An Answer to Unemployment.* An Occasional Paper on the Role of the Economic Order in the Free Society. Santa Barbara, California: Center for the Study of Democratic Institutions, 1964.
Griswold v. State of Connecticut, 381 U.S. (1965).
Harrington, Michael. *The Accidental Century.* New York: Macmillan Co., 1965.
Hayden, Thomas. "A Letter to the New (Young) Left." *The New Student Left.* Edited by Mitchell Cohen and Dennis Hale. Boston: Beacon Press, 1967.
Hollomon, J. Herbert. "Technology and Public Policy." *ASTME Vectors,* American Society of Tool Manufacturing Engineers. 1967, pp. 14–18.
Jacobs, Paul, and Landau, Saul. *The New Radicals.* New York: Vintage Books, 1966.
Jaffee, A. J., and Froomkin, Joseph. *Technology and Jobs.* New York: Frederick A. Praeger, 1968.
Jaffee, Frederick S., and Polgar, Steven. "Family Planning and Public Policy: Is the 'Culture of Poverty' the New Cop-Out?" *Journal of Marriage and the Family,* Vol. 30, no. 2 (May 1968), pp. 228–35.
Kahn, Herman, and Wiener, Anthony J. *The Year 2000.* New York: Macmillan Co., 1967.
Katz, Carol Hecht, ed. *The Law and the Low Income Consumer.* New York: Project on Social Welfare Law, New York University School of Law, 1968.
Keniston, Kenneth. *The Uncommitted.* New York: Dell Publishing Co., a Delta Book, 1965.
Keniston, Kenneth. *Young Radicals.* New York: Harcourt, Brace & World, 1968.

Keyserling, Leon H. "The Problem of Problems: Economic Growth." *Social Policies for America in the Seventies: Nine Divergent Views.* Edited by Robert Theobald. Garden City, N.Y.: Doubleday & Co., 1968.

Kraft, Ivor. "There is No Panacea." *The Nation,* Vol. 208, no. 3 (January 20, 1969), pp. 71–73.

Luce, Phillip Abbott. *The New Left.* New York: David McKay Co., 1966.

McGovern, William Montgomery, and Collier, David S. *Radicals and Conservatives.* Chicago: Henry Regnery Co., 1958.

McKitterick, J. B. "Planning the Existential Society." *Vital Speeches of the Day,* September 15, 1968, pp. 728–32.

McLuhan, Marshall. *Understanding Media: The Extensions of Man.* New York: McGraw-Hill Book Co., 1964.

McLuhan, Marshall, and Fiore, Quentin. *The Medium is the Massage.* New York: Random House, 1967.

Malthus, Thomas A. An Essay on the Principle of Population. Homewood, Ill.: Richard D. Irwin, 1963.

Mitau, G. Theodore. *Decade of Decision.* New York: Charles Scribner's Sons, 1967.

Morley, Felix. "What's Behind the Student Demonstrations." *Nation's Business,* Vol. 54, no. 3 (March 1966), pp. 25–26.

Neil, Robert E. "The More the Merrier?" *Commonweal,* Vol. 87, no. 18 (February 9, 1968), pp. 556–58.

Nelson, Richard R., Peck, Merton J., and Kalachek, Edward D. *Technology, Economic Growth and Public Policy.* Washington, D.C.: Brookings Institution, 1967.

Nelson, Truman. *The Right of Revolution.* Boston: Beacon Press, 1968.

Neubardt, Selig. *A Concept of Contraception.* New York: Trident Press, 1967.

"The New Radicals." *Time,* Vol. 89, no. 17 (April 28, 1967), pp. 27–28.

Nisbet, Robert A. "The Impact of Technology on Ethical Decision-Making." *Religion and Social Conflict.* Edited by Robert Lee and Martin E. Marty. New York: Oxford University Press, 1964.

O'Brien, John A. " 'Humanae Vitae': Reactions and Consequences." *Christian Century,* Vol. 76, no. 9 (February 26, 1969), pp. 288–89.

"Our Future Business Environment." A progress Report on a Continuing General Electric Study of Informed Opinion Outside the Company on Social, Political and Economic Trends of the Next Decade. New York: General Electric, April 1968.

Poverty Law Reporter. New York: Commerce Clearing House, 1968.

Replacing Welfare. *Wall Street Journal,* October 11, 1968.

Schorr, Alvin L. *Poor Kids.* New York: Basic Books, 1966.

Schwartz, Edward E. "A Way to End the Means Test." *Social Work,* Vol. 9, no. 3 (July 1964), pp. 3–12, and 97.

Servan-Schreiber, J. J. *The American Challenge.* New York: Atheneum, 1968.

Shadegg, Stephen C. "Conservatism and Political Action." *Left, Right and Center.* Robert A. Goldwin, ed. Chicago: Rand McNally & Co., 1968.

Somers, Gerald G., ed. *Retraining the Unemployed.* Madison: University of Wisconsin Press, 1968.

218 / SOCIAL WELFARE INSTITUTIONS: PROSPECTS FOR THE FUTURE

Stigler, George J. "The Economics of Minimum Wage Legislation." *American Economic Review*, Vol. 36, no. 3 (June 1946), pp. 358–65.

Theobald, Robert. "American Physical Abundance." *Vital Speeches of the Day*, May 1, 1968, pp. 435–39.

Theobald, Robert. *Free Men and Free Markets*. Garden City, N.Y.: Doubleday & Co., Anchor Books, 1965.

Theobald, Robert, ed. *The Guaranteed Income*. Garden City, N.Y.: Doubleday & Co., 1966.

"The Triple Revolution." *The Ad Hoc Committee on The Triple Revolution*. Santa Barbara, California, 1964.

U.S. Congress. Joint Economic Committee. *Guaranteed Minimum Income Programs Used by Governments of Selected Countries*, by Martin Schnitzer. Joint Committee Print, Study Paper 11. Washington, D.C.: Government Printing Office, 1968.

U.S. Congress. Senate. Committee on Government Operations. *Population Crisis*. S. Rept. 1676, 89th Cong., 1st sess., 1965. Part 2-B.

U.S. Department of Health, Education, and Welfare. *The President's Proposals for Welfare Reform*. Washington, D.C.: Government Printing Office, October 2, 1969.

U.S. Department of Labor. *Technology and Manpower in the Textile Industry of the 1970's*. Washington, D.C.: Government Printing Office, 1968.

U.S. National Archives and Records Service, Office of the Federal Register. *Weekly Compilation of Presidential Documents*. Washington, D.C.: Government Printing Office, August 18, 1969.

Widmer, Kingsley. "Why Dissent Turns Violent." *The Nation*, Vol. 208, no. 14 (April 7, 1969), pp. 425–29.

Williams, William Appleman. *The Great Evasion*. Chicago: Quadrangle Books, 1964.

Wineman, David, and James, Adrienne. "The Advocacy Challenge to Schools of Social Work," *Social Work*, Vol. 14, no. 2 (April 1969), pp. 23–32.

"World's No. 1 Worry—Too Many People." *U.S. News & World Report*, Vol. 66, no. 11 (March 17, 1969), pp. 48–52.

II

The Development of the
Social Work Profession

Chapter Seven

The Social Work Profession:
Growth and Trends

$\mathbf{N}$o profession has been so profoundly influenced by centuries of philosophical searching and contradictory doctrines of social thought as social work. Poverty, dependency, and other kinds of human deprivation have always been in some measure related to morality; to the evils or graces of wealth, property, and governmental structure; and to the improvidence of the idler. There has always been, too, an apparently irrepressible need for rational men to design and reshape social systems and social institutions, thus rearranging people in terms of the totality of their relationships, opportunities, and responsibilities.

Alfred J. Kahn has noted the symbiotic as well as functional interdependence of man, social change, and the development of social responsibility.[1] As long as society itself expands and changes, individual need will occur and change. The changing need becomes more identifiable, more easily interpreted, and finally established as "legitimate." When the primary institutions no longer meet need, helping services must be developed and become a part of the changing order.

Elizabethan England reflected the first expression of individualism and nationalism in public welfare when interest was shifted from the wealth of princes to national economic and social concerns. English Poor Law, although malevolent and punitive, did place more emphasis on individual groups and groupings and "upon the kind of life each should live" than on money and goods. Rural and urban dwellers, the church and the laity, the merchant and the craftsman each had their own orientation and goals as well as their own way of life. Security and well-being meant different things to each. There were fixed wages for workers, regulated apprenticeship for the sons of the wealthy, and work for children of the poor. The local community directed its own affairs, protected its members,[2] and designated the Overseers of the Poor as guardians of the economic, social, and moral welfare of those who could not function within the clearly defined segments of society.

Under this system the poor and other inadequate persons were helped to fit into their role as paupers but were not enabled to escape from their assigned status. The mentally and physically handicapped, the able-bodied poor, and the deviate were not readily absorbed by society despite its tacit commitment to the Judeo-Christian ethic. Yet changes occurred, not because of any change in the nature and degree of man's compassion, but primarily because men could no longer control the socioeconomic milieu in which they were forced to live.

[1] Alfred J. Kahn, ed., *Issues in American Social Work* (New York: Columbia University Press, 1959), p. 16.
[2] T. H. Marshall, "Welfare in the Context of Social Development," in John S. Morgan, ed., *Welfare and Wisdom* (Toronto: University of Toronto Press, 1966), p. 30.

SOCIAL PHILOSOPHY: ITS IMPACT ON THE DEVELOPMENT OF THE PROFESSION

Socrates believed that no man voluntarily chooses to do evil; his dialectic on the meaning of one's own thoughts was deeply set in the psychoanalytical concept of "know thyself" or, more specifically, "know thine own mind." Aristotle wrote of the social instinct, social evolution, and the humanity of man's social nature, yet he placed highest value on the state, stressing that it exists for "the sake of the good life" and has precedence over man because man cannot live without the community of others. Plato was one of the philosophical moralists who did not moralize, but saw the state as the human realization of perfection, and wrote of its usefulness to man.

The evils of private property and the exploitation of the propertyless had long been a concern of social thinkers. Sir Thomas More, the English utopian, wrote scathingly of those who would enlarge their kingdoms and thus deprive others of an equal voice in government. Voltaire, the French Rationalist, had great compassion for the poor, stressed their freedom of expression, and believed that, with proper motivation, they could and would make themselves heard. Count Claude Henri de Saint-Simon, the French philosopher and social scientist who took part in the American Revolution, supported an early version of the guaranteed right to work. His plan provided for an ideal society in which a "right to work" would be guaranteed to all and in which men would be rewarded in terms of their behavior and usefulness to society. The Aristotelian doctrine of the greatest good for the greatest number was adopted by St. Thomas Aquinas, the thirteenth century Scholastic philosopher, who sought to reconcile this viewpoint with the teachings of the Roman Catholic church. Aquinas relied on man's inherent social nature to create a functional society that would respect and support the welfare of all.

Three eighteenth-century philosophers with dissimilar backgrounds gave America a rich heritage in the field of criminal law reform and were influential in designing a contemporary view of the field of corrections. The French publicist Montesquieu, in his epic work *Spirit of the Laws*, offered a significant study in comparative historical-legal developments as well as a treatise on the study of law in relation to other social processes. The famed English jurist William Blackstone, with his *Commentaries on the Laws of England*, and Cesare de Beccaria, author of *Essays on Crime and Punishment*, contributed two of the most scholarly volumes on criminal law reform. Beccaria, an Italian nobleman, recommended change in the severity of punishment of offenders and pointed out that the prevention of crime was more advantageous to society than punitive and retributive justice. He also advocated abolition of the death penalty, a viewpoint that is still highly controversial almost two centuries later.

Auguste Comte, father of the French positivist or scientific school and a student of Saint-Simon, described sociology as the science of the social order in an evolving society. In his mid-nineteenth-century purview he saw society as a developing, collective organism directed to the public good. Comte showed little inclination toward social reform in his work. His contribution to the social sciences was in clarifying the many diffuse historical and traditional abstractions of society and social interaction. He placed social structure in three distinct universes—theological, meta-physical, and scientific. This classification is still strongly reflected in social work philosophy and method.

The Spencerian philosophy of social evolution had great impact on some sectors of American scholarship. Herbert Spencer, the English phi-losopher, believed that man exists in a state of organic and biological equilibrium with society and that society depends for its very existence on the evolutionary struggle that ensues. Comparing society to a bio-logical unit, Spencer taught that whereas the various units comprising an animal organism exist for the good of the whole animal, the social organ-ism exists for the welfare of its members. Being a laissez-faire individual-ist, Spencer did not support the idea that legislation should deal with social problems, but advocated the need "to unite philanthropic energy with philanthropic calm." A strong believer in private property, he held that the ultimate political organization would be a state in which the products of industrialism would be used for the enhancement of human character and morality.

American sociologists and other social scientists regarded social phi-losophy as the taproot of their newly emerging science. Although the social philosophers lived in different eras and under diverse circumstances and conditions, they contributed to the development of sociological the-ory by providing a basis for theoretical agreement, disagreement, refine-ment, or rejection. The interesting aspect of this "partnership," however, lies in the interpretations and changes made. Sociology emerged as the discipline most closely associated with the study of social organization and the systematized principles of social reform. Sociologists have for the most part identified with the Aristotelian precept that man has a social nature and a desire and need for human interaction, association, and social justice.

Lester Frank Ward, one of America's most distinguished scholars, saw sociology as the social study of man's achievement and emphasized that the most important thing in human progress and association is not what men are, but what they do. He envisioned the social dynamic directed to the satisfaction of needs, the preservation of life, and the modification and manipulation of the environment. Many of Ward's ideas of associated life, diverse modes of interaction, and human relations have been incorporated into social reform and social welfare ideology. Ward saw society as the master of political authority, with the government acting as its agent in the treatment of social problems. He also viewed governmental intervention as the enabler of social progress.

Franklin H. Giddings, the highly respected sociologist and pioneer in social work education, supported Ward's conviction that sociology must give scientific support to social reform. He conceived of the social mind as being many minds interacting in such a way that there is a unanimity of reaction and response by which the group will come to a single decision and act in unison. This concept was premised on his belief in a "consciousness of kind," which caused him to postulate that men tend to be alike in eliciting sympathy, affection, and awareness of others and thus act collectively under a wide variety of stimuli. Giddings placed emphasis not only on the development of community life but on human rights. In assessing the social and psychological characteristics of man and society, he viewed social and group personality as having positive and negative attributes. The positive involved all of the puritanical virtues—vitality, intellect, morality, and sociality—the negative, an increase in the abnormal, the immoral, and the degraded.

Giddings believed that the "pseudo-social class" was composed of congenital and habitual paupers whose "consciousness of kind" is degenerate.

The history of the English Poor Law is one long record of the increase and diminution of pauperism with the rhythmical rise and fall of a maudlin sentimentalism that desired to bestow in alms and parish aid the augmenting wealth of the kingdom. All modern experience of poor relief is an overwhelming demonstration that any community can have all the pauperism and criminality that it cares to pay for.[3]

SOCIAL POLICY: ITS RELATIONSHIP TO THE DEVELOPMENT OF THE PROFESSION

Social work emerged as a profession in America amid turbulent forces produced by a daring, impatient, highly creative, and opportunistic people. It survived the conservative impact of the nineteenth-century individualism inherited from the founding fathers, who spurned aristocracy

[3] Franklin H. Giddings, *The Principles of Sociology* (New York: Macmillan & Co., 1896), pp. 127–29.

to exploit new and free land and to bring about, with singular intent and hard work, a new and free nation. There was less concern historically with differentiating the poor from the rich than the worker from the idler. Men who worked were regarded highly for doing something useful; those who remained idle were considered immoral or debased in nature.

OPPOSITION TO PUBLIC RELIEF

In the nineteenth century there was deep conviction that public relief was unjust because it taxed unfairly one segment of the community for the benefit of another without any compensating return. There was conviction, too, that in most cases public relief subsidized and encouraged immorality, debauchery, and crime. Yet there was also some recognition that not all poor people were unwilling to work and that some situations and circumstances were beyond the individual's control. In such cases public relief was to be given, but the preferred way of providing help was through the almshouse.[4]

There was also a tendency to oppose poor relief on the grounds that it would create in the individual a sense of failure, defeat, and dependency that would lead to crime and would lower the wages of those willing to work. Poor relief was also seen as depriving the individual of "the joys of working" and as leading to generational dependency because it could never meet an individual's or family's total needs. In addition, poor relief would be an injustice to the recipient in that he would assume it to be a right to which he was entitled.

At one point in her role as commissioner of the New York State Board of Charities, Josephine Shaw Lowell wrote to some of the state's municipalities asking for information about the various poor relief programs. In 1883, the superintendent of the poor in Herkimer wrote that considerable money was being saved by sending all disabled transients to the poor house, demanding that all persons able to work do so or go to the poor house, and granting assistance only to those families with young children. The superintendent ended his letter by stating:

> I can safely say that there are not as many paupers in our poorhouse, that there are not as many destitute in our villages, and that there are no complaints from any class of people.
> There is one drawback to our present condition, and that is that the number of insane is increasing; while pauperism is slightly decreasing, insanity is increasing with us.[5]

[4] Josephine Shaw Lowell, *Public Relief and Private Charity* (New York: G. P. Putnam's Sons, 1884), pp. 1–8.
[5] *Ibid.*, p. 65.

One can safely assume that chronic pauperism may at least in part be related to mental illness, yet little association was made between the two. Mrs. Lowell stated:

> In the insane asylums, teaching, moral instruction and employment would usually be found the most efficacious means for the cure of disease. . . . Insanity in the majority of cases is due to excessive indulgence in one form or other of vice, and that frequently the insane are persons who have so long neglected self-control that they finally lose all power of self-control.[6]

This was a significant period in the development of the social work profession, an era in which began a struggle between public and private agencies. The belief continued that unless public relief was given in such a way that the grant was indefinite in amount and duration, chronic dependency would result. There was also a great concern that poor relief administration would lack the humanitarian aspects of the charitable agencies because the giving would not be voluntary and because it would tend to make the recipient feel equal to his benefactor, thus eliminating the charitable quality of the relationship.[7]

The philosophy of the charity organization society movement has been likened to that of a business enterprise. Charity workers insisted that the "buyer" (recipient) be allowed to purchase welfare services from only one seller and that it was not to the seller's or the buyer's benefit "to tell his sad story to several agencies and obtain aid several times over." Seymour J. Mandelbaum described "many small, uncoordinated and even competitive agencies" and reported that "the last three decades of the nineteenth century saw these good souls trying to unite like businessmen in their fields, in order to exercise monopoly power."[8] Another writer considered the charity workers to be dismayed by and distrustful of rapid urbanization, with the result that many turned to history and learned the wrong lesson.[9] There was a tendency to mold government to an ideal characteristic of a far simpler nation. It was difficult for many to accept the changing role of society and the charity workers continued to see themselves as "guardians of the Protestant ethic, where good government reflected management by good people—the middle and upper classes, the affluent, the well-educated and the virtuous."[10]

[6] *Ibid.*, p. 77.
[7] *Ibid.*, p. 89.
[8] Seymour J. Mandelbaum, *Boss Tweed's New York* (New York: John Wiley & Sons, 1965), p. 28.
[9] Alexander B. Callow, *The Tweed Ring* (New York: Oxford University Press, 1966), p. 5.
[10] *Ibid.*

CHANGING ATTITUDE TOWARD POVERTY

The "hereditary pauper" slowly lost his criminal status through a growing insistence on a broader and less provincial understanding of poverty and dependency. Charles R. Henderson submitted that society must have more knowledge of the interrelatedness of social and economic conditions in order to evaluate the degree and causes of pauperism and treat it accordingly. He explained that in 1890 it was necessary for a working man to earn $520 a year to support a family minimally but the national average income was only $192. Because the per capita cost of living was estimated to be 75 cents to $1.25 a week exclusive of shelter costs, it seemed obvious that the family would suffer drastically if earnings fell below $1.00 per week per person.[11] Henderson argued that the causes of crime —immorality, poverty, and deprivation—were related to causative environmental factors and that poverty could not continue to be viewed as indigenous only to the pauper but must be recognized as a condition common to many workingmen in the United States. He also pointed to the fact that the "vices" so freely associated with poverty were not confined to the economically deprived:

> The more individual causes of poverty, namely ignorance, shiftlessness, intemperance, premature marriages, the habits of gambling and borrowing are to be found not alone in any one class of the community, but infect the whole social body, deadening that spirit of devotion to social tasks by which alone men become strong.[12]

Robert Hunter, associated with the University Settlement in Chicago, stated that pauperism was one of the greatest fears of the workingman in the early part of the twentieth century. He differentiated pauperism and poverty by defining the pauper as "one who depends upon public or private charity for sustenance." A person could not be a pauper unless he received some kind of charitable aid, yet thousands lived at the poverty level.

Hunter reflected the convictions of his era when he expressed his judgment that "the sins of men should bring their own punishment, and the poverty which punishes the vicious and the sinful is good and necessary. Social and industrial institutions that save men from the painful consequences of folly are not productive of the greatest good."[13] Simultaneously, however, many concerned persons began to question their right

[11] Charles R. Henderson, *Modern Methods of Charity* (New York: Macmillan Co., 1904), p. 381.
[12] *Ibid.*, p. 385.
[13] Robert Hunter, *Poverty* (New York: Macmillan Co., 1912), p. 9.

to judge the poor on moral grounds or to take responsibility for validating such judgment. The need for social reform was becoming ever more apparent by the nature and impact of the multivariant social problems relating to regular employment, fair wages, safe working conditions, the prevention and control of contagious and crippling diseases, the yardless tenement, and the abuse and misuse of child labor in hundreds of sweat-shops. There was also a growing concern about the social and economic exploitation of the immigrant and the need to respond intelligently and responsibly to new ethnic, racial, and nationality groupings. Hunter elaborated eloquently on the human condition as he studied and perceived it:

> The mass of the poor are bred of miserable and unjust social conditions, which punish the good and pure, the faithful and industrious, the slothful and vicious, all alike. We may not by going into the homes of the poor be able to determine which are in poverty because of individual causes, or which are in poverty because of social wrongs; but we can see by looking about us, that men are brought into misery by the action of social and economic forces. And the wrongful action of such forces is a preventable thing.[14]

The attitudes expressed by Hunter were in marked contrast to those of earlier scholars. In 1883, William Graham Sumner, the colorful, ministerial-trained Yale sociologist, described "the forgotten man" as "the simple, honest laborer ready to earn his living by productive work." This man, Sumner believed, receives little attention because he is independent and self-supporting and "does not appeal to the emotions or the excitement of the sentiments." [15] Sumner had small patience with philanthropists who were constantly concerned with "the shiftless, the imprudent, the negligent, the inefficient, the idle, the intemperate, the extravagant and the vicious." In the same lecture Sumner made these pithy observations:

> We hear constantly of "reform" and the reformers turn out to be people who do not like things as they are and wish that they could be made nicer. We hear a great many exhortations to make progress from people who do not know in what direction they want to go. Consequently social reform is the most barren and tiresome subject of discussion amongst us, except aesthetics.[16]

Sumner attributed the rise of a wealthy class to freedom from the problems of state interference and the ultimate development of "socialistic enterprise." In an interesting essay titled "The Absurd Effort to Make the World Over," he stated:

[14] *Ibid.*, pp. 62–64.
[15] William Graham Sumner, *The Forgotten Man and Other Essays*, Albert G. Keller, ed. (New Haven: Yale University Press, 1919), p. 476.
[16] *Ibid.*, p. 468.

The captains of industry and the capitalists . . . if they are successful, win, in these days, great fortunes in a short time. There are no earnings which are more legitimate or for which greater services are rendered to the whole industrial body. . . .[17]

Sumner remained a latter-day Spencerian who strongly believed in free enterprise, private interests, and man's right to become as wealthy as he wished. Edward T. Devine said of Sumner: "What [he] could have to say about crop restriction and the N.R.A. codes baffles the imagination, or at least the feebler powers of expression, of this degenerate age, as he no doubt would have called it." [18]

Other sociologists writing in the early years of the twentieth century did not share Sumner's views about big business. E. A. Ross was especially concerned about the "ruthless exercise of corporate" might, which he labeled "sinning by syndicate." In his thinking,

corporations are necessary, yet through nobody's fault, they tend to become soulless and lawless. . . . Nothing but the curb of organized society. . . . can keep them from grinding into dividends the stamina of children, the health of women, the lives of men, the purity of the ballot, the honor of public servants, and the supremacy of laws.[19]

Thorstein Veblen, the economist-philosopher, while far apart from Sumner on matters concerning big business and capitalistic enterprise, nevertheless called philanthropies "essays in pragmatic romance." [20] He pointed out, however, that work was always considered a virtue for the poor but that it had a far different meaning for the wealthy. Veblen noted the "pecuniary emulation" of those involved in "conspicuous leisure." It was traditionally considered a mark of inferiority for the rich to engage in useful occupation. If a wealthy man worked, he was considered to be unworthy of his status. Paradoxically, the Puritan ethic decreed that hard work paved the poor man's road to Heaven, but Veblen indicated that for the rich man, "abstention from labour was not only an honorific or meritorious act, but it presently becomes a requisite of decency." [21] In retrospect, then, it is clear that there was a double standard of societal expectation: in the case of the poor, useful employment

[17] William Graham Sumner, *War and Other Essays*, Albert G. Keller, ed. (New Haven: Yale University Press, 1911), p. 201.

[18] Edward T. Devine, *When Social Work Was Young* (New York: Macmillan Co., 1939), p. 37.

[19] Edward A. Ross, *Sin and Society* (Boston: Houghton Mifflin Co., 1907), pp. 130–31.

[20] Thorstein Veblen, *What Veblen Taught: Selected Writings of Thorstein Veblen*, Wesley C. Mitchell, ed. (New York: Viking Press, 1936), p. xix.

[21] *Ibid.*, p. 235.

was seen as necessary in order to avoid personal degradation and wrong-doing; for the wealthy, work was regarded as dishonor.

NEW VALUES AND CONCERNS

The early twentieth century brought increasing intellectual, moral, and political cynicism. It was a time of ambivalence in which snatches of the old ethnic were retained while an attempt was made to find new values. It was a period of "judgmental science" and penetrating muck-raking. At an earlier date, Richard L. Dugdale, who created the genetically dismal Jukes family, stated without equivocation that "whatever is physiologically right is morally right and whatever is physiologically unsound is morally rotten." [22] Lincoln Steffens, the socio-moralist, indicated that hypocrisy in solving social problems persisted in the first decade of the twentieth century. Chafing at the pseudo-propriety of the times, he stated: "Oh, we are good on Sunday, and we are fearfully patriotic on the Fourth of July," [23] and "The Fourth of July oration is the front of graft . . . there is no patriotism in it, but treason." [24] E. A. Ross, writing of the pretension of American "holiness," exhorted his students "not to be good, but to be rational." [25]

The cynicism and skepticism of those days tended to create a new dynamic, that of a beginning displacement of charitable and political paternalism by educational and democratic processes. When the National Conference of Charities and Correction was established in 1879, its major concerns related to problems encountered by state boards of public charities. Philanthropy did not as yet state these concerns. There was a growing movement, however, toward unity and coordination of effort and an increasing recognition that the volunteer or "friendly visitor" needed to have knowledge of his objectives in working with the poor.

TRAINING FOR SOCIAL WORK

In 1893 Anna Dawes, a highly regarded social worker, presented a significant paper titled "The Need for Training Schools for a New Profession" at the Chicago meeting of the International Congress of Charities. At the 1897 meeting of the National Conference of Charities and Correction, Mary Richmond further expanded the new concept, stating that training for social work was an educational function and should be provided by institutions for higher learning. She advocated a close relation-

[22] R. L. Dugdale, *The Jukes* (4th ed.; New York: G. P. Putnam's Sons, 1877), p. 87.
[23] Lincoln Steffens, *The Shame of the Cities* (New York: McClure, Phillips & Co., 1904), p. 11.
[24] *Ibid.*, p. 15.
[25] *Op. cit.*, p. viii.

ship between the professional school and social agencies, both public and private, to permit students to observe social problems and social work practice and to provide a functional tie between classroom instruction and the experience gained in the agency.

A year later the first Training Class in Philanthropy was established in New York City under the auspices of the Charity Organization Society. It became the Summer School in Philanthropic Work and the first school of social work in the country. In 1904 the program was expanded to a full year of study and the name was changed to the New York School of Philanthropy.

In 1919 the school, which had offered a two-year graduate program since 1912, was renamed the New York School of Social Work. It continued under the direction of the COS until 1939, when the COS merged with the Association for Improving the Condition of the Poor and the two became the Community Service Society. In 1940 the school formally affiliated with Columbia University and began to grant a master of science degree, although it remained a part of CSS until 1950.

A similar pattern was followed in Chicago where the Institute of Social Science was planned as part of the Extension Division of the University of Chicago, in 1903. The Chicago School of Civics and Philanthropy became an independent entity in 1908 and in 1920 the program was returned to the University of Chicago as its graduate School of Social Service Administration. The Simmons School of Social Work founded in 1904 was initially supported by Simmons College and Harvard University but was solely identified with Simmons after 1919. By 1915 seven schools had been established, and in the next four years this number nearly tripled.

SOCIAL WORK AS A PROFESSION

In 1915 Abraham Flexner, a renowned educator, developed criteria identifying the characteristics of a profession. Using the medical model, he perceived a profession as (1) combining intellectual involvement and individual responsibility, (2) drawing its knowledge from the sciences and other branches of learning, (3) applying this knowleldge to practical and definite objectives, (4) tending toward self-organization, and (5) becoming increasingly more altruistic in its client relations. Flexner did not feel that social work had achieved professional status at that time since, in his opinion, it had no definite ends, it lacked the discipline of individual responsibility, and it was but one aspect of many related fields.[26]

[26] Abraham Flexner, "Is Social Work a Profession?" *Proceedings of the National Conference of Charities and Correction* (1915), pp. 576–90.

Writing in the next decade, Robert D. Kohn stated that the criteria of a profession should be developed by a member of that profession. Kohn, an architect, expressed his conviction that a professional objective is

the perfection of a service, and the most important reward of that perfection is not to the extent to which it is paid, but to the extent to which the service is appreciated by those best competent to judge it—by those who practice the same profession.[27]

Kohn listed his criteria of a profession: (1) its work must be done in the public interest, (2) it must have the means to improve in the public's mind, (3) it must have useful intra- and interprofessional relationships and interests, (4) there must be a continually improving admissions policy for entry into the field and adequate educational qualifications for practice, and (5) public needs must have priority over professional desires or rights. Kohn also stressed the importance of creating favorable public opinion if a profession is to be understood and accepted. He wrote: "Nothing is more evident than that today the inexpert is listened to more freely, perhaps more trustfully than the expert, on questions of public policy. Even when the expert speaks officially, he is suspect as to his motives." [28]

Social work continued to have difficulty in defining its function and establishing itself as an independent discipline. Charity and social work were not clearly differentiated. Stuart A. Queen commented that there continued to be a strong conviction growing out of the Elizabethan Poor Law heritage that the poor and otherwise needy are the responsibility of the government and that charity is never able to meet need adequately. The church and other sources of private philanthropy drew attention away from the significant issues involved in poverty and dealt only with the obvious suffering. Donors were often motivated by selfish, maudlin sentimentality. More important, they reflected paternalism rather than justice and charity rather than democracy. If social work were to remain charity, then it could not be a profession, but merely one function of many other professions. Queen believed that social work was not a profession prior to 1920 for yet another reason: the persistence of the apprenticeship system in social work education.[29]

There was still a charity ring to the treatment of the poor by the female do-gooder, reminiscent of Caleb's conversation with Meredith in *The*

[27] Robert D. Kohn, "The Significance of the Professional Ideal," *Annals of the American Academy of Political and Social Science*, Vol. 101, no. 190 (May 1922), p. 2.

[28] *Ibid.*, p. 4

[29] Stuart A. Queen, *Social Work in the Light of History* (Philadelphia: J. B. Lippincott Co., 1922), pp. 307–8.

Golden Fleece in which he observed, "Why that merry black-eyed damsel, Lucy Langton . . . can play at charity when she has nothing better to play at, hunt out 'cases' when there's no other game to hunt."[30] Despite these traditionalisms, the period from 1900 to 1920 was one of growing significance in the development of the profession. The social sciences slowly began to make an impact on the legitimation of social concerns. Social reform had been primarily concerned with social conditions and those facets of American life that could be handled as impersonal entities. Social work emphasis on causation was then a long way from Benjamin E. Youngdahl's contemporary observations on "Group Morality Through the Law," in which the social worker challenges the status quo, which tends to accept or at least tolerate illiteracy and other human problems.[31]

THE BEGINNINGS OF A METHODOLOGY

In the second decade of this century the emerging profession of social work was faced with the necessity of creating a more "scientific" approach to the prevention and cure of human problems. There was movement toward increasing governmental support of agencies and recognition that a means must be devised to measure the effectiveness of work with clients. In addition there was a growing tendency to worry somewhat less about the duplication of charity organization services "in which children were baptized seven times in seven other churches . . . and whose parents received Protestant fuel and Catholic groceries." There was agreement, however, with Mary E. Richmond's belief that "the indiscriminate and insensitive donor would never win Heaven by making other human beings less human."[32] Miss Richmond would have indeed agreed with Everett C. Hughes that "professionals profess." "This," Hughes states, "is the essence of the professional idea and the professional claim."[33]

Miss Richmond's most valued legacy to the profession is believed by many to be her classic volume *Social Diagnosis*.[34] Hers was a sociological approach to casework and, although there was stress on individualized need, she paid scant attention to the psychological factors that affected social and emotional functioning. Service was always directed to material or financial need and "diagnosis" was used in its most literal sense—that is,

[30] A.L.O.E., *The Golden Fleece and Zarda's Notebook* (New York: Robert Carter & Bros., 1876), p. 19.

[31] Benjamin E. Youngdahl, *Social Action and Social Work* (New York: Association Press, 1966), p. 33.

[32] Mary E. Richmond, *The Good Neighbor in the Modern City* (Philadelphia: J. B. Lippincott Co., 1907), p. 150.

[33] Everett C. Hughes, "Professions," in Kenneth S. Lynn, ed., *The Professions in America* (Boston: Houghton Mifflin Co., 1965), p. 2.

[34] New York: Russell Sage Foundation, 1917.

to discover the need and attempt to meet it. There was something more, however, to the Richmond approach. She believed deeply in the value of knowing how to obtain information from the client and from collateral sources, how to record the findings, and how to make appropriate referrals. There was also a scholarly insistence on the social worker's attitudes and behavior. Miss Richmond believed in the professional value of sincerity, directness, and the need to remain impersonal in relation to the client, but never detached. She had expressed this belief a decade before *Social Diagnosis* was published, when she wrote: "What we win through authority, we lose; what we win through influence, the influence of understanding and caring, we keep." [35]

A significant step in the recognition of social work as a profession came in 1918 when the Training School of Psychiatric Social Work at Smith College was asked to train social workers to treat and reeducate soldiers suffering from war-related neuroses. Schools of social work up to that point had done little to bring social workers closer to the center of the totality of American life with its many new problems and needs. Even then, as Edith R. Spaulding reported, the school questioned whether it was "too risky" to introduce theories and the "actualities of mental illness" and whether the students were "old enough to assimilate what has caused many an older person mental and emotional indigestion." Because their training was designed to "cultivate in them comprehending and sympathetic attitudes towards the problems of mental disease," it was finally decided that the students would be given a course in the concepts of normal and abnormal behavior, a short course in mental testing, information on alcoholism and the physical basis for emotional illness, and skills in history-taking.[36]

In the 1920s Americans experienced their first reactions to the consequences of a world war. There was a changing and urgent demand on the profession not only for services to relieve immediate distress but for the expansion of service to a new group of people—the returning psychologically and physically damaged war veteran who could not be expected to fit into the charity mold. As a result, social work practitioners and educators began to turn seriously to theories of behavior and psychopathology for direction in helping the battle-fatigued or "shell-shocked" veteran.

Mary Van Kleeck and Graham R. Taylor made the observation that, of all the professions, social work is the only one in which from its begin-

[35] Richmond, *The Good Neighbor in the Modern City, op. cit.,* p. 157.
[36] Edith R. Spaulding, "The Training School of Psychiatric Social Work at Smith College," *Proceedings of the National Conference of Social Work,* 1919 (Chicago: Rogers & Hall Co., 1920), pp. 606–8.

nings the practitioner has been mandated by one group to give services to another.[37] It is not only expected to serve, but to make its objectives and techniques a common possession for the common good. Edward T. Devine had earlier called attention to social work "as a common possession" in pointing out that it was never reactionary or utopian and that anyone—liberal or conservative—willing to face the new order of needs in dynamic America could take part in it. But the young profession had difficulty in achieving its own identity for, as Devine stated: "The spirit of what we now call social work has emerged many times in the past and is even now taking new forms." [38]

It was this flexibility, however, that allowed social work to develop as a profession. Rosa Wessel observed that it operated without the burden of accumulated theory or intellectual and symbolic content, but long faced the pragmatic test of "does it work?" [39] On the other hand, it is this fluidity of program and practice that has limited society's knowledge of what the social worker does and how he is educated to do it. Unlike the practice of medicine, law, teaching, or nursing, the community does not ask whether a social worker is trained for his task, but it expects him to be knowledgeable and competent and it invests in the social agency, which the community supports both ideologically and materially, accountability for producing this competence.[40]

This viewpoint is historically well supported by Michael M. Davis and Andrew R. Warner, who described the functions of a social worker in a medical setting as broad and varied, but aimed in particular at "medical efficiency to gain medical results." The social worker was expected to assist the physician in the education of patients and the control of their environment, judge the level of the patient's intelligence for diagnostic purposes, teach hygiene, communicate with other agencies, and take social histories. He was defined as a person who has learned how to make critical but sympathetic judgments about the human problems presented and how to deal effectively with such problems in practice. The only question raised as to the educational preparation for this "effective judgment" and skill was whether social workers should be trained as nurses! [41]

Alfred North Whitehead wrote that "education is the requisite of the

[37] Mary Van Kleeck and Graham R. Taylor, "The Professional Organization of Social Work," *Annals of the American Academy of Political and Social Science,* Vol. 101, no. 290 (May 1922), p. 158.

[38] *Op. cit.,* pp. 3–5.

[39] Rosa Wessel and Goldie Basch Faith, *Professional Education Based In Practice* (Philadelphia: University of Pennsylvania School of Social Work, 1953), p. 17.

[40] *Ibid.,* p. 7.

[41] Michael M. Davis and Andrew R. Warner, *Dispensaries* (New York: Macmillan Co., 1918), p. 101.

art of the utilization of knowledge." [42] Gordon Hearn maintained that theory-building in professional education and practice will be influenced by "our beliefs about the nature of knowing and . . . the extent to which we think one can achieve certainty." Each, he continued, will reflect influences of society "by his view of man and the universe, for he will tend to notice and incorporate only that which fits, while rejecting that which violates, his philosophy and value orientation." [43]

MILESTONES IN THE PROFESSION'S DEVELOPMENT

An important step in the development of social work as an art and a science was taken when the American Association of Social Workers was created in June 1921. The constitution of the new organization stipulated its purpose

. . . to bring together professional social workers for such cooperative effort as may enable the group more effectively to fulfill its function in service to society. To this end the Association may formulate and seek to establish preparation and training, disseminate information concerning social work as a profession and conduct research . . . and such other activities . . . appropriate to this purpose. [44]

During its first five years the association studied, defined, and classified positions in social work and their required qualifications; published a monthly journal to provide information for its members; published a series of pamphlets describing family, psychiatric, and medical social work for students contemplating social work as a career; cooperated with the training schools in recruitment; and acted as a representative in the professional interest of its members. Although social workers employed in all settings were eligible for membership in AASW, creation of the organization did not impede the trend toward separate identification of those employed in special settings.

CONTRIBUTIONS TO THE LITERATURE

During this period the professional status of social work was enhanced by important contributions to its literature. In 1922 Mary E. Richmond's

[42] Alfred North Whitehead, *The Aims of Education* (New York: Macmillan Co., 1929), p. 6.
[43] Gordon Hearn, *Theory Building in Social Work* (Toronto: University of Toronto Press, 1958), pp. 12–13.
[44] "American Association of Social Workers' Constitution," cited in Esther Lucile Brown, *Social Work as a Profession* (New York: Russell Sage Foundation, 1935), p. 48.

What Is Social Case Work? [45] clarified the casework process and in 1924 Karl de Schweinitz' classic, *The Art of Helping People Out of Trouble*, offered an interpretation of social work to the layman.[46] The first *Social Work Year Book* was published by Russell Sage Foundation in 1929. This volume presented in encyclopedic form the history and current development of activities within the social service field and established a model for the periodic issuance of Year Books until 1960. (The first edition of the Year Book's successor, the *Encyclopedia of Social Work*, was published in 1965 by the National Association of Social Workers.) *American Charities and Social Work*, by Amos G. Warner, Stuart A. Queen, and Ernest B. Harper,[47] joined Mary Richmond's *Social Diagnosis* as a standard text for many educational programs in social work and the *Proceedings of the National Conference of Social Work* continued to bring new ideas and knowledge to the field.

Professional knowledge was also enriched as monographs and papers were made available by the U.S. Children's Bureau, Child Welfare League of America, Family Welfare Association (now the Family Service Association of America), American Association of Social Workers, and National Committee for Mental Hygiene. The monthly journals published by these organizations, the *Jewish Social Service Quarterly*, and the periodicals published by Survey Associates *(Survey Graphic, Survey Midmonthly*, and later *The Survey)* also contributed to a growing body of knowledge. These resources were augmented by *The Social Service Review*, a quarterly journal published by the School of Social Service Administration of the University of Chicago.

IDENTIFICATION OF SOCIAL WORK METHODS

One of the most significant reports published was the summary of deliberations, analyses, and conclusions reached by representatives of eight national organizations who attended four annual meetings at Milford, Pennsylvania, to discuss and clarify pertinent issues related to the practice of social casework.[48] The group concluded that, while social casework is a definite entity, "the problems of social case work and the equipment of

[45] Mary E. Richmond, *What Is Social Case Work?* (New York: Russell Sage Foundation, 1922.)

[46] Karl de Schweinitz, *The Art of Helping People Out of Trouble* (Boston and New York: Houghton Mifflin Co., 1924.)

[47] Amos G. Warner, Stuart A. Queen and Ernest B. Harper, *American Charities and Social Work* (New York: Thomas Y. Crowell Co., 1930.)

[48] *Social Case Work: Generic and Specific Studies in the Practice of Social Work* (New York: American Association of Social Workers, June 1929), which is usually referred to as the Milford Conference report.

the social case worker are fundamentally the same" regardless of the setting in which he works, and suggested that social casework be recognized as a generic process:

> In other words, in any discussion of problems, concepts, scientific knowledge or methods, generic social case work is the common field to which the specific forms of social case work are merely incidental. At the present time the practice of social work is more precise than the formulations of philosophy, knowledge, methods and experience.[49]

The conferees concluded that "there is no greater responsibility facing social case work at the present time than the responsibility of organizing continuous research into the concepts, problems and methods of its field."[50] The most significant value of the report for contemporary practice, however, was its recognition that "social work is a unified profession and not an aggregate of specialties" and that "generic social work is as valid and important a conception as generic social case work."[51] The fundamental social work methods were listed as social casework, community organization, group work, social research, and administration, and it was emphasized that these should all be included in social work education.

This report greatly influenced the development of social work as a profession and, more specifically, the future pattern of social work education. For some time many of its implications for practice were not fully accepted by agencies intent on the medical model and on preempting the teachings of psychiatry. This delay was perhaps accentuated by the publication of Virginia P. Robinson's *A Changing Psychology in Social Case Work*, which proved to be another milestone in the development of professionalism. Miss Robinson fully accepted the Milford Conference belief in a common social casework methodology. Her emphasis on the individual and on the importance of the caseworker's relationship with him as a means of enhancing treatment, however, served to focus professional attention on personal change. She stated:

> If it be granted that therapy, not history for its own sake, is the excuse for the case worker's intrusion into the lives of other human beings, then we must examine the first contacts from the angle of the treatment relationship which is being created there and determine each move by our judgment of its effect upon this relationship as a criterion.[52]

This was, indeed, a new and lasting concept in treatment.

[49] *Ibid.*, p. 11.
[50] *Ibid.*, p. 12.
[51] *Ibid.*, pp. 66 and 88.
[52] Virginia P. Robinson, *A Changing Psychology in Social Case Work* (Chapel Hill: University of North Carolina Press, 1934), p. 138.

The effects of the Milford Conference report in other areas were more immediate. In 1930 the Association of Training Schools for Professional Social Work appointed its first curriculum committee, and by 1935 courses in all five social work methods were available. However, the varied content of the courses in group work and community organization continued to reveal that the scope of these two fields had not yet been clarified or the differences between community organization and administration fully identified.[53]

OTHER PROFESSIONAL DEVELOPMENTS

Another significant innovation occurred in 1929 when plans were made for organization of the American Association of Public Welfare Officials during the National Conference of Social Work. As established in 1930, the American Public Welfare Association was principally concerned with the improvement of existing public welfare programs. When its first annual meeting was held in June 1931, however, the problems resulting from mass unemployment absorbed the attention and energies of its members and a committee was appointed "to work for increased public relief appropriations, especially in distressed rural areas and to promote better standards of administration."[54]

With the onset of the Depression in 1930, social work received increasing recognition as its members assumed an active role in identifying the problems brought about by existing economic conditions and in stimulating corrective legislation. During this crisis the growth and development of social work as a profession was greatly influenced by the changing national scene. There were new alignments in the responsibilities of public and private agencies as well as new concepts relating to the role of government on a local, state, and federal level.

There were other professional developments of great import during the Depression and post-Depression years. When the Group Work Section of the National Conference of Social Work was established in 1935, it set in motion a series of events that was to make social group work the most rapidly growing social work method. Interest in the meetings of this section resulted in the creation in 1936 of the American Association for the Study of Group Work. In 1946 the American Association of Group Workers was formed, with membership requirements that gave equal recognition to professional training and experience in education, recreation and social work.

[53] Wayne McMillen, "The Content of Professional Courses in Community Organization," *Social Service Review*, Vol. 9, no. 1 (March 1935), pp. 68–69.
[54] Josephine C. Brown, *Public Relief, 1929–1939*, (New York: Henry Holt and Company, 1940), p. 85.

At an earlier date group work had been limited primarily to character-building or youth-serving agencies and social settlements, but as social group work became an identifiable method, its value in other settings was recognized. There was a demand for professionally trained social group workers in child guidance clinics, hospitals, summer camps, day nurseries, and institutions for children, as well as in various types of adult facilities. By 1946 group therapy had also become a new method of serving the emotionally disturbed and the social group worker had become a member of the traditional clinic team in psychiatric settings.

A somewhat similar development began in 1938 when the Community Organization Section of the National Conference of Social Work was established. In six cities discussion groups were formed in which the objectives and techniques of community organization were discussed for later presentation at the section meetings. The Association for the Study of Community Organization was created in 1948. During subsequent years papers presented at the national conference, articles appearing in *Social Work Year Book*, and the publication of Wayne McMillen's *Community Organization for Social Welfare* [55] initiated "a scientific orientation to the concept of community organization as a process." [56] This achievement was regarded as one of the most significant developments in social welfare in the United States during the first half of the twentieth century.

THE PROFESSIONAL ORGANIZATIONS

The social work profession is generally considered to have come of age with the merger of the seven professional membership associations into a single organization. Stimulated in part by the American Association of Schools of Social Work, five of these seven associations had begun by 1949 to examine the feasibility of creating a single professional association of social workers, with the result that in 1950 the Temporary Inter-Association Council of Social Work Membership Organizations (TIAC) was formed. After a long period of study, planning, and negotiation, the National Association of Social Workers came into existence on October 1, 1955. Thus the social work profession is currently represented by a single membership association that gives recognition to the need for specialization in certain settings.

The purposes of the National Association of Social Workers are out-

[55] Wayne McMillen, *Community Organization for Social Welfare* (Chicago: University of Chicago Press, 1945.)

[56] Leonard W. Mayo, "Community Organization in 1946," *Proceedings of the National Conference of Social Work, 1946* (New York: Columbia University Press, 1947), p. 129.

lined in Article II of its bylaws. These purposes are broad but definitive and give direction to the growing responsibilities and goals of the profession. Among these responsibilities are the promotion of activities appropriate to strengthening and unifying the social work profession as a whole, the promotion of sound and continuous development of the various areas of social work practice in which the profession contributes to the meeting of specific aspects of human need, and the promotion of efforts in behalf of human well-being through methods of social action. The ultimate purpose of the Association, however, is to work toward maintaining and promoting high standards of practice in alleviating poverty and distress through the use of social work methods.

In October 1960 the NASW Delegate Assembly authorized establishment of the Academy of Certified Social Workers to identify and give recognition to individuals meeting specified standards of professional experience and education. The Academy was also seen as providing a means of fixing on its members the responsibility imposed by the profession in the absence of the state licensure legally incumbent on other professions. Qualifications for admission are membership in NASW, possession of the master of social work degree from a school accredited by the Council on Social Work Education, and two years of employment in one agency under the supervision of a member of the Academy. Members are issued a certificate and are authorized and encouraged to use the initials "ACSW" as their generic professional designation.

PROFESSIONAL EDUCATION IN SOCIAL WORK

During the mid-1930s marked progress was made in establishing a basic curriculum in professional social work education. As increasing agreement was reached regarding the fundamental principles and processes of social work, the American Association of Training Schools of Professional Social Work, established in 1919, sought to establish uniform basic curriculum emphasis, content, and requirements for all member schools. In 1944 this goal was achieved and a manual of accreditation was issued as a basis for the admission of new schools to the association.

In August 1946 another significant step was taken when the National Council on Social Work Education was formed to bring together representatives of the professional membership groups, professional schools of social work, colleges, and universities. Its primary purpose was to make an extensive assessment of current social work education. Through a grant from the Carnegie Corporation, a comprehensive and systematic study was made in 1948 by Ernest V. Hollis and Alice L. Taylor. Published in 1951, their report stimulated considerable discussion and led to the establishment of the Council on Social Work Education in 1952.[57] This new organization replaced the National Association of Schools of Social Work and the National Association of Schools of Social Administration (the latter was established in 1942 to develop an experimental undergraduate and graduate degree program). The new council included representatives from accredited schools of social work, undergraduate departments offering preprofessional courses, professional associations, and employing agencies.

One of CSWE's major projects was a 3½-year national curriculum study designed to develop educational objectives for use in creating appropriate learning experiences.[58] The 13 volume report published in 1959 dealt separately with content related to the values and ethics of the profession, human growth and social environment, social welfare policy and services, administration, research, casework, group work, community organization, undergraduate social work education, and education for social workers in the corrections field, in the public social services, and in rehabilitation of the handicapped.

The official statement of curriculum policy for the master's degree in social work was approved by CSWE's board of directors in October 1961. It includes a succinct statement of educational goals based on the following definition:

Social work as a profession is concerned with the restoration, maintenance, and enhancement of social functioning. It contributes, with other professions and disciplines, to the prevention, treatment, and control of problems in social functioning of individuals, groups and communities. . . . It has its own identity drawing from knowledge, values, and techniques applied in professional practice.[59]

As one of its major functions CSWE accepts responsibility for the accreditation of schools of social work granting the two-year MSW degree or a similarly designated degree. It does not accredit undergraduate social welfare programs, but schools offering such work may hold constituent membership.

[57] Ernest V. Hollis and Alice L. Taylor, *Social Work Education in the United States* (New York: Columbia University Press, 1951).

[58] Werner W. Boehm, director and coordinator, *Social Work Curriculum Study* (13 vols.; New York: Council on Social Work Education, 1959).

[59] "Official Statement of Curriculum Policy for the Master's Degree Program in Graduate Professional Schools of Social Work" (New York: Council on Social Work Education, October 1961), pp. 1–2. (Mimeographed.)

Summary

Social work, like other dynamic social movements, reflects the dislodgement of traditional social and economic symbols and values. It drew from many disciplines but it gained its professional status through the development of useful and defensible educational objectives and democratic service goals.

The history of social work is rooted in social philosophy, the Elizabethan Poor Law, philanthropy, and organized charity. These have often been opposing forces, attempting to justify or ameliorate poverty and dependency by the same or by quite different means. Social work emerged as an art, a science, and a profession in a relatively short period of time under various circumstances.

One writer has supplied a dramatic backdrop on which professional social work practice and education may be vividly projected. He predicted that the twentieth century will be called the "Age of the New Nation," "Age of the Psychoanalytical Revolution," "Age of Mass Society," and "Age of the Global War." The major themes of this century reflect cultural and social protest, a newly emerging social and political involvement, and a liberalizing interpretation of civil and human rights.[60]

It is abundantly clear that this century of concern has given the nation a new kind of community with a larger sense of personal and collective identity than ever before. It is also apparent that this development has given the social work profession significant impetus. During this era social work has developed the requisites for a profession and has legitimated its role and function in the nation. It has done so by accepting its responsibilities and by developing the identifiable components of professionalization.

Selected Bibliography

Devine, Edward T. *The Principles of Relief*. New York: Macmillan Co., 1939.
Devine, Edward T. and Lilian Brandt. *American Social Work in the Twentieth Century*. New York: The Frontier Press, 1921.
Follett, Mary Parker. *The New State*. New York: Longman's, 1934.
Hamilton, Gordon. "Helping People—The Growth of a Profession," *Social Work as Human Relations*. New York: Columbia University Press, 1949.
Howard, Donald S. *Social Welfare: Values, Means and Ends*. New York: Random House, 1969.

[60] S. N. Eisenstadt, *Modernization: Protest and Change* (Englewood Cliffs, N.J.: Prentice-Hall, 1966), pp. 32–33.

244 / THE SOCIAL WORK PROFESSION: GROWTH AND TRENDS

Kahn, Alfred J. "The Function of Social Work in The Modern World," in
Issues in American Social Work, Alfred J. Kahn, Editor. New York:
Columbia University Press, 1959.

Kasius, Cora (ed.). *New Directions in Social Work*. New York: Harper &
Row, 1954.

Konopka, Gisela. *Eduard C. Lindeman and Social Work Philosophy*. Minneapolis: The University of Minnesota Press, 1958.

Lowell, Josephine Shaw. *Public Relief and Private Charity*. New York: G. P.
Putnam's Sons, 1884.

Queen, Stuart A. *Social Work in The Light of History*. Philadelphia: J. B.
Lippincott Co., 1922.

Robinson, Virginia, P. *A Changing Psychology in Social Case Work*. Chapel
Hill: University of North Carolina Press, 1934.

Sumner, William Graham. *What Social Classes Owe Each Other*. New York:
Harper & Row, 1883.

Tufts, James H. *Education and Training for Social Work*. New York: Russell
Sage Foundation, 1923.

Warner, Amos G., Stuart A. Queen and Ernest B. Harper. *American Charities
and Social Work*. New York: Thomas Y. Crowell Co., 1930.

Weinberger, Paul E., Editor. *Perspectives on Social Welfare*. New York: The
Macmillan Co., 1969.

Chapter Eight

Methods of Social Work

THE OFFICIAL STATEMENT of curriculum policy issued by the Council on Social Work Education in 1962 listed casework, group work, and community organization as the primary methods of social work practice, with administration and research cited as enabling methods. The current thrust to dissipate social alienation and satisfy the yearning for human dignity and creative expression of individual and collective differences has placed new demands on social work practice. As a result, the profession must now address its skills to the broad spectrum of contemporary social problems by utilizing new knowledge and theory to strengthen the effectiveness of traditional social work methods and by developing innovative approaches in the use of these methods in a broad gestalt to achieve newly defined objectives. As task forces appointed by CSWE and NASW seek to determine whether any new classification of basic social work methods is needed to reflect the "emerging awareness that individual achievement and social change are the central activities of professional helping," [1] it is still useful to examine the essential characteristics and purposes of the traditional methods.

SOCIAL CASEWORK

A survey of social work literature over the past five decades reveals a score of definitions relating to the nature and function of social casework. Mary E. Richmond's much-quoted statement in 1915 that "social work is the art of doing different things for different people" [2] was soon followed by more analytic descriptions. Mary C. Jarrett regarded social casework as

. . . the art of bringing an individual who is in a condition of social disorder into the best possible relation with all parts of his environment. It is the special skill of the caseworker to study the complex of relationships that constitute the life of an individual and to construct as sound a life as possible out of elements found in the individual and his environment.[3]

Several years later Miss Richmond broadened her philosophical perceptions of social casework and displaced her onetime simplistic view that the art of helping is merely the use of "common sense in uncommon situations." She wrote dramatically of the ultimate high purpose of social

[1] Edwin J. Thomas, "The Socio-Behavioral Approach: Illustrations and Analysis," in Thomas, ed., *The Socio-Behavioral Approach and Applications to Social Work* (New York: Council on Social Work Education, 1967), p. 2.
[2] Mary E. Richmond, *The Long View* (New York: Russell Sage Foundation, 1930), p. 374.
[3] Mary C. Jarrett, "The Psychiatric Thread Running Through All Social Case Work," *Proceedings of the National Conference of Social Work*, 1919 (Chicago: Rogers & Hall Co., 1920), p. 587.

casework: "If we would understand *what* social casework is, we must understand *why* it is. . . ." [4] She stated further:

It is not enough for social workers to speak the language of democracy; they must have in their hearts its spiritual conviction of the infinite worth of our common humanity before they can be fit to do any form of social work whatsoever. Life itself achieves significance and value not from the esoteric things shared by the few, but from the common experiences of the race—from the issues of life and death, of affection satisfied and affection frustrated, from those chances and hazards of daily living that come to all men. Unless these conditions common to all humanity strongly appeal to us, or until they do, we are not ready to adopt social case work as our major interest.[5]

In 1920 Jessie Taft alluded to the practice of social casework this way:

The caseworker alone in all the world is attempting to handle human behavior undiluted, and in its actual setting. Only the caseworker leaves hospital, clinic, office . . . and observes the individual in action—at home, at work, in school, playing, loving, toiling, hating, fearing, striving, succeeding, failing—an organic part of the social context.[6]

In the aftermath of the Great Depression, Gordon Hamilton wrote of "the unity of the case work process" and developed the concept of social casework as "a living event" with economic, physical, mental, emotional, and social components. She elaborated:

A social case is always composed of internal and external, or environmental factors. We do not deal with people in a physical sense or with environment in a physical sense, but we treat people who have not only social experiences but also feelings about their experiences. . . . While we are asking a person about his situation we are also trying to establish a relationship with him—in a sense we are treating him.[7]

Somewhat later, Miss Hamilton wrote of Freud's influence on social casework:

Freud's creative genius did for the human spirit what political revolutions sometimes aim to do and sometimes partially succeed in doing—free the mind and actions of the common man for further self-realization and

[4] Mary E. Richmond, *What Is Social Case Work?* (New York: Russell Sage Foundation, 1922), p. 128.
[5] *Ibid.*, p. 249.
[6] Jessie Taft, "The Social Worker's Opportunity," *The Family*, Vol. 3, no. 6 (October 1922), p. 151.
[7] Gordon Hamilton, *Theory and Practice of Social Case Work* (New York: Columbia Press, 1940), pp. 34-35.

self-development . . . a new liberty, a power to choose, hitherto circum-
scribed by ignorance . . . and our own neuroses.[8]

She explained, too, that "it was not Freud's fault that the pendulum
swung too far. . . . It is not the first time teachers have been caught
indoctrinating instead of teaching." [9]

Swithun Bowers saw casework as an art having a method, a process, and
specific techniques that are used creatively to help the client make necessary adaptations. He viewed casework as a process drawing on a science
for knowledge and contributing data and clinical experience. He wrote:

The subject matter of social casework is the individual human being as he
exists in reality, that is, in a total situation. Social casework does not deal
with attitudes, difficulties, or relationships, but with persons who have
attitudes, difficulties, and relationships. . . . Casework does not deal with
some particular segment of the individual, but with the individual as a
whole person. Casework does not deal only with the socially maladjusted
individual or the socially inadequate individual, but with any person whose
adjustment to all or any part of his physical, social, and cultural environment can be more satisfactorily resolved through casework competence.[10]

CSWE defined social casework as "a method of social work which in-
tervenes in the psycho-social aspects of a person's life to improve, restore,
maintain, or enhance his social functioning by improving his role performance." [11] Florence Hollis has stated that "central to casework is the
notion of the person-in-his-situation." [12] In another connection she explained:

The treatment of any problem is inevitably determined in large part by
one's understanding of its nature. . . . In casework, diagnosis is the attempt
to define as accurately and fully as is necessary for casework treatment
the nature of the problem, its causative factors, and the person's attitude
toward the problem.[13]

Social casework's origins were in family social work and the literature
reveals that often the definition of social casework was more in concert

[8] Gordon Hamilton, "A Theory of Personality: Freud's Contribution to Social
Work," in Howard J. Parad, ed., Ego Psychology and Dynamic Casework (New
York: Family Service Association of America, 1948), p. 12.
[9] Ibid., p. 35.
[10] Swithun Bowers, "The Nature and Definition of Social Casework. Part III," Journal of Social Casework, Vol. 30, no. 10 (December 1949), p. 416.
[11] Werner W. Boehm, The Social Casework Method in Social Work Education,
Vol. X of the Curriculum Study (New York: Council on Social Work Education,
1959), p. 44.
[12] Florence Hollis, Casework: A Psychosocial Therapy (New York: Random House,
1964), p. 10.
[13] Florence Hollis, "Personality Diagnosis in Casework," in Parad, ed., op. cit., p. 83.

with agency policy and services than with the building of a specific practice base. Anita J. Faatz stated that "it marks a singular advance both in the profession and in the individual helper, that this compelling pressure to define has at last given way to the greater strength of a wholly different kind of precision." Miss Faatz recognized that to "some who are oriented within the older natural science philosophy . . . and its veneration of reason and logic to the exclusion of emotion" there is still the insistence that social casework have the precision of a science.[14] But to others, "casework belongs with that philosophical movement in human experience which seeks new ways to comprehend the dynamics of living, and at last acknowledges the inescapable fact that life will not yield its meaning to him who would attempt to force it into the rigid mold of causal determinism." [15]

Whatever the definition of social casework, it is important that its function be understood in terms of a helping process. Casework relates to helping in the manipulation of a problem and affording opportunity for the amelioration of a situation, whether through provision of medical care, food, housing, training for the handicapped, or some other service. It offers a supportive relationship during a time of stress and makes available understanding, empathy, and sympathetic listening to help the client endure his pain. Help is given to the client in interpreting and classifying his problem to facilitate discovery of ways in which he might handle his difficulties.[16]

In considering the goals of social casework, it is well to understand what transpires in the life of the client before he comes to the agency as a "help-seeker." He must decide that something is wrong—some need is not being fulfilled, some obligation is not being met, or some social or personal standard is being violated. He must recognize that his family, friends, employer, and others may learn of his distress and that in coming to the agency he is admitting his inability to solve or handle his own problems without help. He must recognize that some self-esteem will be lost through placing himself in a dependent situation by asking for help and he must decide for himself if he wants to take the risks of therapy and whether he will be able to adjust to the new behaviors that may emerge.[17]

[14] Anita J. Faatz, *The Nature of Choice in Casework Process* (Chapel Hill: University of North Carolina Press, 1953), p. 6.
[15] *Ibid.*
[16] Elizabeth Nicholds, *A Primer of Social Casework* (New York: Columbia University Press, 1960), pp. 18–19.
[17] David Landy, "Problems of the Person Seeking Help in Our Culture," *The Social Welfare Forum*, 1960 (New York: Columbia University Press, 1960), pp. 144–45.

Helen Harris Perlman has written that "to attempt to define social casework takes courage or foolhardiness or perhaps a bit of both," [18] yet she developed a perceptive description of the casework method as a problem-solving process premised on the function of role and on the fact that vital growth-producing relationships between people arise out of shared and emotionally charged situations.[19] The casework process is also seen as having a sustaining, supplementing, and fortifying function. Mrs. Perlman stated: "The interest of the casework process is to engage the person himself in working on and in coping with the one or several problems that confront him and to do so by such means as may stand him in good stead as he goes forward in living." [20] These means include the offering of a therapeutic relationship that sustains the client, gives him a professional structure and climate in which to talk about and work with his problems and provides the resources necessary to meet his needs.

In her impressive book *Persona*, Mrs. Perlman puts the tasks of social work in yet another way:

> The moments of felt crisis are moments when the iron of personality structure and patterning is white hot. This is because of the pervasive inner sense of shake-up and disorganization; emotion is intense; self-mobilization to fight or to flee, to struggle or to collapse, is high, though it often cannot be sustained for long and may end in capitulation. The feeling is that something radically different must happen at once on the outside or within the self.[21]

SOCIAL GROUP WORK

In 1949 an American Association of Group Workers committee chaired by Grace L. Coyle outlined the functions of group workers. This definition reflected a belief that the group worker enables various groups to function in such a way that both group interaction and program activities contribute to the growth of the individual and the achievement of desirable social goals. The group worker also assumes the responsibility of providing for personal growth according to the client's capacity and need in relation to other persons, groups, and the wider society. Although there has since been some elaboration of these functions, they have remained basically the same.

[18] Helen Harris Perlman, *Social Casework: A Problem-Solving Process* (Chicago: University of Chicago Press, 1957), p. 3.
[19] *Ibid.*, p. 64.
[20] *Ibid.*, p. 58.
[21] Helen Harris Perlman, *Persona* (Chicago: University of Chicago Press, 1968), p. 30.

Social group work has always been directed in practice to the sharing and integration of ideas, experiences, and knowledge and to the development of understanding among different ethnic, cultural, religious, and socioeconomic groups. The group worker must possess knowledge of individual and group behavior and skills in leadership that will stimulate group members in using their capacities to create socially constructive group experiences. He also makes use of his relationship to the group and his knowledge of programs and group process.

Group work and recreation have often been thought of as similar processes used by the "happy agencies." Miss Coyle pointed out that "while people play they are doing much more" in terms of associating with others and "achieving deep delight . . . in the mutual interactions of a democratic and creative group." In differentiating the role of the social group worker from that of the recreation worker, she wrote:

> What contribution does group work as a method have to fulfilling . . . the recreation function? [It does so] in three specific areas: first, its contribution to the increase of enjoyment by more satisfying human relations, second, the help it can be to individuals who are not able to enjoy themselves because of personal difficulties of some kind; and third, its contribution to the significant by-products of the recreation experience.[22]

Gertrude Wilson and Gladys Ryland defined group work as an enabling method through which group members acquire new ideas and develop new skills while their attitudes and behaviors are changed "through participation in a group process wherein they make the decisions and take the social action necessary to accomplish the purposes of the group." Group work was also seen as a method "through which group life is affected by a worker who consciously directs the interacting process. . . ."[23]

Harleigh B. Trecker projected the definition of social group work into the agency itself so that a clearer distinction can be made in terms of the practitioner, the group, and the setting:

> Social group work is a method through which individuals in groups in social agency settings are helped by a worker who guides their interaction in program activities so that they may relate themselves to others and experience growth opportunities in accordance with their needs and capacities to the end of individual, group and community development. . . .

[22] Grace L. Coyle, "Group Work and Recreation," in Harleigh B. Trecker, ed., *Group Work: Foundations and Frontiers* (New York: Whiteside & William Morrow & Co., 1955), pp. 94–95.
[23] Gertrude Wilson and Gladys Ryland, *Social Group Work Practice* (Boston: Houghton Mifflin Co., 1949), p. 61.

The group itself is utilized by the individual with the help of the worker as a primary means of personality growth, change and development. The worker is interested in helping to bring about individual growth and social development for the group as a whole and for the community as a result of guided group interaction.[24]

Ruth E. Smalley seemed to take some exception to Trecker's implication that social group work is a compatible function in all social agencies. She believed that the traditional voluntary agency offering many services, including leisure-time activities, could help persons in groups to meet their needs for individual and social development because the agency's function was diffuse and not as clearly defined as it is now.[25] William Schwartz appeared to support this premise in his description of the social agencies in which social group work originated. These agencies, he explained, were established to educate and reform their clientele; serve youth; aid large numbers of immigrants; help retain cultural, ethnic, racial, and religious identifications; "preserve the middle-class ethic"; and "exert a benevolent moral pressure on those whose low position in society rendered them especially susceptible to the confusions and temptations of the time." [26]

Miss Smalley recognized that the contemporary agency has a more specific purpose that gives both form and content to what is done in the group and believed that the "group *as a group* has little or no importance in the agency established to meet a 'problem.' It is what each individual can achieve *through* the group which is primary." [27] The services of the contemporary casework agency may therefore include group work with clients, but it is seen as a therapeutic resource rather than as a process used to teach the skills of democratic interaction and socialization.

Robert D. Vinter wrote of the several dimensions of group organization and process that are basic to all small groups. He defined the worker's major concerns in group development as (1) the social organization of the group with its pattern of participant roles and statuses, (2) the activities, tasks, and operative processes, (3) the culture, norms, values, and shared purposes of the group, and (4) the group's relationships to its external environment, including the agency in which it is served. Vinter also pointed out that the practitioner's concern is not merely the fostering

[24] Harleigh B. Trecker, *Social Group Work* (New York: Association Press, 1955), p. 5.
[25] Ruth E. Smalley, *Theory for Social Work Practice* (New York: Columbia University Press, 1967), p. 210.
[26] William Schwartz, "Group Work and the Social Scene," in Alfred J. Kahn, ed., *Issues in American Social Work* (New York: Columbia University Press, 1959), p. 116.
[27] *Op. cit.*, p. 210–11.

and achievement of "groupness" but the development of supportive patterns that will help in achieving treatment goals.[28]

Philip Klein has stated that "perhaps the best way to describe this technique [social group work], despite the earnest efforts of its practitioners to give it a coordinate status with casework—is to say that it actually does not exist." Klein expressed regret that group work did not stay fully aligned and identified with the many leisure-time and constructive activities in which it offered greatly needed recreational resources in American communities. "For some reason," he wrote, "perhaps by way of competition with the technical self-assurance of the casework field, personnel in group work has worked hard to establish a professional content for group work as a process."[29]

Despite Klein's reluctance to accredit group work as a social work method, the use of group techniques has now been extended to the therapeutic area. Group work has, in fact, broadened its base of concerns to the multipractice of group therapy and conjoint family therapy and has begun to relate to community social problems in a far more comprehensive way than ever before.

Traditional forms of social service are rapidly changing as new services develop around community models and in therapeutic community settings, which do not lend themselves to the practice of individual treatment. There is growing emphasis on treating the whole family group as a unit of service and group methods are also used in social action, community organization, and community planning.

William Schwartz's definition of a group reflects the new emphases and accompanying changes in group work practice. The group is seen as "an enterprise in mutual aid, an alliance of individuals who need each other, in varying degrees, to work on common problems."[30] Schwartz described group work as a "helping system in which the clients need each other as well as the worker. This need to use each other, to create not one but many helping relationships, is a vital ingredient of the group process and constitutes a common need over and above the specific tasks for which the group was formed."[31]

Schwartz further explained that the group is a system of relationships that affords many forms of interaction in terms of social objectives, social

[28] Robert D. Vinter, "Social Group Work," in Harry L. Lurie, ed., *Encyclopedia of Social Work* (New York: National Association of Social Workers, 1965), p. 719.

[29] Philip Klein, *From Philanthropy to Social Welfare* (San Francisco: Jossey-Bass, 1968), pp. 172–73.

[30] William Schwartz, "The Social Worker in the Group," *The Social Welfare Forum, 1961* (New York: Columbia University Press, 1961), p. 158.

[31] *Ibid.*

resources, and values. It is an organic whole made up of interdependent human beings, each acting out his changing relationship to society. "The group worker acts to help others act and the emphasis upon new ways of moving, of interacting, is more realistic and productive than the concern with total being, with discrete characteristics, and with totalistic concepts of change." [32]

In its effort to develop new methods of using the group to achieve therapeutic objectives, social work has borrowed heavily from the methods and techniques of other disciplines. These approaches have been variously called "sensitivity training," "T-group," "group encounter," "group therapy," "milieu therapy," and "multiple counseling." Despite differences in nomenclature, these techniques are used in small groups to stimulate therapeutic interaction involving here-and-now experiences and learning.

Maxwell Jones described the rationale of the institutional therapeutic community as a treatment process in which the patient's subservient role and status are changed by allowing and encouraging patient participation in many treatment and administrative activities. The patient's new role, status, and function result in a peer relationship with the treatment staff, thus changing his perception of his institutional experience as well as the institution's traditional social organization. [33]

Robert N. Rapoport outlined "the themes of therapy" in a therapeutic community as democratization, permissiveness, communalism, and reality confrontation. Democratization refers to the belief that each member of the group or "community" should share equally in therapeutic and administrative decision-making. Permissiveness allows individuals to "expose" behavioral problems and encourages others to react freely to these so that relationship patterns can be mutually exposed. Communalism is characterized as developing "tight-knit, intercommunicative and intimate sets of staff-patient relationships." In confrontation the patient is continuously presented with interpretations of his behavior as it is perceived by others. [34]

John and Elaine Cumming stated that the therapeutic milieu must offer a clear, organized, and unambiguous social structure in which policy is made and executed in the interests of the milieu and problems can be solved in a variety of protective settings. It should also provide information, facilities, and support that aim at equipping the patient to act in

[32] *Ibid.*, p. 159.
[33] See Maxwell Jones, *The Therapeutic Community* (New York: Basic Books Inc., 1953).
[34] Robert N. Rapoport, *Community as Doctor* (Springfield, Ill.: Charles C Thomas, 1962), pp. 54–63.

clearly defined roles powered by different values. Problems must be solved in groups in which everyone has full membership and opportunity to learn and participate with staff in lifelike situations.[35]

The CSWE curriculum study of social group work relates group work to community planning and other task-oriented coordinating activities. Committees represent their constituencies in the assessment of social problems that have an impact on the community and its neighborhoods. The ability of the members to make decisions will be affected

> to the extent to which each has maintained close communication with the groups he represents. . . . The social worker's role is to participate in the committee meetings in such a way that the meaning of this responsibility is made clear to each of the members. . . . Community planning and coordinating committees offer channels for such interpretation and opportunity to work with other agencies and groups to initiate the necessary social action to control or change the undesirable situations.[36]

COMMUNITY ORGANIZATION

A community is a social system and a social structure reflecting the behavioral norms and values of a group within a common geographic area. It is functionally interdependent, with individuals and groups contributing to the permanence of the structure.[37] The community has a pattern of leadership that influences decisions and a social ranking of members based on what it values most highly. Members of the community tend to conform to acceptable patterns and norms, are aware of their uniqueness and separate identity as a group, and are resistant to change or outside influences. The community's solidarity results from shared interests and goals. For most purposes the community has become a functional concept rather than a geographic one.[38]

To a considerable degree the framework of community policy is determined by local, state, and national governments, often with substantial subvention for local programs. Despite this fact, community structure has lagged and has often demonstrated a marked resistance to change. This

---

[35] John Cumming and Elaine Cumming, *Ego and Milieu* (New York: Atherton Press, 1962), p. 71.

[36] Marjorie Murphy, *The Social Group Work Method in Social Work Education*, Vol. 11 of the Curriculum Study (New York: Council on Social Work Education, 1959), pp. 154–56.

[37] Blaine E. Mercer, *The American Community* (New York: Random House, 1956), pp. 26–27.

[38] Charles R. Adrian, "The Community Setting," in Adrian, ed., *Social Science and Community Action* (East Lansing: Michigan State University Board of Trustees, 1960), p. 3.

lag has been attributed to an absence of any adequate conceptual scheme for identifying the crucial elements in community structure and their relationship to socioeconomic inequities in the community. The impingement of social structure on significant social institutions has been recognized but insufficient attention has been given to the effect of local governmental structure on communities.[39] The sociological definition of community expressed earlier by Robert E. Park and Ernest W. Burgess as "a constellation of social forces"[40] and by Jesse Steiner as "a social unit of significant social reconstruction"[41] has now been broadened to embody the concept of functionalism in which community reorganization and community planning and development are seen as processes by which citizen participation is motivated and professionally and technically supported and directed.

COMMUNITY ORGANIZATION AS A SOCIAL WORK METHOD

Community organization has faced some of the same difficulties in achieving recognition as a social work method experienced by social group work. In fact, like group work it was originally related to the field of recreation. In 1939 Stuart A. Queen and Lewis F. Thomas described the problem of definition this way:

During the years immediately following the World War there was much loose talk about "community organization," but the underlying ideas were rather vague. Some people identified the term with public recreation. Others meant by it the enlisting of popular support for social work organizations. Still others had in mind church unity, consolidated schools, "Americanization" and doubtless other pet projects. All of these efforts contained the germs of social planning, but none of them was sufficiently comprehensive to warrant the use of that label.[42]

This ambiguity is not surprising since community organization as such was not included in the programs of the National Conference of Social Work until 1910, when Jane Addams was its president. By 1939, however, papers on community organization were contributed and a clearer definition and description of the process emerged. Stress was placed on such concepts as mobilizing resources to meet needs, initiating social services through community social action, coordinating the services of

[39] Peter H. Rossi, "Theory, Research and Practice in Community Organization," in Adrian, ed., *op. cit.*, p. 22.
[40] Robert E. Park and Ernest W. Burgess, *Introduction to the Science of Sociology* (Chicago: University of Chicago Press, 1924), p. 493.
[41] Jesse L. Steiner, *Community Organization* (New York: D. Appleton-Century Co., 1930), p. 14.
[42] Stuart A. Queen and Lewis F. Thomas, *The City* (New York: McGraw-Hill Book Co., 1939), p. 488.

welfare agencies, setting agency standards, and facilitating relations among organizations, groups, and agencies. The conference proceedings since that time have covered the history of community organization and presented community planning and development as ideological approaches, processes, and methods related to effective adjustment between social welfare and other community resources and needs.

The early definitions of community organization reflected the orthodox sociological point of view presented by Steiner:

> Community organization when considered in its broadest terms, may be said to be chiefly concerned with the problems of accommodation and social adjustment. More specifically it is concerned with the interrelationships of groups within communities, their integration and coordination in the interest of efficiency and unity of action. In a wider sense it may also include the adjustment of a local community to the larger social unit of which it is a part. . . . Community organization is, therefore, not merely an essential process; it is also a continuous process in which adjustments are being made and remade to keep pace with changing conditions.[43]

Wayne McMillen formulated a concept of community organization that related its components to a series of questions: How are social needs identified in a community? How are priorities established among these needs? What methods are most successful in formulating programs to meet identified needs? What procedures are most promising in promoting the adoption of programs already formulated?[44] McMillan's questions had a functional direction rather than a definitive purpose, since he stated that "in the field of social work there is no definition of the term 'community' to serve all occasions."[45]

Clarence King viewed community organization as a process of building a "community interest" or "common interest group" that would be developed into an association of persons and organizations to meet need.[46] More recently, Murray G. Ross and B. W. Lappin characterized community organization as a process by which a community identifies its needs or objectives, orders them, develops the confidence and will to work at them, finds the resources (internal and/or external) to deal with them, takes action in respect to them, and in so doing extends and develops cooperative and collaborative attitudes and practices in the community.[47]

[43] Steiner, *op. cit.*, p. 170.

[44] Wayne McMillen, *Community Organization for Social Welfare* (Chicago: University of Chicago Press, 1945), p. 25.

[45] *Ibid.*, p. 29.

[46] Clarence King, *Organizing for Community Action* (New York: Harper Bros., 1948), p. 18.

[47] Murray G. Ross with B. W. Lappin, *Community Organization: Theory, Principles, and Practice* (2d ed.; New York: Harper & Row, 1967), p. 40.

CSWE's curriculum study identified the processes involved in community organization as a social work method. In this connection Violet M. Sieder defined community organization as

. . . a method of social work practice which helps a community determine and achieve continuously more desirable program goals, which meet constantly changing social welfare needs by facilitating the interaction of its constituent parts (organizations, institutions, individual leaders, and geographical subdivisions) in such a way as to make maximum use of its internal and external resources . . . to undertake the solution of new and more difficult problems. Its focus is upon helping individuals and groups increase their capacity and motivation to work together to bring about progressive change and better integration in the social services of the community.[48]

COMMUNITY WELFARE COUNCILS AND FUNDING

Community organization is not accomplished through structure alone, but must also have a financial base. The mechanism for bringing community action to bear on the creation of education, health, and welfare services is variously called a welfare federation, council of social agencies, united community service, or health and welfare council, depending on tradition or community preference. Such voluntary associations of lay, professional, and indigenous groups are created for the purpose of guiding the community in eliminating duplication of effort, determining unmet needs, coordinating existing services, promoting needed public understanding, and making planning, policy, and budget decisions.

Community welfare councils exist in all urban areas of America and in nearly all areas of 100,000 or more population. Council membership includes representatives from tax-supported and voluntary agencies and from civic, business, and industrial groups; policies are established by a board of directors.

Traditionally, councils have been closely related to the funding resource, known generally as the Community Chest, United Crusade, or United Fund. Most councils and chests are now distinct agencies, each with its own professional staff and board. It is the function of the Community Chest or other designated body to develop a system of federated funding to support all voluntary agencies having membership in the council. This represents a marked departure from practice prevalent in the Charity Organization Society era when each agency was respon-

[48] Violet M. Sieder, "The Tasks of the Community Organization Worker" in *The Community Organization Method in Social Work Education*, Vol. 4 of the Curriculum Study (New York: Council on Social Work Education, 1959), p. 249.

sible for meeting its own financial needs through annual drives. The proliferation of voluntary agencies necessitated many fund-raising drives, which proved expensive, duplicative of effort, and confusing to the donor. Contributors and participating volunteers now prefer one campaign planned, promoted, and administered by a separate fund-raising agency. More money can be raised through one drive, and a single effort provides an opportunity for continued interpretation to the public and for sustained budgeting, planning, and promotional activities. No community beginning federated funding has ever gone back to the multiple-drive system.

All voluntary member agencies submit their annual budgets to the fund-raising agency, which reviews them. A goal based on the combined budgets of all member agencies is then determined and presented to the community. If the goal is reached, the individual agencies will receive their budget requests; if it is not achieved, a new budgeting process must be undertaken. Few voluntary agencies have sources of income other than those derived from the annual drive, client fees, or other private sources.

Community Development and Planning

"Community development" is a recent term that has been defined as the process of educating community members to take action for change. "Neighborhood community development" is seen as community organization effort designated to serve the lower socioeconomic class, minority groups, and urban slum residents. It involves direct engagement of the poor in the decision-making process and the realignment of "the power resources of the community by creating channels through which the consumers of social welfare services can define their problems and goals and negotiate on their own behalf." [49] Services include clubs dealing with such social problems as housing and social welfare issues, block organization, and social movements relating to civil and welfare rights. [50]

Community development is characterized as a *process* because it moves from one social condition to another and reflects a progression of changes. Irwin T. Sanders regards "community development" as a neutral, scientific term that is subject to precise definition and measurements. *People* make decisions about common concerns and problems and the process places emphasis on what happens to *people* socially, psychologically, and economically.

[49] Charles F. Grosser, "Community Development Programs Serving the Urban Poor," *Social Work*, Vol. 10, no. 3 (July 1965), p. 15.
[50] *Ibid.*, p. 21.

Community development is also a method and therefore has defined objectives. It is a means to an end and may involve state, national, and local levels of government as well as private agencies in efforts to achieve some definitive end. As a method, community development has a set of procedures and activities. When the process is highly formalized, its emphasis is on activities, whether in the field of health, welfare, agriculture, industry, recreation, or whatever program is involved.

Community development tends to assume the characteristics of a crusade or a cause to which people become committed. It carries an emotional impact because people are either for or against it.[51] This ambivalence regarding social issues has always been apparent in community action program and service efforts. Eduard C. Lindeman pointed this out almost half a century ago:

> Discontent with current political, economic, and social organization appears to be well-nigh universal. Men everywhere are attempting to work out a new way of living together. We live in a period which is likely to produce many theories. Extremists of one sort will want the entire structure of the present destroyed. Extremists of another sort will insist on keeping the old machinery intact. In the meantime, a few men and women here and there will be attempting to evaluate the resources of the present world; these have abandoned all short-cuts to progress, and have set for themselves the task of building the future out of the materials at hand.[52]

Because community development is dedicated to progress it is also a philosophical concept. Progress in community development must be viewed with reference to goals and values that differ under varying political and social systems. It is a movement that tends to become institutionalized while building its own organization, structure, procedures, and professional practices.[53]

Much of the recent effort in community development can be attributed to Title II of the Economic Opportunity Act of 1964, titled "Urban and Rural Community Action Programs." This federal program provides stimulation and financial incentive for urban and rural communities to mobilize their resources to combat poverty through community action programs. Approved programs are designed to develop employment resources and improve human performance, motivation, and productivity for learning, living, and working. They are planned, conducted, coordinated, and administered by public or private nonprofit agencies with

[51] Irwin T. Sanders, *The Community* (New York: Ronald Press, 1966), p. 521.
[52] Eduard C. Lindeman, *The Community* (New York: Association Press, 1921), p. vii.
[53] Sanders, *op. cit.*, p. 505.

maximum feasible participation of neighborhood residents and thus provide a means of bringing together the poor and the nonpoor, professionals and laymen in efforts to meet local problems through the exploration of needs, planning, decision-making, and action.

Thus the older concept of community organization as being almost solely related to the Community Chest and planning council has changed. This is due in large part to the War on Poverty and the programs included in the Economic Opportunity Act, which moved social welfare planning back to the neighborhoods and to the constituency of those neighborhoods. Indeed, there has been a return to the settlement house ideology so valiantly espoused and practiced by the earlier social workers of this nation.

RESEARCH

The objectives of social work practice and social work research are mutually directed to the analysis, improvement, and expansion of that which is already known and to the exclusion of methods and procedures that are no longer useful or feasible. Mary E. Richmond reiterated the imperative need for knowledge many years ago when she wrote: "Affection and kindness unlock many doors, straighten out many complications. But when to affection and kindness we are able to add that knowledge of the workings of the human mind . . . we have a new power in the world added to the older power of just loving one another." [54] These dimensions were broadened as she elaborated: "'If development of personality is our task—then personality as it is now, together with the ways in which it came to be what it is now, must be discovered. . . .[55] It is not always enough to adjust to the present environment, but to make changes in it too." [56]

Contemporary social work research is directed to practical issues related to services, policies, and clientele and is used in program evaluation and planning, in developing more efficient and effective methods of practice, and in the enrichment of existing services. Mary E. MacDonald elaborated on the function of social work research:

Neither subject matter nor method serves to define and delineate social work research. The idea of function is more useful. The function of social work research is to contribute to the development of a dependable body

[54] Richmond, *op. cit.*, p. 9.
[55] *Ibid.*, p. 101.
[56] *Ibid.*, p. 103.

of knowledge to serve the goals and means of social work in all its ramifications.[57]

There is conviction that professional "goals are translated best into services through a systematic attempt to think of objectives, methods and content of programs together." [58] Every objective must have its methodology and content clearly articulated and "every activity its objectives and methods matched to it. . . . The implication of the importance of research is reflected by placing goal-setting and reassessment of service as an on-going process." [59]

Research in social work is imperative to permit an agency to express accountability and to meet its responsibilities to its various supporting publics. Each agency is obligated to review the goals of its services and to determine whether these goals have been appropriately selected and directed toward useful and feasible ends. The agency must also review its practices, policies, and procedures to evaluate their efficiency, determine whether its program leads to the goals that have been established, and examine the effectiveness of the agency's operations.[60] Social work research contributes to these processes and to the development of new knowledge that can be used by agency staff to refine practice skills.

Recognition of research as a significant social work method is a recent development. Throughout the years, however, intermittent studies have been effective in changing public opinion and have ultimately influenced the extent and quality of social welfare services. Although their work was descriptive rather than empirical, Dorothea Dix's painstaking analysis of her observations of the care of the mentally ill and the impressive variety of works by Mary E. Richmond, Grace and Edith Abbott, Florence Kelley, Edward T. Devine, Frank J. Bruno, Enoch C. Wines, and others provided social work with needed ideology, substance, and structure. Charles Booth, the English reformer who described the conditions of a segment of London's population in *Life and Labour of the People in London* (1904), and the Pittsburgh survey made in 1907 provided patterns for more intensive research, but until the three-year St. Paul (Minn.) Family-Centered Project was concluded in 1957 there were few in-depth casework studies of this kind. The St. Paul project was devoted to a study

[57] Mary E. MacDonald, "Social Work: A Perspective," in Norman E. Polansky, ed., *Social Work Research* (Chicago: University of Chicago Press, 1966), p. 1.
[58] Alan F. Klein, "Individual Change Through Group Experience," *The Social Welfare Forum*, 1959 (New York: Columbia University Press, 1959), p. 144.
[59] *Ibid.*
[60] Martin Wolins, *A Proposed Research Program* (New York: Child Welfare League of America, 1959), p. 1.

of the multiproblem family, "distrustful families," "unwilling clients," and the agencies available to meet their needs. As Alice Overton, Katherine H. Tinker, and their project associates explained, the main intent of their research was "to stick close to the earth of practice." [61]

Research seeks knowledge rather than change, although much social work research is designed to provide knowledge that can be utilized to achieve change. There are, however, some significant similarities between the researcher and the practitioner. Harris K. Goldstein pointed out that both must raise questions and develop hypotheses that can be used to direct their observations. Both must make observations, but practitioners designate theirs as part of "the study process," while research workers refer to this activity as "data gathering." Both look for relationships between the things they observe. Practitioners know this process as "diagnosis" while researchers call these activities "the development of explanations." Both must make judgments in the process of knowledge-gathering and both can use the same standards to evaluate their knowledge of clients and programs. [62]

The value of research in social work is premised on the following beliefs: (1) there is a common body of theory and attention given to any researchable problem is within the framework of that theory and contributes to its clarification, (2) there is sufficient similarity in organization and use of casework services that research in one setting has some applicability to other settings or unique features can be identified and understood, and (3) social work is a profession with a value system sufficiently structured to presume a commonality in the major purposes or ends to be served by its research enterprises. [63]

Social work research contributes to learning that will increase the practitioner's skill. The practitioner, in turn, can be expected to make a contribution to the development of research knowledge and techniques. [64] Samuel Mencher identified the research-related capacity of the practitioner as the ability to (1) apply logical and orderly thinking to problems that are evident in his own practice, (2) develop an attitude of scientific inquiry and a willingness to question the theory and method on

[61] Alice Overton, Katherine H. Tinker, and Associates, *Casework Notebook* (St. Paul, Minn.: Greater St. Paul Community Chests & Councils, 1959), Preface to the 2d ed.

[62] Harris K. Goldstein, *Research Standards and Methods for Social Workers* (Ann Arbor, Mich.: Edwards Bros., 1968), pp. 16–19.

[63] Lilian Ripple, "Plans for Obtaining Judgment Data," *Use of Judgments As Data in Social Work Research* (New York: National Association of Social Workers, 1959), p. 55.

[64] Samuel Mencher, *The Research Method in Social Work Education*, Vol. 9 of the Curriculum Study (New York: Council on Social Work Education, 1959), p. 3.

which his own practice is based, (3) organize and present his own practice experience objectively and clearly, (4) develop an appreciation of the contribution that research can make to the field of practice and a knowledge of sources of research, and (5) critically evaluate new contributions to method and theory.[65]

There are a number of methodological approaches to social work research. These may depend on the purposes to which the research is addressed but research usually centers around problem identification. It may be quantitative or descriptive in nature and may use the same formulations as the sociological study. Quasi-diagnostic studies are made of single agencies or groups of agencies. Other studies evaluate the results of technical operations relating to wider community problems or to the clients served. The validity of techniques and their components are also a subject of study.[66]

Although the practical purposes served by research are important, it is essential to prevent these from overshadowing social work's desperate need for new knowledge validated by research. As Herbert Stroup has written:

All of us live in an essentially inchoate society. The growth of complexity in human affairs has been so remarkable that there remains today no known power by which society can be either rationally understood or controlled. Current ideas of regulation and control, drawn from biology and engineering as well as from the social sciences, are widely employed to present a model of the self-regulating society inspired by democratic values. Yet these are inadequate means to explain the setting of human desires and apprehensions, goals, and standards. Human values cannot be defended as adaptations to the stress and strain of existence. They must be founded on more than a reaction; they must find an apologetics which is substantial.[67]

SOCIAL WORK ADMINISTRATION

The administrative process in social work is best understood in terms of the functions to which it is applied. Kenneth L. M. Pray described the typical concerns to which social agency administration is related:

The problems with which social work deals are not problems of social structure, as such, nor of individual personality, as such. They are not definable in terms of particular sets of circumstances or of particular

[65] *Ibid.*
[66] Philip Klein, *op. cit.*, p. 183.
[67] Herbert Stroup, "Social Work's New Era," *The Social Welfare Forum*, 1960 (New York: Columbia University Press, 1960), p. 72.

forces or qualities, either in the social environment or in people themselves, that may obstruct or frustrate satisfying and fruitful living. They are the problems which people find in the actual process of adjustment to each other or to any part or aspect of their social environment. That is to say, they are problems of relationships.[68]

John C. Kidneigh has defined social work administration as "the process of transforming social policy into social services . . . and the use of experience in recommending modification of policy." [69] Harleigh B. Trecker saw it as "a creative process of thinking, planning and action inextricably bound up with the whole agency . . . [with] the real focus of administration [being its] relationships with and between people . . . and [requiring] leadership with unusual insight into behavior plus skill in helping people relate to one another so that a unity of purpose and effort is created." [70] James D. Thompson wrote of three major functions performed by the administrative process: (1) "organization-directing" is concerned "with what the organization as a total entity is now, is becoming, and should become, and with making sure that the organization continues to fit into the changing scheme of things," (2) "organization-managing" is concerned with "acquiring, assigning and planning for the orderly coherent utilization of resources, namely, finances, personnel, physical facilities and materials, and authority," and (3) "supervisory function" is directed toward the coordination of technical or professional activities, making sure that these are done at appropriate times and places and in generally accepted fashion.[71] Sue Spencer observed that administration involved making judgments that require the use of professional knowledge and skill that while not wholly peculiar to social work nevertheless differ considerably from the knowledge and skill required in business administration.[72]

Stated another way, the administration of social work programs, whether in the public (bureaucratic) or voluntary agency, is concerned with the assignment of personnel, standardization of service operations,

[68] Kenneth L. M. Pray, "What Is Community Organization Social Work Practice?" in Donald S. Howard, ed., *Community Organization: Its Nature and Setting* (New York: American Association of Social Workers, 1947), p. 4.

[69] John C. Kidneigh, "The Quest for Competence in Welfare Administration," *Social Service Review*, Vol. 29, no. 2 (June 1950), p. 175.

[70] Harleigh B. Trecker, *Group Process in Administration* (rev. ed.; New York: Women's Press, 1950), pp. 2–3.

[71] James D. Thompson, "Common Elements in Administration," in Ella W. Reed, ed., *Social Welfare Administration* (New York: Columbia University Press, 1961), pp. 19, 20, and 21.

[72] Sue Spencer, *The Administration Method in Social Work Education*, Vol. 3 of the Curriculum Study (New York: Council on Social Work Education, 1959), p. 17.

and utilization of human resources. This necessitates concern for program structure and use of staff in order to facilitate optimum efficiency. The administrator must also be concerned with community action and social processes, because community forces must always be considered.[73]

Social agency administration requires a recognition that American social policy is shaped and reshaped by a number of factors and that the objectives of a social work program and the value system of society cannot be considered separate entities. It has been pointed out that "the characteristics of one cannot be radically different from the other, or be changed without inevitably changing the characteristics of the other." [74] At a meeting on community planning in public welfare held in the nation's capital in the spring of 1967, Mildred Arnold emphasized this point when she spoke of the ever-changing nature of society and the consequent need for the development of programs and services as a never ending process. She explained that as the nation has become more aware of its social problems, it has recognized the need for community action, participation in urban development, improved education, public housing, and alleviation of poverty and economic inequities.[75] These are national as well as local burdens to which the American social agency structure must respond by shedding the residuals of philanthropy still present in many areas of the country. Miss Arnold emphasized that social work is dealing with a different kind of client who has different needs and expectations and lives in a phase of national history quite different from the past. As the character of the nation changes, as social inequities become more visible and urgent, agencies will have to respond in more meaningful ways.

It is generally agreed that contemporary social agencies do not meet the many and varied needs of urban communities with their large concentrations of heterogeneous and deprived populations. It has been pointed out, too, that social agencies are essentially middle class in their preception of service and clientele and that admission of this characteristic would enable them to serve the community in a more democratic manner and to relate standards and services more realistically to the clients they serve. Agencies should also select out of the community culture those qualities, characteristics, and practices to which the client can psychologically and culturally respond and reject those to which he cannot relate. They should not hold out unrealistic hope for opportunity but should develop pro-

---

[73] *Ibid.*, pp. 21–25.

[74] *A Guide for Training: Local Public Welfare Administrators* (Washington, D.C.: U.S. Department of Health, Education, and Welfare, 1964), p. 25.

[75] Mildred Arnold, "Criteria for Adequate Provision for Community Organization," *Community Planning in Public Welfare* (Washington, D.C., Department of Health, Education, and Welfare, 1968), p. 56.

grams that will strengthen individual, family, and community life. The social agency also has a deep responsibility to teach, through work with individuals and groups, about the complexity of the nation's diverse cultures and to develop, foster, and stimulate social values and behaviors which will enable all member groups to become integrated through a system of sound social services.[76]

To ensure the relevance of agency goals and programs to contemporary community needs, the administrator must develop appropriate ways to ensure (1) continuous staff participation in the identification of needed client services, planning long-range implementation, and the development of policies and procedures, (2) organizational structure that supports the implementation of services and the analysis and classification of tasks required to attain agency goals, (3) recruitment, retention, and utilization of staff premised on recognition of the different skills necessary to implement agency programs and attain community goals, and (4) adequate staff training to provide effective service to clients.[77]

Summary

There is still a great deal of ambiguity and confusion in social work terminology. This lack of clarity is due in part to the youth of the profession, the variety of auspices under which social services have traditionally been given, the diversity of the clientele, and the influence of psychoanalytic and sociological systems on social work practice. The broadening scope of public welfare services has added another dimension to the already diffuse concept of practice, since these services are provided within a bureaucratic structure in accordance with the agency's legally assigned tasks.

The concepts of community organization, community planning and community development have remained as difficult to define as other social work methods. This is due in part to a change in goals. Although these goals continue to include the objective of ensuring the availability of needed services, they are also expected to reflect a greater degree of problem awareness and social action within the community to conform with the objectives brought to the neighborhood by the various federally funded programs.

There is yet another reason for the lingering instability of definition

[76] Alan F. Klein, *Society, Democracy and the Group* (New York: Women's Press, Whiteside & William Morrow & Co., 1953), p. 117.

[77] Joanne T. Bell, *Staff Development and Practice Supervision* (Washington, D.C.: U.S. Department of Health, Education, and Welfare, 1968), pp. 5–6.

and purpose. The public knows little about what the social worker does, what he is trained to do, or where to place him among the professions. It is apparent in reviewing this chapter that social work methods and processes have been defined and redefined—generally with other practitioners in mind instead of the public and, perhaps more important, instead of the client, who is social work's special public. The acquisition of new knowledge from other fields and the enhanced status of the social worker achieved through the rediscovery of poverty and other forms of dependency and deprivation may help the profession to identify its own purposes and methods more clearly as it is forced to define its role in new approaches to the solution of social problems.

Selected Bibliography

Bernstein, Irving. *The Lean Years.* Boston: Houghton Mifflin Co., 1960.

Biddle, William W., and Loureide J. Biddle. *The Community Development Process: The Rediscovery of Local Initiative.* New York: Holt, Rinehart & Winston, 1965.

Bremner, Robert H. *American Philanthropy.* Chicago: University of Chicago Press, 1960.

Building Social Work Knowledge. New York: National Association of Social Workers, 1964.

Community Planning in Public Welfare. Washington, D.C.: U.S. Department of Health, Education, and Welfare, 1967.

Dunham, Arthur. *Community Welfare Organization: Principles and Practice.* New York: Thomas Y. Crowell, 1958.

Feldman, Frances Lomas, and Frances H. Scherz. *Family Social Welfare.* New York: Atherton Press, 1967.

Garton, Nina R., and Herbert A. Otto. *The Development of Theory and Practice in Social Casework.* Springfield, Ill.: Charles C Thomas, 1964.

Gordon, William E. "Professional Base of Social Work Research—Some Essential Elements," *Social Work Journal,* Vol. 33, no. 1 (January 1952), pp. 17–22.

Gouldner, Alvin, and S. M. Miller eds. *Applied Sociology: Opportunities and Problems.* New York: Free Press, 1965.

Hollis, Florence. *Casework: A Psychosocial Therapy.* New York: Random House, 1964.

Konopka, Gisela. *Social Group Work: A Helping Process.* Englewood Cliffs, N.J.: Prentice-Hall, 1963.

Marris, Peter, and Martin Rein. *Dilemmas of Social Reform.* New York: Atherton Press, 1967.

Phillips, Helen U. *Essentials of Social Group Work.* New York: Association Press, 1965.

Polansky, Norman ed. *Social Work Research*. Chicago: University of Chicago Press, 1960.

Reed, Ella W., *Social Welfare Administration*. New York: Columbia University Press, 1961.

Ross, Murray G., with B. W. Lappin. *Community Organization: Theory, Principles and Practice*. 2d ed.; New York: Harper & Row, 1967.

Shepherd, Clovis R. *Small Groups: Some Sociological Perspectives*. San Francisco: Chandler Publishing Co., 1964.

Smalley, Ruth E. *Theory for Social Work Practice*. New York: Columbia University Press, 1967.

Trecker, Harleigh B. *Social Group Work*. Revised edition; New York: Association Press, 1955.

U.S. Welfare Administration. *Cities in Crisis: The Challenge of Change*. Publication 20, Washington, D.C.: Government Printing Office, 1967.

Zald, Mayer N. ed. *Organizing for Community Welfare*. Chicago: Quadrangle Books, 1967.

Chapter Nine

The Fields of Social Work

J. ROBERT OPPENHEIMER, one of America's most brilliant scientists, wrote of the great power of common effort and of man's dependence on the totality of his environment:

Each of us knows from his own life how much even a casual and limited association of men goes beyond him in knowledge, in understanding, in humanity, and in power. Each of us, from a friend or a book or by concerting of the little we know with what others know, has broken the iron circle of his frustration. Each of us has asked help and been given it, and within our measure each of us has been offered it. Each of us knows the great new freedom sensed almost as a miracle, that men banded together for some finite purpose experience from the power of their common effort. . . . Each of us knows how much he has been transcended by the group of which he has been or is a part; each of us has felt the solace of other men's knowledge to stay his own ignorance, of other men's wisdom to stay his folly, of other men's courage to answer his doubts or his weakness.[1]

These ideas form the nucleus of the philosophy and social intent expressed in social work's traditional pattern of service to others and, more recently, in the complex programs of income maintenance and public services that reflect the concept of a "welfare state."

In the early years of this century, social work began to gain recognition as an identifiable profession. As other professions perceived the need for social services, social workers were gradually employed in a variety of settings. Because there are marked differences in the social tasks assigned to each type of setting and in the central problems presented by the clientele served (e.g., physical and/or mental illness, child abuse or neglect, poor educational progress, and law violation), it soon became apparent that these factors necessarily determine the specialized knowledge needed and affect to some degree the process and methods used to fulfill the tasks of a specific agency. As a result, the principles and techniques basic to social work as a profession assumed different configurations in different settings. Today these differences are identified by reference to a constellation of "fields of practice"—e.g., medical and health, mental health, child welfare, school social work, and corrections. In the sections that follow, the historical development of the major fields of practice will be traced and their contemporary characteristics described.

THE MEDICAL AND HEALTH FIELD

Social work within the medical field had its origins in the "community dispensary" or outpatient clinic. Boston Dispensary, the oldest medical in-

[1] J. Robert Oppenheimer, *Science and the Common Understanding* (New York: Simon & Schuster, 1953), pp. 91–92. Reprinted by permission of Simon & Schuster, Inc.

stitution in this country, was established in 1798 to ensure (1) "that the sick, without being pained by separation from their families, may be attended and relieved in their own homes; (2) that the sick can, in this way, be assisted at less expense to the public than in any hospital; and (3) that those who have seen better days may be comforted without being humiliated, and that the poor receive the benefits of a charity, the more refined as it is the more secret." [2]

In 1902 Dr. Charles P. Emerson developed a program through which medical students at Johns Hopkins Hospital could acquire some knowledge of the patient's home and social environment. Plans made with the Charity Organization Society of Baltimore enabled students serving as volunteer workers, to study the relationship between the patient's illness and the socioeconomic conditions under which he lived.

In 1905 Richard C. Cabot, physician and social philosopher, created the first social service department in the outpatient clinic at Massachusetts General Hospital in Boston. The services provided by this department were quite different from those initiated in 1895 by the London Charity Organization when a social worker was first stationed at the reception desk of the Royal Free Hospital in London. The English "lady hospital almoner" received applications for hospital admission and rejected those from patients considered suitable for outpatient treatment.

Dr. Cabot saw the function of the social worker as extending far beyond the scope of determining eligibility for service. He stated:

> Clearly the supplementary information thus secured by the social worker will count for nothing unless clearly explained to the doctor, and taken up by him as part of the evidence on which he bases his diagnosis and treatment. It is absolutely essential that the social worker should not merely make her visits and record them in her notebook, but should incorporate her findings in the medical record and deliver them not formally but effectively to the doctor's mind.[3]

It was Cabot, too, who stressed the value to social workers of following the medical model to differentiate their function from that of "the charities." He wrote:

> When the social worker begins the difficult task of acquiring her influence in a family she starts with a great deal in her favor if she appears in the home as *the agent of the physician.* He has prestige . . . he is not thought to have any axe to grind. He is assumed to be genuine in his desire of

---

[2] Cited in Ida M. Cannon, *On The Social Frontier of Medicine* (Cambridge, Mass.: Harvard University Press, 1952), pp. 28–29.

[3] Richard C. Cabot, *Social Work, Essays On The Meeting-Ground of Doctor and Social Worker* (Boston: Houghton Mifflin Co., 1919), pp. 12–13.

helpfulness. Therefore anyone who appears in his name, as his assistant has a great deal in her favor, especially when compared with the visitors of societies which might be supposed to begin with economic or moral suspicions about the family.[4]

In 1905 social workers were employed in three other hospitals (Johns Hopkins, Bellevue Hospital in New York City, and Berkeley Infirmary in Boston). As a result the hospital began to be recognized as a medical-social agency. Homer Folks, addressing the annual conference of the American Hospital Association in 1909, described the hospital as existing to care for and cure the sick; to provide food, clothing, and shelter; and to "relieve overcrowded homes and overworked housekeepers." He reminded resident and attending physicians of "the charitable origin, nature and purpose of hospitals." Folks also elaborated on the responsibility of the hospital to teach patients the skills needed in raising their standards of living in respect to "the art of living." Curiously, despite these social work concerns, Folks did not refer to social workers as a part of the medical team.[5] By 1915, however, social service departments had been established in more than 100 hospitals.

CONTEMPORARY PRACTICE

Social work in the medical and health field is meeting new demands caused by broader public and prepaid sickness and disability coverage, expanding medical technology, new techniques in physical and occupational therapy, and the development of a variety of other types of therapy. The increasing number of patients seeking medical and accompanying social services is reflected in the fact that the total annual public and private health cost in the nation was approximately $43 billion as of June 30, 1966.

The social services offered by hospitals and outpatient clinics now include services to individuals, families, and groups through the use of social casework and social group work methods, community organization and planning, educational and research activities, and consultation to other agencies and health facilities.

As she described the services provided for the patient and his family, Harriett M. Bartlett clearly delineated the shared responsibility of the social worker and physician:

The social worker shares the aura of authority in the medical institution, which encourages the patient to have confidence in the social worker's

[4] *Ibid.*, p. 7.
[5] Saval Zimand, ed., *Public Health and Welfare: Selected Papers of Homer Folks* (New York: Macmillan Co., 1958), pp. 76–77.

understanding of the medical problems and social expertness. The social worker does not, however, carry responsibility for the medical aspects of care and does not make medical recommendations. The physician's position is based on a scientific and professional analysis of the situation which enables him to recommend to the patient what can be regarded as the "best" action to be taken, in the light of medical knowledge. The social worker focuses on the individual's particular life situation and its meaning to him. These positions of the physician and the social worker are complementary in contributing toward a more exclusive understanding and handling of the problem than if each were meeting the patient's needs alone.[6]

Leonora B. Rubinow stressed the need for individualized services and explained the physician can give such service only when he understands the needs and circumstances influencing the patient and the impact these factors willl have on his illness. She emphasized that social work services should be utilized fully to help the patient receive the medical care available to him "and to work out a pattern of life that is at the same time consistent with his physical limitations and satisfying to him." [7] In describing the social worker's approach to the patient, Miss Rubinow stated that "the social worker is not concerned with the name of the disease, but what it does to the patient, how he feels about it—what his capacity for adjustment is." [8]

In elaborating on the traditional approach to illness and its implications for social work in medical settings, Sigmund L. Friedman stated:

> Disease meant a disease of an organ, not a disease of a patient. This isolation of disease from the patient was purely a device of the intellect. . . . This fashion has begun to change with increasing recognition that man's social environment affects his mental and physical health and well-being and that it can either produce disease of itself or alter other diseases.[9]

This highlights especially the social worker's need for knowledge of cultural aspects relating to health, illness, and medical care. John M. MacLachlan pointed out that "culture is a dynamic factor related to virtually every state of health and disease" and that "being sick is a cultural phenomenon in itself and may or may not accompany clinically definable ill health." [10] It is also recognized that attitudes toward good and ill health

---

[6] Harriett M. Bartlett, *Social Work Practice in the Health Field* (New York: National Association of Social Workers, 1961), p. 86.

[7] Leonora B. Rubinow, "Medical Social Service," in Dora Goldstine, ed., *Expanding Horizons in Medical Social Work* (Chicago: University of Chicago Press, 1955), p. 15.

[8] *Ibid.*, p. 17.

[9] Sigmund L. Friedman, "The Medical Social Worker Sees The Human Being First," in Goldstine, ed., *op. cit.*, pp. 4–5.

[10] John M. MacLachlan, "Cultural Factors in Health and Disease," in E. Gartley Jaco, ed., *Patients, Physicians and Illness* (New York: Free Press, 1967), p. 95.

and ways of treating illness are culturally derived and must be understood within the total culural context. As Lonis Liverman has written:
"appropriate individual behavior during illness, family responsibility for
the ill person, the role of the medical practitioner—all are culturally prescribed and intimately related to the way in which family roles, work
roles, religious beliefs, and other values are perceived by the group." [11]

The majority of social workers employed in medical settings are on
the staffs of public and private hospitals, voluntary and public health
agencies, public welfare agencies, sanatoriums, and rehabilitation agencies
under government auspices. Special attention should be given, however,
to the broadening use of social work in the public health field. Public
health now plays a far greater part in the life of the American community than ever before and its responsibilities are therefore becoming more
clearly defined. Public health is now considered to include all those activities that promote the health of the community and its members. Environmental health involves the identification of health problems in the total
environment in terms of the biological, physical, chemical, and social
stresses on man. Environmental health reaches into almost all human activities, including the public and private sectors of community and national life.[12] Disease prevention and control, the most traditional of the
public health services, is now classified as one of the categories of environmental health.

The number of social workers in the public health field almost tripled
between 1951 and 1964, increasing from 363 to 918.[13] The unmet need for
social workers in this field is reflected in the fact that in 1966, 31 percent
of the available positions on the state level and 20.4 percent of those in
local health departments were vacant. It is estimated that in the year 1970
some 6000 social workers are needed in public health agencies throughout
the country.[14]

SOCIAL WORK'S PLACE IN THE MEDICAL SETTING

Regardless of the type of medical setting or patient problem, social
work practice is generic in nature. Leonard Shotland emphasized this
point when he wrote of work with the chronically handicapped:

The fact that in a case of cerebral palsy the caseworker is dealing with a
specific disability does not make the basic casework approaches any differ-

[11] Lonis Liverman, "Cultural Dimensions: Attitudes Toward Health, Illness and
Medical Care," Social Work Papers, Vol. 9 (Los Angeles: School of Social Work,
University of Southern California, 1962), p. 10.
[12] Third Annual Conference on Public Health Training (Washington, D.C.: U.S.
Department of Health, Education, and Welfare, Public Health Service, 1967), p. 4.
[13] Ibid., Table 12, p. 55.
[14] Ibid., Table 13, p. 56.

ent than if the worker was working with any other client or any other problem. All the same basic generic casework principles apply to work with the chronically handicapped as well as to work with any other group or individual needing help.[15]

Steven K. Chough also stressed the generic aspects evident in work with the deaf. These he identified as (1) assessing factors in the client's personal and social development, (2) helping him come to terms with the reality of his problem and move toward personally acceptable and realistic goals, (3) helping him locate and use various community resources, and (4) assisting in coordinating the services he elects to use in his rehabilitation program.[16]

There is also a generic quality to the social worker's involvement in the education of medical personnel. Traditionally, the social worker was expected to teach physicians, nurses, and other medical staff members how his services could be used—that is, how to acquaint the patient with what the social worker had to offer. The emphasis has shifted in contemporary medical education, however. As a result, the social worker now teaches generic content in terms of "(1) the concept of the community as an integrated helping force, (2) the impact of illness on individual and family dynamics, and (3) the interrelationships of these aspects." [17]

THE MENTAL HEALTH FIELD

The term "psychiatric social work" was first used at the Boston Psychopathic Hospital in 1913 when the social service department was established under the direction of Mary C. Jarrett. Writing a decade later with E. E. Southard, director of the hospital, Miss Jarrett stated:

> The history of psychiatric social work is the focusing of various influences leading to more attention to the mind in social practice, under pressure from psychiatry demanding more attention to social needs in medical practice.
>
> . . . . . .
>
> We claim no novelty or originality for the social work of the Psychopathic Hospital, but rather, we would claim to have created the part that the social worker is to play in the mental hygiene movement and to have given it a name—psychiatric social work.[18]

[15] Leonard Shotland, "Social Work Approach to the Chronically Handicapped and Their Families," Social Work, Vol. 9, no. 4 (October 1964), p. 73.

[16] Steven K. Chough, "Casework with the Deaf: A Problem in Communication," Social Work, Vol. 9, no. 4 (October 1964), p. 81.

[17] S. Eric Edelson, "The Changing Role of the Social Worker in Medical Education," Social Work, Vol. 10, no. 1 (January 1965), p. 83.

[18] Mary C. Jarrett and E. E. Southard, The Kingdom of Evils (New York: Macmillan Co., 1922), pp. 518 and 521.

World War I had a deep impact on the mental health field because it brought increased knowledge of the relationship between the biological, psychological, physiological, and sociological aspects of human behavior. The concept of personality lost some of its abstract qualities and became identified as an entity to be recognized, understood, and studied much as the continuum of physical growth was being studied. Foreseeing the mental hospital of the future and the part that psychiatric social work and "social psychiatry" would play in the American community, Richard C. Cabot advised conferees at the 1919 National Conference of Social Work:

We should welcome the influx of social workers from the psychiatric side. This psychiatric eruption is the best thing that has happened in the history of social work during the last thirty years.[19]

By 1929 psychiatric social work was perceived as having two dimensions. It was seen as a social casework service given in a psychiatric or medical setting. It was not regarded as a specialized field, however, "but rather as social casework in whatever field whose practitioners have at their command an adequate working knowledge of mental hygiene."[20] This is the premise on which all contemporary psychiatric social casework is based.

CURRENT CLINICAL PRACTICE

Social workers are employed in a variety of mental health settings. The largest number work in local, state, and federal hospitals and outpatient clinics, but others are employed in voluntary or proprietary hospitals, residential treatment facilities, and mental health clinics. Their assigned tasks vary from direct service to mentally ill or mentally retarded individuals receiving inpatient care to work with patients on convalescent leave in their own homes or in family care homes. Psychiatric social workers are also employed in schools and by public health departments.

Traditionally, the social worker was assigned to compile the patient's medical and social history and to assist the patient and his family to locate and use ancillary health and welfare services. The family was helped to understand and accept the nature of the patient's illness and to work toward modifying the stressful environment or situation that may have contributed to the onset of mental illness. The work of the psychiatrist and the social worker was interrelated but separate in terms of function and relationship to the patient. The social worker did not assume the role

[19] Richard C. Cabot (informal discussion), *Proceedings of the National Conference of Social Work,* 1919 (Chicago: Rogers & Hall Co., 1920), p. 524.
[20] Porter R. Lee and Marion E. Kenworthy, *Mental Hygiene and Social Work* (New York: Commonwealth Fund, 1931), p. 161.

of diagnostician and usually did not function as a therapist in work with the patient.

Gerald Caplan outlined some basic concepts and assumptions about mental health services that are reflected in contemporary social work practice in mental health settings. Caplan perceived therapy as a "segmental" process even though the patient is the focus of all service offered. The service begins with casefinding and proceeds through the comprehensive process of diagnosis, individual and/or group treatment, and rehabilitation. Whenever possible the treatment regimen should begin and end with the patient at home with his own family and ensure continuity of therapy in the aftercare process.

The patient's mental disorder is now seen as a life experience and psychiatric intervention as an artifact in his life. The patient is viewed as being constantly affected by his interpersonal and social relationships and environment, with the major purpose of therapy being to return him as quickly as possible to normal life-style functioning.[21]

THE CHILD GUIDANCE MOVEMENT

Dr. William Healy directed the first clinic for children operated in connection with a juvenile court. Although it is often described as the first child guidance clinic, it initially lacked the staffing pattern now considered characteristic of such clinics. When established in 1909, this clinic was known as the Juvenile Psychopathic Institute of Chicago, but it is now the Institute for Juvenile Research.

The first child guidance clinic was in fact opened in St. Louis in 1922. It was staffed by a team consisting of a psychiatrist, a psychologist, and a social worker. After 1922 work in the child guidance field developed into a distinct movement to which the Commonwealth Fund made impressive contributions through the support of demonstration clinics in various parts of the country. In some communities these clinics became permanent resources for children after the five-year demonstration period ended.

Since these early beginnings, psychotherapy with children and their parents has become an indispensable service. Parental and environmental influences, evident in developmental, personal, and social history, are still considered important clues to the cause of a child's problems. Major emphasis, however, is now placed on a treatment process in which the patient and the therapist are involved in a professional relationship based on the total needs of the patient, whether parent or child. The treatment process often includes conjoint therapy in which the family is treated as a unit.

[21] Gerald Caplan, *An Approach to Community Mental Health* (New York: Grune & Stratton, 1966), pp. 233-35.

The child guidance clinic is a diagnostic and treatment facility for children with behavioral problems stemming from emotional and mental disturbance. The professional service offered follows the traditional staffing pattern. Each member of the team (psychiatrist, psychologist and social worker) has his own contribution to make to the patient's rehabilitation and their functions are often interchangeable despite their differences in professional training. The psychiatrist, who is a physician familiar with patterns of deviation, is usually engaged in direct therapy with the patient; the psychologist administers various tests, observes the patient, and participates in the treatment process. The social worker often handles the intake interview and, like other members of the team, works with children, parents, and related agencies.

As previously implied, child guidance clinics and other mental health facilities that include a service for children have been developed under a variety of auspices. Those established by voluntary groups are often supported by community chests, but in many areas, both rural and urban, the child guidance clinic functions as part of a larger program administered by a state agency, a local health department, or a local board of education. Outpatient clinics operated by state hospitals for the mentally ill may also accept children for diagnosis and treatment, although they usually serve former patients of the hospital who have recovered sufficiently to live in the community. In some rural areas a psychiatric service may be available to a child despite the lack of any agency. This is accomplished most often by the use of a "mobile clinic" that takes the treatment team to the area in which the child lives.

THE CHILD WELFARE FIELD

The child welfare field includes a range of specialized services for children designed to protect and promote their welfare. These services have evolved separately in different eras but are now considered essential to any comprehensive pattern of resources for children.

INSTITUTIONAL CARE

After the first almshouse was established in Rensselaerswyck, New York, in 1657, the continued demand for custodial care for homeless children and dependent adults led to the construction of many additional institutions of this kind. The Revolutionary War, the Indian wars, and widespread epidemics caused the death of many parents and thus created a need for some type of care for orphans and half-orphans.

The orphanage was America's first step toward giving dependent children a form of care that was solely child-focused. The first such institution was established by the Ursuline Sisters in New Orleans in 1729, to care for children orphaned by Indian raids and massacres during that year. The first recognized public orphanage in the United States was established in 1794 in Charleston, South Carolina.

In New York State, where public funds had been available for private congregate care since 1811, the number of children in almshouses increased from 3000 in 1847 to more than 26,000 in 1866. The Civil War caused the major increase in the number of orphans and the number of institutions established. By 1874 state support of private institutions was terminated by law, but local governmental units assumed responsibility for continued financial subsidy. Despite the continued availability of care in institutions operated under voluntary auspices, the number of homeless or otherwise dependent children committed to mixed almshouses did not decline. The negative impact of mass child care was dramatically and forcefully reflected when an 1834 report of the Poor Law Commission of New York included this stark and melancholy description of an almshouse:

> . . . the building . . . occupied by sixty to eighty paupers, made up of a dozen or more neglected children (under the care, perhaps, of a pauper), about twenty or thirty ablebodied paupers of both sexes, and probably an equal number of aged persons, proper objects of relief. Amidst these the mothers of bastard children and prostitutes live without shame and associate freely with the youth, who also have the examples and conversation of the inmates of the county gaol, the poacher, the vagrant, the decayed beggar, and other characters of the worst description. To these may be added a solitary blind person, one or two idiots, not infrequently are heard, from among the rest, the incessant ravings of some neglected lunatic. In such receptacles the poor sick are often immured.[22]

In the decades that followed, other states responded to the problem of the dependent child in a variety of ways. The Monson Primary School, established in Massachusetts in 1866, apprenticed the children in its care to various tradesmen. Staff from an auxiliary agency visited the children to become familiar with the conditions under which they would live during their apprenticeship. Ohio's efforts to remove childrren from mixed almshouses resulted in the establishment of county children's homes. Beginning in 1866 these institutions provided care for orphaned and other dependent children under the age of 16. Whenever possible this was considered temporary care, with indenture or adoption as the final plan for the child.

---

[22] "Report of the New York Poor Law Commission, 1834," as cited in H. W. Thurston, *The Dependent Child* (New York: Columbia University Press, 1930), p. 27.

Another plan of institutional care was provided in the State School at Coldwater, Michigan. This facility was set up on the cottage plan, with small groups of children of similar age and sex living together under the supervision of a houseparent. This school represented a pioneer effort in simulating family living for the child who had to be institutionalized.

The development of child welfare in America was significantly affected by the contributions made by voluntary agencies. Their activities led to changes in basic thinking about the needs of children as well as to the creation of new programs and facilities.

Although the first orphanage in America was established under Catholic auspices, a Jewish orphanage and several Protestant institutions were established during the Revolutionary War. The nineteenth century however, was the era in which many institutions for children were established under a variety of religious auspices. Simultaneously there was increasing realization that large institutions could not meet the individual needs of all children. It was recognized, too, that large-group congregate care deprived children of meaningful parental models and a pattern of family life that would enable them to form their own perceptions of family living. In more recent years, many institutions have sought to eliminate those deficiencies through the cottage plan inaugurated in the Coldwater school.

There is current agreement that the cottage plan is superior to large-group care, but a cottage of 15–45 children cannot approximate the family constellation deemed so necessary for the socialization and emotional growth of a child. As a result, thinking about institutional care for children has made two distinct pendulum swings. The philosophy of child care first moved to concensus that the needs of the homeless and dependent child can best be met through custodial care in a large institution and then to an era in which there was deep conviction that group living of any kind would prove detrimental to a child's growth and development. Recent decades have brought about a sensible compromise, based on knowledge that group living can meet the needs of some children if the traditional accouterments of large-group congregate care are minimized or completely absent.

A concept new to the field is evident in the increasing use of group homes. An agency group home (operated in a house owned or leased by an agency or institution) gives the child a family living experience coupled with the security of institutional care, because child care staff employed by the agency cannot insist on removal of a child because of his behavior or a change in their own personal plans. This knowledge can be of real comfort to a child previously shunted from one foster home to another.

FOSTER CARE

As indicated in an earlier chapter, Charles Loring Brace, a Protestant clergyman was moved and troubled by the numbers of homeless children seen each day on New York City streets or sleeping in doorways. These were the deserted or orphaned children of immigrants living in the city's ethnic pockets.

Brace conceived a foster home plan whereby children would be transported by the trainload from the city to the farms and villages of the Midwest, where they would work for their keep and become permanent members of the families with whom they lived. To achieve the objectives of this program, Brace sent agency representatives in advance of the scheduled departure of the children so that plans could be made to receive them. He also sent letters to farmers describing the children who would arrive and asking that they be considered for placement.

The plan was crude in its beginnings because the children did not know where they were going or in whose home they would live once they arrived at their destination. Children were encouraged to use whatever talents they might possess to attract foster parents and help them be selected. When Charles Loring Brace, Jr., succeeded his father in directing the New York Children's Aid Society, he made sustained attempts to locate many of the children his father had been responsible for placing. Although his father's methods were cumbersome and sometimes damaging to the children he hoped to serve, he and the New York Children's Aid Society provided a significant pattern for modern child placement programs.

In its current context the term "foster care" is applied to any type of care for children who must live apart from their parents. Such care is usually arranged in another family home, but the term may be used to include group living in an institution or school. Some children require foster care only during a family crisis; others may need it for a more prolonged period until necessary changes can occur in their parents' circumstances. For still other children, foster care will be necessary until they can assume full responsibility for themselves as adults.

The length of time a child remains in foster care depends on his individual situation and the auspices under which he is placed. Child welfare agencies plan to separate children from their families only as long as the child's needs and the family's circumstances warrant. If the child is placed in foster care by order of the juvenile court, it is generally incumbent on the court to rescind the placement order before the child can be restored to the custody of his parents. However, the juvenile court judge will be guided in his decision to return the child to his own home by the recommendation of the probation department or a social agency to which the placement assignment was given. Experts in the child welfare field believe that a child's future adjustment is directly related to the opportunity to continue his contacts with his parents and that he should also be encouraged to talk about them as much as possible during the time he is in placement. Out-of-home care will have lasting value only when a child is encouraged to evaluate the totality of his experience while in the new environment and to understand that this experience is preparing him to return to his own home when it has been rehabilitated. The need for continuing parental ties is well stated by a noted authority:

> Strange to say, we sometimes fear the child's love for a delinquent parent. We are afraid of this love because we all know that a child often becomes like the person he loves. On the surface it seems that if we tell a child that of course he should love his mother or father, we are telling him to become like the parent . . . This need not be so.[23]

The professional dictum, then, is that the importance of the parent in the life of the placed child be recognized. As Jolowicz stated:

> . . . the more we come to know and to like the parent, and the more we come to respect him or her as a human being, the less often shall we place a child too hastily and without making every effort to preserve him for his own niche in this universe, which is simply his place in his own home.[24]

ALTERNATIVES TO FOSTER CARE

Because a continuing relationship with his own parents is so important to a child, all possible alternatives should be explored before temporary out-of-home care is planned. Family pressures and crises may be alleviated by the use of *day care*, in which the child returns to his own home at night. Such a service will allow a mother to work while assuring her of child care or it may relieve an overburdened mother who has too many responsibilities and too few coping strengths.

Another resource is *homemaker service*, which provides an effective means of avoiding family breakdown. Such services are provided by voluntary and public agencies in many communities to keep the family intact when the illness of the mother or some other family crisis would otherwise require the placement of children in foster homes. The homemaker is a woman employed by an agency to help with various aspects of family living. She may feed, clothe, and care for the children or help mothers

---

[23] Almeda R. Jolowicz, "A Foster Child Needs His Own Parents," *The Child*, Vol. 12, no. 2 (Washington, D.C.: U.S. Children's Bureau, August 1947), p. 20.
[24] *Ibid.*, p. 21.

to achieve these skills. The homemaker is often used to give guidance to mothers in handling such problems as delinquency or dealing with a physically handicapped or mentally retarded child. In most instances homemakers also offer families facing problems a measure of stability during the crisis.

ADOPTION

Adoption is the legal act whereby one person assumes parenthood of another. It entails the same rights and obligations on the part of parent and child as those incurred in natural parenthood. Although its legal status in the United States is comparatively recent (the middle of the nineteenth century), adoption of orphaned children has been a part of the custom and tradition of almost every nation of the world from earliest times. Only in this century, however, has it come to be seen as a legal-social process requiring the involvement of a social agency.

Each state now has its own adoption laws but some still permit exploitation of both the natural and the adoptive parents. The black market in child adoptions is significantly related to legislation in which loopholes result in lack of protection for all parties concerned.

An adequate adoption law prohibits the placement of a child by any person other than an authorized and qualified employee of a licensed child-placing agency. It requires investigation of each adoptive applicant to determine the suitability of the home as well as the type of child best fitted for this specific family. It also requires, after placement, a period of supervision by a qualified agency and a detailed report to the court, with recommendations as to the wisdom of permitting the adoption to become final. In addition, the law prohibits hasty surrender of the child by natural parents or, in fact, any relinquishment on their part that is not fully understood, carefully considered, and voluntary in nature. State adoption laws meet these requirements in varying degrees.

There was a time—not too distant—when it was considered a great gesture of humanity for any couple to want to adopt a child. Friends, neighbors, relatives, and, indeed, social agencies thought of adoption as a benevolent act and adopted children as fortunate indeed. If the adoptive parents were often rigid in their expectations of the child, this was, if not approved, at least tolerated, on the grounds that the child was "better off" than he would be in an institution or in an unwholesome family situation. In spite of the current overabundance of babies eligible for adoption and a dearth of suitable adoptive parents, placement standards remain high and laws are constantly being amended to bring a wider measure of protection to the children.

Adoptive homes are selected from among a wide variety of applicants who vary in socioeconomic level, education, ethnic heritage and race. Most states require that the natural parent's religious preference be respected in the child's placement. As nearly as possible national origins, race, and the physical appearance of the child and the adoptive parents are matched so that there will be no gross differences in appearence as the child matures. There has been concern in the child welfare field because the number of adoptive applicants from Negro and other racial groupings is far less than the number of children available for adoption. This imbalance has produced a modified point of view on "total matching" and cross-racial adoptions are now being permitted or even encouraged.

Children may be placed for adoption by their natural parent(s) and released directly to the adoptive family. In these placements the state department of social welfare usually acts as legal agent for the child and his parent and determines the suitability of the adoptive home. Adoption is also handled directly through voluntary and public agencies licensed or otherwise authorized to provide an adoption service. In such cases the child is relinquished to the agency and the agency chooses the adoptive parents. In agency placements the natural parents are not told the identity of the adoptive family and that family is, therefore, accorded more security in knowing that the natural parent cannot claim the child at some future time. Most states require that a child be in a home under agency supervision for a specified period of time before the court is petitioned for a final adoption decree. This is true in independent adoption in which the natural parent is actively involved in the selection of the adoptive parents, and in agency adoption, in which the natural parent asks the agency to select the best adoptive family to meet the child's needs.

PROTECTIVE SERVICES

In 1874 a group of concerned people were interested in the welfare of a child who was being cruelly treated but could find no agency that could legally remove her from her abusive foster parents. After much exploration and dismay, the group brought the child's plight to the attention of the New York Society for the Prevention of Cruelty to Animals. The case was accepted by that agency on the basis that the child could be considered an abused animal, and after legal procedures were duly initiated the child was removed from the custody of her guardians, who received a prison sentence for their mistreatment of their ward. In the following year the New York Society for the Prevention of Cruelty to Children was founded and by 1909 more than 160 agencies were providing protective services for children.

In recent years the increasing number of children coming to the attention of law enforcement and social agencies because of extreme physical abuse has made many communities aware of the need for expanded child-protective services. As child abuse has become more prevalent, a "child-abuse syndrome" has been identified. It usually involves young parents who feel the many pressures and demands of parenthood but lack the emotional and financial supports needed to meet their obligations in a responsible way. The depth of their desperation is often apparent in the kinds of sadistic and unwarranted abuse they heap on small children. An appropriate casework service should be offered these parents to alleviate their need to express their hostile feelings in brutality toward their children.

Casework service for children in their own homes is made available by many agencies when parents seek help in coping with some problem in family living, child-parent relationships, or difficult child behavior. When a member of the community, an agency, or the school reports that a child is being neglected or abused the service given is generally referred to as a "protective service."

Protective services were initially developed by private agencies either as a part of the total service provided by a family agency or as a specialized service given by a child protective agency. The absence of voluntary agencies in many rural areas and the impetus provided by the Social Security Act have led many state and local welfare departments to employ professionally educated child welfare staff to provide both protective and other casework services to parents seeking help with problems in family life.

As previously indicated, a protective service differs from a casework service for children in their own homes chiefly in the fact that in the latter, it is the parent who has sought the agency's help. When the welfare of a child is in jeopardy, the agency providing a protective service responds to information about child neglect or abuse by offering service to the parents. The primary purpose of this service is to help the parent find more acceptable ways of dealing with stress and coping with the kinds of behaviors and reactions that encourage the neglect or abuse of children.

SCHOOL SOCIAL WORK

In 1906 and 1907 Boston, New York City, and Hartford developed a "visiting teacher" or school social work program and proposed this kind of child welfare service to their respective public school systems. Two staff members of Hartley House and Greenwich House were assigned to work in three New York slum areas in 1906, and in Boston the Women's Education Association employed a visiting teacher to work in one school. In 1913 Rochester, New York, became the first city in which a board of education employed its own visiting teacher.

The greatest stimulus for the development of social work in the schools came about through programs inaugurated by the Commonwealth Fund in 1921. One project authorized the Public Education Association of New York City to organize a National Committee of Visiting Teachers that would initiate programs to demonstrate the value of social work in the schools. School systems in some 30 localities in 23 states were used as demonstration areas. By 1930, when the Commonwealth Fund withdrew from the field, 92 communities in 30 states had developed school social work programs. Since that time the term "visiting teacher" has been changed to "school social worker" and social services have become an integral part of the school's guidance programs in an increasing number of school districts, especially on the elementary school level.

CONTEMPORARY PRACTICE

The primary purpose of providing a social work service in a school setting has been described as enabling "those children with social and emotional difficulties to achieve their optimum potential and to make the fullest use of their school experiences." [25]

Rachel Dunaway Cox has written that the school social worker's major function is to help foster ego development. She pointed to three significant developmental steps relating to "the tasks of childhood": the child's acceptance of "separateness" from the home, his readiness for discipline in body and mind, and his need and opportunity to find his place in the social group where he can strive for recognition and find new roles for himself.[26] The school social worker is also concerned with helping the child to develop his own strengths to deal with "the facts and demands of his chronological age" in the way society deems behavior appropriate for that age. The social worker must also help the child to accept responsibility for using the education society provides and to "help him achieve, with a nice balance between dependence and independence, a strong individuality, secure enough in its new function that it need not fly in fright from a certain degree of conformity." [27]

The school has come to be regarded as the major socialization force in a child's life. As such it is the center of his earliest efforts to adapt and relate to the demands of others outside the parental and familial structure. Cornelia T. Biddle explained, however, that "education does not begin when the 5- or 6-year-old enters kindergarten or first grade. It begins when the child first draws breath. . . . The school does not begin the edu-

[25] John J. Alderson, "The Relationship of School Social Work to Child Welfare Services," Child Welfare, Vol. 44, no. 9 (November 1965), p. 504.
[26] Rachel Dunaway Cox, "Social Work in Elementary Schools," Social Work, Vol. 8, no. 2 (April 1963), pp. 78–79.
[27] Ibid., p. 81.

cational process; it furthers it." [28] The report on a substantial demonstration of school social work also included these findings:

> The school is rarely the community agency to make the first identification of the child whose problem behaviors may be associated with belonging to a family that is the recipient of public welfare or the child who belongs to the multiproblem family. Usually these families are identified long before the child enters school, and the primary responsibility for identification and intervention might well be assumed by the agencies to which the families are known. . . .[29]

When there is a continuum of problems and stresses for the child and his family, the school social worker shows a continuity of concern for the treatment of these problems. In so doing he coordinates and gives consultation to other social service systems, thus placing the school within the community of social agencies. The school social worker is not only concerned with the child from the multiproblem family but works with all children referred by the teacher and other school staff. The teacher shares with the social worker the responsibility for understanding the child as his own "change agent" with the help and support of those who care about him. Ruth E. Smalley wrote eloquently of the child in his search for the opportunity to change:

> It is the social characteristics inherent in the child's nature which make him able to use help. He is a growing, changing, self-directing organism who has the power and the necessity to use his own resources, as well as outside resources, of which we may be one, to accomplish his own development. He is a unique individual with his own purpose and integrity, constrained to use help in a way which is *his* way in order to achieve a self identifiable as his own self, a self which he will not let be pushed around, violated, obliterated, or transformed into something it is not and for which he, therefore, would not, could not, and should not take responsibility. He is a social individual who is just as organically and necessitously part of a whole as he is a differentiated unit within it.[30]

SOCIAL WORKER–CHILD–PARENT RELATIONS

It has been pointed out that the family must be seen as a therapeutic unit in which interactional experiences and intrapsychic forces are ap-

[28] Cornelia T. Biddle, "Casework Intervention in a School," in *Ego Psychology and Dynamic Casework*, ed. Howard J. Parad (New York: Family Service Association of America, 1948), p. 184.

[29] Charlotte D. Elmott, Jane Criner, and Ralph Wagner, *The Troublesome Ten Percent* (Santa Barbara, Calif.: Santa Barbara City Schools, California State Department of Social Welfare, and Junior League of Santa Barbara, 1961), p. 23.

[30] Ruth E. Smalley, "The Social Worker Helps the Troubled Child," *Social Work*, Vol. 1, no. 1 (January 1956), p. 105.

praised as the patient is treated in the presence of his family.[31] The school social worker deals with family dysfunction with the focus of intervention on the person, the family, or the social structure, depending on the nature of the problems for which service is needed. Change in the child and his parents may involve any aspect of physical or emotional health that interferes with appropriate and satisfying role performance. Change in the family system will require role support from other members of the family so that role expectations can be met and role performance can lend equilibrium to the family structure and family functioning. Specifically, emotional sensitivity would be needed and mutuality of gratification in terms of child-rearing, home management, and fulfillment of other expectations. Changes in the social structure would ensure the availability of social welfare, health, and educational services all brought within "an operational system [so that] the existing services can be deployed and coordinated in a way that brings them to bear effectively upon the problems of the family whose functioning is impaired." [32]

Howard J. Parad and Gerald Caplan described the "impact of crisis" and identified the need to see "the life-style of the family as a backdrop against which the crisis drama takes place." [33] They reviewed five related "aspects of the perceptual meaning of crisis to the family," (1) the stressful event poses a problem that is by definition insoluble in the immediate future, (2) the problem overtaxes the psychological resources of the family, since its resolution is beyond their traditional problem-solving methods, (3) the situation is perceived as a threat or danger to the life goals of the family members, (4) the crisis period is characterized by tension, and (5) the crisis situation awakens unresolved key problems from both the near and distant past.[34]

Borrowing again from Boehm, these are the kinds of problems that become the "focus of intervention" and demand the "tactics of intervention." In the school setting the intervention processes may involve a number of specialists who are members of the treatment team serving the child in school—the school physician, nurse, psychometrist, social worker, psychiatrist, counselor, and attendance officer. Each of these persons contributes to the broader understanding of the individual child for whom the teacher has major responsibility.

[31] See Virginia M. Satir, Conjoint Family Therapy (Palo Alto, Calif: Science and Behavior Books, 1964).

[32] Werner W. Boehm, "The Family as the Basis of Diagnosis and Treatment." Unpublished paper, April 1967.

[33] Howard J. Parad and Gerald Caplan, "A Framework for Studying Families in Crisis," Social Work, Vol. 5, no. 3 (July 1960), p. 11.

[34] Ibid., pp. 11–12.

The contemporary dimensions of school social work were set forth some 30 years ago by Dean E. George Payne of New York University:

The social changes and adjustments, which amount to a revolution in our social life, have made a new theory practice inevitable and these have changed the theoretical emphasis from that of knowledge-getting to that of developing a unified personality in a complex social life. The theoretic emphasis has changed from the knowledge aim to the personality aim, from knowledge to behavior as the outgrowth of school endeavor. This change of front on the part of educators has brought education directly into the realm of social work, for the emphasis of the social worker from the beginning has been upon personality and behavior.[35]

FEDERAL LEGISLATION

Three recent pieces of federal legislation have been enacted to strengthen and broaden programs on the local school district level and within the state departments of education. This legislation also has a direct relationship to social work in the schools.

Title II of the Economic Opportunity Act of 1964 (PL 88-452) relates to community action groups and contains provision for educational programs for preschool children who live in economically and culturally deprived areas. Head Start programs provide part- and full-time school social workers whose efforts are directed toward stimulating the interest and participation of community groups, locating children in need of a preschool learning and socialization experience, involving the parents of these children in program planning and cooperation, and helping families to meet health and welfare needs. Head Start programs follow the preschool or nursery school model and may be established in conjunction with local school districts or conducted independently of a school system.

Titles I, III, and V of the Elementary and Secondary Education Act of 1965 (PL 89-110) also bear a close relationship to school social work. Under Title I funds are given to local school districts through the state department of education to improve the quality of education and expand educational and social services to meet the needs of educationally deprived children in districts where need is apparent.

Title I provides educational opportunity for all children, whether in public, private, or parochial schools. The school social worker may supervise untrained personnel and, in some situations may be used as a consultant to teachers and other school staff. Title III also provides funds directly to local school districts that have innovative programs or projects directed to professional team participation in strengthening educational, vocational,

---

[35] E. George Payne, "The Social Worker in Education," *The Compass Needle*, Vol. 2, nos. 3-4, (November–December 1935), p. 5.

health, and school-home-related social services. Title V is designed to strengthen state departments of education. School social workers may be hired as consultants to school districts to establish such services. A federal-state-local partnership is reflected in Title V, which also provides staff funding on the local level.

The National Defense Education Act under Title V provides for the establishment of guidance services for public elementary schools. Funds are given for training and activities designed to encourage local school districts to develop such programs. The school social worker employed under this title would not be used as a consultant but would primarily be engaged in working directly with children and their families and with social and collateral agencies.

THE CORRECTIONAL FIELD

Most rational persons conform to societal expectations and to statutory law because they know that violation of established norms may bring social rejection and/or legal penalty. The degree of conformity is varied, but most individuals value social acceptance and freedom enough to allow or want their behavior to be controlled by others through sanctioned social forces. When the person finds it impossible to conform to mandated forms of social control, however, the community must be protected by law enforcement, judicial processes, and mandatory correctional services. Correction has been defined as

a social process by which society maintains legally identifiable offenders as members of the community in temporarily handicapped status. The necessities of this task require both control over the behavior of the offender during the period of his penalty and services designed to help him achieve a less socially dangerous mode of participation in the community.[36]

The correctional process

is administered through a system of operating agencies which are a part of the formal system of social control and are authorized to use, under limitations, the force of the state to protect the community against unlawful acts. . . . [These are] primarily governmental agencies, established by legislation which authorizes their activities and makes the service mandatory for both agency and client.[37]

In short, the social worker in the correctional setting is working within the framework of the administration of criminal justice.

[36] Elliot Studt, *Education for Social Workers in the Correctional Field*, Vol. 5 of the Curriculum Study (New York: Council on Social Work Education, 1959), p. 7.
[37] *Ibid., p.* 8.

The role of the social worker in corrections is characterized by its direction to resocialization of the offender while he is incarcerated or on probation or parole.[38] The social worker in the correctional setting often experiences functional and ideological conflict, however. Lloyd E. Ohlin and his associates pointed this out clearly:

> The social worker in corrections . . . soon recognizes that the community consists of a number of interest groups with varying and conflicting demands upon him and the offender client. He finds that many officials and citizens have a negative attitude toward his client and that this is reciprocated by the client. His task is not only to alter both conceptions, but to deal with the problems raised by these conflicts of ideas. . . . He finds himself subjected to pressures to act in ways which violate his own conception of the proper role and function of the social worker.[39]

The authors outlined "the three conditions which structure the occupational dilemmas of the social worker" as (1) the nature of the clientele, (2) agency organization, and (3) community organization.[40]

THE SOCIAL WORKER'S TASKS

The basic tasks of social workers who enter the correctional system as probation or parole officers or as employees of correctional institutions have been carefully articulated: [41]

1. To act as an officer of the court or of any other quasi-judicial body by investigating and reporting on the offender and his social situation so that appropriate and meaningful legal decisions can be made.

2. To supervise the client in such a way that violations of the condition of his status and success in meeting those conditions can be reported and controls and other services provided to stimulate conforming behavior, inner growth, and the potential for self-control.

3. To help the involuntary client to handle the stresses produced by the law enforcement and correctional processes and to become motivated to ask and use help in modifying his behavior in terms of societal expectations.

4. To work with other individuals and agencies associated with the client's life and with group and community resources.

[38] Elliot Studt, "Correctional Services," *Encyclopedia of Social Work* (New York: National Association of Social Workers, 1965), pp. 221–22.

[39] Lloyd E. Ohlin, Herman Piven, and Donnell M. Pappenfort, "Major Dilemmas of the Social Worker in Probation and Parole," in Mayer N. Zald, ed., *Social Welfare Institutions* (New York: John Wiley & Sons, 1965), p. 534.

[40] *Ibid.*, p. 528.

[41] Studt, *Education for Social Workers in the Correctional Field, op. cit.*, pp. 15–16.

5. To administer a case load appropriately and responsibly so that legal and administrative deadlines and expectations are met and client emergencies handled.

6. To work in partnership with other professions in making shared decisions in behalf of a client.

7. To assume a responsible part in the development and enhancement of agency service by contributing to policies based on professional knowledge.

8. To contribute to the growth of knowledge and practice in social work in the correctional field.

Subsumed under these responsibilities are the generic social work methods—social casework, group work, community organization, administration and research.

The social worker in the correctional field needs to understand delinquent and criminal behavior as a form of social deviance as well as the psychological and social pressures that tend to influence such behavior. The offender must be accepted without condoning his antisocial behavior. The social worker is therefore obligated to respect and have concern about the total welfare of persons rejected by the community because of illegal acts. As an administrator of criminal justice and its stress-provoking practices and procedures, the social worker must view objectively the offender, his past behavior, and his current needs as he proceeds to carry out the purposes of law and justice. He must have knowledge of the techniques the offender learned in order to commit the crime and be able to view criminality as a subcultural entity with its own unique system of interpersonal relationships. To work realistically with the offender, the social worker must also have knowledge of the dynamics of stress, skill in a variety of diagnostic and treatment techniques, and an understanding of the unique problems encountered in application of social work concepts to the corrections case load.[42] In short, the social worker in the correctional field is working with the client subculture as well as the correctional subculture and he must have knowledge of the relationship between them and the free community.

THE PROBATION PROCESS

Juvenile and adult probation systems are generally administered under county auspices and mandated by state legislation. Probation is extended to persons who have been arrested but are not considered serious risks in the community.

[42] *Ibid.*, pp. 33–37.

Probation has been defined as "a form of disposition under which a court suspends either the sentence or execution of judgment of sentence on selected offenders, releasing them conditionally on good behavior, under prescribed terms and rules and subject to the control, guidance and assistance of the court as exercised through officers appointed to supervise them." [43] The probation officer is in effect an arm of the court with responsibility for the prehearing or pretrial study, supervising the probationer, helping the offender to meet satisfactorily the conditions of his probation, and assisting him to effect the changes in attitudes and goals necessary for his rehabilitation. The probation officer is also responsible for helping the probationer to locate and use needed community social, educational, and health services and for recommending the termination or revocation of probationary status at an appropriate point.

There is general agreement that probation work with juveniles or adults involves giving help to the person by imposing responsibility on him and assisting him to become more positively related to the wider community. Probation is seen in its widest sense as "a process of helping the individual accept and live within the limitations required by society . . . and should never be permitted to deteriorate into mere watchful supervision or routine reporting: an individual approach to each case is necessary." [44]

CORRECTIONAL INSTITUTIONS

The primary purpose of incarceration is to protect society by isolating the offender and deterring him from present and future involvement in criminal activity. This form of protection is in effect legally mandated punishment, but it is also directed toward rehabilitation of the offender. The offender is kept out of the community and is expected to learn how to function more adequately as a member of society. The correctional institution is therefore forced to assume a paradoxical dual role as the locus of punitive justice directed toward rehabilitative ends. The duality and duplicity of the correctional facility's roles has been well stated by Hall, Williams, and Tomaino:

> It begins to appear that a different perspective toward the field of corrections is needed, and the objectives of corrections may provide the context for this perspective. . . . The task of the correctional worker, when stripped of its most essential elements and presented in its most incisive form, is one of changing individuals from offender to non-offender status, with the

[43] Charles L. Newman and Milton G. Rector, *Sourcebook on Probation, Parole and Pardons* (2d ed.; Springfield, Ill.: Charles C Thomas, 1964), p. 72.

[44] William H. Sheridan, *Standards For Juvenile and Family Courts* (Washington, D.C.: U.S. Department of Health, Education, and Welfare, Children's Bureau, 1966), p. 90.

result that the public will then be protected and the offender can be considered to be rehabilitated.[45]

It has also been pointed out that the prison is to be regarded as a "people-changing organization" and that "the issue of priority of tasks about which one hears so much—the protection of society versus the treatment of offenders, evades a basic reality. The only means by which society can achieve its desired protection is a resocialization of the deviant which leads to his reintegration into society." [46] Thus custodial and rehabilitative goals are each an integral part of the reintegration and socialization-resocialization process.

Since relatively few incarcerated persons spend the remainder of their lives in prison, treatment is centered around eventual parole and readjustment to living in a free community. In short, preparation for parole begins, at least indirectly, at the time of entry into the institution. This is done by moving the offender through a classification system in which the appropriate work, school, and treatment programs are identified. The initial diagnostic workup is generally done at a reception or guidance center where the inmate is retained until the case study is completed. The skills and services of the total institution are utilized as his medical, psychiatric, educational, and vocational needs are evaluated. The new inmate is also assessed as to the type of custody he will need—that is, whether he should be held under minimum, medium, or maximum security.

The social worker or correctional counselor who has been assigned a specific case load within an institution has responsibility for helping the inmate make a satisfactory prison adjustment, for assisting him to retain contact with his family, and for giving support and encouragement as he engages in the total rehabilitative experience.

Parole

Like most rehabilitation programs, parole supervision was initiated by volunteers. The first paid public parole agent was employed in Massachusetts in 1845 to do "aftercare" supervision. Parole as a correctional process, however, is rooted in the traditional practices of indenturing servants and apprentices, transporting criminals by "ticket of leave" procedures, and granting conditional pardons.

[45] Jay Hall, Martha Williams, and Louis Tomaino, "The Challenge of Correctional Change: The Interface of Conformity and Commitment," in Lawrence Hazelrigg, ed., *Prison Within Society* (Garden City, N.Y.: Doubleday & Co., 1968), p. 311. Reprinted by special permission of *The Journal of Criminal Law, Criminology and Police Science* (Northwestern University School of Law) Copyright (B) Vol. 57, no. 4, 1967.
[46] Hazelrigg, *Prison Within Society, op. cit.,* Introduction to chapter on "The Therapeutic Function of Prisons," p. 267.

As a contemporary correctional service, parole is premised on three basic concepts: (1) it represents a conditional remission or commutation of part of the sentence, (2) it is a contract between the recipient of parole and the authority granting it, and (3) it requires the establishment of provisions for helping the parolee to fulfill the legal obligations of his status and to succeed in the total rehabilitation process.[47] The fundamental purpose of parole is to afford the offender an opportunity for conditional release after he has served part of his sentence in a correctional institution. The parole process is based on the assumption that the offender now has more value to the community and to himself than he would have if he remained incarcerated.

The criteria for "parolability" include some factors that can be questioned in terms of their reliability in relating prison adjustment to success or failure on parole. Some inmates are able to make an acceptable adjustment to prison life and routine because expectations are well ordered and defined. The assessment of an inmate's potential for success on parole seems to be necessarily premised on his record of prison behavior because that is the only basis for judgment available from the date of initial incarceration to the time of parole consideration. The parole board or other appropriate decision-making authority must base its assessment on such factors as educational achievement, work record, and the quality and kinds of peer and staff relationships observed during the time of imprisonment. Other factors taken into consideration include the nature of the crime for which the person was convicted, the length of time spent in prison, the inmate's previous criminal record, his motivation and capacity to make personality and behavioral changes, the willingness and ability of his family to help him fit into family and community life, and his seeming readiness to use supervision.

The social worker in the parole setting has responsibilities similar to those of the probation officer since he must help the offender to succeed in satisfactorily carrying out the conditions of his parole. There is no uniform pattern of parole because each state institutes its own procedures. Most states, however, have some conditions in common that determine the parole officer's involvement in the life of the parolee. It is usual to require the parolee to obtain the permission of his parole officer before changing his residence or employment and to follow a prescribed system of reporting his activities. The parolee must not marry without the parole officer's knowledge and consent, must not use narcotics or alcohol, must not use or carry weapons, and must not associate with others having a criminal record.

The commission of a new crime results in revocation of parole as does

[47] G. I. Giardini, The Parole Process (Springfield, Ill.: Charles C Thomas, 1959), p. 5.

any violation of the conditions of parole. Revocation therefore means that the parolee will be returned to the correctional institution to serve the time remaining from his previous sentence with or without credit for the time already spent successfully on parole.

Parole may be terminated at the end of the period covered by the offender's sentence or at an earlier date. It may also continue for life or as long as the paroling authorities believe necessary. These options in terms of parole status add importance to the role the parole officer plays in the welfare and life of the parolee.

HALFWAY HOUSES AND OTHER COMMUNITY SERVICES

Halfway houses were first established in the early 1950s. Some facilities initiated under private or religious auspices later received state subsidy. Others have been operated and financed by state departments of corrections, youth authorities or the federal Bureau of Prisons. The first two short-term (three to four months) pre-release guidance centers for juvenile and young offenders were opened by the Bureau of Prisons in New York City and Chicago in September 1961.

The purpose of the halfway house is to offer "permissive but supportive housing to the person who leaves the institution without a job, a home or both" and to "offer some degree of personal help" to the parolee so that he can become more easily and properly adjusted to free society.[48] Halfway houses sometimes serve special groups only, such as persons classified as narcotic addicts or alcoholics.

There are other interim facilities and services designed to help the individual make a gradual transition from the institution to the community. Outpatient diagnostic and treatment centers often provide psychiatric and social work services for those who were not considered suitable for probation but did not require a long period of institutionalization. Clinical service is available in some communities to those on probation or parole who are not making an adequate adjustment at home or at work but are not considered to need institutional care. Detention centers in some jurisdictions also offer a diagnostic or short-term treatment service and act as a prerelease guidance center for offenders who are granted probation or parole. Some communities offer a work release or work furlough program that allows the offender sentenced to serve a jail term an opportunity to work or attend school. In these programs the participants usually return to the institution at night and remain there on weekends and holidays until the imposed sentence has been served.[49] In some communities the offender

[48] Paul W. Keve, *Imaginative Programming in Probation and Parole* (Minneapolis: University of Minnesota Press, 1967), p. 223.
[49] John J. Galvin, ed., *Treating Youth Offenders* (Washington, D.C.: Correctional Research Associates, 1966), pp. 31-33.

may be permitted to live in his own home during the workweek and spend only the weekends in jail or at a boys' ranch.

Whether the parolee lives in the free community under the auspices of a halfway house, in his own home, or by himself, the role of the parole officer is one of support, guidance, and referral to need-meeting resources. The social worker employed in a parole system works within a legal setting but uses social work methodology in helping the parolee to meet the expectations imposed by his involuntary status and to use the parole period to enhance his social functioning.

PUBLIC WELFARE

Public welfare is considered a separate field of practice even though its responsibilities include those commonly associated with the fields of child welfare and health. In some states a public welfare department may also perform functions usually classified as falling within the correctional field and/or mental health, for example, services for delinquent children and youth and operation of institutions, detention facilities for children, and mental health clinics.

The parameters of public welfare are related to the source of its funds and mandated functions rather than to the nature of the problems presented by its clientele or the specific tasks undertaken to alleviate those problems. As a field of practice public welfare may be defined as including any social work activity legally assigned to a federal, state, or local public welfare department or undertaken by such agencies to fulfill their legal responsibilities. (Activities involved in administration of the social insurance programs are not included in this definition.)

The three-level network of governmental agencies responsible for administration of the current public welfare system had its origins in legislative action taken more than a century ago. In 1858 a special commission appointed by the Massachusetts legislature expressed concern about the founding of nine unrelated state institutions and recommended "the creation of a permanent State Board of Charities to be entrusted with the duty of constantly supervising the whole system of public charities, in order to secure the greatest usefulness without unnecessary expense." [50] The board created in 1863 was empowered to investigate and supervise municipal and state institutions and make recommendations related to the care of inmates. The states of Ohio and New York established similar boards in 1867. By 1913 only 10 states had no legally constituted control agency and the U.S. Bureau of the Census reported

[50] Robert W. Kelso, *The History of Public Poor Relief in Massachusetts, 1620–1920* (New York: Houghton Mifflin Co., 1922) p. 142.

that "there is not a single state that does not in some form recognize its duty to secure better care for those who cannot care for themselves." [51] The U.S. Children's Bureau played an important role in encouraging states to adopt legislation that would improve the quality of care available to children through state supervision and control. Its influence was most evident in legislation that expanded the functions of state agencies to include responsibility for the licensing of child-placing agencies, maternity homes, child-caring institutions, and foster homes and for the administration or supervision of mothers' aid programs. It was also evident, however, in the type of structure developed to administer these laws. In Minnesota, the advice of the Children's Bureau staff was used in formulating recommendations that resulted in the enactment of 35 statutes in 1917. This legislation centered in the Board of Control broad responsibility for the administration of a child welfare program and permitted the establishment of county child welfare boards. The latter were to act as agents of the state Board of Control in protecting children and were authorized to administer mothers' pensions and poor relief if requested to do so by local officials. Other states soon established similar agencies.

The first system of state-county administration of a total public welfare program was also established in 1917 by Illinois and North Carolina. This pattern was rapidly followed by 13 other states and by 1929 there appeared to be widespread agreement that

> the state can perform certain functions better than the local government, but in the performance of these duties, it has become increasingly clear that the functions . . . of the state and the local community must be made a correlated state and county responsibility. . . .[52]

Despite this concurrence in philosophy, no unified pattern of administration or financing emerged before 1935, although 27 states had adopted laws providing cash assistance to the blind. Some 34 had authorized grants to the needy aged, all but three states had sanctioned mothers' aid programs,[53] and 40 states had established licensing requirements for the care of children[54] and in some instances for the care of the aged. In most states the laws authorizing financial assistance were permissive and many states made no provision for state supervision or for participation

[51] U.S. Bureau of the Census, *Summary of State Laws Relating to the Dependent Classes* (Washington, D.C.: Government Printing Office, 1913), pp. 312–29.
[52] Grace Abbott, "The County vs. the Community as an Administration Unit," *Social Service Review*, Vol. 4, no. 1 (March 1930), pp. 12–16.
[53] Arthur P. Miles, *An Introduction to Public Welfare* (Boston: D. C. Heath & Co., 1949), pp. 192, 196, and 202.
[54] Gladys Genevra Fraser, *The Licensing of Boarding Homes, Maternity Homes, and Child Welfare Agencies* (Chicago: University of Chicago Press, 1937), p. 5.

in the financial cost of programs administered by the localities. Basic changes in state laws were therefore necessary to enable states to obtain the grants-in-aid made available under the Social Security Act.

The Social Security Act required states wishing to obtain federal grants-in-aid to submit a plan for the operation of each public assistance category and for the child welfare service program defined in the act. For the public assistance categories it also stipulated that the state plan provide for operation in each local unit of the state and for the administration or supervision of the plan by a single state agency. Because it did not specify the form of organization to be used, states that had previously established a network of county welfare departments usually authorized these agencies to assume responsibility for all programs under the supervision of the state department of public or social welfare. Other states elected a plan of state administration with local operation delegated to branch offices. A few states continued an existing pattern through which federally aided programs are administered or supervised by two or more state agencies.

THE CONTEMPORARY SCENE

All states have federally aided programs of old age assistance, (OAA), aid to the blind (AB), and aid to families with dependent children (AFDC). All states except Nevada also have a program of aid to the permanently and totally disabled (APTD) and in 1970 each state will need to establish a medical assistance program (MA or Medicaid) or forfeit the large amounts of federal funds previously available for medical assistance to the aged. Specialized services for the aged—homemaker service, day centers, and other programs designed to further self-care and independent living—have also been developed in many states. Federal funds for child welfare services have been allocated to all states since 1936 but are no longer available unless a state can show satisfactory progress in implementing a plan for the provision of necessary child welfare services for children in all parts of the state by July 1, 1975. Some form of general assistance is provided through state and/or local funds for persons not eligible to federally aided programs, but the assistance given is usually limited in amount and duration and may be available only in emergency situations.

The 1956 amendments to the Social Security Act indicated clearly that it was the objective of each public assistance program to furnish appropriate social services to strengthen family life and to help aged, blind, and disabled persons achieve independent living. The 1962 amendments contained incentives and requirements designed to encourage and—in effect—force the states to provide needed services. In signing this bill President John F. Kennedy stated:

This measure embodies a new approach—stressing services in addition to support, rehabilitation instead of relief, and training for useful work instead of prolonged dependency. . . . Our objective is to prevent or reduce dependency and to encourage self-care and self-support—to maintain family life where it is adequate and to restore it where it is deficient.[55]

The 1967 amendments required that child welfare services and services for children receiving AFDC be administered by the same organizational unit at the state and local levels and stipulated that the state plan for AFDC provide for the development of a comprehensive program of family and child welfare services for each child and relative receiving AFDC. In addition these amendments required that the state plan for each of these programs provide "for the training and effective use of subprofessional staff, with particular emphasis on the full-time or part-time employment of recipients and other persons of low income as community aides and . . . for the use of . . . a volunteer social services program in providing services to applicants and recipients. . . ."[56]

To meet these changes in federal requirements, states wishing to obtain maximum federal reimbursement for the services and financial benefits they provide will need to develop new organizational patterns for their delivery and in most instances will need to initiate some new services not currently available, such as day care and family planning.

ROLE OF THE SOCIAL WORKER

During the Depression public funds for unemployment relief were to a large extent administered under the direction of social workers. Regulations and policy statements issued by the Federal Emergency Relief Administration (FERA) therefore made it abundantly clear that the administration of public relief was considered a social work function. As a result agencies responsible for implementing these regulations made every effort to employ professional social workers and to train other staff in the essential elements of family casework. This philosophy continued as staff in these agencies assumed responsibility for administration of the new social security programs.

The original Social Security Act did not specifically assign to staff any responsibilities not clearly related to the equitable determination of eligi-

[55] "Handbook of Public Assistance Administration: Transmittal No. 4, Part I" (Washington, D.C.: U.S. Government Printing Office, December 8, 1966), p. 1.
[56] Social Security Act as amended by Public Law 90-248, Secs. 402 and 422.

bility for financial assistance. To ensure equitable treatment, appropriate individualization of need, and accountability for the expenditure of tax funds, mountains of instructions and policy statements appeared in manuals and multiple forms were required to route needed information to appropriate persons or agencies. As a result workers engulfed by paperwork and frustrated by their inability to spend needed time with the people in their case loads sometimes questioned whether their activities could be considered social work.

Despite the redefinition of function contained in the 1956 amendments to the Social Security Act, many public assistance workers continued to find their jobs unrewarding because their case loads were not reduced. Their discontent was heightened by the rising tide of public resentment against the increased cost of welfare programs, the resultant criticism directed against these programs, and in some states the harsh measures taken to meet the hostility vented on the AFDC program—for example, "midnight raids" to detect the presence of a man in the home and grant reductions based on the assumption that support was available from an absent father or a man "assuming the role of spouse."

Since 1962 the picture has changed. Federal funds are now available to meet a major portion (75–85 percent) of the administrative costs involved in the provision of needed services, federal regulations limit the size of service case loads, and many states are now using simplified methods of determining eligibility and the amount of grants—"eligibility workers" or paraprofessionals to process initial applications, determination of continuing eligibility by client affidavit, and computer determination of grant amounts. For the first time, perhaps, social workers employed in public assistance programs are now finding it possible to use their knowledge and skill to help individuals and families achieve more effective social functioning; to participate in the training and supervision of community aides; and/or to become involved in the development and operation of new programs such as multiservice centers, community organization in ghetto areas, and development of homemaker services.

Social workers employed to provide child welfare services in public welfare departments assume responsibility for a wide variety of activities depending on the specific services provided by the agency. Many local agencies have a comprehensive program of services for children that includes adoption, services to unmarried mothers, foster care, protective services, day care, homemaker services, specialized services for children living in their own homes, and licensing of foster family and day care homes. Child welfare workers employed by state departments of social welfare may assist in developing policy and informational materials and have an assigned responsibility for protecting the welfare of children through the licensing of adoption and/or child-placing agencies, institutions for children, day nurseries, and/or maternity homes. All these activities fall within the definition of child welfare services included in the 1962 amendments to the Social Security Act:

> Child welfare services means public social services which supplement, or substitute for, parental care and supervision for the purpose of (1) preventing or remedying, or assisting in the solution of problems which may result in the neglect, abuse, exploitation of children, or delinquency of children; (2) protecting and caring for homeless, dependent, or neglected children; (3) protecting and promoting the welfare of children of working mothers; and (4) otherwise protecting and promoting the welfare of children including the strengthening of their own homes where possible, or when needed, the provision of adequate care of children away from their homes in foster family homes or day care or other child-care facilities.[57]

Social workers employed to provide services for aged, blind, or disabled adults may also be engaged in a wide range of services designed to protect the welfare of these persons or to help them to achieve or retain capacity for self-care. Their assigned responsibilities may include the licensing of boarding homes for aged persons or activities to assist their clients in obtaining needed medical, rehabilitative, vocational, or legal services or appropriate out-of-home care. Social workers employed in state departments of social welfare may be assigned to the licensing of institutions for aged persons or engaged in formulating policy or preparing informational materials.

Social workers are also employed in administrative and supervisory positions in local, state, and federal agencies and may carry responsibility for a variety of community organization activities as client needs are identified and new services developed.

In local agencies extensive use is made of the casework method in providing direct services but group methods are receiving increased recognition as effective means of achieving defined objectives. Local agencies are also utilizing techniques of community organization.

PRIVATE PRACTICE IN SOCIAL WORK

The social worker in private practice provides social services on a fee basis independently of any agency structure. Although this is a relatively new field of practice, greater numbers of private practitioners are making their services available, especially in large urban areas.

Private practice has been a controversial issue among professional social workers. Many believe that social work should not be practiced with-

---

[57] Compilation of the Social Security Laws, 1962, Sec. 521, p. 153.

out direct supervision by and accountability to an agency sanctioned by law or an organized voluntary body representative of the community. As Ruth E. Smalley has explained:

> The dilemma for the private practice of social work, with support of individual practitioners by individual persons through payment of fee, lies in its appearing to wipe out society's stake in a social service, society's ultimate responsibility for its direction, and the social worker's responsibility to society as well as to the individual, not only for a method of helping but also for a program of service, with the helping method inextricably linked to the service.[58]

The point relating to private practice as "appearing to wipe out society's stake in a social service and society's ultimate responsibility for its direction" appears to be the very reason private practice has evolved so rapidly. Society has not in fact faced up to its responsibility to help the troubled person who is too affluent for public service yet not affluent enough to purchase sustained psychiatric treatment. In voluntary agencies purporting to serve such clients, long waiting lists have resulted from the lack of professionally qualified therapists and/or the financial resources needed to employ them.

Sidney Levenstein pointed out:

> When an institution's major concern is with social change, as social work's is, and its own norms are being challenged and modified, there needs to be some understanding of the process, its roots, and the extent and direction of change. Knowing itself and its struggles with change more fully may help social work to fulfill its social change functions. The minor revolution, the challenge, is private practice.[59]

The question of whether social work can be practiced outside an agency structure has now been answered somewhat substantially. Many changes have taken place since Mrs. Lee Steiner was forced in 1936 to list herself as a "personal consultant" because the manager of the building where she maintained her office feared the reaction of other tenants if she placed the MSW designation after her name.[60]

In December 1962 the Delegate Assembly of the National Association of Social Workers gave tacit approval to private practice by establishing standards of competence. These include (1) graduation from a school of

---

[58] Ruth E. Smalley, *Theory for Social Work Practice* (New York: Columbia University Press, 1967), p. 5.

[59] Sidney Levenstein, *Private Practice in Social Work* (New York: Columbia University Press, 1964), p. 3.

[60] *Ibid.*, p. 42.

social work accredited by the Council on Social Work Education, (2) membership in the Academy of Certified Social Workers, and (3) five years of acceptable full-time experience in agencies providing supervision by professionally trained social workers, of which two consecutive years must have been in one agency under such supervision, giving direct service and using social work methods.

OTHER FIELDS OF PRACTICE

Family social work is usually included in any listing of fields of practice but its characteristics do not differ in any essential way from those of the "service for children living in their own homes" provided by many public welfare departments or the services given by a school social worker or a child guidance clinic.

Historically this term originated when services to children and their families were customarily provided by voluntary agencies. It was therefore useful in describing the services of a Charity Organization Society or its successor, a family welfare agency. It also served to differentiate the services given to a voluntary applicant from those initiated by a child protective agency. In that era, too, the service of the family agency differed in an obvious way from that provided by other child-serving agencies because the functions of the latter were usually limited to the provision of institutional or foster family care and did not include service to children living in their own homes.

The term "family social work" is still used to describe in a general way the services provided by more than 300 voluntary agencies affiliated with Family Service Association of America. These agencies, however, serve individuals faced with stressful situations as well as families. They customarily employ staff qualified by professional education to provide marital counseling, help with problems involving parent-child relationships, and assist in developing plans for the care of aged parents. Many of these agencies are also active in conducting family life education programs. Casework and a variety of group methods (e.g., family counseling sessions, parent groups, and adolescent groups) are used and psychiatric consultation is usually made available to staff. These agencies derive a portion of their financial support from community chests or united crusades but their clients are also charged a fee for each session, based on their ability to pay.

Similar services are provided by other voluntary agencies operating under various religious auspices—Lutheran welfare agencies, Catholic welfare bureaus, Jewish social service agencies, the Salvation Army, Volunteers of America.

Group services represent another indentifiable field of practice. These services are usually associated with neighborhood centers and a variety of leisure-time group-serving agencies—YM-YWCAs, YM-YWHAs, Jewish service centers, Campfire Girls, boys' clubs, Boy Scouts, Girl Scouts. Many organizations of this type do not employ social workers but draw their staff from the fields of recreation or education. Others, however, like the Jewish service centers, have staff skilled in social group work and may also employ one or more caseworkers to provide help with individual or family problems.

Community planning and development is a field of practice long identified with councils of social agencies or community welfare councils. Today, however, the need for staff skilled in research and community organization techniques is increasingly recognized as public and voluntary organizations attack the problems that beset the inner-city ghettos and rural slums and attempt to help the poor achieve a better opportunity system.

The preceding chapter described the processes involved in the use of community organization as a social work method and provided rather detailed information about the settings in which this method is practiced. It also presented the objectives, philosophy, and characteristics of the process currently known as community development and indicated that much of the recent efforts to engage the poor in decision-making and in action designed to ensure a more equitable distribution of community resources received its impetus from Title II of the Economic Opportunity Act of 1964.

Federal funds allocated under this title are granted on a formula based on the percentage of public assistance recipients, the number of unemployed persons, and the number of related children under 18 living in families with annual incomes of less than $1000. Other considerations include the concentration of low-income families with children, extent of persistent unemployment and underemployment, number of migrant or transient low-income families, school dropout rates, military rejection rates, and other evidences of low educational attainment and high incidence of disease, disability, infant mortality, crime, delinquency, and poor housing. Programs with emphasis on research, training, and demonstrations are given priority and approved programs are funded on a grant-in-aid basis (PL 88–452). Under the Economic Opportunity Act amendments of 1967, a community action agency may be established at the state level to provide an agency site for antipoverty efforts.

Other community action programs are Head Start, legal services for the poor, Upward Bound, and tutorial programs. These attempt to bring local citizens together to work toward the easing and elimination of poverty. A community is eligible for a community action program if it provides a suitable organizational structure and has the motivation and commonality of interest needed for sustained involvement in a program with approved objectives.

Other classifications of fields of practice. In this chapter the nature of the setting and its assigned tasks have been used as the primary factors in differentiating the various fields of practice. It is well to note, however, that for some purposes increasing use is being made of a classification based on the central problem of the persons to be served—such as mental retardation, mental illness, poverty, unmarried parenthood, drug addiction, aging. A classification of this type is useful in planning a comprehensive and coordinated program of services needed by a specific group of troubled or handicapped persons and in stimulating the development and dissemination of knowledge essential to the provision of needed services.

SOCIAL WORK MANPOWER

The projected national population of 226 million by 1975 reflects an age distribution in which there will be many more older people and children. It is estimated that by 1980 there will be 5.3 million children under the age of 5 as compared with 3.9 million children under the age of 6 in 1967.[61] Since the aged and children represent the nation's most dependent persons, the increased need for social services for the elderly and in the field of child welfare is quite apparent. Each year there will be a marked increase in the number of persons reaching the age of 18 and many of these adults will be mobile. Families and individuals will move from rural to urban areas; some will add to and perpetuate the squalor and poverty of the inner city while others will become a part of the broadening middle-class sector with its symbolic and compulsive thrust toward mortgaged affluence. The total population will in some way be affected by the welfare state and the nation's rising concern about the well-being of greater numbers of people.

There are assumed to be some 10,000 unfilled social work positions in the nation. This is probably an underestimate, considering the growing demand for social services in both public and private agencies and institutions. Four out of five social workers do not have a master of social work degree and most have no graduate education at all. It is thus apparent that most social services are given by paraprofessionals or by

[61] U.S. Department of Labor, Bureau of Labor Statistics, Special Labor Force Report No. 49 for March 1960, March 1963, and 1967.

clients and others who have been educated to work in new careers. The nature of chronic dependency or illness, crime, unemployment, and other social problems is such, however, that unless professionalism is built into the social work system, public welfare programs in particular will con-tisue to broaden without meeting the basic needs of the clients—namely, those related to achieving self-sufficiency and self-support. The public assistance field attracted only 5 percent of the MSW graduates in 1960. The majority of the new MSWs went into social work practice in psychi-atric, medical, child welfare, and family service settings.[62]

Summary

This chapter has described the recognized fields of social service, their evolution, social tasks, and social sanction. In this process it became appar-ent that social work methodology, as characterized in Chapter VII, bears a functional relationship to the settings in which services are given.

Selected Bibliography

Aptekar, Herbert H. "American Societal Values and Their Influence in Social Welfare Programs and Professional Social Work," *Journal of Social Work Process*, Vol. 16. Philadelphia: University of Pennsylvania Press, (1967).

Fromm, Erich. *The Sane Society*. New York: Fawcett World Library, 1968.

Goode, William J. "Encroachment, Charlatanism and the Emerging Profession: Psychology, Sociology and Medicine," *American Sociological Review*, Vol. 25, no. 6 (December 1960).

Grosser, Charles F. "Changing Theory and Changing Practice," *Social Case-work*, Vol. 50, no. 1 (January 1969).

Hollis, Florence. "And What Shall We Teach? The Social Work Educator and Knowledge," *Social Service Review*, Vol. 42, no. 2 (June 1968).

Kohs, S. C. *The Roots of Social Work*. New York: Association Press, 1966.

Pumphrey, Ralph E., and Muriel W. Pumphrey eds. *The Heritage of American Social Work*. New York: Columbia University Press, 1961.

Smith, Edmund A. *Social Welfare—Principles and Concepts*. New York: Asso-ciation Press, 1965.

Titmuss, Richard M. *Essays on the Welfare State*. New Haven: Yale University Press, 1959.

Trends in Social Work Practice and Knowledge. New York: National Associa-tion of Social Workers, 1966.

[62] *Salaries and Working Conditions of Social Welfare Manpower in 1960* (New York: National Social Welfare Assembly, 1961), Table 18, p. 39.

Trost, Mary Ann. "The Preventive Role of Social Work in a Social Setting," *Child Welfare*, Vol. 47, no. 7 (July 1968).
Wilensky, Harold L., and Charles N. Lebeaux. *Industrial Society and Social Welfare*. New York: Russell Sage Foundation, 1958.
Youngdahl, Benjamin E. *Social Action and Social Work*. New York: Association Press, 1966.

Chapter Ten

American Involvement in the Development of International Social Work

THE INTERNATIONAL social welfare movement reflects in large part a humanitarian response to the intercountry conflict, migration, disaster, and despair that are always present somewhere in the world community. In each crisis or tragedy men and women have responded to their suffering fellows across the earth. In many instances they have ignored all questions raised about their responsibility for feeding or harboring the "foreigner." Motivation for a show of love for the unfortunate has often been rooted in the donor's religiosity as he sought to repay God for His blessings or in his inability to withstand philanthropic peer pressure. Whatever the personal or ideological persuasion of the giver, persons and nations who because of sentiment or conviction were sensitive to human need have always made contributions in time of international hardship and stress.

Assistance in the constant series of world crises has been given by persons and organizations with little else in common. Samuel Gridley Howe, on completing Harvard Medical School in 1825, became deeply involved in the Greek struggle for freedom in the war for independence they waged against the Turks. Howe organized hospital services on the Greek battlefields and became chief surgeon in the Greek army. In 1828 he returned to the United States with two orphan boys, the first of many to be adopted by American families. This could well be regarded as one of the first intercountry adoptions emanating from an international conflict.

The great Irish famine of 1845 stimulated the establishment of the Society of Friends of Dublin in several American cities and aroused the interest of Robert Dale Owen, Daniel Webster, and Senator John J. Crittenden of Kentucky. Crittenden had hoped to see successful passage of his bill authorizing Congress to make financial help available to Ireland, but Webster stated his belief that assistance should be given not by one government to another but from one people to another, and Horace Greeley held that any bill authorizing foreign aid was unconstitutional. Consequently legislative efforts ceased in favor of voluntary funding.

Clara Barton, who later founded the American Red Cross, went to Europe in 1870 to aid those wounded in and displaced by the Franco-Prussian War. She also gave assistance to the victims of the Russian famine of 1891. Eight years later, at the age of 76 she accepted one of the most difficult responsibilities of her long and distinguished career—that of helping to alleviate starvation in Cuba after its tragic struggle for independence from Spain.

Religio-missionary work has played a significant role in American history since colonial times. Cotton Mather and Jonathan Edwards believed America had a special need to evangelize the earth, as did John Stuart Mill. Dr. Peter Parker became the first Protestant medical missionary in

China in 1834 and in 1850 Dr. William J. Wanless developed one of the greatest medical centers in Asia. In 1849 the Mormons established the Perpetual Emigrating Fund and Stewart Parnell created the politically significant Irish Land League. The *Christian Herald* popularized the story of the gross suffering of hundreds of thousands of people in the Indian famine of the 1890s and aroused nationwide concern at the number of deaths caused by starvation. The Hebrew Sheltering and Immigrant Aid Society was formed in 1909 and James Loeb, a prominent lay social actionist, established and financially supported the German Institute for Psychiatric Research in Munich in 1911.

Wars produced international philanthropic activity that was impressive and timely. Andrew Carnegie established the Andrew Carnegie Hero Fund Commission in 1904 and the Carnegie Endowment for International Peace in 1910. The World Peace Foundation was created in the same year by Dr. Edward Ginn. In 1915 Henry Ford chartered a "Peace Ship" and the Red Cross Mercy Ship brought much-needed medical supplies and personnel to Europe.

Governmental and voluntary agencies also became functionally involved in international assistance. The efforts of the Salvation Army were significant in two world wars. The American Society of Friends was actively engaged in many international activities. In 1919 the American Relief Administration was established with Herbert Hoover as its general director. In 1939 Catholics organized the Bishop's War Emergency and Relief Committee and in 1950 the Council of Churches established a Committee on Foreign Relief Appeals. Catholic Relief Services, the Church World Service, the Lutheran World Federation, the Baptist World Alliance Relief Commission, and the Hebrew Sheltering and Immigration Service, among many others, contributed to displaced persons in need of assistance and shelter in two world wars and in the Korean conflict.

In this sphere of human concern social work has had an impressive influence on the nature and character of foreign aid as a technique of statecraft, on the intercountry movement of people, and on many aspects of the international social order. As the contemporary social revolution gained momentum to keep pace with the spiraling technological revolution, social work has contributed effectively to the multi-nation movement against ignorance, social and economic injustice, deprivation, and the traditional inequities of other decades.

Twentieth-century international social-foreign policy has given major impetus to a deepening concern for human welfare and human rights. This concern has been accelerated by the increasing population of underdeveloped countries; by the displacement, refugee status, and homelessness of thousands during the wars that have taken place within this century; and by the neo-humanistic world trends emerging to offset the dehumanizing effect of totalitarianism, colonialism, and international power politics.

INTERNATIONAL SOCIAL WORK

International social work is directed to intercountry cooperation in matters of social and economic security. More specifically, it attempts to make migration and separation from the home country a less devastating experience for persons whose family ties are seriously affected by distance and whose potential adjustment in another land is made more difficult by ignorance of the immigration process or of the ways of their new country. The impetus for international social work grew out of experience gained in World Wars I and II, but its scope and function have broadened under the various programs of the United Nations and voluntary agencies. However, the first concerted interest in international social work predated World War I by six decades, although it too was related to wartime circumstances and tragedy.

In 1859 a young Swiss businessman, Jean Henri Dunant, was shocked at the carnage he saw on the battlefield at Solferino, where the French and Sardinians fought the Austrians at great loss of life and with many gross injuries. He wrote his impressions of the suffering of the wounded soldiers in a small book entitled *Un Souvenir de Solférino* (1862) and at his own expense sent copies to all the leading members of the governments of Europe. He also lectured before the Society of Public Utility in Geneva and gained the interest of many prominent persons. Through his efforts an international convention was held in Geneva in 1864, at which the first Geneva treaty was created and a permanent International Committee established with headquarters in Geneva. In addition, a basic plan for the development of permanent national relief societies was adopted.

One of the first objectives of the International Committee was to seek recognition of neutrality for hospitals, for the sick and wounded, and for persons and equipment connected with rescue operations. Identification was to be achieved through a uniform sign or badge, a red cross on a white ground, to be worn on the arm of all persons in the service. The colors of this symbol were the colors of the Swiss flag, reversed.[1] These were the early beginnings of the Red Cross.

[1] Clara Barton, *The Red Cross in War and Peace* (Washington, D.C.: American Historical Press, 1899), pp. 23–24.

INTERNATIONAL SOCIAL SERVICE

The International Social Service evolved from a service established by another international organization. The World's Young Women's Christian Association had been concerned traditionally with the problems of the woman who traveled to the United States with little knowledge of the situations she might encounter and little protection from her home or receiving government. Because the numbers of women coming to the United States had increased by 1921, the YWCA engaged in a survey to determine the needs of immigrants. The study, titled "The Welfare of Migrants," resulted in the establishment of Cooperative Service Bureaus in seven countries and gave the YWCA an opportunity to bring the hardships of the immigrant to the attention of the League of Nations and the International Labor Office. These actions received support because concern for the immigrant multiplied after the United States passed its first quota law, a forerunner of the Quota Act of 1924.[2]

Ruth Larned wrote dramatically of this post-World War I era when "lines of cattle cars, crowded with migrants moved westward on Europe's newly repaired rail lines with migration to the United States as their goal." The immigrants faced more difficulties in being admitted to this country since for the first time passports and visas were required and decisions regarding admittance were made at the port of entry.[3]

In the interim the YWCA had exhausted all funds available for its international program. Funds to continue the service were provided for an additional three months by the Laura Spellman Rockefeller Memorial Fund until the International Social Service was established with headquarters in Geneva, Switzerland.

The International Social Service continued to expand in coverage, function, and the number of persons served. In 1940 it established a United States Committee for the Care of European Children, which developed a program to find American homes for orphans and children fathered by American soldiers in foreign countries. This committee worked with paternity problems and other legal complications that must be solved to permit international placement of children for adoption. The work of its intercountry adoption program is financed in part by the World Adoption International Fund, which has received generous support from prominent persons in the entertainment world.[4]

[2] Ruth Larned, *The Story of the International Social Service: A History* (New York: American Branch of the International Social Service, 1960), p. 5.

[3] *Ibid.*, pp. 5–6.

[4] *Ibid.*, p. 30.

INTERNATIONAL CONFERENCE OF SOCIAL WORK

Credit for creation of the International Conference of Social Work (ICSW) is often given to two Europeans, Dr. Clotilde Mulon, a Parisian, and Dr. René Sand, a Belgian. It was actually Dr. Sand who founded ICSW, however. He had been aware of the long histories of the National Conference of Social Work in the United States and the European International Conferences on Charities and Welfare that began to meet as early as 1856. It appeared to Sand that social work and growing social problems were not unique to one continent and that the time had come to develop a mutuality of interests and concerns that would have a global perspective.

The first ICSW held in Paris in July 1928 was funded and sponsored by seven organizations representing prominent foundations and voluntary agencies. Some 2500 conferees came from 42 countries to discuss pertinent social work issues and the responsibilities incumbent on the various nations at that time.

When the third conference opened in London in 1936 the Lord Mayor of London, Sir Percy Vincent, pointed out in his welcoming speech that this conference was indeed being held in an historic place as far as the history of public and private social services was concerned. At that meeting Dr. Ellen C. Potter read a paper prepared by Katharine F. Lenroot, then chief of the U.S. Children's Bureau. Although more than 40 years have passed, Miss Lenroot's astute evaluations still have wide domestic and international meaning for social work and social welfare:

Both in philosophy and method, social work is now sharply challenged. Not only is it attacked from the right by those having economic power and willing to yield only to the minimum they concede to be necessary for social safety, but is also challenged from the left by those who are disillusioned as to the possibility of gradual improvement and dominated by the philosophy of class conflict. In some countries social work finds sacrificed much that it has gained through years of struggle for social amelioration; in others it finds advance strongly resisted by economic and sometimes by professional interests. On the other hand, in certain nations it sees incorporated in government and universally applied some or many of the measures which elsewhere it has sponsored and developed tentatively within limited areas and fields of service.[5]

The growing emphases on social justice and the need for more equitable opportunity for development and growth in the physical, emotional, and motivational sense continued to make an impact on forthcoming inter-

[5] Report of the Third International Conference of Social Work (London: LePlay House Press, 1938), pp. 21–22.

national conferences. At the twelfth ICSW, held in Athens in 1964, the theme was "Social Progress Through Social Planning." Nikolaos Bancopoulos, Greek minister of social welfare, eloquently described the human condition as it has evolved through the ages:

> "Everything changes" (Ta panda rhi), the aphorism of our forefather, the philosopher Heracletian [Heracleitus], still retains its intrinsic truth today. The influence of this natural law has gradually transformed the general concept of man as a unit of society through the ages. The "slave" is now enfranchised and he that is "weak" is not alone. He benefits from the assistance of the embodiment of society, the State. And this, not merely from pity or love for truth. He benefits because he has this "social right," a right that is recognized, to a great extent by law, not only in his individual interest but in the common interest.[6]

UNITED NATIONS RELIEF AND REHABILITATION ADMINISTRATION

The United Nations Relief and Rehabilitation Administration (UNRRA) was a wartime agency established in November 1943 to relieve the suffering of people who experienced deprivation, disease, or national disaster. It was directed by a council composed of one representative of each of the 48 nations supporting the agency and was established as a temporary body. When the United Nations came into being in 1945 the United States proposed that the operations of UNRRA be brought to a close within two years. The United Nations would have considered the problems that UNRRA handled even if the agency had continued, for its functions were relatively restricted.[7] Former President Harry S Truman stated that a major difficulty confronting UNRRA was the undefined role that it had been given. It had been organized to help countries unable to provide for their own needs "but there was no fixed limit of the field of rehabilitation into which UNRRA was entitled to go."[8] In spite of these limitations UNRRA dealt with the devastation of World War II by serving thousands who were homeless and without clothing, food, or medical care. It participated in the relief and rehabilitation of war-ravaged countries and communities but had insufficient funds to restore and rebuild the industrial and economic systems needed to

---

[6] *Social Progress Through Social Planning—The Role of Social Work, Proceedings of the XIIth International Conference of Social Work,* (New York: International Conference of Social Work, 1965), p. 41.

[7] Harold Karan Jacobson, "Economic and Social Matter," in Franz B. Gross, ed., *The United States and the United Nations* (Norman: University of Oklahoma Press, 1964), p. 233.

[8] Harry S Truman, *Year of Decision,* Vol. 1 (Garden City, N.Y.: Doubleday & Co., 1955), p. 466.

enable the victimized residents to become involved in their own rehabilitation and reconstruction activities.

Since one of UNRRA's major responsibilities was to give service to some eight million refugees and displaced persons, it worked closely with voluntary social agencies as well as intergovernmental agencies in many parts of the world. It assisted in locating missing persons by establishing a Central Tracing Bureau. Thousands of refugees and displaced persons from slave labor camps were fully dependent on UNRRA's help. The magnitude of assistance given by UNRRA in food and other materials is apparent in the fact that it distributed 25,000 tons or 6000 shiploads of goods costing some three billion dollars.

INFLUENCE OF THE UNITED NATIONS

When the United Nations was created in 1945, its charter reflected several steps that had been taken previous to its creation. The London declaration had been signed at St. James's Palace in June 1941 by representatives of 14 nations. This document read in part:

> The only true basis of enduring peace is the willing cooperation of free peoples in a world in which, relieved of the menace of aggression, all may enjoy economic and social security. . . .

The Atlantic Charter signed in August 1941 by President Franklin D. Roosevelt and Prime Minister Winston Churchill declared in Clause 5 that

> the signatories desire to bring about the fullest collaboration between all nations in the economic field with the objective of securing, for all, improved labor standards, economic advancement and social security.

The UN charter was drawn up by representatives of 50 countries at the UN Conference on International Organization, which met in San Francisco from late April to the latter part of June 1945. The charter was signed on June 26, 1945, and the UN became an official international body on October 24, 1945.

When the UN was formed UNRRA was not formally associated with it, but there was a significant symbolic and intellectual relationship between them as well as a sharing of major purposes. It was postulated that if the newly chartered UN were to achieve political maturity and a secure position through international socioeconomic improvement, it would have to become concerned with war relief for devastated nations and provide assistance and rehabilitative services to great numbers of refugees and displaced persons.[9]

The UN's most important programs in social welfare were inherited

---

[9] Jacobson, *op. cit.*, p. 232.

from UNRRA and the League of Nations. The UN became responsible for UNRRA's advisory social welfare services, technical assistance to nations seeking to reconstruct their governments and cities, housing, income maintenance, family and child welfare, and community development. In short the UN was obligated to assume the responsibilities and the scope of functions for which UNRRA had been created.[10]

The purposes of the UN were spelled out in its charter:

1. To maintain international peace and security.
2. To develop friendly relations among nations.
3. To cooperate internationally in solving economic, social, cultural and humanitarian problems and in promoting respect for human rights and fundamental freedoms, and,
4. To be a centre for harmonizing the actions of nations in attaining these common ends.

The UN gave its major social work, medical, and educational service responsibilities to the Economic and Social Council (ECOSOC). ECOSOC receives recommendations from the Social Commission, which now numbers 21 members who meet once a year to determine policy and plan programs and services designed to meet international social welfare concerns.

The work of ECOSOC is directed specifically to promoting higher standards of living, full employment, and economic and social progress to facilitate the development and search for solutions to health and social issues that affect peace and international security. It is mandated by the charter to make recommendations on these matters in cooperation with the Social Commission, make and initiate studies, develop reports, call international conferences, and negotiate agreements with specialized agencies defining their working relationship with the UN. Basic to these functions is ECOSOC's responsibility for promoting universal respect for and observation of human rights and individual freedoms.

On recommendation of the Social Commission, ECOSOC, at its thirty-ninth session in 1965, adopted resolutions in regard to a proposed conference of ministers responsible for social welfare for family, child, and youth services, for the training of social welfare personnel, and for reappraisal of the UN's social service program. These resolutions reflect the UN's continuing responsibility in international social work. The proposed conferees were asked to

discuss social welfare programs in national development in order to examine national and regional variations in the approach to social welfare and identify common elements in social welfare functions and services, to

[10] *Ibid.*, p. 239.

clarify the role of social welfare in economic and social development, and to focus attention on ways of making full use of the contribution of social welfare programmes to human development and to raising the levels of living.[11]

ECOSOC requested the Secretary-General to prepare monographs on the developmental and operational facets of the UN's social welfare services to families and children and to study the effects of rapid population growth, urbanization, and labor mobility on family life and the means of assisting families and individuals under these conditions and circumstances. The study was also expected to include an exploration of the use of volunteers, especially in youth development programs, an assessment of the social welfare needs and unique problems of youth, and recommendations on how these needs can best be met.

ECOSOC also requested that the Secretary-General develop priorities in giving assistance to developing countries in the establishment and expansion of social welfare training programs consonant with local circumstances and social welfare manpower needs and requirements. Special emphasis was placed on the need for social welfare training programs for teachers and "trainers"; for personnel in key positions in program planning, policy development, and administration; and for auxiliary social welfare workers. A further request was that appraisal of services and manpower be cast within the framework of the UN in a manner that would accommodate and facilitate carrying out its responsibilities of leadership, research, and technical assistance in the social welfare field.[12]

WORLD HEALTH ORGANIZATION

The constitution of the UN World Health Organization (WHO) was adopted on July 22, 1946, by the International Health Conference called by ECOSOC. It reflected a deep conviction that health, sanitation, and epidemics are of worldwide concern. Dr. William P. Forrest emphasized the apolitical characteristics of this concern when speaking before the fourth International Conference of Social Work:

. . . these sixty-one nations recognized that those problems which are no longer purely national must be solved by international action and on a world-wide basis, at that. Governments have long realized that they are not able to deal with epidemics independently, because these epidemics

[11] UN General Assembly, Official Records: Twenty-first Session, Supplement No. 1 (A/6301) *Annual Report of the Secretary-General on the Work of the Organization* (New York: United Nations, June 1966), p. 95.
[12] *Ibid.*

treat national frontiers with a fine disregard for any political considerations and it has been remarked . . . that bacteria cannot read.[13]

The principles on which WHO is based include a definition of health as "a state of complete physical, mental and social well-being and not merely the absence of disease or infirmity." Health is established as a fundamental right, without distinction "of race, religion, political belief, economic or social condition." The constitution also stated that "the health of all peoples is fundamental to the attainment of peace and security and is dependent upon the fullest cooperation of individuals and states." It pointed out, too, that the "unequal development of different countries in the promotion of health and control of communicable disease is a great and common danger." Governments are seen to have a responsibility for healthy child development and for the broadening of medical, psychological and other knowledge. The constitution concludes that "governments have a responsibility for the health of their peoples which can be fulfilled only by provision of adequate health and social measures." [14]

WHO is concerned specifically with assistance to individual nations for medical research and with the development and adoption of regulations relating to environmental sanitation and quarantine, causes of death, and disease nomenclature. It is also concerned with standards for pharmaceuticals, vitamins, antitoxins, and vaccines for the prevention of communicable diseases or parasitic infections. In addition it provides training support for education in the various fields of medicine.

The 1963 United Nations *Report on the World Social Situation* stated that world health was better in 1960 than it had been a decade before. Although precise comprehensive information is lacking for a large proportion of mankind and no single index of the level of health has been devised for even the statistically most advanced countries, the broad trend in world health is unmistakable.[15] The report also commented on the significant interdependent relationship among the medical, biological, and social sciences, which must be appraised:

> In order to assess the present health situation, however, one must look beyond the contributions of these newer advances [in the medical and biological sciences which continue to provide new weapons to attack and prevent disease] and recognize the continuing effect of the discoveries of the previous decade and their much wider deployment. One must also align with them the benefits that have accrued from social, educational

[13] William P. Forrest, "World Health Organization," Proceedings: Fourth International Conference of Social Work" (New York: International Conference of Social Work, 1948), p. 30. (Mimeographed.)

[14] *Ibid.*

[15] *Report on the World Social Situation* (New York: United Nations, 1963), p. 23.

and economic improvement. Of the various determinants of health, the social and economic factors, though long recognized, have been amongst the last to be given due weight.[16]

INTERNATIONAL LABOR ORGANIZATION

The International Labor Organization (ILO) was established on April 11, 1919, when its constitution was adopted as Part XIII of the Treaty of Versailles. When the League of Nations was established, ILO became affiliated with it. The United States became a member of ILO in 1934. Since 1946 ILO has had the status of a specialized agency associated with the UN. Through intergovernmental agreement ILO is composed of 24 members representing governments, 12 representing management, and 12 representing labor. Its chief function is to formulate international policy relating to labor relations through international labor conferences and recommendations.

ILO's interests relate to all facets of industrial welfare and working conditions, including income maintenance legislation, employment insurance, workmen's compensation, and financial protection against illness and old age. It is also concerned with pay scales, family allowances, maternity benefits, public subsidies for low- or below-cost food for infants and schoolchildren, and international considerations relating to child labor and the rights of aliens and migrant workers.

The work of ILO has significance for the social work profession because its conferences cover broad areas relating to human welfare. Financial need with its accompanying multiple deprivations, frustrations, and failures can only be ameliorated by working conditions and a work opportunity system that afford the individual a secure and adequate way of life in every country throughout the world.

INTERNATIONAL REFUGEE ORGANIZATION

In the years preceding the invasion of Poland in 1939, hundreds of thousands of persons fled their homes in Germany and Austria because of deepening Nazi suppression. After World War II ended these persons were unwilling and usually unable to return because of fear of political reprisal or loss of national identity. The latter occurred because many territories were annexed to new governments and former residents of these areas became, in effect, aliens in the countries in which they were born.

When UNRRA was discontinued in 1947, the International Refugee Organization (IRO) was established by the UN General Assembly. IRO found homes for over 800,000 displaced persons, repatriated another

[16] *Ibid.*

71,500, and assisted thousands of aged, ill, and handicapped persons before it was terminated on January 31, 1952. In its six-year tenure IRO helped over 1.5 million refugees by providing food, clothing, shelter, and social welfare services. It also developed a child tracing and search program, camps, and other child welfare services. IRO's repatriation and resettlement program included more than 100,000 minors under the age of 18, some 5 percent of whom were refugees unaccompanied by a parent or guardian.

IRO worked closely with the U.S. Displaced Persons Commission, which was concerned with the selection of immigrants, their children and displaced orphans to be admitted to the United States. "Eligible displaced orphans" were defined as displaced persons from specified European areas who were under the age of 16, were orphans because of the death or disappearance of both parents, and for whom satisfactory assurances had been provided that if admitted to the United States they would be given proper care and guardianship. The Displaced Persons Commission, on recommendation of the U.S. Children's Bureau, entered into arrangements through which the U.S. Committee for the Care of European Children acted as a clearing-house for the majority of applications made for the sponsorship of orphans. This committee worked in close cooperation with major Protestant, Catholic, and Jewish child care agencies in the United States. These agencies received the children when they arrived, made arrangements for temporary shelter care, and provided them with foster homes in accordance with standards established by the Children's Bureau. Working cooperatively under this program, IRO, the Displaced Persons Commission, the U.S. Committee for the Care of European Children, the voluntary agencies, and the Children's Bureau were therefore able to provide American homes for displaced orphans and minor unmarried dependent children of displaced persons who were admitted with their parents.[17]

In 1949 plans for the termination of IRO were made and a Provisional Intergovernmental Committee established to assume responsibility for those refugees and displaced persons awaiting assistance. Because of the remaining volume of work, however, IRO remained active under the Office of the UN High Commissioner for Refugees (UNHCR) for six months after that office was established.

OFFICE OF THE UN HIGH COMMISSIONER FOR REFUGEES

Since 1951 UNHCR, headquartered in Geneva, has had a 25-nation executive committee that also advises the high commissioner. UNHCR

---

[17] *Programs of the Federal Government Affecting Children and Youth* (Washington, D.C.: Interdepartmental Committee on Children and Youth, 1951), p. 68.

provides assistance and protection to refugees and stateless persons and seeks solutions to their problems through repatriation or assimilation by new nations. The high international status and growing prestige of UNHCR became readily apparent when it won the Nobel Peace Prize in 1954.

The UN General Assembly agreed to retain UNHCR on January 1, 1964. The office continues to offer legal protection to refugees and to address itself to the multiple problems of displacement and resettlement. In 1965 UNHCR projects benefited some 223,000 refugees migrating to various countries. Many refugees have been granted asylum in developing countries where their resettlement is closely linked with development programs and projects.[18]

FOOD AND AGRICULTURE ORGANIZATION

Plans for a permanent food and agriculture organization were made at the United States Conference on Food and Agriculture at Hot Springs, Virginia, in 1943. The constitution drafted for the Food and Agriculture Organization (FAO) by an interim committee was subsequently accepted by more than 20 governments. FAO became a legal body of the UN on October 16, 1945, when the constitution was signed at the opening of the first FAO conference in Quebec.

The purposes of FAO are to raise the levels of nutrition and standards of living and to promote improvements in all food and agricultural products coming from farms. It is also concerned with forests, reforestation, fisheries, and the general improvement and development of basic soil and water resources. It gives attention to the international exchange of new types of plants and foodstuffs, irrigation engineering, and the prevention and control of animal diseases and infestation.

The International Freedom from Hunger Campaign was one of the achievements of the UN development decade. This campaign, initiated in January 1960, gave FAO leadership responsibilities in working cooperatively with the governments of UN member nations and with nongovernmental agencies to create international awareness of the problems of hunger and to stimulate a new and deeper interest in hunger and malnutrition.

It was President John F. Kennedy's conviction that American agricultural abundance offered a significant opportunity for the United States to promote the interests of international peace and human welfare. Consequently Title III of Public Law 480, the Agricultural Trade Development and Assistance Act of 1954, was broadened on January 24, 1961, to become the Food for Peace program under the administration of the U.S.

[18] *Annual Report of the Secretary-General* . . . (A/6301), p. 110.

Departments of State and Agriculture, with food distribution through FAO. This program allowed needy countries to buy American farm surpluses at their own currency value as mandated in the 1954 legislation and permitted the United States to make large food donations for refugees and other needy persons. Food was given in lieu of wages on development projects and to unsettled families until such time as their first crop could be harvested.

UN EDUCATIONAL, SCIENTIFIC, AND CULTURAL ORGANIZATION

The constitution for the UN Educational, Scientific, and Cultural Organization (UNESCO) was drawn up at a conference held in London in November 1945 and accepted by its 20 signatories. UNESCO has broad and significant responsibilities in the dissemination of educational materials through all national and international mass communications media available to the various nations. Its major objective is the promotion of social and economic progress through education, the sciences, and the arts. It offers financial support to public and private agencies to facilitate national and international meetings and to publicize pertinent programs. It also makes funds available for the international exchange of persons having experience in education, the arts, and the sciences.

UNESCO has placed much emphasis on the need for compulsory education, free tuition, and other opportunities to combat illiteracy on an international scale. "Putting knowledge to work" as a fundamental right is seen as a primary method of raising socioeconomic standards and broadening the opportunities of all people to know and understand diverse cultures and ways of life.

UNITED NATIONS CHILDREN'S FUND

The United Nations Children's Fund (UNICEF) was established by the General Assembly in 1946 and has been concerned with the welfare of areas in which two-thirds of the world's population and three-fourths of all children on the earth live in great need. These 55 million children are in 120 countries, many of them located in the tropics or semitropics.

Two-thirds to three-fourths of the parents of these children are engaged in agriculture, but poor tools, lack of transportation, and the absence of technological aids cause their income to be inordinately inadequate. In Asia, for example, more than 100 man days of labor are required to harvest one acre of ground as compared to two days in the United States. The average weekly income is $10 per family. The depressed condition of the underdeveloped countries is perhaps most evident in the fact that they are in parts of the world where one-third of all children born will die before the age of 5 and one-half of all surviving children will go to school but will be malnourished.[19] UNICEF has a wide variety of concerns. It attempts to fulfill its economic and social mission in the area of socioeconomic international policy and practice by allocating funds to train local personnel for services benefiting children. Such personnel includes health workers, food technologists, teachers, social workers, and administrators. It also

> . . . pursues this objective through its support of field projects to work out and demonstrate measures that can be taken up on a larger scale by national ministries (disease control and social welfare projects, for example), by private industry (the commercial production of high-protein foods), or by local agencies and people (community development . . . UNICEF also makes some grants to projects with national coverage designed to solve problems of particular importance to children such as those to strengthen maternal and child health services on a nation-wide basis.[20]

In assessing the worldwide implications of UNICEF's activities, it is important to evaluate concurrently the vast cultural, geographic, and national differences in wealth and economic opportunity and in the kinds of problems that cause deprivation. About 35 percent of the world's population lives in the tropics and semitropics where malaria is still prevalent.[21] Warmth and humidity are favorable to the transmission of yaws, a communicable disease causing disfigurement and a crippling condition. Children are especially susceptible to leprosy. In 1962 more than a million persons, half of them mothers and children, were being treated by the UNICEF leprosy control project. Bilharzia or schistosomiasis is a parasitic disease caused by larvae of the Schistosoma fluke that results in blood loss and tissue damage, especially of the liver. This disease is on the increase today because no appropriate means have been found to arrest transmission of the parasite. Whatever the disease, the goal of UNICEF has been to reduce and if possible eradicate the sources of infection through environmental sanitation and medical technology and thus protect the present and future health of children in these areas.

UNICEF has recognized that a billion of the world's people lack adequate diet and that 500 million never have enough to eat. It has therefore assisted in dry milk distribution, education in nutrition, and food production.

[19] *Children of the Developing Countries, A Report by UNICEF* (New York: World Publishing Co., 1963), pp. 2-3.
[20] *Ibid.*, p. 13.
[21] *Ibid.*, p. 30.

UNICEF has also made funds and personnel available for education and vocational training and for family and child welfare during times of great social change. The current period is one of transition for many families because developing countries are becoming urbanized, families are being separated, and the hardships created by the impersonality of the newly emerging systems are becoming apparent. The traditional primacy of the village will not be readily replaced by the technological partnership of man and machine, mechanized communication, or sophisticated politicality. The underdeveloped countries have for the most part been rural in their orientation and values. They have also been isolated from the developed countries to whom they now look for leadership in alleviating conditions that jeopardize survival but were fatalistically accepted in an earlier era.

The developing countries have a great need for social services in all phases of human betterment during this period of national growth and development. This seems apparent from the vastness and multiplicity of problems inherent in an unsettled and increasing world population at a time in history when concerns for man are becoming more universal and national perimeters have in effect been eradicated by science and technology.

UNITED STATES AID TO UNDERDEVELOPED COUNTRIES

The countries of the world are classified as either poor or rich. A distinction is also made among underdeveloped, developing, and developed countries: the first two are considered to be poor and the third, rich. Since 1960 the population of the poor countries has increased 67 percent; it is estimated that this will further increase from a projected 72 percent in 1980 to 76 percent at the end of the century. The world population is expected to increase by 1.3 billion persons in the period 1960–80, and 1.079 billion of these people will live in underdeveloped and developing countries. Of the 1.7 billion population increase predicted between 1980 and the year 2000, 1.463 billion persons will live in poor countries and a mere 283 million in rich countries. This suggests the vast needs that will be presented by 2 billion persons, or nearly three-fourths of all persons living in the 100 underdeveloped and developing countries.[22]

Population projections recently made by the UN Secretariat indicated that in many developing countries the rate of population growth is now 3 percent per year or more. This rate, if sustained, is sufficient to double

[22] *Population Crisis,* Hearings of the Subcommittee on Foreign Aid Expenditures, 89th Cong., 1st Sess. (Washington, D.C.: Government Printing Office, 1965), pp. 78–80.

the population in less than 25 years. Mortality in these regions has been declining while fertility has remained at a stable—but high—level. Conditions affecting the level of fertility are slow to change while mortality readily responds to public health and economic measures. If mortality continued to decrease and a decline in fertility were to begin within the next two decades in many developing countries, world population would still rise from the 1960 figure of approximately 3 billion to 4.3 billion by 1980 and 6 billion by the end of this century.[23]

What is an underdeveloped country? It is defined as an area dominated by poverty where there is begging in the streets of the cities and the rural villagers eke out a bare existence. It has no factories of its own and there is generally an inadequate supply of power and light. Its roads and means of transportation are insufficient as are its governmental services and communication systems. It has few and poor public health facilities, few institutions of higher learning, and most of its people are illiterate. The economy is poor because earning levels are greatly depressed, the banking system is inadequate, and its exports to other countries consist mainly of raw materials. There are a few wealthy people but they live removed and isolated from the great majority of those who are in great need. Paul G. Hoffman pointed out that while some of the underdeveloped countries are new, others such as India and China are ancient centers of civilization, knowledge, and culture. He believes that the life of the average man is worse there today than it has ever been because the great population expansion cannot be sustained by the medieval forms of agriculture and production still in use or by the too-slowly evolving technology.[24]

THE PEACE CORPS

The Peace Corps was established as a permanent program under the Department of State in September 1961. Its antecedents can perhaps be traced to Christopher Columbus' voyage to the New World; St. Benedict's mission of young affluent men who went to work in underdeveloped countries of northern Europe; John Winthrop and William Penn, the Christian missionaries and peace advocates; William Ellery Channing; and William James. James did in fact suggest a "peace army" made up of young men who would be drafted for the purpose of eliminating war, poverty, ignorance, and disease. He saw this approach as "a moral equivalent of war." In a recent cartoon Carmack of the Christian Science Monitor portrayed a male Peace Corps volunteer with tool box in hand and spade, rake, and pitchfork on his shoulder following a directional

[23] *Annual Report of the Secretary-General* . . . (A/6301), p. 93.
[24] Paul G. Hoffman, *One Hundred Countries: One Quarter Billion People* (Washington, D.C.: Committee for International Economic Growth, 1960), p. 9.

marker stating "Battle Against Hunger, Inexperience and Apathy." Carmack titled his cartoon: "To Wage a Better Kind of War."

While all these approaches have something in common, the goals of the Peace Corps are not limited to efforts to wage a war on international poverty and deprivation. Instead its primary intent is to develop creatively more meaningful people-to-people and nation-to-nation communication through "doing." The broad objectives of the Peace Corps have been established by Congress as follows:

1. To aid social, cultural, and economic development through the provision of trained manpower to nations that request such help.

2. To increase knowledge of the United States in other countries.

3. To increase American understanding of other people.

Harold B. Textor comments that the "Peace Corps was to be the New Frontier's most original, most visible bequest to history . . . and perhaps its noblest." [25] Surely it was one of the most successful adventures into international statecraft; by the fall of 1965 there were 12,000 Peace Corps volunteers in 46 countries. Textor further developed the rationale of the Peace Corps:

> Members of the Peace Corps, staff and volunteers alike are actionists. They crave a direct, personal involvement in developmental activities in economically less fortunate nations. This direct involvement, they believe, should be as non-bureaucratic as possible. The ideal they seek is "people to people" contact with ordinary citizens—not just the elite—of the countries of the developing world.[26]

Thus Textor implied that the volunteer will search for cultural and transcultural meanings, that he can use as learning experiences in a way that is not missionary in the sense of conversion but mutually meaningful to him and to those with whom he works in the host country. It is significant that unlike the AID personnel (to be described next) the Peace Corpsman serves as if he were an employee of the host country. John D. Montgomery described the Corpsman in this way:

> For the Peace Corps technician now in Latin America, Africa and Asia, the experiences of the missionary as an individual teacher working in a strange culture is intensely relevant. It is possible that the Peace Corpsman has more in common with the missionary in terms of techniques and approaches than he has with the foreign aid technician.[27]

[25] Robert B. Textor, *Cultural Frontiers of the Peace Corps* (Cambridge, Mass.: Massachusetts Institute of Technology Press, 1966), p. 1.

[26] *Ibid.*, p. 6.

[27] John D. Montgomery, *Foreign Aid in International Politics* (Englewood Cliffs, N.J.: Prentice-Hall, 1967), p. 11.

A great many interesting developments have taken place since November 1960 when 100 students and business leaders met at Princeton University to discuss the formation of the Peace Corps. The volunteer has emerged as a reluctant folk-hero and as a symbol of American brotherhood and goodwill. He has been to many Americans and to host countries a welcome eradicator of the image of the ugly americans so vividly portrayed by Burdick and Lederer. The Peace Corps volunteer has settled into a substantive and useful role as a catalyst to stimulate host community involvement and self-help. To give that community and the volunteer a mutually worthwhile experience he may be placed in community development, education, agricultural technology, public health or ancillary assignments.

Only a few months before the Princeton meeting, leaders from 40 countries located on five continents met at the Weizman Institute of Science at Rehovoth, Israel, to attend the International Conference on Science in the Advancement of New States. Problems of new nationhood were discussed because 17 new African and Asian nations were entering the United Nations.

The late Reverend Solomon B. Caulker attended that conference. When he addressed its members he spoke autobiographically because he was born in a jungle village. As dean of the faculty at Furah Bay College in Freetown, Sierra Leone, the oldest institution of higher learning south of the Sahara Desert, Reverend Caulker stated:

> Show me, how science can answer the witch doctor. In Sierra Leone, 8 out of every 10 infants die before one year . . . Most of our people die of leprosy, malaria, undernourishments of all kinds. . . . This is a primary problem: whether typhoid is caused by drinking dirty water or whether it is caused by someone who has bewitched you. Whether your babies are dying because you are not feeding them properly, or whether they die because someone who hates you has put sickness on them. . . . There is a holy impatience in us that too many of our people are living subnormal lives.[28]

AGENCY FOR INTERNATIONAL DEVELOPMENT

The Agency for International Development (AID) found its model in other foreign aid programs such as the Marshall Plan, Point Four, and UNRRA. However, AID is concerned with broader aspects of socioeconomic progress than were its predecessors. AID emerged in 1961 from the Development Loan Fund authorized by the Mutual Security Act of 1957 and is a semiautonomous body within the U.S. Department of State.

[28] Ruth Gruber, ed., *Science and the New Nations* (New York: Basic Books, 1961), p. x.

AID has stressed the philosophy and practice of self-help in making funds and technical assistance available to countries requesting such assistance. However, Seymour J. Rubin pointed to some of the problems that exist when incomes are low and the absence of organized capital inhibits economic growth and buying power:

> Difficulties are inherent in the self-help doctrine. Those who need aid are likely to be those least capable of the kind of organization and administration which enacts, then enforces fair tax laws, efficiently carries through land reform, and does the other things usually thought to be within the self-help concept.[29]

Personnel hired by AID is sent to "strong self-help countries"—those that have made determined efforts to help themselves. Supervision emanates from AID headquarters and staff is not supervised by personnel from the host country. In 1966 two-thirds of the $1.667 billion expended went to seven countries that fulfilled John F. Kennedy's expectation that AID funds would be spent where there had been a demonstrated effort at self-help. In 1963 President Kennedy had stated to the Congress:

> Special attention [will be given] to those nations most willing and able to mobilize their own resources, the necessary social and economic reforms, engage in long range planning and make the other efforts necessary if they are to reach the stage of self-sustaining growth.

In 1966 Brazil, Chile, Nigeria, Tunisia, India, Pakistan, and Turkey fell in the "strong self-help" category.

Development loans are used for road-building, factory construction, education, medical care, and other needs. AID has worked closely with the Food for Freedom program authorized by the Agricultural Trade Development and Assistance Act, which permitted the sale of surplus commodities abroad. As a result commodities valued at $1.5 billion leave America annually for impoverished countries.

AID supplied paper and technicians to produce 20 million textbooks in the Philippines. Malaria was greatly arrested on the Pacific Coast of Guatemala as well as in India and Indonesia. Iranian peasants were taught to farm and were given instruction in basic home economics and sanitation. As Montgomery wrote, however:

> Describing the accomplishments of foreign aid in terms of hundreds of rivers and streams dammed, thousands of miles of roads built, tens of thousands of schoolrooms in operation, hundreds of thousands of literacy classes conducted, or millions of people vaccinated will not satisfy critics

[29] Seymour J. Rubin, *The Conscience of the Rich Nations* (New York: Harper & Row, 1965), p. 36.

of costly foreign aid programs. The issue is not what American dollars have *bought* but what they have *done*. Dams, schoolrooms, classes, and the improvement of public health are only means of approaching the basic objectives of American foreign policy.[30]

AID is the largest single aid-giving agency. Any evaluation of its work must include its relation to international social policy and politics. David A. Baldwin capsulated this concept well:

Foreign aid should be studied within the context of foreign policy. The primary assumption . . . is that foreign aid is first and foremost a technique of statecraft. It is, in other words, a means by which one nation tries to get other nations to act in desired ways. To the extent that national desires conflict, foreign aid involves international politics.[31]

It is perhaps this international ideological and political variability that makes the Peace Corps and the AID program so attractive to many young Americans. They welcome an opportunity to engage in a people-to-people program in which they will encounter political and cultural differences. This opportunity to become involved in the cultural and social changes occurring in newly emerging countries and in underdeveloped older communities also offers social workers and the social work profession one of their finest challenges.

INTERNATIONAL SOCIAL WORK EDUCATION

As need expands and greater demands are placed on intercountry social welfare practice, it becomes increasingly urgent to develop a science of international social work and a teaching-learning format commensurate with the responsibilities of the American social worker abroad. It becomes apparent, too, as Alva Myrdal points out, that the demand for social work in foreign countries will increase because "the increasing moral sensitivity on the part of the more privileged peoples and . . . growing impatience on the part of others . . . are not disconnected. They strengthen each other." [32] Understanding and acceptance of these assumptions are necessary to the development of a philosophical entrée to international social work education. These issues also reflect principles emerging from the value systems of nations and communities to which American social

---

[30] *Op. cit.,* p. 71.

[31] David A. Baldwin, *Foreign and American Foreign Policy* (New York: Frederick A. Praeger, 1966), p. 3.

[32] Alva Myrdal, *America's Role in International Social Welfare* (New York: Columbia University Press, 1955), p. 4.

workers will bring their expertise. International social work, like that generically practiced in the United States, should be directed toward closing the gaps that scientific and technological intervention has broadened.

When the United States first became involved in providing foreign aid through the earlier Point Four Program in Technical Assistance for Economic Development, relatively little if any emphasis was placed on the impact of social change or the way in which people would be affected, individually or as a group, by being moved into industrialization or reconstruction of their country. In 1959 Christopher H. Phillips, UN representative to the Economic and Social Council, pointed out that social development is often treated as entirely distinct and separate from economic development. He emphasized the fact that there is a strong tendency to attach great importance to economic progress on the assumption that social adjustments will automatically follow. The significant issue, Phillips felt, was not the establishment of bigger and better factories, but the basic goals of higher standards of living, more educational opportunity, secure incomes, and the general well-being and satisfactions of the individual.[33] Mydral supported these conclusions and further elaborated on them by stating that it is far easier to transfer engineers and technical knowledge from one country to another than to export social skills and convert these into meaningful and useful practices in another country. This is especially true of social work methods, which may not lend themselves to the traditional value system of the nation to which these skills are brought.[34]

There are historical reasons for the American social work approach but this does not ensure that a similar process will be of value in a developing or less advantaged country. Social work in the United States has been perceived and practiced along the lines of the medical model, which primarily involves work with an individual in a one-to-one relationship. Such an approach is not likely to be useful to the person whose meaningful and sustained relationships are invested in his peer group, family, neighborhood, and village. This basic difference in life-styles affects role perception, expectation, and function, and consequently cannot be considered unrelated to an understanding of the meaning of behavior within a specific cultural context.

The way in which social services are developed and used in an underdeveloped country also differs from that of a capitalistically oriented nation such as the United States. Here capital was developed first and as

[33] Christopher H. Phillips, "United States Information News Release," July 14, 1959.
[34] Myrdal, *op. cit.*, p. 43.

human need emerged from deprivation of the lower socioeconomic classes, social welfare programs and resources were created to meet that need. Foundations endowed by wealthy individuals and families furnished a useful reservoir from which funds could be drawn for use in many areas of human welfare for the enhancement of well-being. It is unlikely that social workers will find such sources of funds in underdeveloped or developing countries. It is unlikely, too, that these nations will move quickly in establishing an adequate tax structure or a sophisticated political system through which adequate public welfare programs can be easily or readily developed. The concept of cultural lag is universal once a nation becomes industrialized and it can be assumed that the technology that creates jobs but also displaces men from employment will move ahead far more quickly than the provision of legislation and public funds to meet need caused by technological breakthrough.

Social work and social welfare services succeed best in the developing community when local responsibility is reflected in local self-government and free access to democratic processes and procedures. International social work is, in effect, intercountry social work within another nation. It assumes that skills are brought to the host country by the "giving country" without full recognition that the "givers" also learn new skills in communication and in individual and group relations. Herbert H. Aptekar commented on the "mutuality" of the help-giving and help-taking processes and the difficulty we face in thinking of ourselves as needing and taking as much as we give. He stated:

> They [the foreign country] know they have something to give us in return for our giving and they are pained, when they see that we do not know it. In many ways they show they want to help us too, but we seldom let them.[35]

Presently there is little specialized training for international social work, although social workers have successfully filled positions in refugee programs and in various programs within the UN as well as in voluntary agencies. The dimensions of American social work education would seemingly have to be broadened in several curriculum areas to meet the full demands of international social welfare responsibilities. Greater stress would need to be placed on studies of cultural variance, community planning and development, and the language training demanded in other branches of foreign service. Training centers in foreign countries have

[35] Herbert H. Aptekar, "The Preparation of Americans for Social Work Abroad," *Social Work Education Reporter*, Vol. 13, no. 2 (June 1965), p. 19.

been suggested as a means through which American social workers and social work educators could learn about the cultural and socioeconomic environment in which they will work. To date, however, an interchange of information and experience has occurred primarily through the enrollment of foreign students in American schools of social work and through the assistance of American social work educators in establishing schools of social work in foreign countries for students interested in social work as a career.

Summary

Humanitarian efforts to bind the wounds caused by armed conflict began more than a hundred years ago. In the twentieth century recurrent world wars brought widespread devastation, displacement of millions of people, and massive attempts to alleviate personal tragedy through intercountry mobilization of resources and social services.

With the founding of the United Nations in 1945, a new era in international social welfare began. Its focus is no longer limited to an amelioration of the aftermath of war and natural disasters. Instead, its purposes are similar to those of the United Nations as set forth in its charter: "To cooperate internationally in solving economic, social, cultural and humanitarian problems and in promoting respect for human rights and fundamental freedoms. . . ." These purposes are pursued through programs developed by the United Nations, by specialized agencies associated with the United Nations, and by individual nations with membership in the UN. The last group includes intergovernmental and people-to-people programs—such as the Peace Corps and AID—established by the United States to aid underdeveloped countries.

American social workers and social work educators have assumed a significant role in international social welfare programs. For more than 40 years they have participated in or cooperated with the International Conference of Social Work, the International Social Service, and a changing array of agencies established to meet specific problems (e.g., UNRRA, IRO). As individuals or as representatives of the United States government, they have assisted other nations in planning a wide variety of social welfare programs and in establishing their own schools of social work. Enrollment in American schools of social work has been made available to foreign students who can return to their own countries to apply the principles they have learned, and in recent years an increasing number of schools have developed special courses in international social work.

Selected Bibliography

Austin, David M. "Social Work's Relation to National Development in Developing Nations." *Social Work*, Vol. 15, No. 1, January 1970.

Brooks, Rhoda and Earle. *The Barrios of Manta*. New York: New American Library, 1965.

Brown, Malcolm. "Social Work Values in a Developing Country." *Social Work*, Vol. 15, No. 1, January 1970.

Chandler, Edgar H. S. *The High Tower of Refuge*. New York: Frederick A. Praeger, 1959.

Curti, Merle. *American Philanthropy Abroad*. New Brunswick, N.J.: Rutgers University Press, 1963.

de Jongh, Jan F. "Western Social Work and the Afro-Asian World." *Social Service Review*, Vol. 43, No. 1, March 1969.

Eichelberger, Clark M. *U.N.: The First Twenty Years*. New York: Harper & Row, 1965.

Madison, Bernice Q. *Social Welfare in the Soviet Union*, Stanford, California: Stanford University Press, 1968.

Madow, Pauline. *The Peace Corps*. New York: H. H. Wilson, 1964.

Mason, Edward J. *Foreign Aid and Foreign Policy*. New York: Harper & Row, 1964.

Mukundarao, K. "Cultural Variants and Social Work Practice in India." *Journal of Education for Social Work*, Vol. 5, No. 1, Spring 1969.

Rubin, Seymour J. *The Conscience of the Rich Nations*. New York: Harper & Row, 1966.

"Urbanization: Development Policies and Planning," *International Social Development Review*, no. 1. New York: United Nations, 1968.

Chapter Eleven

The Social Work Profession:
Prospects for the Future

NEW DIRECTIONS in American social work are premised on the nation's changing needs, expectations, and concept of individual fulfillment. These are reflected in the formulation and implementation of social policy, in practice, and in the new dimensions of social work education.

Poverty and dependency were historically regarded as conditions to be ameliorated only by the provision of tangible assistance—by the giving of something to assuage the pain of hunger and deprivation. The contemporary shift has been toward recognition that the dimensions of social responsibility must be reexamined within the context of social institutional change, wider acceptance of the right to democratic involvement and action, and an understanding of the gross implications of poverty in a nation so abundantly endowed with the means for the good life. As Herbert Aptekar stated:

> The priority currently given to the social component in social work in the American scene, of course, has a great deal to do with a developing conception of social responsibility in American society. Known sometimes as an individualistically oriented people, we are moving at this point in our history towards greater and greater awareness of the need for social orientation in order to carry out many of our national ideals.[1]

More than a quarter of a century ago a writer in *Survey Midmonthly* jocularly referred to the social worker as "Sallie Carter, Applicant for Kingdom Come" and the classified advertisements carried an appeal for a "man-caseworker, social service training, white, Protestant, mature. Work involves establishing paternity." [2] Social work has not yet arrived at Kingdom Come but it would be illegal today to designate race, religion, or sex in seeking an applicant.

In the same issue Gertrude Springer wrote of the U.S. Children's Bureau:

> The bureau believes in standards in social work, and it has been steadfast in adhering to them. But it realizes that it is no longer the only keeper of the faith, that it has no monopoly of the conviction that sound social growth must begin at the grass roots. It knows that many county welfare workers . . . have rooted their programs deep in community understanding and have gone forward steadily "from lower to higher" in community participation and in broadening the social content of the services they administer.[3]

[1] Herbert Aptekar, "Education for Social Responsibility," *Journal of Education for Social Work*, Vol. 2, no. 2 (Fall 1966), p. 7.

[2] Mary L. Rogers, "Sallie Carter, Applicant for Kingdom Come," *Survey Midmonthly*, Vol. 77, no. 2 (February 1941), p. 54; and the classified advertisements in that same issue, p. 72.

[3] Gertrude Springer, "In Predominantly Rural Areas," *Survey Midmonthly*, Vol. 77, no. 2 (February 1941), p. 40.

In the present century we have discovered and rediscovered the grass roots many times, just as we have rediscovered the social worker's responsibility in a rapidly changing social order.

In 1935 Linton B. Swift wrote of change through growth or evolution as opposed to change through revolution.[4] The nation's scholars support the social problems, social systems, and sociophilosophical approach and identify as areas of strong societal risk the population explosion, the challenge of automation, and the issues associated with race and integration.[5] These become starkly significant in terms of a projected national population of 344 million by the year 2000 and 907 million in 2060 at the present rate of increase.[6]

In describing the current search for "new and viable human orders," Maxine Greene commented on the changing attitudes toward moral principles, conflicts in ethical choice, and the dilemma of the teacher and learner regarding values associated with equality and those associated with standards of achievement. There are hidden preconceptions and assumptions: Are the poor responsible for their condition? What does "adjustment" mean? [7]

To Miss Greene's theme may be added Richard M. Titmuss's thesis of "the welfare state, its image and reality in Western democratic societies." Titmuss wrote:

> Political man likes collective abstract phrases; scientific man does not. . . . The broad historical assessment that isolates and takes account only of material indicators is not, we may conclude, a fruitful approach to the problem of definition [of the welfare state]. . . . We have to particularize; we have to examine the causal factors at work in each society; we have to understand the social costs of change, which are continually creating new areas of dependency; and we have to recognize that the aims of welfare include the enlargement of personal freedom and the discovery and maintenance of more and more justice.[8]

Thus, while not turning away from the Freudian orientation of individuation emphasized in the post-World War I period, social work is looking

---

[4] Linton B. Swift, "The Social Worker's Responsibility Toward a Changing Order," *The Family*, Vol. 15, no. 9 (January 1935), p. 283.

[5] Eveline M. Burns, "Tomorrow's Social Needs and Social Work Education," *Journal of Education for Social Work*, Vol. 2, no. 1 (Spring 1966), p. 10.

[6] Donald J. Bogue, "Population Growth in the United States," in Philip Hauser, ed., *The Population Dilemma* (Englewood Cliffs, N.J.: Prentice-Hall, 1963), p. 72.

[7] Maxine Green, "The Humanities and Social Work Education," *Journal of Education for Social Work*, Vol. 2, no. 1 (Spring 1966), pp. 23, 28–29.

[8] Richard M. Titmuss, "The Welfare State: Images and Realities," *Social Service Review*, Vol. 37, no. 1 (March 1963), p. 1.

more sharply than ever at all models that will give substance to and help to reshape the generalized ideas of social reform. Models must be found that are social action directed, not only toward ending the squalid impoverishment of the inner cities and the agonies of Appalachia, but toward alleviation of deprivation for all those in the poor or welfare classes.

SOCIAL WORK'S NEW ROLE

Involvement of the poor in policy formulation and protest had its roots in social work's advocacy of client rights, especially as these related to the "fair hearings" mandated by the Social Security Act. As the social worker became more involved in protecting the client's rights, the latter was encouraged to demand an opportunity to act in an adversary role and to make himself heard.

Involvement of the poor in policy-making and protest emerged as one of the significant movements of the 1960s. Although settlement house workers at the turn of the century attempted to encourage resident participation in identifying and meeting community needs, these activities progressively diminished as the profession developed. In the 1960s, however, under the impetus of the Office of Economic Opportunity, the Peace Corps, VISTA, and a revitalized welfare rights movement, the adversary system has become a reality in the client–social worker relationship, especially—but not exclusively—in public welfare.

Since 1965 public welfare recipients have organized on the neighborhood level and in 1966 the National Welfare Rights Organization was created in the nation's capital. The NWRO claims a membership of some 30,000 AFDC mothers, who seek more substantial support for their children. OEO has funded the work of attorneys who have won major court decisions and thereby extended welfare coverage and limited the discretion of local agencies in denying assistance. The *Wall Street Journal* commented on the fact that "the Poor People's March on Washington in 1967, won a commitment from the Department of Health, Education, and Welfare to furnish legal help to recipients whose right to relief was challenged" and stated that agitation by NWRO and various antipoverty agencies has forced welfare departments to publicize their granting procedures in intelligible form for the first time. Clients, the paper stated, "were helped to battle the welfare bureaucracy which produced more applications for aid and more liberal local administration." [9]

In describing the client advocacy role Martin Eisman explained that social work attempts to clarify the relationship between the recipient and

[9] *Wall Street Journal*, April 24, 1969.

the welfare department and "encourages the recipient to develop and express moral indignation at efforts to punish and humiliate him for claiming his rights." The new social work approach also "helps the individual and group (1) become conscious of the existence of their class, (2) discover their class style and ideology, and (3) develop class goals and ways of reaching them that are in keeping with the welfare-class style and strengths." [10]

The advocacy challenge has also reached the schools of social work, which are advised that they "must back their students in unflinching criticism and attempts at changing the settings they are in when those settings hurt the people they (and the schools) serve." [11] The schools' power is limited but the dehumanization apparent in some fields of social work practice has become of increasing concern to the student. David Wineman and Adrienne James have stated that some agencies have the characteristics of a prison, which they define as "a social arrangement in which a captor-captive relationship exists." Elaborating on this concept, they explain: "Public assistance, probation, and parole agencies are prisons without walls. All forms of incarceration—jails and mental hospitals—are virtual prisons. And the American public school system chronically oscillates between potential and actual prisonhood." [12] These authors summarize school and student advocacy this way:

> Thus, if social work's dream of the client-advocating professional is a real dream, the profession, along with the schools, ought to welcome the challenge of the shift to advocacy of social work faculties and to back this one tiny but tough step toward bringing that dream closer to reality.[13]

FUTURE DIRECTIONS IN SOCIAL WORK FUNCTION AND EDUCATION

The social work profession will continue to be influenced by the need to create new treatment and service models to meet growing demands. The social worker will assume a more realistic professional stance in starting with the client, his problems, and his needs rather than the methods to be used in meeting need. The social work system must learn ways of fitting methodology to people rather than relating people to available methods of treatment. This will involve helping the client to change his

[10] Martin Eisman, "Social Work's New Role in the Welfare-Class Revolution," *Social Work*, Vol. 14, no. 2 (April 1969), p. 83.

[11] David Wineman and Adrienne James, "The Advocacy Challenge to Schools of Social Work," *Social Work*, Vol. 14, no. 2 (April 1969), p. 28.

[12] *Ibid.*, p. 23.

[13] *Ibid.*, p. 32.

behavior and situation more appropriately. The profession is also engaged in and will continue to expand the process of changing the social service structure and those parts of the larger social system that undergird the social services. Thus the new emphasis is on social intervention, which seeks to alleviate troublesome social situations in the client's experience, and on societal intervention, which will focus on social welfare programs, policies, and resources.[14]

Werner W. Boehm identified the current concerns of social work as self-actualization, social functioning, habilitation, rehabilitation, resource provision, and prevention of dysfunction. He believes that these will become part of the enlarged responsibility of social work as the need to care for the poor diminishes, since poverty will probably be decreased through a guaranteed minimum annual income. The social worker will no longer deal merely with economic deprivation but will become involved in ridding society of the causes of deprivation. The profession will become more concerned with the human consequences of alienation, inequality, health, housing, and social planning.[15]

Louis Lowy has suggested that social work educators should be concerned not with coverage of subject matter but with teaching the student how to learn, how to find relevance in the concepts with which he must deal, and how to link them to further understanding.[16] Lowy recognized that clinical and nonclinical skills cannot be taught in the same curriculum. He also raised four significant questions in relation to social work education as it attempts to revise curriculum to meet the expanding role of the professional in the delivery of social services:

1. What must learners know and feel in order to effect behavioral and social change?
2. What is known, what is tentatively known, and what is not known at all?
3. How can such knowledge be organized efficiently and effectively so that it can be communicated for learning purposes?
4. How can the learner learn and practice skills based on attitudes developed and knowledge acquired? [17]

Henry S. Maas suggests another approach: "We need more than goals and strategies related to social structure and power, set in a crisis time-

---

[14] Werner W. Boehm, "Common and Specific Learnings for a Graduate of a School of Social Work," *Journal of Education for Social Work*, Vol. 4 no. 2 (Fall 1968).
[15] *Ibid.*, pp. 16–19.
[16] Louis Lowy, "Whither Social Work Education Amid Social Change?" *Journal of Education for Social Work*, Vol. 4, no. 1 (Spring 1968), p. 34.
[17] *Ibid.*

perspective and a conflict model for social change. We need to allow for human variation in tempo, values, compassion, and competence." [18]

NEW CAREERS FOR THE POOR

Social workers will not only need to be trained for their new advocacy role but for the education of indigenous workers who enter social work as a new career. These workers may be recruited from target neighborhoods or from public agency clientele and may be assigned to perform a wide variety of social service functions.

Frank M. Loewenberg reported the activities of some 24,000 indigenous workers associated with various OEO programs.[19] Among the responsibilities of this group are service delivery functions in which they act as interpreters, mediators, or expediters to make public social services more available and acceptable to the poor. Their role in giving service also has a therapeutic value in that they are learning skill and effectiveness in the use of self, and "for those who have always been losers, gaining self-respect, identity, and skill is no small achievement." [20]

Loewenberg pointed out, however, that there are some problems connected with the indigenous worker–social worker relationship, especially in antipoverty programs that are not social work oriented. Among these are the indigenous workers' lack of awareness of the rules of the profession, their lack of understanding of bureaucratic mandate and accountability, and the professional workers' discomfort in finding themselves without agency colleagues, isolated from professionals outside the agency, and perhaps working in positions subordinate to nonprofessionals.[21] These and other related problems have affected adversely the social worker's involvement in the War on Poverty. The social work profession must be more actively involved in training the indigenous worker, however, because the 1967 amendments to the Social Security Act require that clients be employed as case aides in public welfare departments. Robert Pruger and Harry Specht recognized that some barriers will be encountered in implementing this requirement:

Although it is acknowledged that resistance to attempts at broad social and institutional reform is inevitable, there is still, at least at first glance, fair reason to wonder if there must be such an inevitable reaction to the

[18] Henry S. Maas, "Social Work, Knowledge and Social Responsibility," *Journal of Education for Social Work*, Vol. 4, no. 1 (Spring 1968), p. 41.
[19] Frank M. Loewenberg, "Social Workers and Indigenous Nonprofessionals: Some Structural Dilemmas," *Social Work*, Vol. 13, no. 3 (July 1968), p. 66.
[20] *Ibid.*
[21] *Ibid.*, p. 71.

development of new careers for the poor. As a strategy to eliminate poverty, for example, it is certainly less controversial and abrasive than organizing the poor for political power or vesting such power in their organized representatives.

. . . . .

. . . The new careerist, born and raised in the low-income life-style so different from the middle-class professional's, implicitly, if not explicitly, challenges the organization's morally buttressed modus operandi.[22]

Such programs as Project ENABLE (Education and Neighborhood Action for Better Living Environment), a national project involving three voluntary social agencies, demonstrated that it is of great importance to delineate the role to be assumed by the nonprofessional aide in social work and to determine "whether or not his role is a vital one." This project, in fact, raised questions as to whether some assignments are not carried out best by nonprofessionals. This is an important question to be faced by the profession since most of the Project ENABLE aides had little formal education although they were able to read and write. Few had graduated from high school and many had been welfare recipients. Yet the aides were aggressive, alert, verbal, and capable of carrying the role of helper and of acting in a supportive capacity.

The aides in this project were seen to have considerable strength and ability in working with poor people characterized as unmotivated, hard core, and unreachable. They also demonstrated an ability to use on-the-job training to learn to do meaningful, satisfying, and essential tasks effectively. There was evidence that the nonprofessional could work co-operatively with the professional toward the achievement of common goals, and could use his professional co-worker as a role model in developing professional attitudes, values, and behavior. It was pointed out, however, that "perhaps their most vital contribution to the field of social work and for themselves was the destruction of many myths that have been barriers to the achievement of the universal goals of making families stronger and communities healthier." [23] Thus in its one-year demonstration period this project contributed some significant impressions and conclusions that could well be used in developing the teaching content needed in work with the nonprofessional aide.

In correctional agencies there is also a significant move to utilize the

[22] Robert Pruger and Harry Specht, "Establishing New Careers Programs: Organizational Barriers and Strategies," *Social Work*, Vol. 13, no. 4 (October 1968), pp. 23 and 24.
[23] Martin L. Birnbaum and Chester H. Jones, "Activities of the Social Work Aides," *Social Casework*, Vol. 48, no. 10 (December 1967), pp. 631–32. (*See* entire edition for description of Project ENABLE).

ex-offender as a staff member, thus making available another untapped manpower resource. This concept does not represent an innovation since for some time offenders have been helping to reconstruct the lives of other offenders, although this has never been formally recognized as a therapeutic technique. J. Douglas Grant, in describing the current use of this concept in the development of a new careers program, stresses the need for a viable staff climate in which career lines can be built by doing and reaching others.[24]

Each field of social work practice will begin to recognize the value of developing training programs for the utilization of the nonprofessional worker. While problems will undoubtedly develop around role discrepancy and role amalgamation, the client can bring deeper understanding of the problems created by need and of the reasons such needs exist. Perhaps one of social work's great errors has been in the evolution of a monolithic hierarchical system in which a director and/or board has the power to decide what is good for the client without client involvement or active participation in planning and decision-making. The profession consequently has lost the value of one of its most meaningful sources of knowledge, the client himself.

This epilogue might best be summed up by examining the social work profession within the context of Charles Frankel's *The Democratic Prospect*. Frankel posed, in another framework, a charge that could well be directed to social work as a professional entity:

> Our commitment to science and technology is irreversible. Moreover, it is difficult to think that the distinguishing characteristics of the scientific style of mind—a recognition of the evidence to support one's beliefs, a preference for qualified argument over sweeping generalization, a habit of acting on the basis of ideas examined in advance, a willingness to use our actions to test and revise these ideas—it is difficult to think that these have nothing to contribute to humane civilization.[25]

[24] J. Douglas Grant, "Vital Components of A Model Program Using the Offender in the Administration of Justice," *Offenders As a Correctional Manpower Resource* (Washington, D.C.: Joint Commission on Correctional Manpower and Training, 1968), p. 60.
[25] Charles Frankel, *The Democratic Prospect* (New York: Harper, Colophon Books, 1962), p. xi.

Selected Bibliography

Adelson, Gerald and Anthony R. Kovner. "The social health technician: a new occupation." *Social Casework*. Vol. 50, No. 7 (July 1969).

Brody, Stanley J. "Maximum Participation of the Poor: Another Holy Grail?" *Social Work*. Vol. 15, No. 1 (January 1970).

Changing Services for Changing Clients. Published for the National Association of Social Workers. New York: Columbia University Press, 1969.

Diesing, Paul. *Reason in Society*. Urbana, Illinois: University of Illinois Press, 1962.

Freeman, Howard B. and Norman R. Kurtz. *America's Troubles: A Casebook on Social Conflict*. Englewood Cliffs, New Jersey: Prentice-Hall, 1969.

Gilbert, Neil. "Neighborhood Coordinator: Advocate or Middleman?" *Social Service Review*, Vol. 43, No. 2 (June 1969).

Gyarfas, Mary. "Social Science, Technology and Social Work: A Caseworker's View." *Social Service Review*. Vol. 43, No. 3 (September 1969).

Levy, Charles S. "The Social Worker as Agent of Policy Change." *Social Casework*. Vol. 51, No. 2 (February 1970).

Lubove, Roy. "Social Work and the Life of the Poor." *Nation*. Vol. 202, No. 2 (May 16, 1966).

McCormick, Mary J. "Social Advocacy: A New Dimension in Social Work." *Social Casework*. Vol. 51, No. 1 (January 1970).

Shattuck, Geralom and John M. Martin. "New Professional Work Roles and Their Integration into a Social Agency Structure." *Social Work*. Vol. 14, No. 3 (July 1969).

"Special Issue of the Future of the Social Services." *The Political Quarterly*, Vol. 40, No. 1 (January–March 1969).

Name Index

Subject Index

355